The
WORD OF CHRIST
and the
WORLD OF CULTURE

The
WORD OF CHRIST
and the
WORLD OF CULTURE

Sacred and Secular
through the Theology of Karl Barth

PAUL LOUIS METZGER

William B. Eerdmans Publishing Company
Grand Rapids, Michigan / Cambridge, U.K.

Wipf and Stock Publishers
199 W 8th Ave, Suite 3
Eugene, OR 97401

The Word of Christ
and the World of Culture
Sacred and Secular through the
Theology of Karl Barth
By Metzger, Paul Louis

ISBN 13: 978-1-59752-407-0
Publication date 10/1/2005
Previously published by
William B. Eerdmans, 2003

Distributed and managed by
Wipf and Stock Publishers.
For all orders and inquiries
please contact us at:

http://www.wipfandstock.com
info@wipfandstock.com
orders@wipfandstock.com

255 Je ;03 /

Library of Congress Cataloging-in-Publication Data

Metzger, Paul Louis.
The word of Christ and the world of culture : sacred
and secular through the theology of Karl Barth / Paul Louis Metzger.
p. cm.
Based on the author's thesis (doctoral) — King's College, London.
Includes bibliographical references (p.) and index.
ISBN 0-8028-4946-6 (pbk. : alk. paper)
1.Christianity and culture — History of doctrines — 19th century.
2. Barth, Karl, 1886-1968. I. Title.
BR115.C8 .M296 2003

261'.092 — dc21

2002029657

www.eerdmans.com

To Mariko,
my earthly joy
and partner
in life's journey

Contents

Foreword

Recent Barth studies have done much to counter the many misapprehensions that continue to cloud the question of his message and meaning. One misunderstanding that dies hard is that Barth's obsession with Mozart was an exception to the general rule that he was uninterested in and blind to the theological meaning of culture. Paul Metzger's fine study will here serve a double function: of explicating Barth's complex relation to culture and of showing his broad significance for those who would develop a theology of culture for the present. As the author points out in his introduction, Barth himself worked in a political context that involved an extreme divinization of culture, not unlike the context today as America's distorted religious culture itself attempts to come to terms with an Islam it finds difficult for theological reasons to understand.

Even the early Barth, with his critique of culture Protestantism, is not *against* culture, as is often asserted; where he differs from his cultured predecessors is not there, but in the starting point from which culture is approached. For the later Barth, christology and analogy are the two keys to the relation. In the analogy between the divine and human in Christ is to be found a theological account of the relationship between sacred and secular, the church and the broader culture within which it is set. By means of what he calls "analogical extensions," Dr. Metzger is able to show the bearing of trinitarian and Chalcedonian categories on this world. Over against the positions adopted by Schleiermacher and Tillich, he proceeds to argue that only such a concept of analogy makes it possible to avoid the twin — and opposite — perils of the secularization and divinization of culture.

What kind of connection can then be made between theology and culture? There are two main focuses for the discussion. On the one hand is the capacity of the Word to enculturate itself, and thus to allow Christians to retain their cultural identity — to be, for example, both Christian and truly Japanese. On the other is the capacity of Barth's theology to allow a proper secularity both in politics and in human activity more generally. Barth on Mozart is not an isolated episode in the theology, but a symptom of this theologian's more general capacity to let the world be the world — as God's world.

This is not a "Barthian" book in the sense that Barth is presented as beyond criticism. Indeed, the imbalance in some of his doctrines, Christology and election in particular, is shown to make a proper affirmation of the created order more difficult than it ought to be. It is not that Barth holds that grace destroys nature, but that we need to go beyond Barth to be able to understand grace more adequately as the means of the created order's elevation. Yet what is made clear above all is that Barth is a modern theologian, aware of the need for a theology of culture "after Christendom" and going a good way toward providing one.

Colin Gunton
King's College, London

Preface

While this study on Barth is written with the American church and its culture in mind, it was birthed in Japan where I lived from 1992 to 1994. Infatuation and fascination are apt words to describe how I approached life in Japan, a land immersed in contradiction, the historic home of the samurai warrior and also of haiku, whose people venerate both the chrysanthemum and the sword.[1]

Perhaps I am immersed in contradiction. I am a Protestant committed to historic Christianity but equally committed to appreciating much of Japanese society, whose history is so striking. To some, it might appear an even greater contradiction that my stay in a land not even remotely Christian, yet so appealing to me, would have led to an analysis of culture through the theology of none other than Karl Barth. In fact, many would argue that in contrast to Friedrich Schleiermacher's "cultured despisers" of religion, Barth was a "religious despiser" of culture. But the story is not so simple.

Barth himself spoke of a similar contradictory or paradoxical situation that engendered puzzlement in the minds of others — namely, that one such as he, "an evangelical Christian," a Protestant, could champion the "so Catholic" Mozart, "a Freemason," who was "no more than a musician, albeit a complete one."[2] For was not this the same Barth who spoke so

1. Reference here is made to Ruth Benedict's classic study of Japanese culture, *The Chrysanthemum and the Sword: Patterns of Japanese Culture* (Tokyo: Charles E. Tuttle Company, 1974), especially p. 2.

2. Karl Barth, "Mozart's Freedom," in *Wolfgang Amadeus Mozart,* with a foreword by John Updike (Grand Rapids: Eerdmans, 1986), pp. 56-57.

forcefully and effectively against a profoundly cultured European society at the turn of the century? What could this Münzer[3] have to do with one such as Mozart?

Perhaps the answer to the question as to why I would look to Barth, whose wide following among Japanese Christians this past century had much to do with the radical nature of his thought,[4] is found in the dialectical union of his very radical denunciation of the deification of culture with his equally radical affirmation of culture, that is, when culture immerses itself in a secularity that is nothing other than human and creaturely. Japanese history bears testimony to the divinization of creation and its culture.[5] But are there not also present in that culture instances of a sensitivity, awareness, and admiration of the *phenomena* of creation as such, free from the imposition of ideology and idolatry, serving as a much-needed relief in view of the propensity found therein to view the creation somehow as divine? Perhaps the paradoxical reality of this culture, immersed as it is in contradiction, extends even this far.

In the present study, one will not find a detailed discussion of Japanese culture, or American culture for that matter. However, both cultures will ever be in view, even as analysis centers on Barth's theological pilgrimage, a pilgrimage in many ways marked by his engagement of the culture of the Europe of his day. And although his theology, like all theologies, is in certain respects dated, bound up with his own *Sitz im Leben,* it speaks with a certain force, transcending his culture and bearing relevance for today. Thus, in what follows, Barth's theology will serve as a paradigm on the basis of which to proceed, providing hints about how to live in this world without being of it, to appreciate culture without being captivated by it, to engage culture positively, theologically, without divinizing it or moralizing on the basis of it.

At the outset, it is important to note that, for Barth, the theme of

3. Eberhard Busch notes that Adolf von Harnack compared Barth to Thomas Münzer. Eberhard Busch, *Karl Barth: His Life from Letters and Autobiographical Texts* (London: SCM Press, 1976), p. 113.

4. Toshio Sato argues that part of the reason for Barth's influence in Japan is the "radicalism" of his theology. Toshio Sato, "The Second Generation," in *A History of Japanese Theology,* ed. Yasuo Furuya (Grand Rapids: Eerdmans, 1997), p. 56.

5. Among other things, I have in mind here the animism so widespread in traditional Japanese culture and the divinization of the State under the emperor system and State Shinto prior to and during World War II.

Christ and culture does not refer ultimately to *Christianity* and culture, as might be assumed in such discussions, but rather to the Word as *Jesus Christ* as the basis of culture, even of the relation of Christianity to culture, as will be shown. The reason for this is that Barth does not focus on Christianity as such, or on the Christian faith, but on Jesus Christ and the relation of both the church and broader culture to him. Therefore, we will center our attention on the Word of God as Jesus Christ in Barth's theology, especially his appropriation of such concepts as *anhypostasis, enhypostasis,* and the *unio personalis,* and how this doctrine of the Word bears upon Barth's understanding of revelation, election, and creation in relation to the theme of culture.

In this work, the phrase "world of culture" is used in its most general sense to refer to that domain which includes the totality of human existence and activity. Through the course of the study, discussion will include those aspects of creaturely life belonging to what Robert Palma terms the "higher branches" of civilization and which Markus Barth calls "the very acme, the summit of human possibilities for which we yearn, which we can never define, which occurs in a great work of art, or in Mozart, or in great persons." This, according to Markus Barth, is what his father has in mind when he speaks of culture.[6] However, reflection on Karl Barth's own definition of culture, where he says that "The Word of God sets culture as the assigned task to realize the destiny of the person in soul and body" ("Die Kultur ist die durch das Wort Gottes gestellte Aufgabe der in der Einheit von Seele und Leib zu verwirklichenden Bestimmung des Menschen"), coupled with attention both to the plethora of themes addressed in his theology and his interest in the lives of ordinary people and everyday events, suggests that although Barth gives special consideration to high culture, his concern for culture as such is not limited to that sphere.[7] In the light of such factors, together with my interest in analyzing

6. See Robert J. Palma, *Karl Barth's Theology of Culture: The Freedom of Culture for the Praise of God,* Pittsburgh Theological Monographs, ed. Dikran Y. Hadidian (Allison Park: Pickwick Publications, 1983), p. 9. See also Markus Barth, "Response," *Union Seminary Quarterly Review* 28 (Autumn 1972): 53.

7. For the German source, see Karl Barth, "Die Kirche und die Kultur," in *Die Theologie und die Kirche,* vol. 2, *Gesammelte Vorträge* (München: Chr. Kaiser Verlag, 1928), p. 368. Dieter Andresen writes, "Barth's cultural receptivity never restricts itself to the creations and consumption of culture in the stricter sense, but rather grasps the elementary workaday life of concrete humanity." Author's translation of excerpt taken from Dieter Andresen, "Karl

the *overall* relation of the Word of Christ to the world of culture through the lens of Barth's theology, culture has been defined in more inclusive terms.

Palma sets forth Barth's mature and multifaceted engagement of culture and argues that Barth offers a theology of culture that conceives culture as free in keeping with the freedom of God and that of the theologian.[8] Palma explicates to a certain extent Barth's discussion of culture and notes its value as a paradigm[9] or model by which to approach culture. However, for all the merits of Palma's work, given the fact that Barth has not given any explicit indication that he is setting forth a theology of culture (which Palma himself acknowledges[10]), Palma is, as Sze Chi Chan points out, "acting as a theologian of culture" on Barth's behalf.[11] As Chan suggests, it would have been better had Palma spoken simply of *"the implicit cultural potential"* of Barth's dogmatic theology.[12] According to Chan, while all theologies are enculturated, not all theologies are theologies of culture, only those explicitly indicated as such.[13]

The purpose of this study is to go beyond Palma by analyzing in greater detail Barth's *explicit* consideration of the theme of culture in view of Barth's doctrine of the Word, while at the same time setting forth *implications* for culture arising from that doctrine, which, as Palma rightly notes, is the rule by which Barth measures culture.[14] Such implications will include both those Barth himself draws out and those that I deduce, especially those relating to the dedivinization, desecularization, and humanization of culture. Thus, this study will go beyond Palma's work in explicating

---

Barth und die Kultur," *Pastoraltheologie* 77 (1988): 229. Andresen gives much consideration to Barth's concern for the higher forms of cultural life, but, as indicated, argues that Barth's interests transcend those bounds (pp. 220-40). Palma's own judgment that Barth "is especially interested in the higher branches" (Palma, *Karl Barth's Theology of Culture*, p. 9) seems to suggest the possibility of considering a wider spectrum of societal phenomena in relation to Barth's theology than simply politics, philosophy, classical music, and the like. That is to say, Barth "is especially interested in" such instances of creaturely life, but not exclusively so.

8. Palma, *Karl Barth's Theology of Culture*, pp. ix, 1.

9. Palma, *Karl Barth's Theology of Culture*, p. 5.

10. See Palma, *Karl Barth's Theology of Culture*, p. 5.

11. Sze Chi Chan, TMs, p. 15, manuscript presented to author by Colin E. Gunton, London, Spring 1997.

12. Chan, TMs, p. 15.

13. Chan, TMs, p. 15.

14. Palma, *Karl Barth's Theology of Culture*, p. 12.

more fully Barth on cultural themes and by drawing out implications arising from Barth's doctrine of the Word for culture, even going beyond Barth's own dogmatic, analogical extensions to culture at points in so doing.

We stated above that we will analyze the Christ-culture theme from the standpoint of the emphasis given to the doctrine of the Word in Barth's theology. The decision to approach the topic in this way — that is, dogmatically, through the doctrine of the Word — bears similarities to Barth's own approach to the subject. Barth refuses to speak non-theologically about the church and broader culture. In his 1926 essay "Church and Culture," Barth makes clear at the outset that he intends to define both church and culture theologically, that is, in the light of the Word of reconciliation.[15] Concerning culture, Barth maintains that *for the church,* consideration of culture must arise in the light of the Word to which it bears witness, setting it

> at the beginning and the end, above all empirical or transcendental principles, as the sole, supreme event which gives law. The Church accordingly knows nothing of human activity in general or in the abstract; but only the activity of a concrete man — who is first sinful and secondly believing and obedient, who lives from the Word of God.[16]

The church knows of "no independent, actual relation between God and nature, God and history, God and human reason." It knows only of such relations between God and the world in and through the mediation of the Word of reconciliation.[17] The church could not accept non-theological definitions of culture "*if* such formulations were to be accepted as determinative and all-inclusive."[18] Such definitions, if absolutized, could only be rejected. But they do possess merit *if* viewed in light of the Word, who makes known the true meaning of culture as indicated in Barth's theological construal.

15. Karl Barth, "Church and Culture," in *Theology and Church: Shorter Writings, 1920-1928,* with an introduction by T. F. Torrance, trans. Louise Pettibone Smith (New York: Harper & Row, 1962), pp. 334, 337-38, 342.

16. Barth, "Church and Culture," p. 338.

17. Barth, "Church and Culture," p. 342.

18. Barth, "Church and Culture," p. 337 (italics added).

Now although the church does not abstract culture from its relation to Christ, Christ is not limited to the sphere of the church. As Jaroslav Pelikan claims in his own preface to *Jesus Through the Centuries,* "Clemenceau once remarked that war was entirely too important a matter to be left to the military. So also, Jesus is far too important a figure to be left only to the theologians and the church."[19]

Barth, the theologian, would have heartily agreed. For Christ himself is not limited to the confines of the church. Rather, church and culture must be defined in relation to him. Thus, Barth stands in the face of that general state of affairs in Christendom, which has so perplexed me, where Christology, perhaps the most important doctrine of the faith, is viewed as having no real bearing on life beyond the walls of the church. Contrary to popular theological opinion, Barth's christologically conceived enterprise is no ghetto theology, sitting on the shelf. For it serves as the foundation for his analysis of culture and as the basis for the relation of the sacred and secular spheres, full of promise that, in the end, "the Redeemer will first speak his 'Behold, I make all things new!'"[20]

19. Jaroslav Pelikan, *Jesus Through the Centuries: His Place in the History of Culture* (New Haven: Yale University Press, 1985; new preface, 1999), p. xv.

20. Barth, "Church and Culture," p. 349.

Acknowledgments

The present study grew out of my doctoral work at King's College London. I wish to express warm appreciation to my Ph.D. supervisor, Professor Colin E. Gunton, for giving generously of his time and guidance, and whose approach to theology and encouragement to pursue publication have served as an inspiration for the present study. I also wish to thank Prof. Georg Pfleiderer, Drs. Ronald Frost, Stephen Franklin, Peter Robinson, and Daniel Bailey for numerous discussions and insights into the subject at hand, and to Profs. Trevor Hart and Alan Torrance for many helpful comments and remarks. Special thanks also goes to the *Overseas Research Student Awards Scheme* and to the *King's Theological Trust,* the Rev. Barry Morrison, Richard Mortimer, the people of Saint Luke's Church of Hampstead and Suzaka Seisho Kyokai, Tak and Kumiko Itano, Robert and Jane Moseley, Dr. Paul Isihara, the faculty, staff, and students of Multnomah Biblical Seminary, including the editorial assistance and perspectives of Joshua Butler and Stephen Woodworth, and most particularly my parents William and Audrey Metzger and my wife's parents Saburo and Yoshie Tomoda, for their various forms of support during the course of my studies and in preparation for them. I am very appreciative of the guidance and encouragement I have received from William B. Eerdmans, Jr., and the staff at Eerdmans in bringing this book into being, most notably Jennifer Hoffman and Charles Van Hof. Lastly, I wish to thank my wife Mariko who, together with our son Christopher and daughter Julianne, has provided me with much joy for the journey and whose sacrifice on my behalf fills my heart with much love and gratitude.

Introduction

In the foreword to *Theology of Culture,* Paul Tillich writes, ". . . most of my writings — including the two volumes of *Systematic Theology* — try to define the way in which Christianity is related to secular culture."[1] Karl Barth, like Tillich, is concerned about the relation of the sacred to the secular, of Christianity or the church to broader culture. While Barth does not pursue a theology of culture as such, he does seek to preserve the proper balance between the sacred and secular, religion and culture. Both theologians seek to guard against the *separation* of the two spheres, which Tillich labels "a dualism of religion and culture."[2] Moreover, they resist the *amalgamation* of the sacred and secular, whereby one overwhelms the other; neither should "the religious . . . be swallowed by the secular, as secularism desires," nor should "the secular . . . be swallowed by the religious, as ecclesiastic imperialism desires," to quote Tillich.[3] However, unlike Tillich, Barth does not wish to discover the *manifestation* of humanity's ultimate concern *in* culture,[4] but rather to view culture *in light of* humanity's ultimate concern, the manifestation of the Logos in human history. In this way, Barth is able to preserve the inseparability of relation involving the secular and sacred dimensions and, at the same time, to affirm the secular in the actualization of its truly secular vocation. Barth engages culture

1. Paul Tillich, *Theology of Culture,* ed. Robert C. Kimball (New York: Oxford University Press, 1959), p. v.

2. Tillich, *Theology of Culture,* p. 42.

3. Tillich, *Theology of Culture,* p. 42.

4. Tillich, *Theology of Culture,* pp. 41-42.

theologically. Yet he does so without seeking to theologize on the basis of secular culture itself, but rather on the basis of the Word of God.

The present enterprise is an inquiry into and appraisal of the relation of the Word of Christ to the world of culture in Barth's theology. Whereas "Word of Christ" refers specifically to Barth's dialectical and incarnational conception of Jesus Christ, the phrase "world of culture" is used in its most general sense to refer to the totality of human existence and activity. For Barth, "Christ and culture" does not signify Christianity and culture, but Jesus Christ and culture.

It will be argued that there is an analogical connection in Barth's thought between the way in which he envisions the relation of the two natures in the person of Christ and his pattern of engaging culture in view of Christ. As in Christology, the church and broader culture, the sacred and secular, stand in distinct though inseparable relation to one another in and through the mediation of the Word of Christ. Barth is largely successful in safeguarding against the confusion or divinization of the sacred and secular spheres, and their separation, which would signify the secularization of culture.

Such issues are by no means irrelevant to our current society. As the present study was nearing completion, a tragic crisis in America began unfolding, involving the call to *jihad* against the Great Satan. America will no doubt have a difficult time coping with the strange and arduous terrain on which it now sojourns as it comes face to face with radical forces within Islam. The difficulty involves this country's compartmentalizing of the sacred dimension. In many ways, Islam belongs to premodernity, if what is meant by that term is the fusion of the sacred and secular. For in much of Islam, a religious war is not so much a fight over a point of doctrine, but rather, a battle waged over a way of life. I am told that in Arabic there is no specific word for "secular." One can only wonder if the phrase, "a secular Muslim state," is a contradiction in terms.

The expressed bewilderment of many Americans over the events of September 11, 2001, in Washington and New York calls to mind Mircea Eliade's comment in *The Sacred and the Profane.* Given the "desacralization" present in modern culture, there is little wonder that it is "increasingly difficult to rediscover the existential dimensions of religious man in the archaic

5. Mircea Eliade, *The Sacred and the Profane: The Nature of Religion,* trans. Willard R. Trask (New York: Harper & Row, 1961), p. 13.

societies."[5] Not only has America (and the West as a whole) been guilty of separating the sacred and secular dimensions of reality, but also it has within itself, especially in conservative Christian circles, the propensity to divinize the American state in times of crisis. In times such as these, how does one guard against the extremes of the total secularization of culture, on the one hand, and the divinization of culture, on the other hand?

As shall be argued in the present study, Barth, who encountered such extremes in his own day, provides a theological paradigm for engaging culture whereby the sacred and secular dimensions stand in distinct though inseparable relation to one another in view of the reality of Jesus Christ, thereby safeguarding against the secularization and divinization of any given culture.

This work documents the development of Barth's Christocentric theology against the cultural backdrop from which it sprang. Moreover, it draws out implications arising from his novel doctrine of the Word, extending them toward the development of a theology of culture. As stated above, Barth's own theological engagement of culture emerged as a response to the extremes of the divinization of culture, on the one hand, and the secularization of culture, on the other. The theological revolution Barth inspired was by no means a dismissive reaction to modern concerns but rather a dynamic and carefully nuanced encounter of the culture of his day. His doctrine of the Word provides a sound basis on which to build a theological model of culture that guards against the two extremes, while nurturing a healthy appreciation for the secular domain.

I wish to trace out and extend analogically the way in which Barth's theology safeguards and promotes the distinct though inseparable relation of God, Christianity, and culture in and through his conception of the Word. Central to Barth's engagement of culture is his concern for the dedivinization of culture — under which I include rejecting the amalgamation of the sacred and secular spheres — and its *desecularization,* which likewise involves resisting a radical separation of the sacred and secular, the church and broader culture.

The first two chapters serve as the *foundations* for the work as a whole, chronicling Barth's theological development in relation to his engagement of culture whereby he comes to conceive the Word of Christ as both dialectical and incarnational. In so doing, he offers a theological model for engaging culture that, in a manner analogous to the pattern found in orthodox Christology for viewing the relation of the natures, preserves the distinction between the divine and human, sacred and secular, as well as the connection between these spheres.

From this fundamental discussion of Barth's theological development and what his maturing theology suggests for a theological engagement of culture, the study proceeds to consider *connections,* showing how Barth's dialectical/incarnational model offers a synthesis, a means by which to overcome the radical division or separation of the divine and human (as well as sacred and secular) realms so evident in the secularization of culture through consideration of the Word in election, revelation, and creation, without on the whole, compromising the distinction between them.

Lastly, attention will be devoted to *distinctions,* namely, how it is that within Barth's proposed synthesis he is able to provide space for the celebration of authentic forms of secularity in the realms of politics, the arts, the sciences, and culture generally. Thus, under distinctions the flow of argument will have come full circle from the discussion of the *dedivinization* and *desecularization* of culture to the prospect of a *humanization* of culture in and through Barth's theology. Although all theologies are enculturated, not all engagements of culture by theologians are dogmatically conceived. In this study, the attempt will be made to show the merits of engaging culture dogmatically in and through the theology of Karl Barth.

In *Jesus Through the Centuries,* Jaroslav Pelikan argues that the dominant images of Jesus in the respective epochs of culture have been instrumental in shaping those periods of history.[6] In developing his thesis, Pelikan refers to Adolf Harnack's claim about Christ in *What Is Christianity?* Harnack writes,

> The great English philosopher, John Stuart Mill, has somewhere observed that mankind cannot be too often reminded that there was once a man of the name of Socrates. That is true; but still more important is it to remind mankind again and again that a man of the name of Jesus Christ once stood in their midst.[7]

Although his Christology is radically different from Harnack's, Barth was convinced that one's perspective on Christology and its placement in one's

6. Jaroslav Pelikan, *Jesus Through the Centuries: His Place in the History of Culture* (New Haven: Yale University Press, 1985; new preface, 1999).

7. Adolf Harnack, *What Is Christianity?,* with an introduction by Rudolf Bultmann (New York: Harper & Row, 1957), p. 1. See also Pelikan, *Jesus Through the Centuries,* p. xxi.

theology impacts greatly one's view of and approach to culture. In fact, Barth's Christocentric theology played a significant role in his keen engagement of pressing concerns in his own cultural context. This work is propelled forward by the underlying conviction that its exposition and extension of Barth's Christocentric model will provide a resource for addressing the complex issues facing the church today in the new millennium.

PART I

FOUNDATIONS

1

The Word of Christ in Cultural Context

The Making of a Modern

In the opening pages of his *Systematic Theology*, Paul Tillich characterizes Karl Barth as a "kerygmatic" theologian. Tillich argues that Barth ultimately fails to do justice to the modern cultural situation, giving rise to the danger of a theology of "repristination."[1] In contrast to this assessment of Barth, it will be argued that Barth is indeed a modern theologian and that one can only understand his theology of the kerygma or Word in the light of the cultural context in which it emerges, and into which Barth is concerned to speak. In what follows, the attempt will be made to place Barth and his doctrine of the Word in that historical context. Consideration will focus primarily on Liberal Protestantism at the turn of the century, its influence on Barth's early theological development, and his eventual critique of it.[2]

In his article, "Evangelical Theology in the 19th Century," Barth writes, "There is hardly any doubt that the distinctive beginnings of 19th-century

1. Paul Tillich, *Systematic Theology*, vol. 1 (Chicago: University of Chicago Press, 1951), p. 5. Refer to Bruce McCormack's discussion of Tillich and Barth here in *Karl Barth's Critically Realistic Dialectical Theology: Its Genesis and Development, 1909-1936* (Oxford: Clarendon Press, 1995), pp. 25-26.

2. This chapter focuses primarily on the years 1904 to 1923, that is, from Barth's university student days to the time immediately following the writing of the second edition of his commentary on Romans. Barth's later works will be analyzed when they bear upon or illumine the context under discussion. The next chapter will consider Barth's theology from 1924 onward.

theology coincide with the publication of Schleiermacher's book, *On Religion, Speeches to Its Cultured Despisers* in 1799."[3] What marked this work and the theology that hailed from it? Perhaps the chief characteristic of this movement was the shared assumption "that theology and even biblical exegesis could only be pursued within the framework of the accepted or prevailing *Weltanschauung* or a generally intelligible view of the totality of things, human, cosmic and divine."[4]

For Schleiermacher, the theologian's task is to show that religion, and theology with it, has a place within the prevailing worldview of human culture. Schleiermacher's *Speeches* is namely an apology for the Christian faith to its cultured despisers, to those who in principle should espouse religion. As E. Graham Waring writes, "Schleiermacher loved that in religion which was alive, and sought at once to show his 'despising' friends that it was not alien to their experience of culture, and to found it in human nature in such a way as to give it independent status."[5] Indeed, Schleiermacher saw himself as belonging to that "higher priesthood" that

> strives to awaken the slumbering germ of a better humanity, to kindle love for higher things, to change the common life into a nobler, to reconcile the children of earth with the Heaven that hears them, and to counterbalance the deep attachment of the age to the baser side.[6]

For this priest, the truly cultured should be the truly religious and vice versa. Schleiermacher conceived religion, especially the Christian religion, as fulfilling the need of cultured humanity to be truly cultured, rather than as sharing in humanity's need before God, as Barth would later maintain.

In keeping with the tendency in Protestant Liberalism to argue that religion fulfills cultured humanity, Neo-Protestantism focused attention on pious man as such.[7] Following the anthropocentric turn in modern

3. Karl Barth, "Evangelical Theology in the 19th Century," in *The Humanity of God* (Atlanta: John Knox Press, 1960), p. 12.

4. Thomas F. Torrance, *Karl Barth: An Introduction to His Early Theology, 1910-1931* (London: SCM Press, 1962), p. 33.

5. E. Graham Waring, introduction to *On Religion: Speeches to Its Cultured Despisers,* by Friedrich Schleiermacher (New York: Frederick Ungar Publishing Company, 1955), p. xii.

6. Friedrich Schleiermacher, *On Religion: Speeches to Its Cultured Despisers,* with an introduction by E. Graham Waring (New York: Frederick Ungar Publishing Company, 1955), p. 8.

7. Significant here is Barth's conversation with Adolf Harnack in 1925 where the latter said that if he were to write a dogmatics he would use the title, "The life of the children of

thought inaugurated by Descartes and perfected by Kant, Protestant Liberalism did not pursue theology from the standpoint of God, but from the standpoint of the pious man, the one who believes in God. Thus, from this perspective, theology is ultimately concerned with the person who believes in God rather than with the God in whom one believes.

Early on in his theological development, Barth entered into this arena of theological discourse and became an active participant in the movement. Although Barth was raised in a conservative theological environment, his university studies took him to the centers of Protestant Liberalism. The three great influences on his thought during his student years were Immanuel Kant, Schleiermacher himself, and Wilhelm Herrmann. Barth also came into contact with other masters, including Adolf Harnack and Ernst Troeltsch. He was very impressed with Harnack,[8] but at Marburg, he found Herrmann's theology far more appealing than that of Troeltsch.[9]

Returning to Kant, Barth says that the philosopher's *Critique of Practical Reason* was the first book that truly spoke to him as a student.[10] This together with Kant's *Critique of Pure Reason* made a great impact on Barth at the time. He writes that when he was a student he believed that one could only enter upon theology through recourse to Kant.[11] Through his study of the *Critique of Practical Reason,* Barth concluded that the gospel and di-

God." Barth's comment on this title is suggestive. Harnack was of the conviction "that dogmatics in the older sense ought now to be replaced by the personal confession of someone who has attained the maturity and serenity of final convictions and spiritual certainties, a confession determined at its very heart by the history of Christianity." Barth goes on to argue, "Harnack was obviously speaking for Neo-Protestantism, whose proper object of faith is not God in His revelation, but man himself believing in the divine." Karl Barth, *Church Dogmatics,* I/2, *The Doctrine of the Word of God,* ed. G. W. Bromiley and T. F. Torrance (Edinburgh: T. & T. Clark, 1956), p. 367.

8. Eberhard Busch, *Karl Barth: His Life from Letters and Autobiographical Texts* (London: SCM Press, 1976), p. 39.

9. Busch, *Karl Barth: His Life,* p. 50. Having said this, Barth's discussions with other students centered on Troeltsch's thought. Barth was wary of Troeltsch even at this time. He considered Troeltsch's outlook the boundary he would not cross in his otherwise firm allegiance to the modern school (p. 50). In this light, Busch conjectures, "Did Barth already suspect what he later remarked about Troeltsch, 'that with him the doctrine of faith was on the point of dissolution into endless and useless talk'?" (p. 50; the translation of Busch's quotation from Barth is taken from the *Church Dogmatics,* IV/1, p. 387).

10. Busch, *Karl Barth: His Life,* p. 34.

11. Busch, *Karl Barth: His Life,* p. 45.

vine truth were simple, not given to abstraction, as was the case in orthodox theology. What mattered was "good will." "This good will is the truth, the divine element in my life." The quest for "the true knowledge of simplicity" drove Barth forward from this point in his theological pursuits.[12]

After immersing himself in Kant, Barth came to Schleiermacher. However, Barth's great theological teacher during his student years was Wilhelm Herrmann. Barth says that his "own deep interest in theology began" on the day he first read Herrmann's *Ethics*.[13] His resolve to study at Marburg where Herrmann was a teacher intensified as a result, to his father's dismay. But finally, his father consented and Barth was allowed to study at Marburg.[14] Barth writes of his days at Marburg that he immersed himself in Herrmann's thought,[15] and describes Herrmann as a disciple of Kant and a student of the early Schleiermacher.[16] "Herrmann was *not* ashamed of the Gospel,"[17] and was adamant in arguing for theology's independence as a discipline whereby it has "its *own* professional fervour."[18] From Herrmann, Barth gained his Christological concentration, which for Herrmann was of paramount significance.[19]

While at Marburg, Barth came into contact with Marburg Neo-Kantianism of which he says, "There has been and there will perhaps be again a philosophical fervor which is almost priestly, as was impressed on us at Marburg in Herrmann's time by the figures of a Cohen and a Natorp."[20] There Barth would also interact with Rudolf Bultmann, whose own immersion in Neo-Kantianism would remain a vital part of his theology throughout his life and would serve in ways to shape his lifelong dialogue with Barth.[21]

12. Karl Barth, a sermon dated 13 October 1912; quoted in Eberhard Busch, *Karl Barth: His Life*, p. 35.

13. Karl Barth, "The Principles of Dogmatics According to Wilhelm Herrmann," in *Theology and Church: Shorter Writings, 1920-1928*, with an introduction by T. F. Torrance, trans. Louise Pettibone Smith (New York: Harper & Row, 1962), p. 238.

14. Busch, *Karl Barth: His Life*, p. 44.

15. Busch, *Karl Barth: His Life*, p. 45.

16. Busch, *Karl Barth: His Life*, p. 44.

17. Barth, "Principles of Dogmatics," p. 258.

18. Barth, "Principles of Dogmatics," p. 256.

19. Busch, *Karl Barth: His Life*, p. 45.

20. Barth, "Principles of Dogmatics," p. 256.

21. As indicated, Bultmann was trained in Marburg Neo-Kantianism. Herman Cohen, the founder of this movement, held that nothing is supplied. Thought produces both content and form. Moreover, thought is the body of scientific knowledge and its unending de-

During his time at Marburg, Barth became editorial assistant of the *Christliche Welt,* a leading journal of the "modern" school of theology, working under the supervision of Martin Rade.[22] Barth considered himself prepared for the task since he had become a true follower of the "modern" school, the reigning theology up until World War I. In accordance with the influence of Schleiermacher and Ritschl, the modern school maintained that Christianity could be examined scientifically as a historical reality, and yet was also to be understood as arising from an experience of the inner person, an experience that was ultimately moral in kind.[23]

The preceding discussion of Barth's theological development during his student days bears witness to the theology of the time and its particular relation to philosophical trends and culture. The presuppositions and categories germane to other disciplines determined the method and content of

---

velopment under transcendental or *a priori* rules that govern mathematical physics; it is not the process of consciousness itself. For Cohen, there is no *Ding an sich* as Kant taught. Nor is there a transcendental ego as maintained by Fichte. All things fall under the constraints of thought, as that is understood. The preceding assessment of Neo-Kantianism is taken in large part from Lewis White Beck's article, "Neo-Kantianism," in *The Encyclopedia of Philosophy,* ed. Paul Edwards (New York: Macmillan and The Free Press, 1967). Another leading figure of Marburg Neo-Kantianism, Paul Natorp, and Bultmann after him, contrasted the individual and religion to this realm of reason. For Bultmann, reason deals with all that can be objectified. The work of reason stands over against nature. Faith, however, stands over against this work of reason. Authentic existence, a theme of all anthropocentric theology hailing from Schleiermacher, but perfected by Bultmann, is to be had in the move away from reason's objectifying constraints to the arena of the faith of the religious individual. Bultmann contrasts the subjectifying process with the objectifying process, faith with culture, soteriology with anthropology. "Objectifying" is, in fact, the key to his demythology program. But one cannot understand Bultmann's program through awareness of his concept of myth, his appreciation of Heidegger, his Lutheran heritage, or his dependence on Marburg Neo-Kantianism in isolation from one another. He borrowed from these various sources and developed his own creative synthesis. That is to say, he was his own master. The foregoing discussion of Bultmann's relation to Marburg Neo-Kantianism is drawn principally from Roger A. Johnson, *The Origins of Demythologizing: Philosophy and Historiography in the Theology of Rudolf Bultmann* (Leiden: E. J. Brill, 1974). See especially pages 36-37, 78-79. And yet, Bultmann was also a true descendant of the theology that hailed from Schleiermacher. In Barth's assessment of Schleiermacher in the twenties, he points to Bultmann as a proponent of the anthropocentric form of theology to which Schleiermacher's thought gave rise. Karl Barth, *The Theology of Schleiermacher: Lectures at Göttingen, Winter Semester of 1923/24,* ed. Dietrich Ritschl, trans. Geoffrey W. Bromiley (Edinburgh: T. & T. Clark, 1982), p. 269.

22. Busch, *Karl Barth: His Life,* p. 46.

23. Busch, *Karl Barth: His Life,* p. 46.

theology rather than its presumed object — God. Whether Christ was interpreted as the moral teacher (Kant) or as the one whose openness to the infinite marked Jesus as a mediator of the infinite in the realm of the finite (Schleiermacher), the content of Christian faith was separated from its historical form. Philosophical themes took theology captive. Barth was also enamored with this movement, carried away by its force. Such is important to note in light of his later attack on it. Barth was no bystander or neutral observer who would later air criticisms of the movement, but one who was a disciple of those figures who dominated the theological terrain at the turn of the century.

The influence of liberal theology on Barth's thought did not end with his university studies but was carried over into his pastorates in Geneva and Safenwil. As late as 1910, one finds in him a committed disciple of the "modern" school. Such is exemplified in an address he gave at a pastoral conference in Neuchâtel that year. There Barth gives consideration to the problem of the relation of faith to history, a central topic of the theology at the turn of the century, especially that of Herrmann.[24] In contrast to the "orthodox" understanding of faith, which Barth believed centers on true propositions, Barth at this time conceived faith as an experience of the inner person that finds its *origin* in the life experience of Jesus. It should be noted that, in accordance with this view, the person of Jesus did not serve as faith's *object* for Barth at the time.[25] And yet as Busch points out, there are occasional indications in Barth's earliest sermons at Safenwil of a different view of theology than the one he espoused then. In such instances, Barth speaks of a theological orientation grounded in the divine descent rather than in the supposed human ascent to God.[26] However, such ideas would not come to the foreground until after the fateful events of 1914, as shall be shown.

During his pastorate in Safenwil, Barth became active in political affairs. He became involved in socialism, especially issues related to the trade union movement.[27] He maintained that what socialism called for could not be realized apart from the good news of Jesus Christ. And yet, he held that

24. Busch, *Karl Barth: His Life,* p. 57.

25. Busch, *Karl Barth: His Life,* p. 57.

26. Busch, *Karl Barth: His Life,* p. 63.

27. Busch, *Karl Barth: His Life,* p. 69. The formation of trade unions became one of Barth's key interests during his time in Safenwil (p. 103). Barth later indicates that his involvement in socialism was driven largely by the needs of the workers rather than by socialist ideas themselves (p. 104).

what socialism sought after was the significant extension of the gospel.[28] Barth identified true socialism with authentic Christianity in the present, the present activity of Jesus, which was not to be confused with the deeds of the socialists.[29] During this time, Hermann Kutter and Leonhard Ragaz, who were largely responsible for the development of Religious Socialism in Switzerland, influenced Barth greatly.[30] Barth's own interaction with the movement spurred him on in his theological quest and participation in socialism. And yet, Barth was wary of Ragaz's systematization of Religious Socialism whereby the latter argued that the church is an appearance of the coming kingdom of God.[31] It would not be too long before Barth would feel compelled to call into question any hint of a connection between the kingdom of God and the kingdom of this world, calling for the total reformation and transformation of humanity's political and ethical systems.

The Twilight of Religion

A series of events that transpired in 1914 made an indelible mark on Barth's thought and would play a significant part in the theological revolution inaugurated by him. Those events were the outbreak of World War I, the appearance of a manifesto favoring the Kaiser's war aims bearing the signatures of most of Barth's theological teachers, the failings of socialism in the current political crisis,[32] and Ernst Troeltsch's decision to leave his chair in theology for one in philosophy. In this light, Barth seriously began questioning everything, including the theology he had inherited from his mentors. He began searching for a more adequate theology than that found in Schleiermacher and the theology arising from him.

Years later, Barth would claim that, in Schleiermacher, one finds the beginning of an era.[33] Later, he would also write that, in Schleiermacher and

28. Busch, *Karl Barth: His Life,* p. 70.

29. Busch, *Karl Barth: His Life,* p. 70.

30. Busch, *Karl Barth: His Life,* pp. 76-77.

31. Busch, *Karl Barth: His Life,* p. 78.

32. Although Barth would become a Social Democrat himself in 1915, he was dumbfounded by European Socialism's inability to offer resistance to the outbreak of the war (Busch, *Karl Barth: His Life,* p. 82).

33. Karl Barth, *Protestant Theology in the Nineteenth Century: Its Background and History* (London: SCM Press, 1972), p. 425.

the theology inaugurated by his *Speeches,* one discovers the seeds for what transpired that fateful day of 1 August 1914 when "ninety-three German intellectuals . . . identified themselves before all the world with the war policy of Kaiser Wilhelm II and Chancellor Bethmann-Hollweg."[34] Barth says of Schleiermacher, "The entire theology which had unmasked itself in that manifesto, and everything which followed after it (even in the *Christliche Welt*), was grounded, determined, and influenced decisively by him."[35] Barth makes the following observation of the signing of the manifesto.

> An entire world of theological exegesis, ethics, dogmatics, and preaching, which up to that point I had accepted as basically credible, was thereby shaken to the foundations, and with it everything which flowed at that time from the pens of the German theologians.[36]

Cultured humanity and its theology were bankrupt. And so, religion's achievements no longer held sway over Barth's thought. In light of the foregoing, the question of God, not humanity's search for God, but God himself, began to plague Barth's mind. No doubt his interaction with Christoph Blumhardt in 1915 was significant in this regard. Blumhardt's emphasis on the kingdom of God and not humanity, God who alone can perform the necessary action, God who radically renews the world, and who is wholly different from anything the world has ever experienced or imagined, made an indelible impression on Barth.[37]

In his essay written in 1916, entitled, "The Righteousness of God," Barth contends, "We make a veritable uproar with our morality and culture and religion. But we may presently be brought to silence, and with that will begin our true redemption."[38] What is needed is the clear recognition that God is God.[39] This is no easy task, but one that "is an ability won only in fierce inner personal conflict. It is a task beside which all cultural, moral, and patriotic duties, all efforts in 'applied religion' are child's

34. Barth, *Schleiermacher,* pp. 246, 263-64.

35. Barth, *Schleiermacher,* p. 264.

36. Barth, *Schleiermacher,* p. 264.

37. Busch, *Karl Barth: His Life,* p. 85.

38. Karl Barth, "The Righteousness of God," in *The Word of God and the Word of Man,* trans. Douglas Horton (London: Hodder and Stoughton, 1928), pp. 23-24.

39. Barth, "The Righteousness of God," p. 24.

play."[40] One must come to terms with God's righteousness, recognizing that God's "will is not a corrected continuation of our own," but that reality which "approaches ours as a Wholly Other."[41] And only as God approaches and redeems does "real progress become possible; morality and culture, state and nation, even religion and the church now become possible — now for the first time!"[42] It is only as God is taken seriously that the state is taken seriously. However, it is regrettable that all too often the state is taken seriously, while God is ignored.[43]

In addition to the events of 1914, Barth's meeting with Blumhardt, and his increasing suspicions of Religious Socialism, there was another factor in Barth's life that had a significant bearing on the change in direction he would make in theological orientation. During his years in Safenwil, tensions had developed between that theology he had inherited and the responsibility he bore as a minister to preach to his congregation.[44] Barth would later write that, after entering the ministry, the theology he had received from Herrmann receded into the background. The sermon replaced it as posing the most significant problem.[45] In the sermon, Barth struggled greatly in the attempt "to speak to the *people* in the infinite contradiction of their life" while at the same time trying "to speak the no less infinite message of the *Bible,* which was as much of a riddle as life." The world and Word often stood before Barth as "Scylla and Charybdis."[46] This led him to question the minister's ability to fulfill the calling of the ministry.[47] "Embarrassment" was and is the situation in which the minister finds himself,[48] and "for which theology desires to prepare" the preacher.[49] Barth would later reflect that his theology arose out of his pastorate in Safenwil.[50]

40. Barth, "The Righteousness of God," p. 24.

41. Barth, "The Righteousness of God," p. 24.

42. Barth, "The Righteousness of God," p. 26.

43. Busch, *Karl Barth: His Life,* p. 87.

44. Busch, *Karl Barth: His Life,* p. 63.

45. Karl Barth, "The Need of Christian Preaching," in *The Word of God and the Word of Man,* trans. Douglas Horton (London: Hodder and Stoughton, 1928), p. 100.

46. Barth, "The Need of Christian Preaching," p. 100.

47. Barth, "The Need of Christian Preaching," p. 100.

48. Barth, "The Need of Christian Preaching," pp. 100-102.

49. Barth, "The Need of Christian Preaching," p. 102.

50. Busch, *Karl Barth: His Life,* p. 61. Perhaps the events that occurred in 1914 gave rise to

> Why, I had to ask myself, did those question marks and exclamation points, which are the very existence of the minister, play really no rôle at all in the theology I knew, so that I had to be surprised by the truth as by an armed man after I became a minister? . . . Why then did the theologians I knew seek to represent the minister's perplexity, if they touched upon it at all, as a condition superable and sufferable, instead of understanding it at all costs, instead of facing it — and thereby perhaps discovering in it, in its very insuperableness and insufferableness, the real theme of theology?[51]

The idea that preaching was to center on the infinite message of the Bible, that is, on God, did not solve the problem of preaching, but rather intensified it. Eberhard Busch points out that "the predicament" in preaching that Barth faced was not for the most part the "technical" problem of how to speak of God, but the more fundamental one, namely, "*can* I, *may* I, speak of God at all?" Busch adds, "the discovery that he now made was this, that to recognise the basic *difficulty* in speaking of God is in itself relevant knowledge *of God.* He felt that this discovery was a profound *change* from his previous theologising."[52] Along similar lines, Barth reflected that no one is disturbed by the skeptic's question as to whether God exists or not. Life only becomes dangerous when one sees that the true question to be asked is the question centering on the actuality of God's existence.[53] According to Barth, this was *the* problem he had failed to see during his student days and at the beginning of his ministry, but which riveted his attention around the year 1915.[54]

A Wholly Other Word

The question of God and the question of human speech about God received an answer when Eduard Thurneysen whispered to Barth in 1916 that

---

the dilemma he faced in the task of preaching God's Word. Regardless though, the question of God and the question of speaking about God were themselves influential forces in the formulation of his theology.

51. Barth, "The Need of Christian Preaching," p. 102.

52. Busch, *Karl Barth: His Life,* p. 91.

53. Busch, *Karl Barth: His Life,* p. 91.

54. Busch, *Karl Barth: His Life,* p. 91.

a "wholly other" theology was needed for service in the church.[55] Schleiermacher's theology could no longer provide the foundation for their ministry.[56] Nor could they look to Kutter in the light of his book, *Speeches to the German Nation,* written during the war.[57] Although thought was given to taking up the study of Kant as well as Hegel, they made the decision to turn to see what the Bible had to offer.[58] There, in Paul's epistle to the Romans, Barth found a message completely different from what he had expected. He and Thurneysen found a strange new world in the Bible, the world of God.[59] Later, Barth would write of this discovery that,

> What the Bible has to offer us, above all, is insight to the effect that the knowledge of God is the eternal problem of our profoundest personal existence, that it is the starting-point at which we begin and yet do not begin, from which we are separated and yet are not separated. . . . No one compels us to turn from the quiet pursuit of our so-called religious or so-called cultural duties to the Bible; but once we have done so, there is nothing for it but that we should find ourselves in perplexity, and in fear and trembling come to respect the necessity under which, as we shall realize, we were living *before* we asked our question or heard the answer.[60]

Through his study of Scripture, especially Romans, Barth came to see that what mattered were not human thoughts about God, but rather, divine thoughts about humanity. Such thoughts formed the content of Scripture. "It is not the right human thoughts about God which form the content of the Bible, but the right divine thoughts about men."[61]

What would be termed the "theology of the Word" or "dialectical theology" emerged during this period.[62] Barth himself considers the prior

55. Barth, *Schleiermacher,* p. 264.

56. Barth, *Schleiermacher,* p. 264.

57. Busch, *Karl Barth: His Life,* p. 97.

58. Busch, *Karl Barth: His Life,* p. 97.

59. Karl Barth, "The Strange New World Within the Bible," in *The Word of God and the Word of Man,* trans. Douglas Horton (London: Hodder and Stoughton, 1928), p. 33.

60. Karl Barth, "Biblical Questions, Insights, and Vistas," in *The Word of God and the Word of Man,* trans. Douglas Horton (London: Hodder and Stoughton, 1928), pp. 59-60.

61. Barth, "Strange New World Within the Bible," p. 43.

62. McCormack argues that the central category in Barth's theology up until 1924 is that of the kingdom of God. (See McCormack, *Karl Barth's Critically Realistic Dialectical Theology,*

phrase more apt than the other to describe the theological movement he inspired.[63] It arose in the light of what Barth had learned during his pastorate in Safenwil, in combination with his appropriation of the Reformers.[64] Busch cites Barth's own definition of the movement in his account,

> "In contrast to the historical and psychological account which the 'religious man' tended to give of himself at the beginning of the century," the characteristic feature of this theology was "its question about the superior, new element which limits and determines any human self-understanding. In the Bible this is called God, God's word, God's revelation, God's kingdom and God's act. . . ."[65]

Romans I was Barth's first major attempt to come to terms with the Word of God's address to humanity in Scripture. It was already in print in December 1918. However, its date of publication was 1919. *Romans I* mainly emphasizes two things. First, God's cause is alone God's cause. No one can claim to stand on God's side against all others.[66] Second, the kingdom of God is not of this world. It does not come forth as a reformation of this age, but as a wholly new era.[67] Busch argues that these themes indicate the

p. 19.) Whether or not this is the case, the doctrine of the Word is a key theme of Barth's writings from a very early stage. Now what was the relationship of Jesus Christ to Barth's doctrine of the Word in his early theology? Will Herberg points out that Barth's theology from the time of *Romans* onward is "radically Christocentric," though becoming "more pronounced and explicit in Barth's later writings." Herberg also notes that Barth's Christocentrism plays a fundamental role in the development of his social views. Will Herberg, introduction to *Community, State and Church: Three Essays by Karl Barth* (Gloucester, Mass.: Peter Smith, 1968), p. 17. In contrast to the preceding, Busch documents that Jesus Christ is not yet the focal point of Barth's theology at the time of the writing of the *Dogmatics* of 1927. Prior to that time, Barth is simply in the process of bringing Christ to the heart of his dogmatic activity. Until that point, Barth speaks chiefly of the *Word* of God as such (Busch, *Karl Barth: His Life*, p. 173). For his part, McCormack argues that in 1924 Barth's emphasis on the kingdom of God "gave way to the centrality of an incarnational Christology" (McCormack, *Karl Barth's Critically Realistic Dialectical Theology*, p. 19). However, he adds (p. 22) that Barth's incarnational theology would not become fully manifest until *Church Dogmatics*, II/1.

63. Busch, *Karl Barth: His Life*, p. 144.

64. Busch, *Karl Barth: His Life*, p. 143.

65. Busch, *Karl Barth: His Life*, p. 144, quoting Karl Barth, letter to Kroner Verlag, 7 March 1954.

66. Busch, *Karl Barth: His Life*, p. 100.

67. Busch, *Karl Barth: His Life*, p. 100.

direction in which Barth's theology was moving at this stage: confronting pietism, Romanticism, and idealism.[68] For Barth, God ever stands over against humanity and its culture, and against its attempts at divinization and search for peace apart from the true God. God alone is on God's side over against humanity. God alone is able to bring true rest. However, such rest only comes through upheaval and unrest.

It was during this time that Barth "secretly" moved away from Schleiermacher and Herrmann and turned away from Ragaz and Religious Socialism.[69] He could no longer affirm in any way what T. F. Torrance calls the virtual "identification" of "the Christian expectation of the Kingdom of God with the socialist expectation for the future" in the thought of Kutter, Ragaz, and the younger Blumhardt.[70] In contrast to this move, "Barth felt compelled to stress the futurity of God as the limit and fulfilment of all human effort and of all time."[71] Reformation, indeed transformation, was in order. Human thoughts about God needed to give way to consideration of God's thoughts about humanity. And the human kingdom must give way to the kingdom of God. Having said this, Barth would soon return to his study of Romans in the light of his concern to distinguish more clearly divine from human possibilities.[72]

The foregoing should not be taken to mean that Barth looked upon human culture only in negative terms. In the same year *Romans I* was published, Barth gave a lecture in Tambach on "The Christian's Place in Society." There, one not only finds consideration of the kingdom of God's critique of human culture and "*attack* upon society,"[73] but also discussion of the occurrence of parables of the kingdom in human culture.[74] In keeping with the latter, Barth can say, "We can permit ourselves to be more romantic than the romanticists and more humanistic than the humanists."[75]

68. Busch, *Karl Barth: His Life,* p. 100.

69. Busch, *Karl Barth: His Life,* pp. 100-101.

70. In view of comments made by Barth to Markus Mattmüller, Ragaz's chief biographer, Paul Bock has argued that Barth would later change his views about Ragaz, placing Ragaz in a more favorable light. See Paul Bock, ed., *Signs of the Kingdom: A Ragaz Reader,* with a foreword by M. Douglas Meeks (Grand Rapids: Eerdmans, 1984), p. xix.

71. Torrance, *Karl Barth: An Introduction,* p. 40.

72. Busch, *Karl Barth: His Life,* p. 100.

73. Karl Barth, "The Christian's Place in Society," in *The Word of God and the Word of Man,* trans. Douglas Horton (London: Hodder and Stoughton, 1928), p. 314.

74. Barth, "The Christian's Place in Society," pp. 303-7.

75. Barth, "The Christian's Place in Society," p. 303.

There is no contradiction here in Barth's thought. The basis for his affirmative claim in the Tambach lecture was his belief in God as creator and preserver of the world, in spite of its present fallen condition. Moreover, he held that human thoughts and actions may reflect the divine, not when human creatures seek to portray the divine, but rather, when they limit their cultural pursuits to the secular sphere, allowing them to remain the secular realities that they are, the objective, creaturely activities that they should be.[76]

For Barth, human culture offers praise to God, not in the attempt to cross the chasm between the divine and human realms, but in the celebration of life in all its creatureliness and secularity. However, humanity is seldom content to exist as the creature that it is. Instead, it seeks after divinity. In the light of this propensity and drive toward divinization, Barth would return once again to Scripture in the attempt to make even clearer the distinction between the divine and creaturely domains and possibilities.

The result of this endeavor begun in 1920 was a revised edition of *Romans,* which appeared in 1922. Barth believed that he had excised the hint of pantheism contained in the original edition.[77] The difference between *Romans I* and *Romans II* according to Busch is the "abundance of *negative* definitions" in the second edition.[78] The purpose of such was to make clear the distinction between the divine and human spheres. Barth had seen in the reigning theology of his day too close an identification of the divine and human, of God and culture, as exemplified in the events of 1914. The aim of Barth's study was to offer a critique of culture whereby the

76. Barth, "The Christian's Place in Society," pp. 303, 308. This view of secular and objective reflections of the kingdom, often neglected by students of Barth, would remain a permanent feature of Barth's thought, surfacing most clearly in his exposition of Mozart years later. Here and in his study of Mozart, Barth compares writers or musicians. In the Tambach article, Barth prizes Dostoyevsky for his objectivity over against Tolstoy's sermonic tendencies (p. 305). In his treatment of Mozart, Barth praises him for his objectivity in music, contrasting his work with the ideology found in Beethoven and the theology latent in Bach's music. See Chapter Six of this work for consideration of Barth's discussion of Mozart.

77. Busch, *Karl Barth: His Life,* p. 118. One may find instances of what Barth would later consider the hint of pantheism present in his early work in Barth's 1916 article, "The Righteousness of God." There one sees considerable emphasis placed on the role of "conscience." Barth would later retract this earlier emphasis on conscience in his introduction to *The Word of God and the Word of Man,* p. v.

78. Busch, *Karl Barth: His Life,* p. 119.

concept of God would be liberated. The concept of God would itself serve as the basis for the critique and means of liberation.

In Barth's commentary on Romans, he looks to figures past and present for inspiration and direction in his attack on an all too human religion. He sees in Calvin the all-important "relentlessness," in Kierkegaard "dialectical audacity," and in Overbeck the "sense of awe." Barth also finds in Dostoyevsky a "hunger for eternity" and in Blumhardt an appropriate "optimism."[79] Kierkegaard may have been the most important influence on Barth's thought at this time. Barth writes that the latter began to make an indelible impression on his theology in the year 1919 when Barth was making the all-important transition from the first to the second edition of his commentary on Romans.[80] The most important contribution Kierkegaard made to Barth's thought in *Romans II* was his rigorous critique of the identification of God and humanity in modern thought.[81]

In his attack on Schleiermacher's non-eschatological theology,[82] Barth turned to Overbeck's critique of Christendom. Overbeck criticized Christendom and its theology with relentless fury. He opposed what he saw as the historicization of Christianity. The only place for Christianity is in the history beyond history *(Urgeschichte),* not in history itself.[83] For Overbeck, Christianity had lost sight of this, and of the parousia. As a result, it had lost sight of itself and its mission.[84] Christianity had become a predicate of history. It had become Christendom. For Barth, the theologian must

79. Karl Barth, *The Epistle to the Romans,* 6th ed., trans. Edwyn C. Hoskyns (London: Oxford University Press, 1933), p. 252. Although reference is made to the sixth edition, it is on the whole a reprint of the second. See page 15 for Barth's remarks on the third edition and page 25 for his remarks on the sixth.

80. Busch, *Karl Barth: His Life,* p. 116.

81. Busch, *Karl Barth: His Life,* p. 116. In addition to this point regarding Kierkegaard's influence on Barth's theology at this time, it is important to note what T. F. Torrance writes of Barth's relationship to Kierkegaard. For all Barth's distancing himself from Kierkegaard in later years, one thing would remain, namely, Barth's understanding of revelation in the light of the lordship of God, which he appropriated with modifications from "Kierkegaard's doctrine of the *Truth in the form of personal being.*" Truth does not arise from within the human consciousness, but through an event whereby God gives himself to be known by humanity in Christ (Torrance, *Karl Barth: An Introduction,* p. 45).

82. See Torrance's discussion of this point in *Karl Barth: An Introduction,* p. 40.

83. Karl Barth, "Unsettled Questions for Theology Today," in *Theology and Church,* with an introduction by T. F. Torrance, trans. Louise Pettibone Smith (New York: Harper & Row, 1962), p. 62.

84. Barth, "Unsettled Questions for Theology Today," p. 64.

"count the cost" before making the journey through the long and narrow passage of Overbeck's critique and "dare" to do theology as eschatology, even if one thinks one knows "something of Blumhardt's *Yes*" that stands at the other end of this passage.[85] Barth coupled Overbeck's critique of the times with Blumhardt's emphasis on hope. Barth writes that the two "stand close together; . . . Blumhardt stood as a forward-looking and hopeful Overbeck; Overbeck as a backward-looking, critical Blumhardt. Each was the witness to the mission of the other."[86]

On first reading *Romans II,* one might come away thinking Barth a pessimist, a preacher driven by a vision of absolute transcendence and divine judgment. Such was not the case. Barth was no pessimist at this stage, or at any point in his development. As indicated by the brief statement on Overbeck and Blumhardt, Barth's theological critique at this time was wed to a theology of hope. Moreover, Barth despised doomsayers, spurning Spengler's *Decline of the West.*[87]

Not only does one discover in Barth's theology at this time the theme of hope, but also one finds here emphasis on the nearness of God and divine compassion.[88] The divine transcendence at this stage in Barth's thinking is the basis for God's nearness.[89] As Torrance indicates, both Kierkegaard and Barth emphasized the encounter between God and humanity as disclosed in the eternal God's "invasion" of time. The focus is not on abstract transcendence, but on the impending approach of the transcendent God. Busch also shows how for the Barth of *Romans* God is not simply transcendent, but also is near to the humble of heart, to those who do not presume to be well acquainted with God.[90]

Not only is the divine nearness central to Barth's thought at this stage, but also, as stated above, God's compassion is highlighted. Judgment and wrath are themselves forms of God's love and mercy.[91] Moreover, Barth attacks Schleiermacher's theology because he finds there an all too human and not divine compassion.[92] In Schleiermacher's thought, there is no real

85. Barth, "Unsettled Questions for Theology Today," p. 73.
86. Barth, "Unsettled Questions for Theology Today," p. 56.
87. Busch, *Karl Barth: His Life,* p. 120.
88. Barth, *Romans,* pp. 177-78.
89. Barth, *Romans,* p. 116.
90. Torrance, *Karl Barth: An Introduction,* p. 44; Busch, *Karl Barth: His Life,* p. 120.
91. Barth, *Romans,* pp. 69-70, 105-6.
92. See Torrance, *Karl Barth: An Introduction,* p. 40.

need for divine compassion since the distinction between the divine and human is blurred. However, divine compassion has a central place in the theology of *Romans II*. Nonetheless, judgment appears to receive more emphasis there in the light of the situation to which Barth speaks.[93]

Through the course of this chapter, consideration has been given to Barth's growing wariness and opposition to Schleiermacher at this time. One could argue that Barth's attack in *Romans II* is aimed principally at the theology inaugurated by him. What was it about Schleiermacher and his *Speeches* that marked the beginning and eventual crisis of a theological epoch? The answer is to be found in what Barth would later say of nineteenth-century theology. The characteristic trait of that theology to which Schleiermacher gave birth, namely its overriding concentration on the "confrontation with the contemporary age," disclosed Schleiermacher's genius and Achilles' heel.[94] For Schleiermacher, the orator, the apologist, one must venture to mediate Christ and culture in such a way that one approaches revelation from the standpoint of human self-understanding.[95] Indeed, "the most significant formal motif" of Schleiermacher's theology is "the principle of mediation."[96] Unlike Hegel's dialectic in which antithesis gives way to a higher form of synthesis or "definable third thing," Schleiermacher's dialectic signifies that truth is to be found in an undefinable center between Christ and human awareness. The all too imminent danger as Barth sees it is that the latter gains the upper hand, leading to the displacement of the distinct identity of Jesus Christ.[97] In place of the Re-

93. T. F. Torrance writes, "Strangely enough, it was his insistence on preserving intact the positive compassion of God, and his fear of losing it again in a secularised Christianity, that pushed into the forefront the emphasis upon the divine *No* of judgement so that it came at times to be heard more clearly and loudly than the great positive *Yes* of God which was the basic content of all that Barth was now seeking to proclaim." Yet to be able to sound the positive note, the negative note had to be sounded in order to break through the unhealthy union of God and humanity (*Karl Barth: An Introduction*, p. 40). David Mueller writes that the primary purpose of *Romans I* and *Romans II* was not to expound "God's judgement of sinful humanity" but to set forth the truth of God's grace in Christ, who comes to humanity "from above" as "the 'Wholly Other' . . . to effect a new creation." David L. Mueller, introduction to *Church and State*, by Karl Barth, trans. G. Ronald Howe, Church Classics (Greenville: Smyth & Helwys Publishing, 1991), pp. xiv-xv.

94. Barth, "Evangelical Theology in the 19th Century," p. 19.

95. Barth, *Schleiermacher*, pp. 244-45; Barth, *Protestant Theology*, pp. 462-63.

96. Barth, *Protestant Theology*, p. 462.

97. Barth, *Protestant Theology*, pp. 453, 464.

formers' emphasis on the Word of God, which "created and sustained" the human response, that is, "the human correlate of faith," Schleiermacher speaks of "religion or piety."[98] In Schleiermacher and his disciples past and present, emphasis is placed on "the presence of God felt in human awareness."[99] For Barth, the rejection of "Tertullian's dictum that *Deus non est in genere,*"[100] which rings true for Schleiermacher and that theology which springs from him in its many forms, called forth a theological counter-response in the form of a "'wholly other' theological foundation."[101]

Whereas Schleiermacher conceives religion "as the noblest of all human works of art,"[102] which finds "its source in the dispositions of humanity," "the pinnacles of the temple" to which Schleiermacher the orator wishes to lead the cultured despisers of religion,[103] Barth perceives religion as the very crisis of culture.[104] Rather than spelling the divinization of human culture, it "spells disruption, discord, and the absence of peace."[105] "Apart from God, it is the most dangerous enemy a man has on this side of the grave. For religion is the human possibility of remembering that we must die."[106] "Religion is not the sure ground upon which human culture safely rests; it is the place where civilization and its partner, barbarism, are rendered fundamentally questionable."[107]

In Schleiermacher, one finds "the Wholly One," the principle of accommodation and mediation, and the ultimate affirmation of the highest forms of cultural life accompanied by an optimism regarding culture's eschatological progression by way of religion. In Barth, on the other hand, one finds in this period of his thought "the Wholly Other" *(ganz anders, totaliter aliter)* and the negation of culture by means of religion. In Schleiermacher and Barth, immanence meets transcendence; optimism meets suspicion. What Barth saw as the divinization of culture by means of religion led him in no uncertain terms to critique culture by

98. Barth, *Protestant Theology,* p. 458.
99. Barth, *Protestant Theology,* p. 453.
100. Barth, *Schleiermacher,* p. 268.
101. Barth, *Schleiermacher,* p. 264.
102. Barth, *Schleiermacher,* p. 246.
103. Barth, *Schleiermacher,* p. 248.
104. Barth, *Romans,* p. 268.
105. Barth, *Romans,* p. 266.
106. Barth, *Romans,* p. 268.
107. Barth, *Romans,* p. 258.

means of a counter-notion of religion and concept of the freedom of God.[108]

Not only was the close identification of Christ and culture exemplified in the thought of Schleiermacher, but also, as already indicated, it was endemic in Protestant Liberalism at the turn of the century. For example, this same tendency surfaces in the writings of Harnack. In a debate with Barth in the journal *Christliche Welt* in 1923, "the head of the liberals" spoke of the possibility of an "'ascent of God' through culture, historical knowledge, morality, and so on." In response to Harnack, Barth claimed Jesus' words, "No one can come to me unless he is drawn by the Father who sent me."[109]

This exchange between Harnack and Barth was not their first. A noteworthy debate had taken place a few years earlier between the two. In 1920, at a conference in Aarau, Harnack voiced strong disagreement to an address delivered by Barth entitled, "Biblical Questions, Insights, and Vistas." In response to the position championed by Barth, Harnack lamented that "the state of affairs was now worse than it had ever been since Kierkegaard."[110] Barth would later write that this "clash" with Harnack "was almost of his-

108. Barth's doctrine of the freedom of God reveals how Barth is truly a modern thinker. Trutz Rendtorff argues that Barth builds on the paradigms of freedom and autonomy generated by the Enlightenment. Barth's theology is the attempt at a second enlightenment whereby the freedom and autonomy of God are championed. Rendtorff argues that without the backdrop of the modern situation Barth's own critique of authority in the light of the freedom and autonomy of God would have been impossible. See Trutz Rendtorff, "Radikale Autonomie Gottes: Zum Verständnis der Theologie Karl Barths und ihrer Folgen," in *Theorie des Christentums* (Gütersloh: Gütersloher Verlagshaus Gerd Mohn, 1972), pp. 161-81. This author is indebted to Bruce McCormack for his discussion of Rendtorff. McCormack points out that this essay by Rendtorff and a work by Friedrich-Wilhelm Marquardt were instrumental in destroying the view that Barth's theology is unconcerned for the modern situation, leading to a revision of the interpretation of Barth. See McCormack, *Karl Barth's Critically Realistic Dialectical Theology*, pp. 25-28. See Friedrich-Wilhelm Marquardt's work, *Theologie und Sozialismus: Das Beispiel Karl Barths* (München: Chr. Kaiser Verlag, 1972). Marquardt champions the view that Barth's theology arises out of political concerns from a socialist perspective.

109. Karl Barth, *Theologische Fragen und Antworten* (Evangelischer Verlag, 1957), pp. 14, 17; quoted in Busch, *Karl Barth: His Life*, p. 147. This debate makes clear Barth's divergence from that school of thought with which he had once aligned himself, but from which he departed in the *Romans* period.

110. Karl Barth, letter to Agnes von Zahn, 23 December 1935; quoted in Busch, *Karl Barth: His Life*, p. 115.

toric significance."[111] According to Busch, one finds in this lecture of Barth's "the first evidence" of his rejection of Schleiermacher's theology.[112] Busch also notes that Barth's clear distancing of himself from Schleiermacher here was the result of Barth's renewed study of Romans undertaken in that same year.[113] In the paper, "Biblical Questions, Insights, and Vistas," Barth argues that humanity's God, its culture and religion, its piety, are rendered problematic by the chief problem of its existence — God. It is only as God presents himself in wholly otherness as the problem of human existence that God offers himself as the solution to its problematic existence.[114] Schleiermacher was blind to this phenomenon, that is, *the radical critique* of all human conceptualities, activities, and cultural forms in the light of God, as was Harnack after him.

It is not the case that in Harnack's theology one finds the uncritical acceptance of cultural thought forms at every turn. Harnack wishes to make a sharp differentiation between the gospel and civilization.[115] The gospel does not have to do with "the affairs of the world." It must not "become entangled in them."[116] And yet, the gospel is the fulfillment of all that is truly good in culture. Ultimately, there is continuity between Christ and culture by means of the line of "ascent." Is such not displayed in the following quotation from Harnack? "We can have no clearer illustration of the fact that in Jesus' view mercy was the quality on which everything turned, and that the temper in which it is exercised is the guarantee that a man's *religious* position is the right one." For Harnack, "the history of religion marked an enormous advance." As he sees it, "The gods were raised to a higher level and civilised; . . . The two great provinces of religion and morality, hitherto separated, were now brought into close relation."[117] Barth, on the other hand, calls into question religion, man's religious disposition, and the type of civilized life it produces.

111. Karl Barth, letter to H. Hag, 16 February 1945; quoted in Busch, *Karl Barth: His Life,* p. 115.

112. Busch, *Karl Barth: His Life,* p. 114.

113. Busch, *Karl Barth: His Life,* p. 114.

114. See especially pp. 58-59, 68-69, 74, 80 and 81 of Barth's essay, "Biblical Questions, Insights, and Vistas" in this regard.

115. Adolf Harnack, *What Is Christianity?*, intro. Rudolf Bultmann (New York: Harper & Row, 1957), p. 118.

116. Harnack, *What Is Christianity?*, pp. 118-19.

117. Harnack, *What Is Christianity?*, pp. 75-76.

In his introduction to Harnack's *What Is Christianity?*, Bultmann puts his finger on one of the central problems with Harnack and Neo-Protestantism, offering the following verdict:

> Harnack never even caught a glimpse of the utter strangeness of the image of primitive Christianity disclosed by the religious-historical school, and which even today at first inevitably shocks a reader of the New Testament.
>
> Harnack evidently never experienced such a reaction of shock. As a result he diluted to the point of harmlessness, as it were, the ever-problematical core of Christianity, of which Kierkegaard, who did not need any such religious-historical lesson, bore the full brunt. The problem is simply this: how is a Christian existence possible in this world when one, in both his work and pleasures, shares in its culture, its tasks, and its worldly goods? It would appear that for Harnack the reconciliation of the Christian with the Goethian conception of the world created no great difficulties. Hence it is quite easy to see that despite all his efforts — a modern reader might even describe them as moving — Harnack possessed no "antennae" for the theology of Karl Barth.[118]

Bultmann concludes this statement by claiming that "it is characteristic" of Harnack "that the Pauline 'as though not' (1 Cor. 7:29-31) played no role in his thought."[119]

Does Bultmann's critique go too far? And was Barth overly critical of Harnack's theological engagement of culture? Before proceeding further, it is important to pause and include the following parenthesis.

Much criticism has been leveled at Barth and the Barthian historiography centering on "Culture Protestantism," which included Harnack, and its relation to the political and cultural crisis at the turn of the century.[120] Mark Chapman criticizes Barth's theological interpretation of the crisis of culture in the early twentieth century.[121] Although Chapman refers to

118. Rudolf Bultmann, introduction to *What Is Christianity?*, by Adolf Harnack (New York: Harper & Row, 1957), pp. x-xi.

119. Bultmann, introduction to *What Is Christianity?*, p. xi.

120. See, for example, George Rupp, *Culture-Protestantism: German Liberal Theology at the Turn of the Twentieth Century*, American Academy of Religion Studies in Religion Series, ed. Stephen Crites, no. 15 (Missoula, Mont.: Scholars Press, 1977).

121. Mark D. Chapman, "Troeltsch, Kant and the Quest for a Critical Public Theology," *Zeitschrift für neuere Theologiegeschichte* 5, no. 1 (1998): 29-59.

other liberal Christian theologians, such as Harnack, who often took a critical stance toward German foreign policy,[122] he concentrates his attention on defending Ernst Troeltsch, who he says prized critical engagement with culture. In fact, for Troeltsch, "the 'greatness of religion lay in its opposition to culture [and] in its difference from science and from utilitarian ethics.'"[123] Chapman maintains that Troeltsch bases his theology of critical engagement in Kant's critical philosophy.[124] Moreover, Chapman seeks to show how Kant's philosophy, which Troeltsch championed, could have "provided some form of religious underpinning for the attempted institutionalisation of a critical and constructive dialogue in the Weimar constitution."[125] In this vein, Chapman points to the limits Kant and Troeltsch place on human reason and knowledge and to Kant's emphasis on teleology.[126] God is that reality beyond human reach that serves as the "final end" in the light of which humanity formulates its moral laws.[127] Since God is always beyond humanity's reach as the final end of history, Kant adamantly refused "to acknowledge a full realisation of the ends of history as possible within history."[128] In the light of Kant's critical philosophical program and Troeltsch's affirmation of it, Chapman makes the following judgment. If the label "'Culture Protestantism' is to remain a useful term to describe such a theology, its meaning will be quite different from that given in Barthian polemics: Troeltsch, though far from a revolutionary, was methodologically critical of his prevailing culture."[129]

In response, let it first be said that certain aspects of Chapman's critique of the prevalent view of Culture Protestantism are illumining and convincing, namely, that certain figures, including Troeltsch, were far more critical in their engagement of culture than is often acknowledged. But were Kant, Troeltsch, and the others critical *enough?* For example, where are the critical

122. Chapman, "Troeltsch, Kant and the Quest for a Critical Public Theology," pp. 33-34.

123. Chapman, "Troeltsch, Kant and the Quest for a Critical Public Theology," p. 35; quoting Ernst Troeltsch, "Die Kirche im Leben der Gegenwart," in *Zur religiösen Lage, Religionsphilosophie und Ethik* (GSII) (Tübingen: J. C. B. Mohr, 1913), p. 100.

124. See Chapman, "Troeltsch, Kant and the Quest for a Critical Public Theology," pp. 41, 55-56.

125. Chapman, "Troeltsch, Kant and the Quest for a Critical Public Theology," p. 33.

126. See, for example, Chapman, "Troeltsch, Kant and the Quest for a Critical Public Theology," pp. 50-52, 58.

127. Chapman, "Troeltsch, Kant and the Quest for a Critical Public Theology," p. 51.

128. Chapman, "Troeltsch, Kant and the Quest for a Critical Public Theology," p. 52.

129. Chapman, "Troeltsch, Kant and the Quest for a Critical Public Theology," p. 57.

limits to human capacities in Kant's thought as reflected in the following quotation taken from his *Opus postumum*? "God is not a being outside me, but merely a thought in me. God is the morally practical reason legislating for itself. Therefore there is only one God in me, about me, above me."[130] And how critical is Kant's engagement with the subject matter of the biblical text if it is the case, as Barth suggests, that the name Jesus never appears in his work? The reason for its absence according to Barth is that Christ serves as a symbol or example of that "archetype residing in our reason."[131] For Kant, the ideal exemplified by Christ "does not require any historical realization."[132] Thus, the identity of the person of Jesus Christ is not of ultimate and indispensable value. He does not serve as the basis or object of faith, but simply as a supreme example of the virtuous life. Ultimate truth lies within, not outside human consciousness in the person of Christ. Given this subjectivist orientation, where are the critical safeguards against the all too human incapacity of human capacities, which Kant refers to as radical evil?[133] Moreover, if Troeltsch builds his theology on the foundation of Kant's philosophy, what is to be made of his system?

Furthermore, what is to be made of Chapman's claim that in the 1920s theologians, who jettisoned the critical theology espoused by Troeltsch, helped bring about the "destruction of . . . the public constitutional sphere, both by their willing retreat from the public domain and by the rejuvenated confessionalism and ecclesiocentricity of so much of their theology"?[134] If Chapman includes Barth in this assessment of such confessionalism, his own historiography is seriously suspect at points. It was due to Barth's strict adherence to the confession and commitment to the church as an agent for social change that he was so outspoken in his criticisms of the German political culture from the teens through the forties.

130. *Kants Opus postumum,* ed. Erich Adickes (Berlin: Reuther & Reichard, 1920), p. 819; quoted in Lewis White Beck, *Studies in the Philosophy of Kant* (Indianapolis: Bobbs-Merrill, 1965), pp. 51-52.

131. Karl Barth, *Protestant Theology in the Nineteenth Century: Its Background and History* (London: SCM Press, 1972), p. 288, quoting Immanuel Kant, *Religion within the Limits of Reason Alone,* p. 175.

132. Barth, *Protestant Theology in the Nineteenth Century,* p. 288.

133. See Immanuel Kant's discussion of the existence of radical evil in human nature in *Religion within the Limits of Reason Alone,* trans., with an introduction and notes by Theodore M. Greene and Hoyt H. Hudson (New York: Harper & Row, 1960), pp. 28, 32.

134. Chapman, "Troeltsch, Kant and the Quest for a Critical Public Theology," p. 59.

Barth was indeed less outspoken in the 1920s; but this was due to the new demands placed upon him in accordance with his change of profession from pastor to professor, and also due to the fact that he was a foreigner residing in Germany.[135] Later, he writes that he wishes he had warned his audience of the Hitler menace in a more direct manner than he had done in the twenties.[136] However, he did become increasingly a vocal opponent of Hitler, a menace and enemy of the state. It can perhaps be argued that no other theologian was as attentive as he was to the political happenings immediately preceding and during Hitler's reign.[137]

As a "confessionalist," not only was Barth a public voice, but also his views regarding his theological predecessors were more nuanced than one might think. One finds in Barth's work, *Protestant Theology in the Nineteenth Century,* and the lectures that gave rise to it, a respectful and charitable presentation of his theological predecessors. In response to surprised readers mindful of his earlier attack on nineteenth-century theology, Barth explains that his views had not undergone change, simply the context in which he speaks of "Culture Protestantism." One should not speak of the dead as one would speak to the living.[138] Moreover, Barth expresses concern over the younger theologians' outright rejection of their predecessors.[139] And he shows signs of displeasure over Emil Brunner's critique of Schleiermacher in *Mysticism and the Word.* The main reason for Barth's disapproval centers on Brunner's outright dismissal of Schleiermacher. For his own part, Barth would never be completely finished with the father of Protestant Liberalism.[140]

135. Busch, *Karl Barth: His Life,* pp. 147-48.

136. Busch, *Karl Barth: His Life,* p. 190.

137. See, for example, page 218 of Busch for his discussion of Barth's critical analysis of fascism in December 1931, a little over a year prior to Hitler's seizure of power in Berlin in January 1933.

138. Busch, *Karl Barth: His Life,* p. 222.

139. Busch, *Karl Barth: His Life,* pp. 221-22.

140. Busch, *Karl Barth: His Life,* pp. 151-52; Barth, *Schleiermacher,* pp. 274-75. Gary Dorrien maintains that, "Barthian theology was a highly creative blend of Reformationist, orthodox, and liberal modernist elements. The latter elements were crucial to its character as a theology of the self-authenticating Word of Christ." In spite of Neo-orthodoxy's attacks leveled at the tradition Schleieirmacher inspired, each major representative, including even Barth, "remained importantly rooted in the tradition of nineteenth-century theological liberalism." Gary Dorrien, *The Barthian Revolt in Modern Theology: Theology without Weapons* (Louisville: Westminster/John Knox Press, 2000), p. 2.

Lastly, Barth does not blame Schleiermacher and the theology he fathered as being responsible for what came to the forefront between the two world wars, namely, the "'people's movement.'"[141] What he does say is that the theology at the turn of the century, including that of Herrmann and Harnack,

> did not provide the necessary safeguards against it. And in virtue of its presuppositions it could not do so. Where the recognition of the distinctive sovereignty of the Word of God spoken in Jesus Christ is as weak as it was in Evangelical theology from the beginning of the 18th century, we must be prepared for the intrusion of false gods. And where this penetration takes place in the evaluation of the state and culture, the erection of a further false god is at least negatively prepared.[142]

The theology hailing from Schleiermacher, including that of Harnack and Troeltsch at the turn of the century, had its faults. But

> the fine humanism of this whole period was enough to prevent them from guilt in this direction. An Harnack would have found it easier to become a Capuchin than to be associated with the champions of the people who came to the forefront in the twenties.[143]

No, according to Barth, Neo-Protestantism did not make positive preparation for what later transpired, only "negative preparation."[144]

The problem Barth and Bultmann see in Harnack discussed above, prior to the parenthetical discussion, is not limited to classical Protestant Liberalism. Barth would later find the same general tendency in the German Christian movement and National Socialism. Moreover, as already indicated, Barth would later argue that Bultmann's theology itself ultimately hails from Schleiermacher. Concerning the German Christians, Barth would criticize them for what he would see as the close identification of Christianity and German culture. As Will Herberg says of Barth,

141. Karl Barth, *Church Dogmatics,* III/4, *The Doctrine of Creation,* ed. G. W. Bromiley and T. F. Torrance (Edinburgh: T. & T. Clark, 1961), p. 307.

142. Barth, *Church Dogmatics,* III/4, p. 307.

143. Barth, *Church Dogmatics,* III/4, p. 307.

144. Barth, *Church Dogmatics,* III/4, p. 307.

> What he was fighting against was essentially the "German Christian" ideology, which closely identified "Germanism" with Christianity *(Volkstum und Evangelium)* and saw in the Nazi revolution an act of divine redemption and a source of divine revelation.[145]

Concerning Bultmann, Barth would find in him once again the "anthropologizing of theology."[146] The focus in each is on the ascent of humanity to God by way of nationhood or religious experience rather than the counter-move by way of a divine descent to humanity.

The true foundation of theology and the Christian community, which theology is to serve, "is not human religious experience but the divine word of revelation directed *to* man."[147] Ultimately, what is at stake in theology is one's approach to the Word. Barth would later focus his attention on this anthropocentric orientation of Protestant Liberalism in his 1927 essay, "The Word in Theology from Schleiermacher to Ritschl," considering the matter of "fundamental" importance.[148] Does Christian preaching (and exegesis) center on God's Word addressed to the creature or on "all which man can say to himself about God"? Does the Word govern theology? Or do human words and experiences govern it? For Barth, two criteria provide the framework for an answer. The first criterion relates to whether or not one is "confronted" time and time again by God's truth, by God's Word, as one who is ignorant of its message and who therefore listens in submission rather than as one who stands over the Word as its master.[149] The first criterion is the

145. Herberg, introduction to *Community, State and Church,* by Karl Barth (Gloucester, Mass.: Peter Smith, 1968), p. 38. See pages 147, 148, 189, and 190 of Busch's work, *Karl Barth: His Life,* on the political problems in Germany from 1920 onward. These matters will be discussed in greater detail in subsequent chapters.

146. Barth, *Schleiermacher,* p. 269. See also Barth's letter of 5 February 1930 to Bultmann where he sets forth his suspicions of the latter along the same lines in *Karl Barth — Rudolf Bultmann, Letters 1922-1966,* ed. Geoffrey W. Bromiley (Edinburgh: T. & T. Clark, 1982), pp. 49-50.

147. The quotation is taken from a lecture delivered in November 1923 entitled "Church and Revelation." According to Busch, *Karl Barth: His Life,* p. 527, note 136, the original can be found in Karl Barth and Eduard Thurneysen, *Revolutionary Theology in the Making,* ed. James D. Smart (Richmond, Va.: John Knox Press and Epworth Press, 1964), p. 193; the quotation here is taken from Eberhard Busch, *Karl Barth: His Life,* p. 150.

148. Karl Barth, "The Word in Theology from Schleiermacher to Ritschl," in *Theology and Church: Shorter Writings, 1920-1928,* with an introduction by T. F. Torrance, trans. Louise Pettibone Smith (New York: Harper & Row, 1962), p. 200.

149. Barth, "The Word in Theology from Schleiermacher to Ritschl," p. 200.

psychological factor.[150] The second criterion is historical in nature. It centers on the relation of the Word of God to history. Is revelation history because God chooses to reveal himself there? Or is history, history as normally conceived, revelation because humanity chooses to place God there?[151] Is history a predicate of revelation, or is revelation a predicate of history, human history, and therefore ultimately that which arises from within humankind? Apart from a few exceptions, Barth finds in the theology of the nineteenth century that approach to the Word according to which humanity in itself and in its history is the measure of all things, even the truth of God.

In the *Romans* period, the Word of God meets human words about God and the world of culture head on, calling them into question, pronouncing judgment upon them, rendering them speechless as to any claim to divine significance so as to offer to humanity divine mercy and compassion. On the whole, the Word of God at this time serves as critical limit to culture's creations rather than as a constructive voice as to how human speech about God and human culture may proceed.[152] Indeed, the God

150. Barth, "The Word in Theology from Schleiermacher to Ritschl," p. 201.

151. Barth, "The Word in Theology from Schleiermacher to Ritschl," p. 201.

152. For an interesting historical parallel to Barth's critique of culture, yet from a very different vantage point, see Allan Janik and Stephen Toulmin, "Culture and Critique: Social Criticism and the Limits of Artistic Expression," in *Wittgenstein's Vienna* (New York: A Touchstone Book, published by Simon and Schuster, 1973), pp. 92-119. There consideration is given to the "critique of the mores of contemporary Viennese society" at the end of the Habsburg era "with its artificiality and aestheticism" by means of "aesthetic expression" (p. 112). Whether it was in the realm of art or the artifact, form or ornamentation ruled the day. Art for art's sake, embellishment as an end in itself, form devoid of content or use, was master (pp. 97, 112-13). Those who critiqued this situation did not wish to put asunder form or ornament, simply the fixation with style and good taste and the "fetish of ornamentation" (pp. 97, 99, 101). The authors quote Oscar Wilde's line on this predicament, "'The first duty in life is to be as artificial as possible. What the second duty is no one has yet discovered'" (p. 113). Barth himself pays tribute to this counter-cultural movement. In his 1919 Tambach essay, he writes, "However strong our aversion may be to the work of the modern expressionistic artists, it is more than clear that for these men the chief concern is the essence, the content, the referring of the beautiful to life's unity, in contrast to that *art for its own sake* which prevailed during the last generation, but which, after all, can cite precedent with certainty in neither Raphael nor Dürer" (Barth, "The Christian's Place in Society," p. 292). The great critic of ornamentation at this time, the architect Adolf Loos, did not consider himself a revolutionary (Janik and Toulmin, p. 99). If anything, he staged a revolution against the revolution, that "reign of terror" that had sabotaged the real purpose of the artifact (p. 101). He was a counter-revolutionary. Is not Barth himself to be viewed in this way? He wished to restore the concept of God to its rightful place, and with it, albeit indirectly at

whose Word it is says "Yes" to humanity in the midst of the utterance of the divine "No." However, this Word, the Word as Jesus Christ, is himself the "Wholly Other," transcending culture rather than being wed to it. It is this Word who comes to the world, to his creatures. Here one finds the radical denial of Plato's doctrine of *anamnesis* which, according to T. F. Torrance, Barth defines as the *analogia entis.*[153] The Word or Logos does not find a point of contact within the human psyche. There is no "immanent continuity" between the Word and humanity.[154] The eternal truth does not lie within, needing simply to be called to mind through a process of discursive reasoning. Knowledge of the wholly other God depends upon God revealing himself to his creation in his Word.

The wholly other God speaks forth a wholly other Word and calls forth a wholly different ethic, exegesis, and theology than those exemplified in the works of Barth's theological mentors. In an essay written in 1922, Barth claims, "The ethics of the *Ritschlian* school" were "the ethics of the bourgeoisie growing prosperous in the time of the consolidation of the Bismarckian empire."[155] It would no longer be possible to sustain such an ethic. In the face of God, ethics arises not from a desire for illumination or from pleasure, but in crisis.[156] One could no longer consider ethics the predictable and "obvious" study of what should be done "to further" an "infinitely imperfect but infinitely perfectible culture."[157] The ethical scandal of the times concerned not the scandalous or "savage" man, but the "moral man" who had been esteemed so highly by those who looked upon dogmatics as a mystifying labor of thought and ethics as essentially a simple task.[158] In opposition to this orientation, one could no longer reduce the gospel to belief in God and love of one's neighbor.[159] One could no longer view following Jesus as a simple endeavor. In fact, his ethic was not so unlike the mysterious and complex dogmatic formulations shunned by the enlight-

---

the time perhaps, culture, too. He wished ultimately to de-divinize culture, to make it truly human culture once again.

153. Torrance, *Karl Barth: An Introduction,* p. 46.

154. Torrance, *Karl Barth: An Introduction,* p. 46.

155. Karl Barth, "The Problem of Ethics Today," in *The Word of God and the Word of Man,* trans. Douglas Horton (London: Hodder and Stoughton, 1928), p. 145.

156. Barth, "The Problem of Ethics Today," pp. 136, 140, 145.

157. Barth, "The Problem of Ethics Today," p. 145.

158. Barth, "The Problem of Ethics Today," p. 147.

159. Barth, "The Problem of Ethics Today," p. 147.

ened European.[160] One could no longer conceive Christianity as the ethic of European culture, for "the ways of European man are now proved impossible in relation to the *ethic* of Christianity."[161] Things were not as obvious or as simple as they once seemed. Instead of raising ethical questions from the standpoint of confident self-assurance, with the answers already to hand, one was now forced to face *the* ethical question. How could it be possible to "be impartial" to the reality of the creator God?[162] In the light of the events of the day, it was indeed impossible to act as if everything remained the same. The certainty with which one had faced the past gave way to uncertainty as to what one was to do in the present. "Whoever now desires certainty must first of all become uncertain."[163] One could not answer the question for oneself. One could not proceed to God, not even by means of "a *via negativa,*" neither by means of "a *via dialectica* nor *paradoxica.*"[164] There could be no point of contact by means of ascent — only by divine descent.[165] God's judgment became the ethical problem, and the forgiveness found in that judgment was the answer to the problem.[166] Only as one faced the wholly otherness of God in his judgment and forgiveness could one be made whole.[167]

160. Barth, "The Problem of Ethics Today," pp. 147-48.

161. Barth, "The Problem of Ethics Today," p. 147.

162. Barth, "The Problem of Ethics Today," p. 148.

163. Barth, "The Problem of Ethics Today," p. 149.

164. Barth, "The Problem of Ethics Today," p. 177.

165. Barth, "The Problem of Ethics Today," p. 179.

166. Barth, "The Problem of Ethics Today," pp. 178, 181.

167. Steven G. Smith argues that Barth was by no means concerned to articulate a doctrine of God as "Wholly Other." Instead the concept functioned in a heuristic manner, serving as "a device for placing theology in the right position before God." Steven G. Smith, *The Argument to the Other: Reason Beyond Reason in the Thought of Karl Barth and Emmanuel Levinas,* American Academy of Religion Academy Series, ed. Carl Raschke, no. 42 (Chico, Calif.: Scholars Press, 1983), p. 48. Smith goes so far as to say that Barth was not attempting to espouse a doctrine of God through the employment of the expression, "the Wholly Other," and that he would come "to dissociate himself almost entirely from talk of the Wholly Other." Smith adds, however, that Barth does so without distancing "himself from the function that this talk served in its place in the theological discussion" (p. 48). In response, it is true that the wholly otherness of God continues to serve a role in theological discussion for Barth. However, this role stems in part from a view of God as "Wholly Other," which Barth continues to espouse. Smith's citation of Barth's own remarks on this earlier view in his essay, "The Humanity of God," as support for his thesis (p. 48), as well as his claim that as a conception of God the wholly otherness of God is logically incoherent and void of content

For the young Barth, God was the "Wholly Other" and as such wholly beyond religion and piety. He was speaking of a God beyond God, religion beyond religion and piety beyond piety. God was not simply the solution to the problem. God was also the problem. God was only the solution as he was the chief problem of cultured humanity's problematic existence, of its religion and piety, which themselves were problems, barriers to humanity's coming to terms with God. "Biblical piety is not really pious; one must rather characterize it as well-considered and definite refusal to regard anything as sacred."[168] Then and now, God confronts humanity's problematic piety and religion. Only as God confronts does God overcome and solve

---

(pp. 48-49), are not convincing. Barth nuanced his dialectical position on the wholly otherness of God. He did not renounce it. Barth could affirm what he earlier wrote while at the same time move beyond it, which he did, as indicated in the essay mentioned above, due to his later employment of the Christological categories of *anhypostasis* and *enhypostasis.* More will be said of this in the following chapter. Moreover, from what Smith says of incoherence, it appears that he is interpreting Barth's concept of God in terms of *opposition* to the concept of humanity rather than in terms of sheer *difference.* The two are not the same. Opposition implies continuum by way of contrast. That is to say, the two concepts could not be contrasted if they did not share some basis for comparison. Barth is wary of the traditional approach to analogy, which involves progression or ascent through the *via negativa* and *via eminentiae.* However, for *qualified* affirmation of the possibility of their use in the consideration of the divine perfections, see Karl Barth, *Church Dogmatics,* II/1, *The Doctrine of God* (Edinburgh: T. & T. Clark, 1957), pp. 347-48. Ultimately, the *via negativa* implies an underlying continuum for the items being contrasted. In their place, Barth espouses difference, and this, above and beyond sheer affirmation and negation. And yet, further to what has already been suggested, Barth would later nuance his viewpoint on analogy, wedding it to a view of God whereby God becomes wholly one with creation. God became wholly one with the creation, while at the same time remaining wholly other in that relation. Now for all this writer's disagreement with Smith, he is correct in arguing that Barth's early formulation served as a therapeutic device for the restoration of theology to its rightful position. However, T. F. Torrance's claim that Barth's "intention" in "*Romans* was by no means an attack on culture as such, but rather the opposite, upon a bogus mystification of culture which required to be disenchanted of its secret divinity before it really could be human culture" goes too far. See Thomas F. Torrance, introduction to *Theology and Church: Shorter Writings, 1920-1928,* by Karl Barth, trans. Louise Pettibone Smith (New York: Harper & Row, 1962), p. 22. For although Barth's critique of classical liberal theology and German culture had the effect of liberating culture to be truly human, the overall *intention* of Barth's earlier critique was as Smith argues to redirect theology to its rightful vocation and to emphasize the distinct existence of God. Barth's concern for the authentic vocation of culture at this point is secondary and indirect.

168. Barth, "Biblical Questions," p. 66.

the problematic state in which humanity finds itself. Schleiermacher did not see this.

The Modern Word of Crisis and the Crisis of the Word

Tillich's discussion of Barth the kerygmatic theologian noted at the outset of this chapter might lead one to conclude mistakenly that Barth's theology is not at all determined by a concern for human culture. Although a theologian of the kerygma or Word, Barth's theology is a theology addressing humanity in modern culture, indeed arising out of that confrontation. The Word always has a direct bearing on the concerns of the church and culture. Indeed one could argue in the light of the foregoing historical discussion that Barth's doctrine of the Word is itself quite modern, having arisen in the light of the modern situation in which Barth was placed. And yet, one cannot reduce his doctrine of the Word to being a predicate of that situation. For Barth believed strongly that theology best serves the concerns of church and broader culture and has the best and most direct bearing on them when the theologian concentrates on those concerns addressed by the Word of God. For as T. F. Torrance argues, Barth found in the theology of the eighteenth and nineteenth centuries the absence of "radical clarity about its own positive task." Barth saw there that "the nature and function of theology were blurred through confusion with the subsidiary task of coming to grips with the spirit of the age."[169]

In contrast to Tillich's assessment, the argument here is that Barth's doctrine of the wholly otherness of God, and later, his dialectical complement to it in the form of the wholly oneness of God, arise out of Barth's engagement with culture. While culture does not dictate the content of Barth's theology, the concepts emerge in direct relation to his concerns for culture. Indeed, each time Barth's theology underwent a transformation it was the result of his having turned to the Word in light of the events of his day and/or as a result of what he might say to the people of his day.

In the end, Barth's theology of the Word demonstrated as much concern for culture as the theology of those orators of speeches of religion

169. Torrance, *Karl Barth: An Introduction,* p. 33.

who preceded him. The difference between them lies in their starting points. Both Schleiermacher and Barth must be understood as preoccupied with two poles of thought, Christ and culture.[170] Yet, in each case, one pole has priority over the other, in effect, if not in principle. For Barth, the Word of God directed to human culture frees culture to be truly human. For Schleiermacher, on the other hand, the oration is in effect a call to awaken and realize what one should already know, namely, the continuity that ultimately exists between the divine and human, between Christ and culture, and that religion is the pinnacle of the cultural sphere. In the end, however, the concepts of God and Christ fall under the scope of human consciousness, reshaped in light of the categories germane to the culture of the day. Thus, the Word of God is at best the predicate of the human word, if not exhausted by it.[171] In Barth's theology, one finds the confrontation of culture. In Schleiermacher, one comes upon the ultimate affirmation of culture, not in terms of what it should be as distinct from God, but in terms of its ultimate union with the divine. Thus, in either event, one pole takes precedent. The key then is to discern which orientation serves best to allow the Word and the world of culture to be what each in fact is. The view adopted here is that Barth's approach to culture proves more satisfactory than its counterpart, in spite of points of tension in Barth's thought, which he would soon seek to resolve.

What is not in *Romans* is the truly integral relation of time and eternity, of revelation and history. In the *Romans II* phase of his thought, Barth conceives revelation as an event in which God veils and unveils himself, albeit in non-historical, non-incarnational terms. In the preface to the second edition of *Romans,* Barth writes that,

> if I have a system, it is limited to a recognition of what Kierkegaard called the "infinite qualitative distinction" between time and eternity,

170. Torrance, *Karl Barth: An Introduction,* p. 36.

171. In his 1920 essay on Ludwig Feuerbach, Barth writes that the question posed by Feuerbach to the theology of Schleiermacher and his disciples concerns "whether and how far religion, revelation, the relation between God and man, can be made understandable as a predicate of man. Theology had let itself be driven by the upsurge of a self-glorifying and self-satisfied humanism from Pietism over the Enlightenment to Romanticism." In the end, was not the result "the apotheosis of man"? Karl Barth, "Ludwig Feuerbach," in *Theology and Church: Shorter Writings, 1920-1928,* with an introduction by T. F. Torrance, trans. Louise Pettibone Smith (New York: Harper & Row, 1962), p. 227.

> and to my regarding this as possessing negative as well as positive significance: "God is in heaven, and thou art on earth."[172]

Barth indicates in this preface that he believes Paul was primarily concerned here "with the permanent KRISIS of the relation between time and eternity."[173] In his exposition of the text of Romans itself, Barth writes that, "As Christ, Jesus is the plane which lies beyond our comprehension. The plane which is known to us, He intersects vertically, from above."[174] It is only later in his development that Barth conceives the relation of time to eternity in integral terms.[175]

Corresponding to Barth's emphasis on the radical distinction between time and eternity at this stage of his thought is his move to stress the deity of God over against what he feared in Schleiermacher's theology, namely, the deification of humanity. In *Romans II,* Barth calls into question the enthronement of God in this worldly sphere by human hands, which in the end is nothing more than the worship of the creature. In this perversion of true piety, humanity sets aside the "contradiction" between time and eternity and God and humanity.

> We confound time with eternity. That is our *unrighteousness.* — Such is our relation to God apart from and without Christ, on this side resurrection, and before we are called to order. God Himself is not acknowledged as God and what is called 'God' is in fact Man. By living to ourselves, we serve the 'No-God'.[176]

Barth was correct to emphasize the distinction. However, he stressed the deity of God and his Word without giving proper consideration to the humanity of God in his Word. Barth would later reflect back saying that he was "at that time only partially in the right."[177] In seeking to compensate

172. Barth, *Romans,* p. 10.

173. Barth, *Romans,* pp. 10-11.

174. Barth, *Romans,* pp. 29-30.

175. As already indicated, although the sixth edition of *Romans* was published in 1928, it is in content virtually a reprint of the second edition published in 1922. The key development in Barth's thought which gave rise to the more integral relation of time and eternity takes place in 1924, as shall be argued in the next chapter.

176. Barth, *Romans,* p. 44.

177. Karl Barth, "The Humanity of God," in *The Humanity of God* (Atlanta: John Knox Press, 1960), p. 42.

for Culture Protestantism's move to make humanity "great at the cost of God,"[178] Barth would come to realize that he had made God great at the cost of humanity.[179] He had viewed the wholly otherness of God "in isolation" from humanity, abstracting it from God's togetherness with humanity.[180] He had "absolutized" this concept and had "boxed" humanity's "ears with it."[181] Only later would he realize that the sovereign Lord is to be conceived in "*togetherness* with man."[182] It is important to conceive God's sovereignty in direct relation to God's togetherness with humanity. God's togetherness with humanity is a "sovereign togetherness with man" as "determined" by God and God "alone."[183] The origin and orientation of this relationship is always from above to below, by divine descent rather than by human ascent. And yet, following on from the incarnation, it is a movement that enables humanity to participate in the divine life as human instead of isolating and ignoring humanity. For as Barth writes, "It is precisely God's *deity* which, rightly understood, includes his *humanity*."[184]

It is only possible to preserve the concept of God's deity, and following on from it, to enable culture to be truly human, through recourse to Barth's emphasis on *diastasis* in the Word event. And yet, by itself, *diastasis* is unable to provide the appropriate categories for the development of a view of theology, and its engagement of culture, that is truly human, truly incarnational. As shall be shown in the next chapter, for Barth, *diastasis* requires *anhypostasis* and *enhypostasis* for a truly incarnational conception of the Word's relation to culture to prosper.

178. Barth, "The Humanity of God," pp. 39, 43.
179. Barth, "The Humanity of God," pp. 42-44.
180. Barth, "The Humanity of God," p. 45.
181. Barth, "The Humanity of God," p. 45.
182. Barth, "The Humanity of God," p. 45.
183. Barth, "The Humanity of God," p. 45.
184. Barth, "The Humanity of God," p. 46.

2

The Word of Christ and World of Culture in Dialectical and Integral Relation

Toward the Critical and Constructive Engagement of Culture

In the year 1924, Barth discovered a way by which he could speak of revelation's relation to history in integral terms without discarding the all-important distinction between the two. Barth's reading of Heinrich Heppe's *Reformed Dogmatics* led him to contextualize the Reformed doctrines of *anhypostasis* and *enhypostasis* to his understanding of this relation.[1] Barth found in the Reformed conception of Christology a means by which revelation could be viewed as taking place "*in* history without becoming a predicate *of* history."[2] It should also be noted that this discovery would enable him to set aside the time-eternity dialectic that had to this point preserved for him the notion of God's sovereignty in the event of revelation whereby God ever remains subject in revelation.[3] The eternal Word reveals himself in history through the otherness of creatureliness.[4]

The Word becomes incarnate in history. This does not mean, however, that the incarnate subject is revealed in a direct manner in human history. For the subject of revelation is not to be understood as a person brought into existence by the union of the divine and human natures, but as the di-

1. Bruce McCormack, *Karl Barth's Critically Realistic Dialectical Theology: Its Genesis and Development, 1909-1936* (Oxford: Clarendon Press, 1995), p. 23.

2. McCormack, *Karl Barth's Critically Realistic Dialectical Theology,* p. 21.

3. McCormack, *Karl Barth's Critically Realistic Dialectical Theology,* pp. 367, 435.

4. See McCormack, *Karl Barth's Critically Realistic Dialectical Theology,* p. 362.

vine person of the eternal Word who takes a concrete human nature to himself in becoming incarnate as Jesus Christ. McCormack writes that,

> The anhypostatic-enhypostatic model was well suited for clarifying what was at stake in speaking of revelation as revelation in concealment, as indirect communication. For the Subject of this revelation is the Person of the Logos who has veiled Himself in human flesh.[5]

5. McCormack, *Karl Barth's Critically Realistic Dialectical Theology*, p. 362. F. LeRon Shults argues that Protestant Scholasticism is responsible for corrupting the dual notion of *anhypostasis-enhypostasis* created by Leontius of Byzantium. See F. LeRon Shults, "A Dubious Christological Formula: From Leontius of Byzantium to Karl Barth," *Theological Studies* 57 (September 1996): 431-46. Shults adds that those influenced by Barth have also fallen prey to error at this point since Barth himself accepts the Protestant Scholastic rendition of the formula (p. 431). In the course of his argument, Shults states that the meaning intended by *anhypostasis* and *enhypostasis* was that the human nature of Christ only subsists "in its union with the Logos in the one person of Christ" (p. 433). He rejects the accompanying notion championed by Loofs, who claimed that for Leontius, the human nature has "its hypostasis . . . in the hypostasis of another nature" (p. 436). One of the points made in his discussion of Leontius is that Loofs errs in taking the "en-" in enhypostasis for "a localizing prefix rather than simply the opposite of an alpha primitive" (p. 437). One should also note Shults's discussion of Marcel Richard, who claimed, "for Leontius all natures . . . are 'enhypostatic'" (p. 440). Shults adds that Richard is absolutely right since enhypostatic "simply means 'hypostasized' or 'subsisting' and, given Aristotelian assumptions, a nature cannot subsist *ante rem* but only *in rebus*" (pp. 440-41). Shults concludes that the Protestant rendering of the formula should be discarded, but adds that Barth's dialectical doctrine of revelation is not dependent on the motif in question, reasoning that, "What seems most important to Barth is not the terms, but a specific kind of relational unity that maintains the asymmetry of the divine initiative . . . an insistence on the creature's total reliance on God's grace" (p. 446). In response, whether or not Shults's interpretation of Leontius is correct, he is wrong about the significance or insignificance of the formula for Barth's theology. Barth does not simply stress *that* there is "asymmetry" in the relationship between God and the creature according to which the creature is wholly dependent on God, but also *how* that asymmetry is expressed, that is, in terms of the human nature of Christ subsisting *in* the divine person. Only in this way could Barth maintain his dialectical understanding of revelation involving concealment. In a recent response to Shults, U. M. Lang, citing McCormack, also argues that the *anhypostasis-enhypostasis* formula plays a most significant role in Barth's theology. U. M. Lang, "Anhypostatos-Enhypostatos," *Journal of Theological Studies* 49, no. 2 (October 1998): 630. Lang agrees with Shults that the *"formula," anhypostasis-enhypostasis,* cannot be found in the church fathers, but then goes on to claim that the "'dual formula' is not found in Protestant orthodoxy either" (p. 631). If anything, this formula originates with Barth. And although the terms are employed in *The Göttingen Dogmatics,* the technical, "'dual formula'" does not emerge until the *Church Dogmatics* (p. 632). Following Brian Daley, Lang maintains

By this means, Barth was able to hold on to his dialectical model that God reveals himself in hiddenness. However, although the Word reveals himself in hiddenness, such concealment actually occurs in history. "The hiddenness of God is a hiddenness in history, because the Subject in whom the humanity of Jesus is made real and exists is a Subject in history."[6] Barth's dialectical theology had now become incarnational.

Not only did the employment of this model lead Barth to set aside the time-eternity dialectic, but also together with related notions, it would provide him with the categories whereby he could solve the dilemma of the strict opposition of the two within the dialectic of their relation. That is to say, he could now set forth a positive view of their relation while also affirming their utter difference. The basis was now laid for Barth to develop a truly incarnational, Christological model of revelation and theology, and as shall be argued, would enable him to set forth a positive yet dialectical conception of the engagement of God and humanity, and Christ and culture.[7] Barth's theology now provided a means by which one could

---

that for Leontius of Byzantium *enhypostasis* does not signify the "in-existence of the human nature in the Logos" (p. 641). Having said this, Lang argues that the *substance* of the doctrine, although not the technical formula, originates in the sixth century in the writings of John of Damascus (pp. 632-33, 656). As such, it was later taken up by the Protestant divines, from whose works Barth acquired it (p. 657). Thus, although the "dual formula" may originate with Barth, the doctrine itself precedes both his work and that of his Protestant forebears.

6. McCormack, *Karl Barth's Critically Realistic Dialectical Theology,* p. 363.

7. Barth never renounces *diastasis* in the development of a more positive theological orientation. Rather, he reshapes his theology in such a way as to promote a holistic view of God's relation to the world, which nonetheless involves the element of *diastasis.* McCormack takes aim at Balthasar's influential interpretation of Barth's theological development, arguing that Barth never ceases to be "a *dialectical theologian,*" even if Barth's method undergoes transformation, becoming more dogmatic in form (McCormack, *Karl Barth's Critically Realistic Dialectical Theology,* p. 18). Balthasar argues that Barth's work on Anselm is the key to understanding Barth's transition to a more dogmatic form of theology. According to Balthasar, Barth renounces dialectical method in favor of analogy. See Hans Urs von Balthasar, *The Theology of Karl Barth,* trans. Edward T. Oakes, S.J. (San Francisco: Communio Books, Ignatius Press, 1992). Among other things, McCormack maintains that Balthasar's interpretation of Barth's development "fails to penetrate deeply enough into the *material* theological conditions in Barth's theology which gave rise to 'dialectic' and 'analogy' in the first place" (McCormack, *Karl Barth's Critically Realistic Dialectical Theology,* p. 19). For McCormack, it was Barth's "anhypostatic-enhypostatic" Christological model, which emerged in 1924, that set the parameters for the development of his doctrine of the *analogia fidei* (p. 19). What occurred as a result was the displacement of the "time-eternity dialectic"

synthesize or harmonize the divine and human realms in the light of Christ, one that would not replace *diastasis,* but rather, enable Barth to incorporate it into his Christological model.

What would the foregoing imply for Christ's relation to culture? The critical engagement of culture found in Barth's response to the reigning worldview at the turn of the century would now find a positive counter-

---

by the newfound Christological model "as the central parable for expressing the *Realdialektik* of God's veiling and unveiling" (p. 367). McCormack says elsewhere that this "*Realdialektik* of veiling and unveiling is the motor which drives Barth's doctrine of analogy and makes it possible" (p. 18). Although McCormack rejects Balthasar's way of speaking of the shift that occurred in Barth's thought, McCormack acknowledges that there is some validity in Balthasar's claim that one finds in Barth's thought a movement from attention on "'the Word'" to attention on "'Jesus Christ'" (p. 22). The basis for agreement here is McCormack's acknowledgment of the gradual development of an incarnational theology in Barth's thought, the "final 'shift'" being evidenced in Barth's exposition "of the doctrine of God in *Church Dogmatics* II/1" (McCormack, p. 22; see also p. 19). Now it is true, as McCormack argues, that Barth's employment of the anhypostatic-enhypostatic Christological model in 1924 gave Barth the Christological basis he needed to develop an incarnational theology that would be true to the "single material insight" and "new starting point" that McCormack says emerged in 1915 (p. 20). McCormack is also correct in claiming that consideration of certain "material problems," namely, those of Christology and the Trinity, led Barth to discover eventually "solutions to methodological questions" (p. 20). Having said this, it should be noted that it was Barth's work on Anselm that provided Barth with the methodological framework to proceed in a concentrated manner from this Christological basis. It was not the turning point; but it did play an important role in the development of Barth's Christological concentration, offering Barth a method that complemented his Christological ontology. Along these lines, see Eberhard Busch's treatment of Barth on Anselm in *Karl Barth: His Life from Letters and Autobiographical Texts* (London: SCM Press, 1976), p. 210. See also Karl Barth, *Anselm: Fides Quaerens Intellectum, Anselm's Proof of the Existence of God in the Context of His Theological Scheme,* The Library of Philosophy and Theology, ed. John McIntyre and Ian T. Ramsey (London: SCM Press, 1960). Lastly, as McCormack shows, the anhypostatic-enhypostatic Christological model Barth employed enabled him to jettison the non-incarnational dialectic of time and eternity without abandoning the dialectic of revelation's relation to history (McCormack, *Karl Barth's Critically Realistic Dialectical Theology,* p. 367). Thus, for all the emphasis on the integral relation of the divine and human, revelation and history, eternity and time, the dialectical element remains a vital part of Barth's theological orientation. It is now simply a matter of *diastasis* being taken up and integrated into his newfound Christological formula whereby the divine and human are viewed both in critical and constructive relation to one another. Gary Dorrien also argues that Barth ever remained a dialectical theologian: "The dialectic of divine veiling and unveiling remained crucial to his thought." Gary Dorrien, *The Barthian Revolt in Modern Theology: Theology without Weapons* (Louisville: Westminster/John Knox Press, 2000), p. 3.

part. Barth could now truly speak of God's transcendence in such a way that it would not threaten the doctrine of the divine immanence. He had always had in mind the doctrine of divine immanence: only the transcendent God can display *divine* compassion. However, the divine immanence, and with it, God's humanity, had not previously received due emphasis. And only as proper attention was given to God's humanity could Barth offer the assurance that humanity and human culture would be preserved, and not annihilated, before God in his Word.

Of course, Barth had set forth the concept of the radical otherness of God to safeguard the doctrine of God. However, it also indirectly served to guarantee the distinct existence of the world and human culture. Only now though, through categories such as *anhypostasis* and *enhypostasis,* was the basis laid whereby the Word and world, including the world of culture, could stand in distinct though positive, that is, integral relation to one another. Thus, the critique of culture, which would remain vital to Barth's engagement of culture, would now be wed to a constructive response. That is to say, Barth's critique of the divinization of the world of culture would not stand alone, but would be matched by a growing concentration on the incarnation of God in history, with implications for *human* culture.

Barth's employment of categories of classical and scholastic theology such as *anhypostasis* and *enhypostasis* brought forth responses, varying "from friendly concern to downright anger, namely, that historically, formally and materially, Barth was going the way of scholasticism."[8] According to Busch, since 1924 when Barth began work preparing "lectures on dogmatic theology," he "was . . . steering an independent course within the circle of dialectical theologians."[9] Barth's use of Heinrich Heppe's *Reformed Dogmatics,* Heinrich Schmid's *Doctrinal Theology of the Evangelical Lutheran Church,*[10] and critical appropriation of categories of "earlier Protestant orthodoxy"[11] were things

> which the others involved in "dialectical theology" could not share, and they could only shake their heads at this remarkable change of direction made by him. His serious consideration of this particular

8. Karl Barth, *Church Dogmatics,* I/1, *The Doctrine of the Word of God,* ed. G. W. Bromiley and T. F. Torrance (Edinburgh: T. & T. Clark, 1975), p. xiii.

9. Busch, *Karl Barth: His Life,* p. 153.

10. Busch, *Karl Barth: His Life,* p. 153.

11. Busch, *Karl Barth: His Life,* p. 154.

heritage marked the point at which their ways had to diverge even more obviously.[12]

In response to the reaction to the new development in Barth's theology, and contrary to what may often be assumed, it was Barth's employment of classical categories that enabled him to remain a dialectical, radical theologian. If he had not appropriated these concepts, he may well have jettisoned the element of *diastasis* in the development of his theology. However, against the backdrop of Kant's critique of authority, and metaphysical and theological speculation,[13] as well as the claim of Harnack and others that the church fathers had hellenized the gospel,[14] Barth's theology may well have appeared to his contemporaries to be a return to dogmatic slumbers.[15]

By no means, though, was Barth's theology a repetition or repristination of an earlier system or school of thought. Constructive it was, conservative it was not. Moreover, it was dogmatic without being systematic, if what is meant by that term is a closed system of theological axioms and propositions.[16] Furthermore, in *returning to* the fathers of the early church and Protestant Scholasticism, Barth intended to go *beyond* them, as well as beyond his previous theological mentors and dialectical peers.

12. Busch, *Karl Barth: His Life,* p. 154.

13. Refer to the following: Immanuel Kant, "What Is Enlightenment?," in *Foundations of the Metaphysics of Morals and What Is Enlightenment?,* trans. and with an introduction by Lewis White Beck (Indianapolis: Bobbs-Merrill, 1959), p. 85; *Kant Selections,* ed. Lewis White Beck, The Great Philosophers, ed. Paul Edwards (New York: Macmillan, 1988), p. 98; and Kant's systematic reformulation of religion in *Religion within the Limits of Reason Alone* (New York: Harper & Row, 1960).

14. See Adolf Harnack, *What Is Christianity?,* intro. Rudolf Bultmann (New York: Harper & Row, 1957), pp. 200-205, where he speaks of the Christian apologists' identification of Jesus Christ as the Logos, and also his discussion of the development of Christian dogma and its relation to Hellenism in *History of Dogma,* vol. 2, trans. Neil Buchanan (London: Williams & Norgate, 1896), pp. 228-29, 246-47.

15. In chronicling Barth's relationship with Tillich, Busch would later point out that, "one of Barth's problems in getting on with Tillich was that he saw to his regret that Tillich (like Niebuhr) still thought of him 'as though I had been asleep since 1920.'" Busch, *Karl Barth: His Life,* p. 437. Busch's quotation of Barth is taken from Barth's correspondence to C. W. Kegley, 9 July 1960.

16. See, for example, Barth's description of his dogmatic enterprise in *Church Dogmatics,* III/4, *The Doctrine of Creation,* ed. G. W. Bromiley and T. F. Torrance (Edinburgh: T. & T. Clark, 1961), p. xiii, and in Busch, *Karl Barth: His Life,* p. 376.

Lastly, Barth was becoming *more critical* than he had been to this point. For only as one is constructive in doing theology in the light of the mystery of the Christian faith can one's critique of theology and culture be truly critical. As modern theological history so painfully indicates, revolution without accompanying construction leads so frequently to further abuses in society. In speaking to the charges of his opponents in the opening pages of the *Church Dogmatics,* Barth counters with his own charge that modern Protestant theology's rejection of "mystery" has resulted in Protestantism being

> punished with all kinds of worthless substitutes, that it has fallen the more readily victim to such uneasy cliques and sects as High Church, German Church, Christian Community and religious Socialism, and that many of its preachers and adherents have finally learned to discover deep religious significance in the intoxication of Nordic blood and their political *Führer.*[17]

By complementing the critical with the constructive, Barth was now in a position to move further along the path first taken in his commentary on Romans. Only through the formulation of a theology that was truly incarnational whereby God becomes human could he fill the void left by his critique of the divinization of human culture, thereby safeguarding against the perpetual inclination of human culture to strive after deification. Struggling against this propensity in humanity, while at the same time desiring to give due consideration to humanity, Barth was resolute in claiming both that the divine becomes human, taking humanity to himself, and that the human thereby becomes truly human without in any way becoming divine.

The ultimate goal of this chapter is to set forth the benefits of Barth's new-found Christological model for a conception of the God-world relationship generally, and theology of culture. To this end, the model must first be set forth, along with what it signifies for the divine and human natures in the person of Christ, including their relation. Only then will it be possible to extend the discussion, arguing for this model's relevance for the general relation of God to the world and of Christ to culture.

17. Barth, *Church Dogmatics,* I/1, p. xiv.

Explication

As indicated in the introduction to this chapter, the reason for Barth's appropriation of the categories of *anhypostasis* and *enhypostasis* was so that he could speak of revelation's relation to history in integral terms without sacrificing his dialectical orientation. For Barth, revelation occurs in and through the veil of creaturely flesh.[18] Humanity never has direct access to revelation. For God always reveals himself in hiddenness and hides himself in revelation.[19] It was only through the employment of *anhypostasis* and *enhypostasis* that Barth could achieve the balance between conceiving ontological union and differentiation as it pertains to the relation of the divine and human in the revelation of God in Christ.

According to Barth, the divine person, the eternal Word, is indeed revealed in history. This person is revealed indirectly through the veil of enhypostasized creaturely flesh. For the subject of revelation is the divine person rather than a person who comes into being through the union of the divine and human natures. In this light, the person's relation to history is always mediated through the veil of creatureliness. And yet, given that the human nature is enhypostasized in the person of the Word, the Word actually reveals himself in history, albeit indirectly through the veil of his humanity.[20]

In his first sustained attempt at dogmatic theology, the *Göttingen Dogmatics,* Barth explains what is expressed by the terms *anhypostatos* and *enhypostatos.* He writes that,

> The humanity of Christ, although it is body and soul, and an individual, is nothing subsistent or real in itself. Thus it did not exist prior to its union with the Logos. It has no independent existence alongside or apart from him. . . . The human nature of Christ has no personhood of its own. It is *anhypostatos* — the formula in which the description culminates. Or, more positively, it is *enhypostatos.* It has personhood, subsistence, reality, only in its union with the Logos of God.[21]

18. McCormack, *Karl Barth's Critically Realistic Dialectical Theology,* p. 362.

19. Karl Barth, *Church Dogmatics,* II/1, *The Doctrine of God,* ed. G. W. Bromiley and T. F. Torrance (Edinburgh: T. & T. Clark, 1957), pp. 199, 343; Karl Barth, *The Göttingen Dogmatics: Instruction in the Christian Religion,* vol. 1, trans. Geoffrey W. Bromiley (Grand Rapids: Eerdmans, 1990), pp. 136-41; McCormack, *Karl Barth's Critically Realistic Dialectical Theology,* p. 362.

20. McCormack, *Karl Barth's Critically Realistic Dialectical Theology,* p. 362.

21. Barth, *Göttingen Dogmatics,* p. 157.

In speaking of the Lutheran and Reformed approval of the early church's designations for Mary "as the *mater Domini, theotokos, deipara,* the God-bearer," Barth concludes, "The one whom Mary bore was not an other or a second; he was nothing apart from being God's Son. He was in human nature, but this human nature was real only in the person of God's Son."[22]

Later, in discussing *anhypostasis* and *enhypostasis* in the *Church Dogmatics,* Barth combats what he calls the "primitive argument" raised in the light of the Latin equivalent for *anhypostasis,* namely, *impersonalitas.* Barth reasons that the argument against the former results from a faulty understanding of the Latin term. *Personalitas* was the word used for "existence or being." The early writers did not deny that what is called "personality" belonged to Christ's human nature. What they denied was that Christ's human nature possessed existence *independent from* its union with the divine person. Christ possessed an *individual* human nature, which involved human personality. But that human nature did not have existence *in abstracto* or apart from its union with the divine person.[23]

Elsewhere Barth affirms the Protestant Scholastics in their employment of the early church's doctrine of the *anhypostasia* or *enhypostasia* of Christ's human nature for the interpretation of John 1:14: *"ut caro illa nullam propriam subsistentiam extra Dei Filium habeat sed ab illo et in eo vere sustentetur et gestetur."*[24] Barth adds that the adequacy of this description is manifest in the "negative statement" being but the delineation of its affirmative counterpart. He concludes, "Because the man Jesus came into being and is by the Word of God, it is *only* by the Word of God that He came into being and is. Because He is the Son of God, it is only as such that He is real man. . . ."[25]

22. Barth, *Göttingen Dogmatics,* p. 157.

23. Karl Barth, *Church Dogmatics,* I/2, *The Doctrine of the Word of God,* ed. G. W. Bromiley and T. F. Torrance (Edinburgh: T. & T. Clark, 1956), p. 164. See also Barth's discussion of this theme in *Karl Barth's Table Talk,* ed. John D. Godsey (Richmond, Va.: John Knox Press, 1963), p. 49.

24. Karl Barth, *Church Dogmatics,* III/2, *The Doctrine of Creation,* ed. G. W. Bromiley and T. F. Torrance (Edinburgh: T. & T. Clark, 1960), p. 70, quoting *Syn. pur. Theol. Leiden,* 1624, Disp. 25, 4.

25. Barth, *Church Dogmatics,* III/2, p. 70. In addition to their service to Barth, these twin doctrines signified an advance beyond Chalcedon. At this point, it will prove beneficial to retrace briefly the history surrounding Chalcedon. The Council of Chalcedon (451) put forth a resolution to the conflict between the Antiochene and Alexandrian Christological schools. At Chalcedon, the distinction between *hypostasis* and *physis* was established once and for all. According to J. N. D. Kelly, Alexander, Bishop of Alexandria (313-328), for example, conceived

To return to Barth's early dogmatic activity, his employment of the categories of *anhypostasis* and *enhypostasis* provided him with a solution whereby he could conceive the dialectic of revelation to history in an

---

of *hypostasis* and *physis* in "virtually identical" terms. J. N. D. Kelly, *Early Christian Doctrines,* rev. ed. (San Francisco: Harper & Row, 1978), p. 224. At Chalcedon, however, the conclusion was reached that Christ existed as one person ("one *prosopon* and one *hupostasis,*" p. 340; Kelly points out that Flavian's "identification" of the two at the Standing Synod of Constantinople in 448 "marked an important step towards Chalcedon"), who possesses two natures *(physeis):* one divine, the other human (Kelly, p. 331). The upshot of this formulation was to safeguard the personal union while at the same time preserve the properties peculiar to each nature. According to Kelly, each nature was "complete" and retained "its distinctive properties and operation unimpaired in the union" (p. 341). As David Wright indicates, Chalcedon's distinction between the single person *(hypostasis)* and two natures *(physeis),* one divine and the other human, united in the person, was "what Alexandrian theologians called 'the hypostatic union.'" Sinclair B. Ferguson, David F. Wright, J. I. Packer, eds., *New Dictionary of Theology* (Downers Grove, Ill.: InterVarsity Press, 1988), s.v. "Hypostasis," by David F. Wright. However, it should be noted here that Cyril of Alexandria's phrase, "hypostatic union," was abandoned at Chalcedon, much to the dismay of the Alexandrian school (Kelly, *Early Christian Doctrines,* pp. 341-42). And yet, as Kelly argues, "Clearly the divine Word . . . is regarded as the unique subject of the Incarnate, and this is reinforced by the sanction given to the controverted title *Theotokos*" (p. 341). The Chalcedonian model itself speaks of the distinct though inseparable relation of the divine and human natures in the person of Jesus Christ whereby the natures stand to one another "without confusion, without change, without division, without separation" (p. 340). However, in spite of all its benefits, Chalcedon did not resolve all difficulties. For as Wright argues, Chalcedon did not provide a resolution to the dilemma centering "on the integrity of Christ's human nature." What was the status of the human nature? Did it possess a "personal centre"? Or was it "non-personal" *(anhypostasis)?* According to Wright, Leontius of Byzantium (d. *c.* 543) set forth a conceptual framework to resolve the dilemma. Leontius maintained that Christ's human nature was *anhypostatos,* lacking personal existence outside its union with the divine nature in the person of Christ. However, that did not mean the human nature lacked personal subsistence, for it "had its personal subsistence in the person of the Logos." The human nature subsisted in the person of the divine Word *(enhypostatos)* without in any way being jeopardized according to its "properties" (Wright, "Hypostasis"). The significance of the formula lies in safeguarding the union of the two natures in the incarnation and the single hypostasis of the Son, while at the same time giving full weight to the personality of the human nature. Christ was fully human. But his humanity only had existence in being hypostasized in the divine person in the incarnation. In his article, Wright draws attention to a recent study on Leontius by D. B. Evans. (See "Hypostasis.") According to Evans, Leontius held that both natures were "enhypostasized" in Jesus Christ. See David B. Evans, *Leontius of Byzantium: An Origenist Christology* (Washington, D.C.: Dumbarton Oaks Center for Byzantine Studies, Trustees for Harvard University, 1970), pp. 136-43. It follows from this that, "Leontius cannot say that Jesus Christ *is* God . . . for he believes that *both* natures of Christ are enhypostasized"

incarnational manner.[26] On the one hand, the formula enabled Barth to speak of the relation of revelation to history in dialectical terms. For Barth, the subject of revelation is the divine Word who is revealed indirectly, through the veil of anhypostatic creaturely flesh. In this way, Barth was able to maintain his dialectical notion of revelation. However, the model also enabled Barth to move beyond the time-eternity dialectic of *Romans II* whereby he could finally speak of the relation of revelation to history and of the eternal God to temporal creature in integral terms. The eternal Word takes an anhypostatic human nature to himself, thereby becoming human. It follows that the revelation of this subject takes place in history. Barth's doctrine of revelation whose subject is the eternal Word made flesh is now incarnational in orientation.

Through employing and nuancing this model, Barth is now able to speak not simply of the divinity of the Word, but also of the humanity of the same Word. Barth now had the conceptual structure in place whereby he could champion a truly incarnational Christology that would give rise to a constructive engagement of human culture. For Barth, the divine person, the eternal Word, in becoming incarnate as Jesus Christ, is not simply of like nature to humanity *(homoiousios)*. In addition to being of one nature with the Father *(homoousios)*,[27] the Word is also of one nature with human-

(p. 138). On this reading of Leontius, he did not conceive the person of Christ as the person of the eternal Logos. John Meyendorff credits Evans with influencing his own view of Leontius. See John Meyendorff, *Christ in Eastern Thought* (Crestwood, N.Y.: St. Vladimir's Seminary Press, 1975), pp. 30, 61-63, 156, 223, n. 41. Meyendorff differentiates John of Damascus's position from that of Leontius, claiming that for John "the hypostasis of Christ" is "the pre-existent hypostasis of the Logos." He adds, "Chalcedonian orthodox Christology does not conceive the hypostasis of Christ as having come into existence as a consequence of the union of two *enhypostata*, the divine and the human, but as the assumption by the Logos of the human nature in addition to the divine nature that he had possessed from all eternity" (p. 156). For a contrasting view on the subject of the relation of John to Leontius, see Herbert Relton, *A Study in Christology: The Problem of the Relation of the Two Natures in the Person of Christ* (London: Society for Promoting Christian Knowledge, 1917), pp. 77, 84. Wright refers to the following two works as studies that challenge Evans's reading of Leontius. John J. Lynch, "Leontius of Byzantium: A Cyrillian Christology," *Theological Studies* 36 (1975): 455-71; Brian Daley, "The Origenism of Leontius of Byzantium," *Journal of Theological Studies* 27 (October 1976): 333-69. Orthodox faith since Chalcedon has maintained that the person of the eternal Logos was incarnate ἐν δύο φύσεσιν rather than ἐν δύο φύσεων.

26. See McCormack, *Karl Barth's Critically Realistic Dialectical Theology*, pp. 19-21.

27. In one place, Barth speaks of Athanasius' doctrine of the *homoousios* as being of no lesser significance than Luther's concepts of justification and faith and serving as a funda-

ity *(homoousios)*. In the light of this newfound concentration, the basis was now laid for a positive response to human history and the world of human culture. And yet again, it must not be forgotten that Barth ever remained critical of culture's forms. His Christology itself bears witness to the critical and dialectical element of his theology as a whole. It is simply that now he is able to speak in critical *and constructive* terms. Barth's concept of *diastasis* is now wed to *enhypostasis*. However, as McCormack argues, further clarification was required on the subject of Christology, most particularly, the relation of the divine and human natures in the person of Christ, that is, the *unio personalis*.[28]

In his treatment of the *unio personalis* in 1925, Barth follows the Reformed scholastics in their conception of the *communicatio idiomatum*.[29] Let it be noted that the Reformed sought to guard against what they saw as a Eutychean tendency in the Lutheran version of the doctrine, most particularly, the Lutheran notion of the *genus majestaticum*.[30] The Lutheran orthodox conceived the *communio naturarum* in "direct" and "undialectical" terms.[31] That is to say, according to the Lutheran teaching, the divine and

---

mental presupposition for the Reformation's emphasis on faith. For faith concerns revelation, who is the Son of God, "not a second thing alongside God, but a second *in* God." It is because revelation is this subject that one is required to say, "by faith alone" (Barth, *Göttingen Dogmatics*, p. 122).

28. McCormack, *Karl Barth's Critically Realistic Dialectical Theology*, p. 363.

29. See McCormack, *Karl Barth's Critically Realistic Dialectical Theology*, p. 363, for his discussion of paragraph 28 of Karl Barth, "Unterricht in der christlichen Religion," typed manuscript in the Karl Barth-Archiv, Basel, Switzerland.

30. Richard Muller points out that the Reformed scholastics accused the Lutheran orthodox of a tendency in the direction of Eutycheanism, claiming that the latter taught the *communicatio idiomatum in abstracto*. That is to say, the Reformed claimed that their Lutheran counterparts reflected on the relation of the divine and human natures *apart from* their union in the divine person and predicated divine perfections directly to the human nature rather than to the divine person. According to the Reformed, the Lutheran orthodox ran the risk of undermining the distinct identity of the two natures, as was the case with Eutyches. See Richard Muller, "communicatio idiomatum/communicatio proprietatum," in *Dictionary of Latin and Greek Theological Terms: Drawn Principally from Protestant Scholastic Theology* (Grand Rapids: Baker, 1985). Muller defends the Lutheran doctrine against the charge of *"in abstracto."* For his exposition and defense of the Lutheran doctrine against the Reformed scholastic charge, see his entry discussed above as well as his article "in abstracto" in the same work.

31. Karl Barth, "Unterricht in der christlichen Religion," typed manuscript in the Karl Barth-Archiv, Basel, Switzerland, pp. 47-48; quoted and translated in Bruce McCormack, *Karl Barth's Critically Realistic Dialectical Theology*, p. 365.

human natures relate to one another directly, rather than indirectly through the divine person of Christ, as the Reformed maintained. In passing, it should be noted that the Lutheran doctrine of the *genus maiestaticum* served as the logical basis for their view of Christ's real presence in the Eucharist. That is to say, on the Lutheran account, the human nature participates in the divine attributes, which in turn support the Lutheran teaching of the omnipresence of Christ's humanity.[32]

In response, the Reformed scholastics argued that the human nature is in no way capable of the divine: *finitum non capax infiniti.*[33] That is to say, the human nature of Christ does not possess a capacity for the divine nature and its attributes. For the Reformed scholastics, and Barth after them, the approach taken to conceiving the relation of the natures by the Lutherans did not properly safeguard the distinction between them. For Barth, it should be added, this was the same general problem he had seen at work in the theology represented by Harnack who spoke of an ascent to God through human culture.[34] It is interesting to note the connection Barth makes, or which certain idealists have made and to which Barth refers, between Lutheranism and idealism. Barth would later point out that in the light of the Lutheran doctrine of the *communicatio idiomatum* Hegel considered himself a devout Lutheran and Feuerbach claimed Luther as the inspiration for his own view of the oneness of divine and human being.[35]

For their own part, the Reformed, including Barth, argued that the divine and human natures in the person of Christ relate to one another indirectly, that is, through the divine person, thereby safeguarding the distinct existence of each, and its properties. They relate indirectly to one another

32. See Heinrich Schmid, *The Doctrinal Theology of the Evangelical Lutheran Church*, 3rd ed., revised, trans. Charles A. Hay and Henry E. Jacobs (Minneapolis: Augsburg Publishing House, 1899), p. 331.

33. See Heinrich Heppe's discussion of this topic on pages 432-33 of his work, *Reformed Dogmatics: Set Out and Illustrated from the Sources*, with a foreword by Karl Barth, ed. Ernst Bizer, trans. G. T. Thomson (London: George Allen & Unwin, 1950; reprint, Grand Rapids: Baker, 1978). See also Barth's discussion of the Reformed doctrine in *The Göttingen Dogmatics*, p. 159.

34. Refer back to the discussion of Harnack in Chapter One.

35. Karl Barth, *Church Dogmatics*, IV/2, *The Doctrine of Reconciliation*, ed. G. W. Bromiley and T. F. Torrance (Edinburgh: T. & T. Clark, 1958), p. 83. See also Barth's discussion of Feuerbach, Hegel, and the Lutheran doctrine of the *"genus majestaticum"* in Karl Barth, "Ludwig Feuerbach," in *Theology and Church: Shorter Writings, 1920-1928*, with an introduction by T. F. Torrance, trans. Louise Pettibone Smith (New York: Harper & Row, 1962), pp. 230-31.

through the divine person.[36] The Reformed did not, however, speak simply of the indirect relation of the divine to the human nature. They also held that the relation of each nature to the divine person is "direct and undialectical."[37] Thus, to summarize, the divine and human natures relate to one another in "indirect" (and for Barth, dialectical) terms through the person whereas each nature relates to the divine person directly and undialectically.[38] For the Reformed, and Barth after them, the *unio hypostatica* was an immediate union whereas the *communio naturarum* was mediated through the person of the Word.[39]

Barth favored the Reformed model, yet modified it to make even clearer the distinction between the natures. He maintained that the divine person ever wills "moment by moment" to assume or take up the human

36. Muller speaks of a connection at this point between the Reformed scholastic position and Antiochene Christology. He argues that, when "taken to an extreme" as in the case of Nestorius, this approach jeopardizes "the unity of Christ's person" (Muller, "communicatio idiomatum"). In his discussion of the *genus apotelesmaticum,* Schmid combines statements from Quenstedt and the Formula of Concord by which he appears to draw a connection between the Reformed doctrine and what he understands to be the teaching of Nestorius and Paul of Samosata (Schmid, p. 316). Nestorianism is the view that divides Christ into two persons, one divine, the other human. It represents an extreme form of Antiochene Christology, which J. N. D. Kelly refers to as the "Word-man" Christological orientation. This type of Christology is "alive to the reality and completeness of the humanity, but more hesitant about the position of the Word as the metaphysical subject." Kelly contrasts this view with the Alexandrian Christological school which promotes a "Word-flesh" Christology wherein emphasis is placed "on the Word as the subject in the God-man," paying less attention to the "human soul" of Christ. See Kelly, *Early Christian Doctrines,* p. 310; see also p. 281. Charles T. Waldrop argues that Karl Barth's Christology is on the whole Alexandrian in form in *Karl Barth's Christology: Its Basic Alexandrian Character,* Religion and Reason: Method and Theory in the Study and Interpretation of Religion, ed. Jacques Waardenburg, no. 21 (Berlin: Mouton Publishers, 1984). One may argue that the Reformed make more room for Antiochene Christology by arguing that the union of the natures in the person of Christ is indirect. Barth goes even further in this direction by maintaining that the divine Word wills moment by moment to take the human nature to himself in his incarnate existence. (See McCormack, *Karl Barth's Critically Realistic Dialectical Theology,* p. 365.)

37. Barth, "Unterricht," pp. 47-48; quoted and translated in McCormack, *Karl Barth's Critically Realistic Dialectical Theology,* p. 365.

38. McCormack, *Karl Barth's Critically Realistic Dialectical Theology,* pp. 364-65. Heppe writes that one must distinguish between the *unio immediata* (the direct union of the human nature and the personal reality of the λόγος) and the *unio mediata* — the indirect union of the divine and human natures (Heppe, *Reformed Dogmatics,* p. 431).

39. McCormack, *Karl Barth's Critically Realistic Dialectical Theology,* p. 364.

nature to himself.[40] In this way, Barth further strengthened the claim that although the divine "is capable of the human," the human is not capable of the divine.[41]

So far, consideration has been given to the significance of the dual doctrines of *anhypostasis* and *enhypostasis* and the *unio personalis* for Christology proper, revelation, and theology generally in Barth's thought. Now the analysis of these concepts will be extended to see what bearing they might have upon understanding the relation of the Word of Christ to the world of culture. The rest of this chapter will be devoted to making clear their significance for the non-Christological domain. The next section will focus exclusively on consideration of Barth's own extension of Christological categories to the domains of church and broader culture.

Analogical Extensions

An essay written in 1926 manifests an advance beyond the Tambach lecture and the theological engagement of culture found in the *Romans* period. In "Church and Culture," Barth sets forth a critical yet constructive approach to the question of the church's relation to culture. The basis for this approach, however, is not found in the identity and activity of the church, or in the dynamic duality of church and culture, but in the Word of God.[42]

In both this article and the lecture delivered at Tambach in 1919 to which reference was made in the last chapter, Barth speaks of "parables" of Christ or the kingdom. Here, however, he conceives *the basis* for the relation of church to culture in the light of the Word — not some amorphous word, but the Word as Jesus Christ.

Busch draws attention to Barth's 1926 essay, wherein Barth compares his new approach to culture with the address delivered at Tambach seven years earlier. Busch writes,

> As he himself observed, "after seven years . . . he wanted to take a rather different view" of the subject on which he had once spoken at

40. McCormack, *Karl Barth's Critically Realistic Dialectical Theology*, p. 365.

41. McCormack, *Karl Barth's Critically Realistic Dialectical Theology*, p. 366.

42. Karl Barth, "Church and Culture," in *Theology and Church: Shorter Writings, 1920-1928*, with an introduction by T. F. Torrance, trans. Louise Pettibone Smith (New York: Harper & Row, 1962), p. 340.

> Tambach. Barth wanted to consider church and culture in a characteristic way. He sought to see the basis of their relationship "only in the decisive event of the speaking and hearing of the Word of God." As a result of this, on the one hand he could say that "The work of culture . . . *can* be like a parable . . . it can be a reflection from the light of the eternal Logos who became flesh." And on the other, "the hope of the church rests *on* God *for* man; it does not rest *on* men, not even on religious men — and not even on the belief that men *with God's help* will eventually build and complete that tower (of Babel)."[43]

As a result of basing his understanding of the relation of church to culture in the light of this doctrine of the Word, Barth is able to develop a theology for the church that is also for culture. The Word who is present to church and culture also addresses both church and culture. As Barth sees it, *"The theme 'Church and Culture' . . . specifies the question of the meaning of the cultural task for every man as a question answerable only by hearing the Word of God."*[44]

The otherwise unknown God speaks his Word to people. In so doing, he gives them the ears necessary to hear. Thereby he creates fellowship with them. Only then do they have knowledge of God and his Word, this Word — Jesus Christ, God's prophet, priest, and king for them.[45] The church lives by faith in obedience to this Word spoken to it by God, and in turn, speaks forth and acts in the light of God's message of reconciliation through the Word, namely, Jesus Christ.[46]

> All depends on the Word, on faith and obedience, on the act between God and men. In proportion as the Church hears the Word, believes and obeys, the problem and the task of culture become clear. The work of culture takes its place among the earthly signs by which the Church must make God's goodness, his friendship for men, visible to itself and to the world.[47]

43. Busch, *Karl Barth: His Life,* p. 171. The reader is directed to pages 343 and 349 of "Church and Culture" in *Theology and Church* for the quotations taken from Barth by Busch.

44. Barth, "Church and Culture," p. 340.

45. Barth, "Church and Culture," p. 335.

46. Barth, "Church and Culture," pp. 334-36.

47. Barth, "Church and Culture," p. 344.

In the light of the Word who addresses himself to all humanity, the church cannot ignore the concerns of culture,[48] but must concern itself with concrete situations of empirical culture in the light of the "promise" which culture ideally is as proclaimed by the Word of God.[49] Care is required on the part of the church in affirming "the promise" of culture in specific situations.[50] And yet, although

> there can be no thought of a general sanctifying of cultural achievement, such as Schleiermacher accomplished with his idealism, . . . there is even less place for a basic blindness to the possibility that culture may be revelatory, that it can be filled with the promise.[51]

Culture can serve as a sign, but not as the substance of revelation itself, which belongs to God in his Word. It can point to the Word, but can never dispense with God in his Word, serving as its own ground and goal. Nor can it exist autonomously from the church, which bears witness to God in his Word.[52] The church and culture stand in a distinct though inseparable relation to one another in and through the Word of God.[53]

The most striking feature of this development in Barth's thought is his employment of the Reformed doctrine of the *Extra Calvinisticum,* enabling him to maintain "that the Church's own invisible truth is truth also beyond the visible reality of the Church."[54] For the Logos, who is incarnate as Jesus Christ, *"fills heaven and earth."*[55] Here one finds the analogical extension of the Reformed understanding of the *unio personalis* whereby the divine and human natures relate indirectly to one another through the person of the Word. As in the case of the natures, so too in the case of the church's relation to broader culture, the Word mediates the union of the two natures or spheres in such a way that the identity and characteristics of each is in no way communicated to the other. As is true of the Reformed doctrine of the *Extra Calvinisticum,* the Word enfleshed as Jesus Christ whom the church worships and to whom it bears witness as its cen-

48. Barth, "Church and Culture," p. 343.
49. Barth, "Church and Culture," pp. 341, 343-44.
50. Barth, "Church and Culture," p. 344.
51. Barth, "Church and Culture," p. 344.
52. Barth, "Church and Culture," pp. 337-38, 347.
53. Barth, "Church and Culture," pp. 337-38, 341-42.
54. Barth, "Church and Culture," p. 342.
55. Barth, "Church and Culture," p. 342.

ter is present everywhere, filling heaven and earth and therefore human culture as well, indwelling and surrounding it.

Barth would later express reservations about this essay, namely, that strands of natural theology could be detected in it.[56] A hint of "pantheism" is clearly seen in the statement that, "Even the activities peculiar to the Church, . . . can, under the shadow of all cultural achievement, be blessed in Christ, can carry within itself a spark of the seminal logos (λόγος σπερματικός)."[57] That is not to say that Barth lacked critical scrutiny in his assessment of culture at this time. For as already noted, Barth was most wary of the "general sanctifying of cultural achievement" found in the idealism of Schleiermacher.[58] Moreover, Barth's reservation set forth in *"Nein!"* should not cast doubt on his Christological model employed in "Church and Culture." For Barth would later extend Christological patterns of relation to his discussion of the church and state and his treatment of secular witness in *Church Dogmatics* IV/3.1.[59]

In discussing Barth's doctrine of secular witness, George Hunsinger speaks of the "correspondence and extension" of Chalcedonian categories by Barth.[60] He writes,

56. Barth acknowledges Brunner's point that Barth had engaged in natural theology. Karl Barth, "No!," in Karl Barth and Emil Brunner, *Natural Theology,* with an introduction by John Baillie, trans. Peter Fraenkel (London: Geoffrey Bles/Centenary Press, 1946), p. 70. Barth draws attention to his essay, "Church and Culture" and his "Prolegomena" published in 1927 as examples (p. 70). See also Emil Brunner's discussion of Barth's article, "Church and Culture" in the following work: Emil Brunner, "Nature and Grace," in Karl Barth and Emil Brunner, *Natural Theology,* with an introduction by John Baillie, trans. Peter Fraenkel (London: Geoffrey Bles: Centenary Press, 1946), p. 19. As Busch points out, near the end of the twenties, Barth looked negatively at such tendencies and resolved to rid his theology of them (Busch, *Karl Barth: His Life,* p. 196).

57. Barth, "Church and Culture," p. 351. The hint of "pantheism" referred to in the text above is an allusion to Barth's criticism of *Romans I* set forth on pages 118-19 of Busch, *Karl Barth: His Life.*

58. Barth, "Church and Culture," p. 344.

59. For consideration of the extension of Christological categories to the church-state relation, see Chapter Five of this work. See also Karl Barth, "The Christian Community in the Midst of Political Change," in *Against the Stream: Shorter Post-War Writings, 1946-52,* ed. R. G. Smith, trans. E. M. Delecour and S. Godman (London: SCM Press, 1954), p. 93. The extension of such categories for consideration of secular witness to the Word will be discussed in what follows, and in Chapter Four of this study.

60. George Hunsinger, *How to Read Karl Barth: The Shape of His Theology* (Oxford: Oxford University Press, 1991), p. 238.

> It is the mystery of the person of Jesus Christ which sets the terms within which all else is to be explained or understood. Nothing is to be conceived — and this is a basic rule governing all of Barth's later theology — as existing except as together with him. . . . Jesus Christ is, in other words, the grand Mediator *in whom,* as it were, all "externalities" are to be conceived as existing in a complex web of "internal relations."[61]

Hunsinger has in mind here the Chalcedonian categories of "without confusion or change" and "without separation or division,"[62] as well as the asymmetrical ordering of the relation whereby God "retains his transcendental priority and the world its immanent contingency."[63] Moreover, Hunsinger states that internal to the extension of the Chalcedonian pattern of relation is the Trinitarian "pattern of 'dialectical inclusion.'"[64]

> For not only are God and the world thought of as being dialectically included in the Mediator, but in and through the Mediator they are thought of as being dialectically included in one another as well. In Jesus Christ the Mediator, a great catena of relations is thought to subsist in which the whole is always (dialectically) in the part and the part in the whole, without either losing its distinctiveness. All relations between God and the world in Jesus Christ are ultimately conceived, in one way or another, as relations of "coinherence" or of mutual, inner participation.[65]

Thus, the principle that governs Barth's later thought is nuanced in such a way that, in addition to conceiving the coexistence of God and the world in and through the mediation of Jesus Christ, Barth adds that they also coinhere in and through Jesus Christ. This pattern of *coinherence* arises from within the framework of *coexistence.*[66]

61. Hunsinger, *How to Read Karl Barth,* p. 237.

62. Hunsinger, *How to Read Karl Barth,* pp. 237-38.

63. Hunsinger, *How to Read Karl Barth,* p. 238.

64. Hunsinger, *How to Read Karl Barth,* p. 238.

65. Hunsinger, *How to Read Karl Barth,* p. 238.

66. Hunsinger, *How to Read Karl Barth,* p. 238. The terms "coinherence" and "mutual, inner participation" are to be understood to signify the Trinitarian doctrine of *perichoresis* or *emperichoresis,* which refers to the mutual interpenetration of the three hypostases in the divine life. The same terms can be applied to Christology, for the divine and human natures

Not only does this "great catena of relations" include those pertaining to God and the world and God and human culture through the mediator, but also it involves those relations *internal to culture itself,* namely, the relation of the sacred and secular spheres within culture. The sacred and secular spheres stand to one another in distinct though inseparable relation in and through the person of Jesus Christ, resulting in spherical patterns of relation, namely, the inner sphere of the church and outer sphere of broader culture.[67]

Such analogical extensions, however, are not limited to Chalcedonian and Trinitarian patterns of relation. For Barth also makes analogical extensions of *anhypostasis* and *enhypostasis* to speak of non-Christological themes.[68] Now it is important to stress the analogical nature of such statements. For as Balthasar points out, in volume II/2 of the *Church Dogmatics,* Barth "sets off Christ's *anhypostasis* necessarily and definitively from every other form of union with God," including God's presence in the life of the church.[69] Barth makes a similar point in volume IV/2 where he writes that,

> The *enhypostasis* of the human being of Jesus Christ, His existence in and with the Son of God, is sufficiently sharply differentiated from

---

inhere in one another, albeit for the Reformed scholastics and Barth, indirectly through the mediation of the divine person of the Word. Refer to the entry, "unio personalis," in Muller, *Dictionary of Latin and Greek Theological Terms.*

67. Such spherical patterns arise in the light of Barth's employment of the *Extra Calvinisticum.* The sphere of the church pertains to the visible reality of Christ whereas the sphere of culture pertains to Christ's invisible, universal presence beyond the boundaries of the church. The Word incarnate is the center point in this schema, surrounded by the church; but as the Word who also fills the heavens and the earth, he is the circumference within which broader culture is contained, itself encompassing the church. See also Chapters Five and Six of this study for the exposition of this schema.

68. In fact, the term *enhypostasis* has also been used to speak of the *circumincessio* (circumincession or coinherence, that is, *perichoresis* or *emperichoresis*) of the Father, Son, and Spirit in the divine life, existing in one another in the divine communion of being. Thus, what Hunsinger speaks of as the Trinitarian pattern of coinherence (Hunsinger, *How to Read Karl Barth,* pp. 237-38, 261) is the same category of relation applied in a different manner to speak of the union of the human nature to the person of Christ. See the entries for "circumincessio," "enhypostasis," and "unio personalis" in Muller, *Dictionary of Latin and Greek Theological Terms.*

69. Balthasar, *The Theology of Karl Barth,* p. 106. Balthasar's discussion at this point centers on Karl Barth's work, *Kirchliche Dogmatik,* II/2, *Die Lehre von Gott* (Zürich: Evangelischer Verlag, 1942), p. 177.

> the *sustentatio generalis* in which God maintains and accompanies and rules the whole world by the fact that the existence of God is not in any sense identical with that of the world, or the existence of the world with that of God, in virtue of His creative action, but God has and maintains His own existence in relation to the world, and the world in relation to God. It is one thing that God is present in and with everything that is and occurs, that in Him we live and move and have our being (Ac. 17:28), but it is quite another that He Himself became and is man. Even this union and unity cannot therefore be compared or exchanged with the *unio personalis* in Jesus Christ.[70]

One must of course distinguish between *enhypostasis* and the *sustentatio generalis.* Indeed, the union of God and humanity in Christ is different from God's union with the world, humanity, and human culture. One difference between them is that the divine Word takes a concrete human nature to himself, not humanity in general, in the incarnation. Thus, other humans are not hypostasized in the divine Word. This claim is reserved to the humanity of Christ alone. Following on from this, other humans are human persons. Technically speaking, Christ is not. He is a divine person who is human, whose human nature has its personhood in the divine person.

Having said this, it is maintained that for Barth, Christological and Trinitarian categories come to serve as the basis for understanding all other patterns of relation between God and the world and Christ and culture by means of analogical extensions. Barth does not reason in the light of nature and grace, or from nature to grace, but from grace to nature. For Christ is the point of contact between God and humanity. One must work out, think out from him. For this reason, Barth makes such extensions. Christ serves as the basis for how Barth conceives the God-world relation generally, not by way of identity, but by way of analogical extension.

As Balthasar points out, even though Barth distinguishes the union in Christ from all other unions between God and the world, Barth also speaks of the church's relation to Christ as corresponding "to the *anhypostasis* of the human nature of Christ" in the same volume.[71] That is to say, the

70. Barth, *Church Dogmatics,* IV/2, p. 53.

71. Balthasar, *The Theology of Karl Barth,* p. 107, quoting Karl Barth, *Kirchliche Dogmatik,* II/2, p. 236.

church has no independent existence from Jesus Christ, but ever remains inseparably related to him.

In a way analogous to the divine Word taking to himself a non-hypostasized human nature in the incarnation, thereby indicating that the human nature of Christ has no independent existence, so too, the church,[72] humanity in general,[73] and human culture,[74] exist in inalienable relation to God in his Word. The reverse is also true. Not only does the human nature exist solely in its being enhypostasized in the divine person of the Word, but also in becoming human, the divine Word exists in an indissoluble union with the human nature. By extension, God chooses not to exist in isolation from his church, nor humanity in general.

In light of the foregoing analysis, it becomes clear that one of the singular and profoundly ingenious aspects of Barth's theology is his decision to reverse the order in analogical predication. That is to say, he starts not from the human reality, working upward to God, but begins with the Godhead and categories traditionally reserved to the discussion of the divine mystery, making extensions to the human sphere, including that of culture. For Barth, God in Christ is first in the order of being *and* in the order of knowing.[75] Thus, one only understands human concepts and patterns of relation in the creaturely sphere, including that of church and broader

72. See Barth, *Kirchliche Dogmatik*, II/2, p. 236; see also Balthasar, *The Theology of Karl Barth*, p. 107.

73. John Macken makes clear that, contrary to certain modern conceptions of autonomy that signify indifference to and isolation from God, Barth understands human freedom or autonomy as that distinct form of creaturely existence which is awarded to humanity within the parameters of its positive relationship to God. See John Macken, S.J., *The Autonomy Theme in the "Church Dogmatics": Karl Barth and His Critics* (Cambridge: Cambridge University Press, 1990), p. 181. In this study, true autonomy is conceived as the human creature standing in a distinct though inseparable relation to God.

74. Barth rejects "civilization" and *"Kultur"* if such terms are intended to signify self-contained spheres of human life whose ends are self-generated, constructed independently of Christ and his church, signifying indifference to the claim and calling of God's Word (Barth, "Church and Culture," pp. 337-38).

75. For a defense of Barth's view of analogical predication, see Roger White, "Notes on Analogical Predication and Speaking about God," in *The Philosophical Frontiers of Christian Theology: Essays Presented to D. M. MacKinnon*, ed. Brian Hebblethwaite and Stewart Sutherland (Cambridge: Cambridge University Press, 1982), pp. 197-226. For a different approach to the subject, see Paul Edwards, ed., *The Encyclopedia of Philosophy* (New York: Macmillan & The Free Press, 1967), s.v. "Analogy in Theology," by Frederick Ferre.

culture, in the light of God's commandeering of flesh and language in the incarnation.

Through the course of this work, special attention will be given to Barth's own employment of Christological and Trinitarian categories for their bearing on the relation of Christ to culture. Moreover, analogical extensions of Christological categories will be made, using Barth's model as a template for drawing out implications for the theology of culture. Before proceeding further, however, brief consideration will be given to the benefits of Barth's model.

In the light of his employment of the twin doctrines of *anhypostasis* and *enhypostasis,* and with them, the *unio personalis,* Barth is able to set forth a theology that is both dialectical and incarnational. Thus, he can speak both critically *and* positively about God's Word's engagement of the world and human culture. The critical element of Barth's earlier posture on culture remains intact. And yet, now he can speak of a positive relation between Christ and culture. The reality of Christ has positive significance for the church *and* broader culture, making it possible for the church to confront culture about its own secular vocation in the light of its eschatological destiny and limit as set forth in Christ. Neither the church nor culture is confused with Christ or one another in Barth's thought. Nor do they exist independently of Christ or one another. For they coinhere, albeit indirectly, through the mediation of the person of the Word.

The next section will draw out implications from Barth's model for the theological engagement of culture, focusing on the themes of the critique of the deification of culture and the alienation or secularization of culture. The patterns of relation exemplified in Barth's own extension of the doctrines of *enhypostasis, anhypostasis,* and the *unio personalis* will be employed as models for their bearing on the question of the relation of the Word of Christ to the world of culture.

Implications: Contra Deification and Secularization

To this point in the chapter, Barth's Christological model has been set forth. It has also been shown that Barth views the God-world and Christ-culture relation in the light of Christological categories, namely, *anhypostasis/enhypostasis* and the *unio personalis.* In what follows, attention will center on key implications for the theology of culture arising from Barth's Christological doctrine of the Word.

To this stage in the study, it has been argued that Barth's theology during the *Romans* period was aimed primarily at safeguarding the concept of God from the encroachment of a defective anthropology, one that threatened the deity of God. However, in time, Barth came to see that while his earlier theology had been successful in distinguishing the divine and human spheres, he had failed to give due consideration to the humanity of God.[76] As a result, instead of the deification of the human other endangering the deity of God, as Barth had witnessed in Culture Protestantism, the transcendent other threatened to suppress or isolate humanity. The result was either God becoming all (God is everything and humanity nothing), or humanity becoming all in its own sphere (humanity is sovereign in its isolated and alienated state).[77] Concerning the former, Barth was accused of having stood "Schleiermacher on his head, that is, to make *God* great for a change at the cost of *man*."[78] Concerning the latter, the objection was raised against Barth that he had given rise to "a new justification of the autonomy of man and thus of secularism in the sense of the Lutheran doctrine of the two kingdoms."[79]

It was Barth's appropriation of the anhypostatic-enhypostatic Christological model, coupled with his conception of the *unio personalis,* that enabled him to give due account to the humanity of God without jeopardizing the distinction between God's deity and it. As a result, Barth would be able to steer a middle course between two extremes. On the one hand, he was still able to guard against theology's *deification* of humanity and culture (making humanity great at the cost of God), which he had perceived to be so prevalent at the turn of the century, and which still posed a very real threat. And, on the other hand, he was able to guard against giving ground in his theology to the suppression and alienation of humanity by and from God, which had been responsible in part for the growing *secularization* of European culture. The ensuing discussion is an attempt to draw out implications for the theology of culture arising from Barth's dialecti-

76. Karl Barth, "The Humanity of God," in *The Humanity of God* (Atlanta: John Knox Press, 1960), p. 44.

77. Barth, "The Humanity of God," pp. 43-45.

78. Barth, "The Humanity of God," p. 43.

79. Barth, "The Humanity of God," p. 45.

cal-incarnational model, centering on its significance for the dedeification and desecularization of the world of human culture.

The theological and philosophical context in which Barth was placed was a most paradoxical one, within which could be found both the drive toward the deification of humanity and culture and the advance of the secularization of human culture. Even more paradoxical perhaps is that one can observe both lines of thought in the writings of those inspired by one of the fathers of modernism, Hegel.[80] In the light of Hegel's impact on modern philosophy and theology, especially his philosophy's significance for those who promoted the opposing trends mentioned above, it will prove instructive to pause briefly and recount Hegel's legacy and what it signified for the context in which Barth's theology emerged.

Hegel's immediate descendants have been classified according to two groups: right-wing and left-wing Hegelians. Left-wing Hegelians, in contrast to those on the right, who attempted to defend Hegel's orthodoxy, interpreted Hegel's theology along pantheistic lines.[81] Indeed, there is evidence in Hegel's philosophy to support the latter view. In Hegel, God or Spirit requires human consciousness to attain self-consciousness. That is to say, God becomes conscious of himself through human consciousness through the course of history. And since thought coupled with historical process or development are keystones in Hegel's thought, no higher praise could be awarded humanity.[82] Edward Craig writes of Hegel's doctrine

80. J. N. Findlay has gone so far as to call Hegel "the father of 'modernism.'" J. N. Findlay, *Hegel: A Re-examination* (London: George Allen & Unwin, 1958), p. 139. As support for his claim, Findlay argues that Hegel's belief that the "realization" in Christ that God must attain "self-consciousness" in humanity was more significant for Hegel than Christ being the "vehicle" for making this truth explicit (p. 139).

81. See Frederick Copleston, S.J., *A History of Philosophy,* book 3, vol. 7, *Fichte to Nietzsche* (New York: Image Books, 1985), pp. 245-47. On the subject of Hegel's orthodoxy, Charles Taylor writes that Hegel's rational "interpretation" of Christian faith, where it is argued that the ideal must become historical, "restores the decisive events of Christian faith to their central historical importance." Charles Taylor, *Hegel* (Cambridge: Cambridge University Press, 1975), p. 493. For Hegel, the real is the rational, and the rational is the real. But for the rational to be fully true or real, it cannot remain in the realm of the ideal, but must become incarnate in history. See G. W. F. Hegel, *Phenomenology of Spirit,* trans. A. V. Miller (Oxford: Clarendon Press, 1977), p. 586.

82. For Hegel, human consciousness is in effect an incarnation of God, for human consciousness is the historical vehicle through which God becomes self-conscious. See Hegel's discussion of "world-historical persons" who served the "World-Spirit" in this way in Georg Wilhelm Friedrich Hegel, *Introduction to the Philosophy of History,* in *The European Philosophers*

that, "In so far as it is consciousness that is in question, there is nothing to God's thought but what is in our minds — our conscious thought *is* the consciousness of the deity. The Image of God doctrine, the thesis of the divinity of man, reaches its climax."[83]

It was not long, however, before this pantheistic viewpoint gave way to naturalism and atheism.[84] Feuerbach, who did not so much interpret or develop Hegel's thought as transform it,[85] turned Hegel's philosophy upside down, or rather, set it on its feet.[86] In place of "Idea," Feuerbach substituted "Nature."[87] Instead of Spirit or God or Idea coming to self-consciousness through human consciousness in human history, humanity comes to self-consciousness through the objectification of itself through conceiving God. It requires very little to make the transition from claiming that God comes to self-consciousness through human consciousness to argue that God is but the projection of human consciousness or reason. Moreover, for Feuerbach, the sense of ultimate dependence humanity experiences is grounded not in God, but nature, which is the fundamental ground of reality, including human consciousness.[88]

---

from Descartes to Nietzsche, ed. Monroe C. Beardsley (New York: The Modern Library, 1960), p. 564.

83. Edward Craig, *The Mind of God and the Works of Man* (Oxford: Clarendon Press, 1987), p. 180.

84. Copleston, *A History of Philosophy,* p. 247.

85. Copleston, *A History of Philosophy,* p. 293.

86. See Copleston, *A History of Philosophy,* p. 295. For Feuerbach, humanity's God is divinized humanity, whereas for Hegel, God's humanity is ultimately humanized deity. For Feuerbach's view, see Ludwig Feuerbach, *Lectures on the Essence of Religion,* trans. Ralph Manheim (New York: Harper & Row, 1967), p. 17.

87. Copleston, *A History of Philosophy,* p. 295.

88. Copleston, *A History of Philosophy,* pp. 295-96. For all their differences from one another, Hegel and Feuerbach were very much alike. For example, the Lutheran doctrine of the *communio naturarum* symbolized for Hegel and Feuerbach the overcoming of the barrier that separated divine and human being. For the former, the incarnation is the realization in history of the truth that God and humanity are ultimately one. Here one finds the deification of humanity. For Feuerbach, on the other hand, God is but the projection of one's own humanity, infinitely extended. In him, one finds the total secularization of theology and life. Theology becomes anthropology (Feuerbach, *Lectures on the Essence of Religion,* p. 17). In *The Göttingen Dogmatics,* Barth writes, "The whole hubris of certain mystical trends, and in their wake the hubris of speculative idealism, was needed to transform the idea of divine humanity into a universal predicate of the human, that is, to make divine revelation a human attribute" (p. 139).

Engels and Marx, who propagated dialectical materialism, further developed this transformation of Hegel's thought along materialistic lines. Unlike Hegel and Feuerbach, however, the chief thing was not thought, but activity.[89] With Nietzsche and Freud, Feuerbach, Marx, and Engels raised suspicion of the existence of God to a new level, calling for the abandonment of the concept in favor of human progress. Nietzsche's prophet, Zarathustra, speaks for all of them when he claims that, "Dead are all the Gods: now do we desire the Superman to live."[90]

In the face of such extremes, namely, the divinization and secularization of culture, Barth came to conceive God as wholly other, wholly distinct from humanity, yet also, wholly one with it, in inseparable relation to it in the person of Jesus Christ. The divine Word becomes human without the human nature becoming divine. Yet the human nature does not exist independently of the divine, but rather is taken up to participate in the divine life as human. Barth's Christological model was determinative for him in safeguarding against the divinization of humanity and human culture on the one hand, and its secularization on the other.

Contra Deification

Consideration will first center on the subject of "dedivinization" in Barth's thought. The subject of revelation is the divine Word, the second person of the Trinity, who has taken to himself an anhypostatic human nature in the incarnation. As a result, God is revealed in history, not directly, but indirectly through the veil of creaturely flesh, spelling the "dedivinization" of the world, human history, and culture. In speaking of revelation as "concealment" in the incarnation (modeled after his anhypostatic-enhypostatic Christological model), Barth claims, "It means the radical dedivinization of the world and nature and history, the complete divine incognito . . . God's dealings with us exclusively by indirect communication, revelation by law and limit, by distance and judgment."[91]

89. Karl Marx, "Theses on Feuerbach," in *The Age of Ideology: The Nineteenth Century Philosophers,* ed. Henry D. Aiken (New York: New American Library, 1956), p. 195.

90. Friedrich Nietzsche, *Thus Spake Zarathustra,* trans. Thomas Common (New York: Heritage Press, 1967), p. 72.

91. Barth, *Göttingen Dogmatics,* p. 144. See McCormack, *Karl Barth's Critically Realistic Dialectical Theology,* pp. 361-63, for his discussion of this theme. See also pages 138-39 of Barth,

Yet for all its indirectness, the concealment of God in this creaturely form involves the identification of God with this human form as human. The Word did not enter a human individual. No, the Word became human. The Word became Jesus Christ. This man, and this man alone, is to be identified with God. Here one finds that it is not simply the distinction between the divine and human natures, but also the incarnation of God as a concrete human, that safeguards against the deification/divinization of humanity and human culture.

Barth argues that, "the union of deity and humanity could not be multiple. There could not have been several God-men."[92] Since God has become a human, namely, Jesus Christ, in an indissoluble union, and since there is only one God and one revelation of God, God could only have become human once.[93] Multiple incarnations "would mean the dissolution of the union between deity and humanity that we have seen to be an essential mark of the God-man," as well as the denial of the unity and oneness of God.[94] The divine Word becomes a concrete human, taking to himself a potential individual human nature in the incarnation, thereby separating himself from all others, and distinguishing the gospel from paganism, past and present.

Carl Braaten points to Harnack who spoke for classical liberal theology in claiming that the gospel Jesus preached was solely about the Father, excluding consideration of the Son.[95] He goes on to say that Harnack's

> Jesuological gospel has now returned as the centerpiece of the new theocentric pluralists who cannot say that Christ is God, but only that God was in Christ, not exclusively in a categorically unique

---

Göttingen Dogmatics. In a footnote to Barth's argument on page 144, the reader is referred to Kierkegaard's work, *Training in Christianity*. In this work, Kierkegaard endeavors to awaken the reader to the truth that the incarnation is scandalous, the cause of offense. Christ is "the sign of contradiction," concluding from it that, "all direct communication is impossible." Søren Kierkegaard, *Training in Christianity and the Edifying Discourse which "Accompanied" It*, with an introduction by Walter Lowrie (Princeton: Princeton University Press, 1947), pp. 134, 136.

92. Barth, *Göttingen Dogmatics*, p. 139.

93. Barth, *Göttingen Dogmatics*, pp. 139-40.

94. Barth, *Göttingen Dogmatics*, p. 139.

95. Carl E. Braaten, "The Gospel for a Neopagan Culture," in *Either/Or: The Gospel or Neopaganism*, ed. Carl E. Braaten and Robert W. Jenson (Grand Rapids: Eerdmans, 1995), p. 12.

> sense, but inclusively along with other saints, sages, and founders of world religions.[96]

One could of course extend the parameters to include all people. That is to say, the spark of divinity resides in everyone. Braaten identifies this belief as the creed of Neo-paganism, that movement which descends from the ancient mystery religions. All that is needed to attain salvation "is to turn inward and 'to get in touch with oneself,' as people say today."[97]

The claim that God is incarnate as Jesus of Nazareth, and him only, and that salvation comes from him rather than arises from within humanity, has always been, is now, and always will be, "foolishness to the Greeks . . . an insult to human dignity and pride."[98] But what is here foolishness to the wise is the wisdom of God, namely, the gospel *as* Jesus Christ.

> The issue in revelation is not the manifestation of a general relation between the finite and the infinite, between time and eternity, but this concrete, contingent, historically accidental fact in which it becomes objectively possible and apart from which we would know nothing about it because apart from it it would not come to us but would remain an unknown movement in God.[99]

Here, Barth's doctrine of the dialectical Word confronts system. In Hegel's system, for example, the incarnation of Jesus Christ does not create the connection between God and humanity, but is the temporal realization of the eternal truth of the union between God and his creature. The incarnation is necessary in that for truth to be wholly true it must leave the realm of the eternal and ideal and become incarnate in history. But even though the incarnation is necessary, it is not unique or indispensable. For Christ discloses what has always been implied, the divinity of humanity. Along these lines, Diogenes Allen makes note of David Strauss's claim that if there is an underlying unity between God and his creature, as Hegel maintains, no single incarnation could suffice to portray that union.[100] Allen writes,

96. Braaten, "The Gospel for a Neopagan Culture," pp. 12-13.

97. Braaten, "The Gospel for a Neopagan Culture," p. 7.

98. Braaten, "The Gospel for a Neopagan Culture," p. 8.

99. Barth, *Göttingen Dogmatics*, p. 144.

100. Diogenes Allen, *Philosophy for Understanding Theology* (Atlanta: John Knox Press, 1985), pp. 238-39.

> Since *all* human beings are divine in nature, even if only implicitly, an explicit unity *in the race* rather than in an individual would be a higher manifestation of this unity. It is impossible for a single person to partake of or to exhibit the divine-human unity uniquely.[101]

How can it be otherwise since for Hegel "the development of the doctrine of the incarnation" is "the product of human thought and culture, not as response to some transcendent initiative but in terms of spirit's own immanent self-development"?[102]

What does the preceding spell for the uniqueness of Christ? Does it not signify his ultimate displacement? For although he is the vehicle for the Absolute's entrance into history, what does this history do save serve as the copy of an eternally existing union between God and humanity? For history is the manifestation of God, of *God's* other, and the union between the two. As Henry Aiken writes, for Hegel, history is "the progressive incarnation of the Absolute Spirit."[103] In this light, Christ's own incarnation makes explicit what has always been the case, albeit implicitly, and which one day will be true of humanity as a whole, namely, its union with God. Christ is not really unique, and is thus dispensable. This is plainly seen in Hegel's understanding of Spirit's ultimate identity. "Spirit is most essentially itself in the religious community where the Divine Man or Human God is transformed into the members' universal, inward, chastening self-consciousness."[104] Could not the same be said of humanity as a class? Rather than finding its climax in the incarnation of Christ, history will reach its zenith at the end of history in the ultimate synthesis of God and the creature. The incarnation only symbolizes, calls to mind, makes explicit, the already implicit union of God and humanity, which will be perfected by all conscious subjects through whom the Absolute comes to self-consciousness in history. What, then, is the ultimate destiny of the particularity of Jesus Christ on this account? Strauss answers by saying, "it becomes as the faint image of a dream which belongs only to the past, and

101. Allen, *Philosophy for Understanding Theology*, pp. 238-39.

102. Colin E. Gunton, *Yesterday and Today: A Study of Continuities in Christology* (Grand Rapids: Eerdmans, 1983), p. 42.

103. Henry D. Aiken, ed., *The Age of Ideology: The 19th Century Philosophers*, The Mentor Philosophers (New York: New American Library, 1956), p. 81.

104. Hegel, *Phenomenology of Spirit*, p. 588.

does not, like the idea, share the permanence of the spirit which is absolutely present to itself."[105]

In light of the preceding, it was of paramount importance that Kierkegaard and Barth stressed so the particular over against the general.[106] For all Barth's distancing of himself from Kierkegaard after the *Romans* period, Barth did not depart from him here.[107] For in the end, *either* Jesus Christ reveals God and saves humanity *or* humanity saves itself.[108]

On Hegel's account, Christ ultimately serves as a midwife, helping humanity bring forth what has always been there within it, albeit implicitly, namely, its own participation in the divine nature. This view did not originate with Hegel, for it has much in common with Plato's Socrates. As Kierkegaard says of "the Socratic view," "Every human being is himself the midpoint, and the whole world focuses only on him because his self-knowledge is God-knowledge."[109] Now for Socrates, the knowledge of the eternal that lies dormant within humanity, needing only to be recalled, has been there from all eternity. For tied to Socrates' belief that the truth lies within the human self is Plato's doctrine of the eternality of the soul, a soul that only needs to recall what it already knows of the eternal forms, from which it came.

Contra paganism old and new, Kierkegaard exhorts his reader to look outside himself, for within himself he only "discovers his untruth." "For the learner is indeed untruth."[110] Over against the midwife who simply

105. David F. Strauss, *The Life of Jesus, Critically Examined,* trans. Marian Evans (New York: Published by Calvin Blanchard, 1855), p. 896.

106. Allen writes that Hegel's doctrine of the fundamental unity between God and humanity prompted Kierkegaard and Barth to proclaim the wholly otherness of God and the idea that fellowship with God is solely the result of the divine initiative in God becoming human as Jesus Christ (Allen, *Philosophy for Understanding Theology,* p. 238).

107. Barth would later write of Kierkegaard, "I consider him to be a teacher whose school every theologian must enter once. Woe to him who misses it — provided only he does not remain in or return to it." Karl Barth, "A Thank-You and a Bow — Kierkegaard's Reveille," in *Fragments Grave and Gay,* ed. Martin Rumscheidt, trans. Eric Mosbacher (Glasgow: William Collins & Sons, 1971), pp. 100-101.

108. Barth refers to Hegel's "living God" as "living man." He also claims that in Hegel's system, "a new word revelatory in the strict sense, cannot pass between" God and the human creature. Karl Barth, *Protestant Theology in the Nineteenth Century: Its Background and History* (London: SCM Press, 1972), p. 419.

109. Søren Kierkegaard, *Philosophical Fragments,* ed. and trans. Howard V. Hong and Edna H. Hong (Princeton: Princeton University Press, 1985), p. 11.

110. Kierkegaard, *Philosophical Fragments,* p. 14.

serves as an occasion for the discovery of truth, or really untruth, Kierkegaard sets forth the teacher who is more than a teacher, who is "the god himself,"[111] providing the truth and the condition for understanding, even transforming, not simply reforming the learner. The teacher of whom Kierkegaard speaks is *"savior," "deliverer," "reconciler," "judge."*[112] *This one* is the sole wisdom of God, but foolishness to the Greeks and their descendants.

Over against those who would raise the question as to whether the incarnation is essential to the Christian faith, it is maintained here that the gospel perishes without it.[113] For without the incarnation, there is either no salvation, or no need of salvation, or else salvation arises from within the human self. Without the incarnation, Jesus Christ loses his uniqueness and is ultimately dispensable.[114] None of this fits very well with the gospel, only with the neo-Pelagian and pagan cultural context in which Christianity is placed. For Barth, as for Kierkegaard before him, Jesus Christ is not simply a particular of history. He is not simply an illustration of the universal. He himself is the universal, even as the particular of history that he is. It is as such that this particular is scandalous to humankind, robbing it of its supposed claims to divinity.

111. Kierkegaard, *Philosophical Fragments,* p. 15.

112. Kierkegaard, *Philosophical Fragments,* pp. 17-18.

113. The question is raised by Maurice Wiles in "Christianity Without Incarnation?," in *The Myth of God Incarnate,* ed. John Hick (Philadelphia: Westminster Press, 1977), pp. 1-10.

114. Marcus Borg, a leading voice for the Jesus Seminar, calls into question the uniqueness of Jesus Christ. See Marcus J. Borg, *Meeting Jesus Again for the First Time: The Historical Jesus and the Heart of Contemporary Faith* (San Francisco: HarperSanFrancisco, 1994), p. 37. Jesus is significant in that he is "one of many mediators of the sacred" (p. 37). He does not provide salvation for sin, but introduces us to the transforming life found in Spirit (p. 119). Elsewhere Borg claims that, like the Bible, Jesus is a lens through which to view one's relationship with God. But "what matters is not believing in the lens but seeing through the lens." Marcus J. Borg, "A Vision of the Christian Life," in Marcus J. Borg and N. T. Wright, *The Meaning of Jesus: Two Visions* (San Francisco: HarperSanFrancisco, 1999), p. 240. From this it follows that although Christ is significant to the Christian tradition and its path of discipleship, he is ultimately dispensable. Jesus experiences the life in Spirit in a manner quantitatively greater than we do. But he is not qualitatively different from us. How can he be if he is not literally the incarnation of God? For Christians simply *experience* Jesus as the Son of God with post-Easter faith. After Easter, "increasingly he was spoken of as having all of the qualities of God" (Borg, *Meeting Jesus Again,* p. 16). Although Christ serves as a medium, introducing us to life in Spirit, he is not the source or locus of such life. Given this orientation, is it not possible, at least in principle, for each of us to attain the status of mediating the sacred to others?

Contra Secularization

Having spoken of the critique of the divinization of culture, we will now center our attention on Barth's theology from the standpoint of the critique of the secularization of culture. As has been noted already, Findlay claims that Hegel is the father of modernism given the primacy of place awarded to the actualization of the incarnation in the life of the believer over against the story of Jesus Christ in Hegel's system (see note 80 on p. 61 above). The centrality of the faith of the human subject over against the supposed object of faith was indeed characteristic of modern theology up to and beyond the demise of Culture Protestantism. However, a theology emphasizing human consciousness as the focal point of theology is hardly prepared to guard against Feuerbach's critique.[115]

Barth's theology from above enables him to guard against the challenge posed by Feuerbach, namely, the reduction of the source of theology to projections of the human mind and the ultimate secularization of human life. Schleiermacher and his descendants, and Hegel, too, however, were unable to combat this challenge.[116] For if theology begins from below in human consciousness or reason, if knowledge of God is impossible, or if God comes to self-consciousness through the human psyche, Feuerbach's critique is fast approaching.[117] As Barth contends, "To repulse Feuerbach's attack effectively one must be certain that man's relation with God is in every respect, in principle, an irreversible relation."[118]
However, more was required. Attention to the humanity of God was required to offset the alienation of humanity from God and the onslaught of secularization. Barth's primary aim in the *Romans* period had been to reassert the deity of God and at the same time safeguard against the divinization of humanity. Indirectly, such emphasis also served to preserve the distinct, creaturely identity of humanity. However, such preservation would perhaps have been short-lived had Barth not come to give due consideration to the humanity of God. For in the end, disregard for

115. See Barth, *Romans*, p. 236, for Barth's affirmation of Feuerbach's critique of religion.

116. Barth, "Ludwig Feuerbach," pp. 227-28; Barth, *Protestant Theology*, p. 537.

117. Barth, "Ludwig Feuerbach," pp. 227-28. Elsewhere, Barth writes that those who fled from Feuerbach, rejecting the move to ground religion in consciousness, "ran straight into the arms of Strauss" by attempting to found religion in history. Barth, *Protestant Theology*, p. 562.

118. Barth, "Ludwig Feuerbach," p. 231.

humanity gives rise to its suppression, perhaps even its displacement, or else its alienation. The incarnation of God as human helps guard against alienation and inhumanity.[119] For alienated humanity is inhumanity. God has become human, taking a potential human nature to himself in an indivisible union. God does not exist apart from this human. Nor does this human, and by analogical extension, the race he represents before God, exist apart from God.

By emphasizing the *humanity* of God, Barth saw to it that humanity is given its proper due. This is not all though. For Barth also placed stress on the humanity *of God*. Thus, the humanity of Christ, and by extension, all humanity whom he serves as paradigm and mediator, exists in inseparable relation to God. For humanity to exist as truly human, it cannot exist apart from God. On Barth's view, alienated humanity is inhumanity. Without proper place being made for this truth, humanity would exist in isolation, as autonomous, perhaps even perceiving itself to be sovereign in its own sphere, proclaiming itself to be God in that sphere. Barth's doctrine of the humanity of God thus gave due weight to the distinct existence of humanity before God, but also proper place to the inseparable relation of humanity to God. As Barth's theology becomes more incarnational, he is able to stress both the deity *and humanity* of God. As such, Barth's Christological model of theology spells not only the death of the deification of humanity and human culture, but also the rejection of secularization, that is, the alienation of humanity and human culture from God.

Langdon Gilkey argues that Neo-orthodox theology laid the groundwork for the "God is dead" movement.[120] Gilkey claims that Neo-orthodox theology's radical emphasis on revelation as the existential encounter between God and humanity and the accompanying rejection of any capacity for God or point of contact between God and the world in the world set the stage for theological secularism. The danger arose that, once the veracity or authenticity of such an experience or encounter was called into question, the very presence of God in the world was itself called into question.[121]

119. For Feuerbach, on the other hand, belief in the incarnation of God as Jesus Christ spells the alienation of the person from its true self — that it is divine in nature. In the light of this belief, one fails to recognize that the individual is one with "the Infinite" (Allen, *Philosophy for Understanding Theology*, p. 239).

120. Langdon Gilkey, *Naming the Whirlwind: The Renewal of God-Language* (Indianapolis and New York: Bobbs-Merrill, 1969), pp. 109, 117.

121. Gilkey, *Naming the Whirlwind*, p. 117.

Along these lines, Gilkey quotes William Hamilton as saying that it is "a short step, but a critical one, to move from the otherness of God to the absence of God."[122] Gilkey goes on to point out that Hamilton's theology became even more radical with time, whereby "the absence or removal of God ha[s] been replaced by 'the death of God.'"[123]

There appear to be two main causal factors for Neo-orthodoxy's demise according to Gilkey. The first relates to Neo-orthodoxy's absolute emphasis on the faith encounter. The second concerns Neo-orthodoxy's adherence to the wholly otherness of God. The two causal factors are intertwined. For Neo-orthodoxy generally, since God is wholly other, the only access to God is through the subjective faith encounter.[124]

Although there is much truth in what is argued here, it would be wrong to locate Barth in this movement, suggesting that his theology gives pride of place to human subjectivity, as well as claiming that he is in part responsible for the rise of secular theology. Gilkey acknowledges that Barth distanced himself from Neo-orthodoxy by making the sovereignty of God in his Word the focal point of his theology.[125] It should be added (as Gilkey

122. Gilkey, *Naming the Whirlwind,* p. 117, quoting William Hamilton, *The New Essence of Christianity* (New York: Association Press, 1968), p. 55.

123. Gilkey, *Naming the Whirlwind,* p. 117. Gilkey has in mind Hamilton's later work, where Hamilton states emphatically that "God is dead. We are not talking about the absence of the experience of God, but about the experience of the absence of God." William Hamilton, "The Death of God Theologies Today," in Thomas J. J. Altizer and William Hamilton, *Radical Theology and the Death of God* (Indianapolis, New York, Kansas City: Bobbs-Merrill, 1966), p. 28. Harnack made the same link Gilkey does between Neo-orthodox theology and the threat of atheism, that is, secularism, asking, "If God is definitely not all that is said of him in the development of culture and its knowledge and morality, how is it possible to protect this culture and one's self in the long run against atheism?" Adolf von Harnack, "Fifteen Questions to Those Among the Theologians Who Are Contemptuous of the Scientific Theology," in *The Beginnings of Dialectical Theology,* vol. 1, ed. James M. Robinson, trans. Keith R. Crim and Louis De Grazia (Richmond, Va.: John Knox Press, 1968), pp. 165-66. Later, Harnack indicates that it was chiefly Barth to whom he had addressed his questions. See Adolf von Harnack, "An Open Letter to Professor Karl Barth," in *The Beginnings of Dialectical Theology,* vol. 1, p. 171. Barth's response to Harnack's question quoted above is illumining for what it discloses of their different theological orientations. Barth raises the possibility that instead of safeguarding against atheism, those claims made of God in culture, "derived as they are from polytheism," may actually "*plant* atheism." Karl Barth, "Fifteen Answers to Professor von Harnack," in *The Beginnings of Dialectical Theology,* vol. 1, p. 168.

124. See Gilkey, *Naming the Whirlwind,* p. 117.

125. Gilkey, *Naming the Whirlwind,* p. 97. Although often branded an existentialist, Barth

himself observes, using somewhat different categories) that Barth, in contrast to Neo-orthodox theology generally, located faith in the personal revelation event of the Word rather than the Word in the event of faith.[126] Moreover, for Barth, the otherness of God, which has been defined in this study as the utter difference of God in relation to the world rather than opposition to the world, is wed to God's oneness with the world in the light of Barth's newfound Christological model. God is wholly other than the world, but also wholly one with the world in and through the person of Jesus Christ. Lastly, although Barth rejects all forms of natural theology, he does not reject the objective witness of creation to God.[127] The creation does bear witness objectively to God. And in the place of natural theology, Barth moves toward the development of a theology of nature.[128]

Gilkey laments the fact that Neo-orthodoxy, especially in Europe, in-

---

repudiates existentialist theology. (See Busch, *Karl Barth: His Life,* p. 375.) In one place, Barth writes of how "increasingly" he feels "more disgust and abhorrence" in the light "of the thrust of" the "theological existentialists." Karl Barth, letter to Prof. Helmut Gollwitzer, in *Letters, 1961-1968,* ed. Geoffrey W. Bromiley (Grand Rapids: Eerdmans, 1981), p. 61.

126. Gilkey, *Naming the Whirlwind,* p. 117. In passing, it is interesting to note the paradoxical relation of Neo-orthodox theology to Schleiermacher, to which Gilkey also makes reference. In the end, both Schleiermacher and Neo-orthodox theology generally ground the Christian faith in faith rather than in the Word who engenders faith. See Gilkey, *Naming the Whirlwind,* pp. 97, 117.

127. In one place, for example, Barth speaks of the creation as a mirror in its service as a witness to God. See Karl Barth, *Church Dogmatics,* III/3, *The Doctrine of Creation,* ed. G. W. Bromiley and T. F. Torrance (Edinburgh: T. & T. Clark, 1960), pp. 52-53. See also his interpretation of Calvin in "No!," in *Natural Theology,* pp. 106-8. There he rejects Brunner's claim that Brunner finds in Calvin an ally for his conviction that the pursuit of natural theology is of some value, however limited. Barth himself also wishes to make an ally of Calvin. On Barth's interpretation of the Reformer, which appears to be Barth's own view on the subject as well, Calvin maintains that all God's works bear witness to God. As a result, humanity "is without excuse" (p. 108). But neither Calvin nor Paul in Romans maintain "that a 'natural' knowledge of the law of God is to be ascribed to us" (p. 108). The creation objectively bears witness to God (p. 108). But "the possibility of a real knowledge by natural man of the true God, derived from creation, is, according to Calvin, a possibility in principle, but not in fact, not a possibility to be realised by us" (p. 106).

128. See Colin Gunton's development of this way of approaching the subject in his essay, "The Trinity, Natural Theology, and a Theology of Nature," in *The Trinity in a Pluralistic Age,* ed. Kevin J. Vanhoozer (Grand Rapids: Eerdmans, 1997), pp. 88-103.For a provocative defense of Barth as a truly great natural theologian, see Stanley Hauerwas, *With the Grain of the Universe: The Church's Witness and Natural Theology* (Grand Rapids: Brazos Press, 2001), pp. 20, 142, 159.

tentionally divorced "theological discourse from ordinary experience," focusing its attention on the ancient biblical categories, thereby failing for the most part to make sense or to be validated or substantiated in a secular age.[129] The separation of faith and ordinary experience, which earlier had been a virtue at a time of great social turmoil, now became a vice, giving rise to doubt and unbelief rather than faith.[130] Further attention will be devoted to this subject in the course of the next chapter. But for now, brief consideration will be given to two theologies that arose in response to this predicament.

Gilkey pays tribute to Bultmann and Tillich as two theologians who were painfully aware of the inherent weakness of Neo-orthodox theology along the lines indicated above. They attempted to bridge the gap between Christian faith and secular experience, buttressing faith in the Word by setting forth connections with secular experience.[131] However, this author is not so enamored with the supposed merits of the programs of these "mediating figures," who Gilkey claims based their theologies of engagement in Christian revelation.[132] For one, what is in need of buttressing, the divine Word who produces faith, or the human existing in a secular age, who perhaps even believes? For Barth, and notable others before him, it is not the existence of God and his Word that are called into question, but, if anything, humanity before God in his Word.[133] Moreover, it is not at all certain that Tillich actually bases his theology of engagement in revelation. For although he claims to judge even the questions posed by secular man in the light of revelation, it appears that in the end culture's questions shape the agenda and answers framed by this mediating theologian.

Tillich defines his theology as "apologetic," that is, as "answering theology." According to Tillich, "it answers the questions implied in the 'situation' in the power of the eternal message and with the means provided by

129. Gilkey, *Naming the Whirlwind*, p. 99.

130. Gilkey, *Naming the Whirlwind*, p. 99.

131. Gilkey, *Naming the Whirlwind*, p. 99, n. 28. See also the text of page 99.

132. Gilkey, *Naming the Whirlwind*, p. 99, n. 28. See also the text of page 99.

133. See Karl Barth, *Church Dogmatics*, III/1, *The Doctrine of Creation*, ed. G. W. Bromiley and T. F. Torrance (Edinburgh: T. & T. Clark, 1958), p. 6. It is this writer's view that the Word can be "checked" (to use Gilkey's terminology in *Naming the Whirlwind*, p. 99) only when he gives himself to be checked or validated. But ultimately, it is the Word who checks or buttresses the world rather than the other way around.

the situation whose questions it answers."[134] In all fairness to Tillich, he makes a sustained attempt to employ this "method of correlation" without giving priority of place to either the questions or the answers.[135] Moreover, Tillich wishes to safeguard against sacrificing the particularity of Jesus Christ at the altar of the universal principle of the *logos;* in fact, he differentiates the theologian from the philosopher as the one who is concerned for the particular over against the general. Whereas the philosopher focuses attention on "the universal *logos* . . . through rational detachment," the object of analysis for the theologian is "the Logos 'who became flesh,' that is, the *logos* manifesting itself in a particular historical event." And unlike the philosopher, whose "medium" of analysis is "common rationality," that of the theologian is "the church, its traditions and its present reality."[136]

Nonetheless, this writer is left unconvinced that Tillich is able to preserve the particularity of Jesus Christ in his theological program of mediation. Suspicion arises in the light of Tillich's view of the relation of original and dependent revelation, through the mediation of Scripture. As David Kelsey explains, for Tillich, the biblical pictures or symbols *express* "original revelation" — Jesus Christ. However, they also *occasion* "dependent revelation," as Kelsey points out.[137] These biblical symbols have a *direct* bearing on theology when it is focused on "original revelation," but only an *indirect* bearing on theology when "dependent revelatory events" are under consideration.[138] Kelsey asks how it is that the biblical symbols connect the original and consequent revelations.[139] The question arises in light of the fact that when Tillich turns to consider how the biblical picture provides solutions to humanity's existential concerns today, he centers attention on Scripture's ability to "occasion revelatory events now." However, in doing so, Tillich "seems to ignore entirely the intrinsic formal features of the picture."[140] Kelsey concludes that Tillich is unable to show how the biblical

134. Paul Tillich, *Systematic Theology,* vol. 1 (Chicago: University of Chicago Press, 1951), p. 6.

135. Tillich, *Systematic Theology,* vol. 1, p. 8.

136. Tillich, *Systematic Theology,* vol. 1, pp. 23-24.

137. David H. Kelsey, *The Uses of Scripture in Recent Theology* (Philadelphia: Fortress Press, 1975), pp. 71-73.

138. Kelsey, *The Uses of Scripture,* pp. 72, 73.

139. Kelsey, *The Uses of Scripture,* p. 73.

140. Kelsey, *The Uses of Scripture,* p. 71.

picture connects the original and dependent revelations.[141] Kelsey reasons that this inability is "serious" because it seems to suggest that what the theologian has to say about making people whole in society today bears no real tie to Jesus Christ to whom Scripture bears witness.

> If there is no connection between what is said (with only indirect appeal to scripture) about making human life whole today and what is said (with direct appeal to scripture) about the person of Jesus, then Christology would seem to have become logically dispensable for contemporary Christian theology.[142]

Similar instances of the same problem can be found in Tillich's discussion of religion and "New Being." In his discussion of religion in "Invocation: The Lost Dimension in Religion," Tillich distinguishes religion from the religions, arguing that religion is not ultimately about certain beliefs in "gods or one God" or about "institutions."[143] He contrasts "religion in its innermost nature" from the religions. For Tillich, religion "is the state of being concerned about one's own being and being universally."[144] Tillich speaks of those who reject this or that religion for its inability to address "their profound concern," and says that they "are religious while rejecting the religions."[145] This leads Tillich to make the distinction between "religion as living in the dimension of depth from particular expressions of one's ultimate concern," namely, the historic religions.[146] With this foundational definition of religion in mind, Tillich turns to consider the modern religious situation. He writes that in turning "to the concrete analysis of the religious situation of our time," one must bring to bear "the basic meaning of religion" on the situation in order to discern "the predicament of man" in modern society.[147] Tillich concludes from this analysis, using

141. Kelsey, *The Uses of Scripture,* p. 74.

142. Kelsey, *The Uses of Scripture,* p. 74. See also his discussion of the relation between the form and power of the biblical symbol in the following work, David H. Kelsey, *The Fabric of Paul Tillich's Theology* (New Haven: Yale University Press, 1967), p. 142.

143. Paul Tillich, "Invocation: The Lost Dimension in Religion," in *The Essential Tillich: An Anthology of the Writings of Paul Tillich,* ed. F. Forrester Church (New York: Macmillan, 1987), p. 1.

144. Tillich, "Invocation: The Lost Dimension in Religion," p. 1.

145. Tillich, "Invocation: The Lost Dimension in Religion," p. 1.

146. Tillich, "Invocation: The Lost Dimension in Religion," p. 2.

147. Tillich, "Invocation: The Lost Dimension in Religion," p. 2.

this basic definition of religion, that "man in our time has lost" the ultimate concern, and that "the dimension of depth is replaced by life in the horizontal dimension."[148]

The point of concern here is that religion, as Tillich defines it, serves as the basis for his analysis and critique of the modern predicament, not the Word who became flesh, who according to Tillich is *the* subject of study for the theologian.[149] From his discussion of religion and the religions, one has reason to believe that when Tillich moves from what the faith meant to the first Christians to what it means today for those of a more secular orientation, the particularity of Jesus Christ is displaced.

Moreover, in contrast to Tillich who maintains that Christ exemplifies concern for the ultimate and mediates the power of "New Being" to humanity, the claim made here is that Christ *is* humanity's ultimate concern. He is the name for that which concerns all persons ultimately.[150] He is the one who reveals to humankind the modern predicament. Christ does not simply *represent* or *mediate* "the power of the New Being." He is "New Being."[151]

Busch's account of Barth's own debate with Tillich, which began in November 1923, sums up well this author's own disagreement with the latter. The underlying issue in this debate, as Busch points out, is "the status of the person of Jesus Christ in theology."[152] Busch summarizes Barth's account with quotations from Barth.

> "For 'us,' Christ is *the* salvation history," whereas for Tillich Christ was only the symbol of a revelation present and knowable always and everywhere — and thus a revelation which was "given" and not, as Barth wanted to see it, "a very special *event,* revealed only by God and only to be known in so far as we can be known by it."[153]

148. Tillich, "Invocation: The Lost Dimension in Religion," p. 2.

149. See above for Tillich's statement contrasting the theologian and the philosopher.

150. In volume one of his *Systematic Theology,* Tillich writes, "'God' is the answer to the question implied in man's finitude; he is the name for that which concerns man ultimately" (p. 211).

151. In *The New Being,* Tillich writes that Christ "represents and mediates the power of the New Being because He represents and mediates the power of an undisrupted union." Paul Tillich, *The New Being* (New York: Charles Scribner's Sons, 1955), p. 22.

152. Busch, *Karl Barth: His Life,* p. 152.

153. Busch, *Karl Barth: His Life,* p. 152, quoting Karl Barth, "The Paradoxical Nature of the 'Positive Paradox': Answers and Questions to Paul Tillich," in *The Beginnings of Dialecti-*

For Barth, the Logos is not one of many symbols.[154] In fact, it is not a symbol at all. "God's Word means that God speaks. Speaking is not a 'symbol' (as P. Tillich, *Rel. Verwirkl.*, 1930, p. 48 thinks)."[155] God's Word comes to humanity. It does not arise from within the human creature. For Barth, the Logos is not what he claims Schleiermacher understood it to be, namely, "'the spirit in all men,' i.e., in all those united in the Church."[156] Barth refers to Tillich's system as the "realistic end of the same path which Schleiermacher entered upon idealistically."[157] Is it not the case that what Tillich means by the "sacramental situation" is what Barth understands as "proclamation"? And, is it not true that for Tillich, "the historical destiny by which it is created . . . is really the relation between a deepened understanding of self and a deepened understanding of the world, and *vice versa*"?[158] If so, and Barth seems to suggest that such is indeed the case for Tillich, "then we are forced to conjecture that here too man is finally conceived of as conversing only with himself."[159] If so, such an understanding of the Word means in the end that "speech, word, proclamation and preaching" give way to, are made redundant by, "the notion of a general dynamic or even meaning which embraces God and man."[160] On such a view, the Logos "becomes one symbol among many others."[161]

When one turns from Tillich to consider Bultmann, the other mediating theologian to whom Gilkey refers, one is left wondering if "God" him-

---

cal Theology, vol. 1, ed. James M. Robinson, trans. Keith R. Crim and Louis De Grazia (Richmond, Va.: John Knox Press, 1968), pp. 142, 150. In *Beginnings*, Barth draws attention to Tillich's "objection" to Barth's emphasis on "imperceptibleness." Barth counters by saying that Tillich fails to see the centrality of "divine freedom and love, and runs the great danger of letting the justified polemic against the *'man-god,'* once waged by Kierkegaard and Dostoyevsky, be converted into its opposite, the polemic against the *God-man*" (Barth, "The Paradoxical Nature," p. 151).

154. Barth, *Church Dogmatics*, I/1, *The Doctrine of the Word of God*, ed. G. W. Bromiley and T. F. Torrance (Edinburgh: T. & T. Clark, 1975), p. 63.

155. Barth, *Church Dogmatics*, I/1, p. 132.

156. Karl Barth, *Church Dogmatics*, I/1, p. 62, quoting Friedrich Schleiermacher, *Christian Faith*, section 134, no. 3.

157. Barth, *Church Dogmatics*, I/1, p. 62.

158. Barth, *Church Dogmatics*, I/1, p. 62.

159. Barth, *Church Dogmatics*, I/1, p. 62.

160. Barth, *Church Dogmatics*, I/1, p. 62.

161. Barth, *Church Dogmatics*, I/1, p. 63.

self is not in danger of being displaced, given Bultmann's program of demythologizing. Here one is reminded of Fritz Buri's criticism, "The kerygma is a last vestige of mythology to which we still illogically cling."[162] For Buri, Bultmann is inconsistent, unwilling to take the final step and demythologize the kerygma, the divine act in history, into the language of existentialism. Barth, on the other hand, is pleased with Bultmann's decision to refrain from employing the tools of demythologizing at the point of the "Christ event."[163] Nonetheless, Barth is unconvinced that Bultmann has provided a sufficient answer to the question as to whether or not the latter's "retention of an act of God is compatible with demythologizing."[164]

Bultmann wishes to demythologize what he considers to be the mythological statements in Scripture, that is, those statements that "give worldly objectivity to that which is unworldly."[165] This does not mean *eliminating* them, but rather, *interpreting* them so that they can be made accessible to moderns.[166] Bultmann rejects what he considers to be "an ancient worldview which is obsolete," while retaining "the message of Scripture."[167] This message, the kernel to be preserved, is that *God acts.*[168] In this context, Bultmann makes note of the objection raised against him that "to speak of God as acting" is to speak mythologically. Such speech contains "a mythological residue."[169] The conclusion is then drawn by Bultmann's critic that either Bultmann is unable to employ "de-mythologizing consistently" or that "Christian preaching must always remain mythological."[170]

162. Fritz Buri, "Enmythologisierung oder Entkerygmatizierung der Theologie," in *Kerygma und Mythos,* vol. 3, p. 96; quoted in Karl Barth, "Rudolf Bultmann — An Attempt to Understand Him," in *Kerygma and Myth: A Theological Debate,* vol. 2, ed. Hans-Werner Bartsch, trans. Reginald H. Fuller (London: SPCK, 1962), p. 130.

163. Karl Barth, "Rudolf Bultmann — An Attempt to Understand Him," in *Kerygma and Myth: A Theological Debate,* vol. 2, ed. Hans-Werner Bartsch, trans. Reginald H. Fuller (London: SPCK, 1962), p. 116.

164. Barth, "Rudolf Bultmann — An Attempt to Understand Him," p. 116.

165. Rudolf Bultmann, *Jesus Christ and Mythology* (New York: Charles Scribner's Sons, 1958), pp. 18-19.

166. Bultmann, *Jesus Christ and Mythology,* pp. 18, 20.

167. Bultmann, *Jesus Christ and Mythology,* pp. 35, 36.

168. See Bultmann's discussion in *Jesus Christ and Mythology,* p. 43. See also p. 59 as well as chapter five of Bultmann's work.

169. Bultmann, *Jesus Christ and Mythology,* p. 60.

170. Bultmann, *Jesus Christ and Mythology,* p. 60.

Although he defends himself against these criticisms,[171] in the end, Bultmann is willing to admit that such speech is mythological, but adds that such "myth is something very different from what it is as the object of de-mythologizing."[172] How is this so? Bultmann's answer is, "When we speak of God as acting, we do not speak mythologically in the objectifying sense."[173] Yet, how is such non-objectifying talk of God safeguarded from the charge of being completely vacuous? Of what merit is Bultmann's non-objectified mythological talk of "God as acting"? Either one interprets *all* mythology in accordance with the canons of human existence,[174] thereby interpreting "God as acting" along existentialist lines, making God's act a predicate of human activity and existence, or one argues that there are two forms of mythological language, objectifying and non-objectifying, safeguarding the latter from being demythologized, yet also removing the possibility of such language making sense.

Either there is an inconsistency in Bultmann's thought in that he is unwilling to demythologize "God as acting," or incomprehensibility in that he is not able to give any content to the non-objectified mythological talk of "God as acting." In this light, is it not the case that Bultmann himself, the mediating theologian, is guilty of blind faith, of ghettoizing theology in a secular age? In the end, does he not cut himself off without reason from secular, modern culture, by retaining a place for mythological, albeit non-objectified, talk of God, and from the church, because he is unwilling or unable to give any content to "God as acting"? And even if he were to give "God as acting" concrete theological content, he would then be objectifying it, thereby giving rise to the need to demythologize such language. Now, even if, on the whole, Bultmann is successful in making the gospel understandable to modern minds, "he has," as Barth says, "certainly made it difficult, if not impossible, for us to recognize the New Testament message in this new existentialist garb."[175]

Perhaps Bultmann and Tillich are able to mediate faith to secular culture. Perhaps, in their own way, they are able to guard against the utter *secularization* of culture, making space for religion in an age of suspicion. But is Jesus Christ in all his particularity indispensable? In the end, one is

171. Bultmann, *Jesus Christ and Mythology*, pp. 60-61.

172. Bultmann, *Jesus Christ and Mythology*, p. 62.

173. Bultmann, *Jesus Christ and Mythology*, p. 62.

174. See Bultmann, *Jesus Christ and Mythology*, p. 57.

175. Karl Barth, "Rudolf Bultmann — An Attempt to Understand Him," p. 116.

left to consider whether it is possible to mediate between the Word of Christ and the world of culture in such a way that there is perfect symmetry between the two sides. Is this not what is intended by theologies of mediation? In the final analysis, is it not the case that either Christ or culture will attain mastery and sovereignty? Perhaps these theologians of mediation discussed here wish to reserve primacy of place for the Word. But given their apologetic drive to make the gospel palatable to its "cultured despisers," do they not in the end give such primacy to the world of secular culture?

Whatever the case might be, Barth would later warn against the attempt to try to achieve a synthesis between his theological program and those of Tillich and Bultmann. One must choose between his and theirs. There is no middle ground. In the foreword to a new edition of *Rudolf Bultmann* and *Christus und Adam,* published in 1964, Barth would urge his

> colleagues, young and old, who are so keen to find a standpoint "beyond Barth and Bultmann," to stop doing it and instead to follow either the one or the other consistently along his way and to pursue it to the end. They will not find Rudolf Bultmann and me — or Tillich and me . . . as heraldic lions on the left and the right of the door which leads to the paradise of a new and better theology.[176]

In the end, one must choose between a theology of engagement symbolized by an ellipse with two foci as Schleiermacher and these other theologians of mediation maintain, and that alternative which emphasizes the sovereignty of God in his Word, signifying an irreversible relation between God and the world.

Conclusion: Beyond the Impasse

Is a synthesis of any sort between the Word and world possible, indeed ad-

176. Karl Barth, *Rudolf Bultmann* and *Christus und Adam,* new edition, 1964; quoted in Eberhard Busch, *Karl Barth: His Life,* p. 466. In a letter written to Tillich dated 3 December 1963, Barth advises Tillich not "to offer . . . a synthesis" of their theological programs, for although they get on so well on "the human level," "materially" they "can only contradict and oppose one another from the very foundation up." Karl Barth, letter to Paul Tillich, in *Letters, 1961-1968,* ed. Geoffrey W. Bromiley (Grand Rapids: Eerdmans, 1981), p. 144.

visable? Is *diastasis* alone conceivable? Tillich writes in the opening pages of his *Systematic Theology* that,

> No doubt the voices of those who have emphasized the contrast, the *diastasis,* have been louder and more impressive — men usually are more powerful in their negations than in their affirmations. But the continuous toil of those who have tried to find a union, a "synthesis," has kept theology alive.[177]

As shown through the course of the study to this point, Barth himself came to see that *diastasis* alone was not sufficient to preserve theology, but that a positive synthesis with worldly, secular forms was also required. The question is not *whether* a synthesis between Word and world is to be ventured, but rather, *how.* As in Christology proper, so too, here, it is crucial to engage the world of culture, not from below, but from above, proceeding downward. As the divine Word takes to himself a potential human nature in the incarnation, so too, Barth's theology of the Word becomes a theology for the world, and in its own way, a worldly theology.

In the next two chapters, consideration will focus on the synthesis, that is, certain *connections* made between Christ and culture in Barth's thought. Attention will center on the extension of Barth's Christological model to the relation of the sacred and secular spheres, and also on the possibility of Christian and secular witness to the Word. Then, in the final two chapters, reflection will be concentrated on the positive *distinctions* made between the sacred and secular spheres in Barth's theology according to which the world of broader culture is given space to be truly secular.

In Barth's work, the *dedivinization* of culture gives rise to the *humanization* of culture. This reality of dedivinization enables culture to be the human, creaturely reality it is intended by God to be. And although Barth guards against the *secularization* of human culture by emphasizing the significance of the Word for the whole of creaturely reality, not simply the sacred sphere, he is still able to give space to culture to be truly *secular* in light of the Word. Dedivinization and desecularization spell humanization, which in turn spells the celebration of authentic secularity.

In closing, it is wrong to charge Barth with having given rise to secular theology, or to "credit" him with being a mediating theologian. And yet, his dual emphasis on the dedivinization and desecularization of culture en-

177. Tillich, *Systematic Theology,* vol. 1, p. 7.

ables him to mediate between Christ and culture in such a way that broader culture is given the space to be truly secular in distinct though *inseparable* relation to the sacred, in and through the eternal Word who became flesh.

PART II

CONNECTIONS

3

The Constitutive Word, the Sacred, and the Secular

The Secular Awakening and the Demise of *Corpus Christianum*

"The *diastasis* between the Church and the world inaugurated or revealed with the dawn of the modern age has put an end to" the "state of balance" between the church and European civilization.[1] Barth welcomes the "secular" world's discovery or rediscovery of "secularism" through "the emancipation of the world from the Church," which terminated "that doubtful union" or synthesis of the two conceived "in the Middle Ages."[2] Barth's celebration of the dissolution of the *corpus christianum* and secular humanity's coming of age displays once again how much a modern Barth truly is.[3] As Ralph Wood so accurately points out, "Far from being antimodernist, Barth welcomes the radical distinction between church and culture which Western secularization has accomplished."[4]

The fundamental problem with Christendom was its assumption that European society was throughout a Christian world; as a result, it had "very little awareness of the existence of a non-Christian world," thereby

1. Karl Barth, *Church Dogmatics,* IV/3.1, *The Doctrine of Reconciliation,* ed. G. W. Bromiley and T. F. Torrance (Edinburgh: T. & T. Clark, 1961), p. 21.

2. Barth, *Church Dogmatics,* IV/3.1, p. 21.

3. Barth, *Church Dogmatics,* IV/3.1, pp. 20-21.

4. Ralph C. Wood, *The Comedy of Redemption: Christian Faith and Comic Vision in Four American Novelists* (Notre Dame: University of Notre Dame Press, 1988), p. 68.

impeding "a genuine encounter of the Gospel and man."[5] The confrontation of a so very nominal Christendom by a so very "strange" and foreign gospel was urgently needed if there was to be a *true* form of mutual participation.[6] For this reason, Barth donned Kierkegaard's mantle and praised secular humanity's coming of age.[7]

Two things need to be said at this point. First of all, Barth's praise of secularism noted here does not contradict the point made in the previous chapter, namely, that Barth's theology of the Word enables him to guard against the secularization of culture. Barth is not in favor of secularization if what is meant by that term is modern humanity's rejection of God in Christ. What he is in favor of is secular humanity's rejection of bourgeois

5. Barth, *Church Dogmatics,* IV/3.1, p. 20. Closer to home, does not the assumption often found within conservative Christian churches in America that the country was founded as a Christian nation impede a proper engagement of the Word of Christ and the American culture today? Braaten has remarked that such "Christians are so convinced that America was born a Christian nation that they cannot believe that its present inhospitality to Christianity is a phenomenon profoundly rooted in our origins." Carl E. Braaten, "The Gospel for a Neopagan Culture," in *Either/Or: The Gospel or Neopaganism,* ed. Carl E. Braaten and Robert W. Jenson (Grand Rapids: Eerdmans, 1995), p. 16. It is not until the American church completely deconstructs the myth that America was founded as a Christian nation and sees that the Enlightenment's creed was the overarching gospel of the constitutional fathers that, to quote Braaten, "the churches will recognize that they face the challenge of old-fashioned paganism underlying the dominant thought forms" of society, including education, law, and entertainment (p. 16). Of course, as Perry Miller has argued, many of the early colonists such as John Winthrop came to America to create a Christian society. However, the society they envisioned was very different from the one designed by Jefferson and Franklin. See Perry Miller's discussion of Winthrop in *Errand into the Wilderness* (Cambridge: Belknap Press of Harvard University Press, 1956), pp. 4-6. True encounter can only occur when one understands the history and identity of the engagement. Other requirements for true engagement are humility, honesty, and courage — admitting failure. For sometimes the church deserves the antagonism it experiences. For example, it was not until quite recently that the Southern Baptist Conference apologized publicly for its role in the slavery movement in America. How ironic it is (or is it?) that liberal Christians were often at the center of the civil rights activism in the 1960s. In contrast, by and large Evangelicals only got on the bandwagon once the battle was officially over.

6. Barth, *Church Dogmatics,* IV/3.1, p. 20.

7. Wood's reference to Kierkegaard's own attack of Christendom for making authentic Christianity superfluous sheds light on Barth's own concern. (See Wood, p. 68.) As Wood says, for Barth (and here one could add Kierkegaard), there could be no assent whatsoever to Hilaire Belloc's maxim, "Europe is the Faith and the Faith is Europe" (Wood, *Comedy of Redemption,* p. 68).

religion, that which so easily opens the way to the amalgamation and mutual imprisonment of the Word of Christ and world of culture, as Barth witnessed in the theologies of the "Culture Protestants" and "German Christians." Barth claims that "the great hero" of the "emancipation and secularization" of European society[8] may not only have been responsible for freeing culture from the church, but also for freeing the church to be once again "a Church of the Word," that is, "a confessing Church."[9] As "European man" was "awakening to a new awareness of his secularity," the church under the Reformers was awakening to the realization "that everything depends wholly and utterly upon the Word" of God in Christ.[10] The church, which had been reformed by the Word, confronted secular humanity,[11] humanity come of age, with the gospel demand and claim regarding humanity's "new being in and with Christ."[12] It was due to the destruction of "an unprofitable union with the world" that "a materially profitable encounter with the world has been achieved."[13] In this way, "the Church's mainly static being and attitude to the outside world has been changed into a dynamic."[14] Thus, the church has been freed through the secularization of culture to confront that culture with the Word.

Barth does not glory in secularization as such, but secularization for the sake of *diastasis*. But *diastasis* itself is not really the first word. And it is certainly not the last. For the point of *diastasis* is to break up faulty syntheses so that a more wholesome synthesis may be established, one that has in fact already been established with the world through the Word of Christ. This is the second point to be stressed. As Wood says, although the *saeculum* may deny God, "God refuses to deny the *saeculum*."[15] For this reason, although the church confronts secular culture, it exists for that culture. The church is not simply "free in face of" the world of secular culture, but also is free on its "behalf" in the light of the Word addressed to the church and world.[16] This dialectical encounter with the world, based

8. Barth, *Church Dogmatics*, IV/3.1, p. 22.
9. Barth, *Church Dogmatics*, IV/3.1, pp. 21-22.
10. Barth, *Church Dogmatics*, IV/3.1, p. 22.
11. Barth, *Church Dogmatics*, IV/3.1, p. 22.
12. Barth, *Church Dogmatics*, IV/3.1, p. 22.
13. Barth, *Church Dogmatics*, IV/3.1, p. 21.
14. Barth, *Church Dogmatics*, IV/3.1, p. 21.
15. Wood, *Comedy of Redemption*, p. 69.
16. Barth, *Church Dogmatics*, IV/3.1, p. 22.

on "the reconciliation of the world,"[17] the confrontation of this age with the joyful news of the age to come, a synthesis not of something old and new, but a constitutive call to participation in redemption that involves the transformation of the old in light of the new, serves as one of the central themes of this chapter.

The basis for Barth's claim made in CD IV/3.1 that "No Prometheanism can be effectively maintained against Jesus Christ,"[18] to which Wood draws attention,[19] is Barth's doctrine of the election of all humanity in Christ. All humanity is elected in Christ, who is the elect of God throughout eternity and in history. The divine Word, second person of the Trinity, in whom an anhypostasized, that is, a potential human nature is enhypostasized, is the one in whom all those possessing human nature are elect, that is, *constituted* as truly human persons. *And by analogical extension,* not only the church, but also human culture generally, is inseparably related to Christ, having no existence apart from him *(anhypostasis).*[20] This chapter

17. Barth, *Church Dogmatics,* IV/3.1, p. 22.

18. Barth, *Church Dogmatics,* IV/3.1, p. 119.

19. Wood, *Comedy of Redemption,* p. 69.

20. Further to the discussion of the disanalogies in extending the categories of *anhypostasis* and *enhypostasis* to the church and broader culture, the point needs to be emphasized that for Barth, strictly speaking, the divine Word assumes a potential and concrete human nature. For Barth, like John of Damascus before him, the Word does not assume "a human individual," or "humanity, or human nature, in general. It is rather a potential human individual, a nature not yet developed into a person or hypostasis." The quotation is taken from George Park Fisher's discussion of John of Damascus's view in his work, *History of Christian Doctrine* (New York: Charles Scribner's Sons, 1911), p. 159. But in light of the fact that Christ as the elected human is the true ground of humanity and not simply its goal, and that to exercise human autonomy or freedom as heteronomy is an ontological impossibility, the use of the term is being extended to speak analogously of humanity generally. For humanity does not exist independently of Christ. It is interesting to note here what Meyendorff says of Leontius *of Jerusalem's* own version of *enhypostasis.* In contrast to John of Damascus (and Barth), Leontius of Jerusalem seeks to resolve the dilemma of how to conceive a particular of history as the universal of faith by maintaining that the divine Logos assumed a human nature, whose "hypostasis" is "independent of the limitations of created nature." John Meyendorff, *Christ in Eastern Thought* (Crestwood, N.Y.: St. Vladimir's Seminary Press, 1975), p. 75. The problem with this view is that it tends to undermine the concrete particularity of the human nature in favor of its universal significance, which is what Meyendorff refers to as the problem "of Christ's concrete manhood" (p. 75). Barth, on the other hand, besides arguing that the particular of history, namely, Jesus Christ, *is* the universal, posits Jesus Christ as the electing God and elected human who *represents* all other humans before God.

will consider Barth's doctrine of election, that is, the *constitutive* being of the Word and what it implies for the relation of the sacred and secular dimensions in human culture. In this light, discussion will now center on the explication of the doctrine of election itself, including its place in Barth's theology,[21] after which consideration will be given to the relation of the sacred and secular from the standpoint of church and society, and covenant and creation.

Election as Universal Christological Constitution

The primacy of Jesus Christ for Barth's conception of theology generally, and divine and creaturely life specifically, finds definitive expression in his doctrine of election. The Word enfleshed reveals the very being of God and humanity. Jesus Christ is the one in whom God is throughout eternity the electing God and in whom humanity is the elect of God. He is the electing God and elect human.[22]

One must conceive the decree of election in its entirety in the light of Christ, and not as a *decretum absolutum* that stands behind and in opposition to the revelation of God in Christ. As Barth says,

21. McCormack argues that Barth's incarnational theology would manifest itself fully in Barth's doctrine of God and election. According to McCormack, the *transition* to this wholly incarnational orientation was a series of lectures Barth gave on election in Debrecen, Hungary, in 1936, the inspiration for which came from Pierre Maury's lecture on the same topic delivered earlier in that year. McCormack writes that Barth would now consider election from the standpoint of "the election of Christ as Mediator (and of individuals *in Him*) rather than the election of individuals as the effect of a revelation-event in the present." In this light, Barth would reformulate his theology along the lines of "a christocentric concentration" away from "a pneumatocentric concentration," that is, "to a concentration on the *Deus dixit* in the strict sense" from "a concentration on the present actualization of revelation." Bruce McCormack, *Karl Barth's Critically Realistic Dialectical Theology: Its Genesis and Development, 1909-1936* (Oxford: Clarendon Press, 1995), p. 22. The *first evidence* of this wholly incarnational theology was the series of lectures delivered in 1937 on the doctrine of God for Barth's *Church Dogmatics,* II/1 (McCormack, p. 22). McCormack considers this move to be the *final* phase in the development of Barth's singular theological reformation, which began in 1915 (pp. 21-22). For the various phases, including dates, see McCormack, pp. 21-22. The dating of the developments in Barth's singular theological reformation in this work and consideration of the largely theological grounds for them fit roughly those of McCormack.

22. See section 33, located in Karl Barth, *Church Dogmatics,* II/2, *The Doctrine of God,* ed. G. W. Bromiley and T. F. Torrance (Edinburgh: T. & T. Clark, 1957).

> He, Jesus Christ, is the free grace of God as not content simply to remain identical with the inward and eternal being of God, but operating *ad extra* in the ways and works of God. And for this reason, before Him and above Him and beside Him and apart from Him there is no election, no beginning, no decree, no Word of God.[23]

Jesus Christ is the electing God. Moreover, he is in the entirety of his being the elect of God. But Jesus Christ never stands alone. In the loving freedom of the eternal and undivided communion with the Father in the Spirit, he chooses to be with and for humanity and to reconcile the creation to God. Not only is God the God of Jesus Christ, but also God is the God of all humanity in and through and by him. And for its part, all humanity is bound up with God in and through Christ. All humanity is elected in him. In and through his mediation, all humanity is, so to speak, the humanity of God. Just as humanity stands in a distinct though inseparable relation to Jesus Christ, so too, humanity stands in a distinct though inseparable relation to God in and through this one who is true God and true human as expressed in Barth's doctrine of election.

Barth speaks of the distinct though inseparable relation of God and humanity in terms of "Theonomie" and "Autonomie."[24] The lordship of God is everywhere present in Jesus Christ who is himself the kingdom of God. "Da ist also gewiss Theonomie, Gottesherrschaft auf der ganzen Linie. Jesus Christus ist selber das aufgerichtete Reich Gottes."[25] But God does not live in isolation. In the freedom of the divine love, God ever chooses to exist with humanity, taking humanity to himself in and through Jesus Christ. The free and loving God grants humanity freedom to love God in return. In electing humanity in and through and by Jesus Christ, God grants to humanity individuality or particularity ("Eigenheit") and autonomy ("Selbstständigkeit"), or better, a *distinct* existence in inseparable, albeit asymmetrical, relation to his own.[26]

Before proceeding further, it is necessary to discuss the rationale for choosing "distinct existence" instead of "autonomy." The term "distinct" (or distinctive particularity) is a better translation of these words in the light of

23. Barth, *Church Dogmatics,* II/2, p. 95.

24. Karl Barth, *Kirchliche Dogmatik,* II/2, *Die Lehre von Gott* (Zürich: Evangelischer Verlag, 1942), pp. 194-98.

25. Barth, *Kirchliche Dogmatik,* II/2, p. 195.

26. Barth, *Kirchliche Dogmatik,* II/2, p. 195.

the context in which the words are framed, although "Selbständigkeit" is translated as autonomy. The word "autonomy" often carries with it associations of neutrality and indifference, notions that run counter to Barth's view of the doctrine of human being as that creature who lives in loving freedom with and for God and others. Barth himself says in this text that the meaning ("Sinn") and validity ("Kraft") of the eternal election of God is that the creature can and will elect the God who elects it. "Das ist der Sinn und die Kraft der ewigen Gnadenwahl Gottes, dass der von ihm Erwählte ihn selbst wiederum erwählen darf und wird."[27] Thus, as Barth says earlier in this context, God grants to humanity a distinct existence, not that it would exist in detachment from or in opposition to or in conflict with God's sovereignty ("nicht damit es sie ohne ihn, geschweige denn, damit es sie gegen ihn . . . nicht zur Konkurrenz mit seiner Souveränität. . . ."), but rather that humanity would exist ever with and for God in that life of creaturely particularity and distinction in love and freedom as a reflection of the glory of the being in act of the sovereign Lord.[28]

Barth asks rhetorically, "How can there be any question of a conflict between theonomy and autonomy? How can God be jealous or man self-assertive?"[29] How can it be since the divine will "encloses" the "autonomous" or distinct existence of humanity ("seine selbstständige Existenz eingeschlossen ist")?[30] The creaturely reality known as humanity comes forth through the free act of creation by God and is taken to God in the event in which God takes humanity to himself in and through the eternal election in Jesus Christ.[31] In and through God's election in Christ, the world, including human culture, is integrally related to God, but in a manner free of confusion. One finds here a Chalcedonian pattern of relation. Yet, does one not also see evidence here of the extension of the category of *anhypostasis* as argued above? For *in* and *through* Christ's eternal media-

27. Barth, *Kirchliche Dogmatik,* II/2, p. 195.

28. Barth, *Kirchliche Dogmatik,* II/2, p. 195.

29. Barth, *Church Dogmatics,* II/2, p. 179.

30. Barth, *Church Dogmatics,* II/2, p. 181. For the German, see Barth, *Kirchliche Dogmatik,* II/2, p. 198.

31. For a detailed exposition of the subject of autonomy in Barth's thought, see John Macken, S.J., *The Autonomy Theme in the "Church Dogmatics": Karl Barth and His Critics* (Cambridge: Cambridge University Press, 1990). Note especially his summary of various uses of the term "autonomy" in modern thought (p. 21).

tion as the electing God and elected human, humanity, *by analogical extension,* is conceived as having no independent existence from God.[32]

The preceding remarks speak to the originality of Barth's doctrine of election. Barth's conception is markedly different from other treatments in the Western tradition. For one, it is central to his theology, serving as an axis rather than as a mere appendage.[33] This is evident from Barth's deci-

32. Eberhard Jüngel employs the doctrines of *anhypostasis* and *enhypostasis* to expound Barth's doctrine of election, albeit from the standpoint of the time-eternity theme. Eberhard Jüngel, *The Doctrine of the Trinity: God's Being Is in Becoming* (Grand Rapids: Eerdmans, 1976), pp. 81-82. See Macken's discussion and criticism of Jüngel's application of these Christological categories to the "existence" of Christ and the Christian, as well as his remarks on Hans Stickelberger's adoption of Jüngel's view for an understanding of human self-determination (Macken, *Autonomy Theme,* pp. 149-52; see also p. 168). Attention should be drawn to a work by Jüngel, to which Macken refers in this context: Eberhard Jüngel, *Unterwegs zur Sache. Theologische Bemerkungen, Beiträge zur evangelischen Theologie,* Theologische Abhandlungen 61 (München: Kaiser, 1972). See also Hans Stickelberger, *Ipsa assumptione creatur. Karl Barths Rückgriff auf die klassische Christologie und die Frage nach der Selbständigkeit des Menschen,* Basler u. Berner Studien zur historischen und systematischen Theologie, no. 38 (Bern: Lang, 1979). Although Macken believes Jüngel's position is "a restrictive but accurate interpretation of Barth's," he adds that it "is inadequate as an ontology. It formalises Barth's Christological construction in ontological terms" (Macken, *Autonomy Theme,* p. 152). The same criticism is made of Stickelberger (p. 151). Earlier in his study, Macken refers to Stickelberger's claim that in Barth's theology there is a parallel to be drawn between the relation of the divine and human natures in the "hypostatic union" and "the relationship between Christ and other men." Stickelberger employs the categories of *anhypostasis* and *enhypostasis,* arguing that humanity is "truly human" because it has its being "outside of" itself "and in Christ" (Macken, *Autonomy Theme,* p. 59; see note 107). Suggesting that such interpretative parallels between Christology and anthropology in Barth's theology are disputable, Macken then makes a most important distinction. He writes, "What can be said here is that Barth derives *no direct* answer to the question about man from Christology *nor* does he allow of one *derived* from man's self-understanding. He first asks about the humanity of Christ and then talks about man as a *consequence of and in analogy to* Christology" (p. 59; italics added). This study approaches the relation of the Word of Christ to the world of culture by making analogical extensions from the Word proper to the Word's engagement of culture. As argued in Chapter Two and the text above just prior to this footnote, the aim is to draw out implications for humanity and human culture from Barth's Christological doctrine of the Word.

33. Balthasar writes that the doctrine of election is "without doubt . . . the most magnificent, unified and well-grounded section of the whole work. Written with greatest love, it is the heartbeat of his whole theology. . . ." Hans Urs von Balthasar, *The Theology of Karl Barth,* trans. Edward T. Oakes, S.J. (San Francisco: Communio Books, Ignatius Press, 1992), p. 174. Balthasar speaks of this doctrine's appearance in Barth's thought in his commentary on

sion to locate the doctrine of election within the doctrine of God.[34] Second, Christ Jesus himself is central to the doctrine. He is the one in whom God elects and in whom humanity is elected.[35] God's Word is from first to last the enfleshed Word of election.[36] Third, the doctrine of election for Barth is not so much a salvific category as an anthropological one, preceding his doctrine of creation. Election involves humanization. In him, and in the light of him, people are called and exhorted to be human. They are exhorted to be human, to live in the light of Christ.[37] The focus is not so much recognition and reception as it is *constitution*. They are *called* by the *Word* enfleshed to be like him, *to be* human. The doctrine of election in Barth's thought is the doctrine of the *constitutive Word*. Thus, the stress falls on ontology rather than on psychology. Lastly, as has just been indicated, the conception of the constitutive being of Christ concerns *all* humanity. The constitutive Word is addressed to all. Here again, Barth's doctrine of election is different from many in the tradition. All humanity is elected in Christ, that is, called to be in Christ. That is to say, objective constitution extends beyond the confines of the church to include the whole of society.

Having set forth a basic description of Barth's doctrine of election, we will now turn our attention to the discussion of issues that arise in the light of his doctrine of the constitutive Word of God and their implications for the relation of the sacred and secular dimensions in human culture. The topics to be addressed are the relation of church to society and covenant to creation in and through Christ.

Romans as well as the *Church Dogmatics*, IV/4 (p. 174), that is, at the beginning and culmination of his life's work. David Ford writes "that it is where the interrelations of the main topics of Barth's theology are laid out most clearly." Among other things, Ford states that the doctrine of election "is the raison d'être of creation and reconciliation." David Ford, *Barth and God's Story: Biblical Narrative and the Theological Method of Karl Barth in the "Church Dogmatics"* (Frankfurt am Main: Peter Lang, 1981), p. 72.

34. Barth's doctrine of election is the theme discussed in the second half-volume of *The Doctrine of God* in the *Church Dogmatics*. Its placement reflects Barth's belief that God's very being is a being in action, an activity centered in the eternal choice to create communion with the human creature.

35. Barth, *Church Dogmatics*, II/2, pp. 94-145.

36. Barth, *Church Dogmatics*, II/2, p. 95.

37. See Eberhard Jüngel's discussion of Barth's doctrine of election in *Karl Barth: A Theological Legacy*, trans. Garrett E. Paul (Philadelphia: Westminster Press, 1986), p. 121. Jüngel says there that "election" for Barth "determines human beings as human (insofar as they are to be God's covenant partners)."

Church and Society

Now given Barth's claim that through Christ God elects all humanity to be in Christ, how is one to distinguish the church from broader society? Does one find here in Barth's thought the same danger observed in the medieval doctrine of the *corpus christianum,* namely, the blurring of the distinction between the church and broader culture? No, for although all humanity is constituted in Christ, elect *to be* in Christ, although all are in Christ in an objective sense, only some are in Christ in a subjective manner. Another way to put it is to say that Barth's doctrine of the *ordo salutis* is two-tiered. There is the transcendental or objective basis and the empirical or subjective extension. The former concerns Christ's high-priestly response of repentance and faith on humanity's behalf *(de jure).* The latter concerns the individual's appropriation of Christ's work *(de facto).*[38] To put it in Kantian terms, when one speaks of the transcendental ground, one refers to the necessary condition for the possibility of authentic faith. This ground lies not in humanity generally, but in Christ. However, such a model does not negate the importance of the human response. The human response is vital. Indeed, it is what distinguishes the church from the world, and Barth's view from the *corpus christianum* he so despises. The empirical or subjective response of the church concerns those specific acts through which Christ's work and faith are appropriated to individual lives. Barth himself speaks of the distinction between the church and broader culture in the following way.

> We cannot say that they have a share in it, that they are all "in Christ." This would mean that what happened for them had also happened to them and in them. This would mean their recognition and knowledge of its occurrence for them. It would mean their hearing of the Word that became flesh, their receiving of the Spirit from that one place of His fulness. It would mean their gathering to the commu-

38. In his essay, "Gospel and Law," Barth speaks of Christ's work of intercession, which includes his vicarious faith on behalf of humanity. "However, God's grace is Jesus Christ, who intercedes for us with his humanity. He intercedes for us, however, by believing in our place — it took the eternal Word incarnate to do that — and that means by saying 'yes' to God's glory and thus to man's misery." Karl Barth, "Gospel and Law," in *Community, State, and Church: Three Essays,* with an introduction by Will Herberg (Gloucester, Mass.: Peter Smith, 1968), p. 81.

> nity which receives His revelation as true, and their entrance into its service. It would mean their own repentance in reliance on the repentance which that One completed perfectly for all, their own faith in the discipleship of the One who has preceded them in faith, the obedience of their faith as their faith in Him, the placing of their time under the laws of His. We cannot say this when we say that they are fellows of Jesus Christ and that He is their Fellow. What we do say, what we can and must say, is that they have all been chosen from eternity to be "in Christ" in this sense, that this is their determination, and that they exist in their time for this, i.e., with this meaning and higher purpose.[39]

All are elected from all eternity to be "in Christ." As suggested in the quotation above, Barth maintains that Christ died for all, repented for all, believed for all. But still, each must repent, believe, and follow him.[40] That is to say, one must actively participate in Christ. Thus, only the Christian is in Christ in the full sense. Now as the one who participates in Christ (the subjective dimension), the Christian is to turn to the world and bear witness to the world of the objective reconciliation of all humanity in Christ.

What is the Christian task? It is the task of bearing witness to the reality of Christ for all. Since Christ died for all, was raised for all, repented and believed for all, he is the fellow of all humanity. Thus, the church must also be for all humanity, bearing witness to Christ in wider society. And even when the church must go against culture, it is because it seeks to exhort human culture to be fully human — to be what it in fact is called to be.[41] Christ often brings a sword, a sword that inflicts pain, but a form of pain that induces healing.[42] The church exists for the world; and so, its opposition to the world is not permanent, but passing. And even in this opposition, the church exists for the world, calling it back to the Word.[43] The church witnesses to the reality of Christ's kingdom, to which all are *called*,

39. Karl Barth, *Church Dogmatics,* III/4, *The Doctrine of Creation,* ed. G. W. Bromiley and T. F. Torrance (Edinburgh: T. & T. Clark, 1961), pp. 577-78. See also Barth, *Church Dogmatics,* II/2, pp. 419-23.

40. Barth, *Church Dogmatics,* III/4, pp. 577-78.

41. Barth, *Church Dogmatics,* III/4, p. 565.

42. See Barth, *Church Dogmatics,* II/2, p. 212 on Barth's understanding of the relation of wrath to love.

43. Barth, *Church Dogmatics,* IV/3.1, pp. 20-22.

but to which only a few have as yet responded favorably. There are times when opposition is required. But even in opposition, the church militant does not wage war or revolt against anyone, but against disorder.[44] At other times, there is agreement, times when the church definitely aligns itself with the world.[45] There are even times when the church will be in the wrong while broader culture walks in the light.[46] Regardless though, the vocation to which the church is called is to bear witness to the world of the reconciliation of all humanity in Christ.

Christ is the ground of all humanity. Therefore, he is not only the Lord of the church. He is also the Lord of the world. The two are connected given that the Lord of the church is also the Lord of the world. There is no other kingdom. His alone is the kingdom. Outside his kingdom, there exists only "nothingness," that is, the falsehood and the lying imitation of his kingdom.[47] All humanity is constituted in the light of the reality of Christ. He is the one in whom all stand. Therefore, any other constitution is a lie, a falsehood. Nonetheless, the church and broader culture are distinct in that those who are in the church have entered into Christ, repenting and believing in the face of Christ's repentance and faith, whereas the rest of his fellow humans have not as yet done so.[48] Having said this, there are times in Barth's thought when the *de jure* is so stressed that it tends to overwhelm the *de facto,* becoming itself a form of *de facto.*[49] Yet, on the whole, he dis-

44. See Karl Barth, *Church Dogmatics,* IV/4, *The Doctrine of Reconciliation, Lecture Fragments, The Christian Life,* trans. G. W. Bromiley (Grand Rapids: Eerdmans, 1981), pp. 205-6, 210-11.

45. For example, in *Church Dogmatics,* IV/3.1, Barth writes that there are instances when the world of culture guides the church to a deeper involvement in the "*communio sanctorum* of all ages," to which Scripture itself bears witness (p. 127).

46. An example of this would be the successful attempt made by secular humanity to free itself from the *corpus christianum.* Barth speculates that perhaps the liberation of the world from the church led to the liberation of the church from its self-imposed imprisonment in that corrupt union. See Barth, *Church Dogmatics,* IV/3.1, p. 21.

47. Karl Barth, *Church Dogmatics,* III/3, *The Doctrine of Creation,* ed. G. W. Bromiley and T. F. Torrance (Edinburgh: T. & T. Clark, 1960), pp. 525-30.

48. In *Church Dogmatics,* II/2, pp. 419 and 421-23, Barth writes that the number of participants is not fixed. That is to say, the doors of the kingdom are never closed, for God is ever free to increase the number of those who participate in the reality of the kingdom. The matter rests with God. It is God's responsibility. The church, on the other hand, is responsible to bear witness to the reconciliation of all in Christ, and it alone.

49. Geoffrey Bromiley points out that although Barth safeguards against advocating universalism, he nonetheless pleads agnostic concerning the final state of those "outside"

tinguishes the two in a satisfactory manner, thereby safeguarding against a return to the *corpus christianum* where the distinction between the church and world of culture was not adequately maintained.

In light of the preceding discussion, a question arises. What is the purpose of ecclesial existence? Given Barth's mature doctrine of baptism and the Lord's Supper, it is correct to say that the church does not mediate grace, but rather, simply bears witness to the sacramental reality of Jesus Christ. In the fragments of volume IV of the *Church Dogmatics,* Barth argues that Jesus Christ is the only sacrament of God. He is it alone since there are no creaturely capacities or instruments fitted for divine service.[50] For Barth, the church is only a witness. And yet, the church is highly honored, for it is a witness to God's personal act in Christ through which all humanity has been reconciled to God.[51]

Another question requires an answer. What is the significance of the concept of the constitutive being of Christ for all humanity? Its significance lies in the fact that it functions as an ideal, as the *telos* of humanity to which all humanity is called. Christological constitution functions as the

---

Christ. To this, Bromiley replies that contrary to Barth's stance, most exegetes maintain that Scripture is anything but agnostic about the matter in question. Geoffrey W. Bromiley, *Introduction to the Theology of Karl Barth* (Edinburgh: T. & T. Clark; Grand Rapids: Eerdmans, 1979), p. 248. John Colwell has defended Barth against the charge of logical inconsistency in rejecting the doctrine of universalism, making his defense through recourse to analyzing Barth's novel understanding of eternity. See John Colwell, *Actuality and Provisionality: Eternity and Election in the Theology of Karl Barth* (Edinburgh: Rutherford House Books, 1989), pp. 275-83.

50. See Karl Barth, *Church Dogmatics,* IV/4, *The Doctrine of Reconciliation: Fragment, Baptism as the Foundation of the Christian Life,* ed. G. W. Bromiley and T. F. Torrance (Edinburgh: T. & T. Clark, 1969). William Stacy Johnson argues that it is a mistake to interpret Barth's discussion of the sacraments as "an ill-fitting deviation from the rest of his theology." He goes on to write, "To reject Barth on this point may be to have misunderstood him on all the other points." Barth's exposition of baptism "in the final fragments of the *CD* is but the consistent outworking of a theology that is reticent to speak of a 'real presence' of God in earthly media." William Stacy Johnson, *The Mystery of God: Karl Barth and the Postmodern Foundations of Theology,* Columbia Series in Reformed Theology (Louisville: Westminster/John Knox Press, 1997), p. 8. Even in Christ, the divine presence is indirectly or dialectically communicated through the cloak of creaturely flesh, as was indicated in Chapter Two.

51. Barth's esteem for the church is evident in his claim that its proclamation can become a form of the very Word of God. See Karl Barth, *Church Dogmatics,* I/1, *The Doctrine of the Word of God,* ed. G. W. Bromiley and T. F. Torrance (Edinburgh: T. & T. Clark, 1975), pp. 88-99.

basis for the call to sanctification, that is, humanization. All are called to "Be human!"[52] In this light, one can see that for Barth sanctification precedes justification, not in the sense that one is justified through sanctifying acts, but in the sense that *all* are elected or called to participate in Christ, the ground and goal of humanity as the elected human. As Jüngel writes, ". . . sanctification is nothing but a demand to realize our essence."[53] Thus, the Word of Christ, the electing Word, has relevance and positive significance, not only for the church, but also for all humanity, since Christ is the one by whom and in whom and for whom all are elect to be created and reconciled in order that they might be fully human. As Barth sees it, just as God *calls* all humanity into being by the Word, Jesus Christ, so too, God *calls* all humanity to live in the light of him.

Earlier in this chapter, consideration was given to Barth's praise of the *diastasis* between the church and society that emerged with the rise of secularism in the modern period for its bearing on liberating the church to confront the world with the gospel. Now attention will be given to implications that arise in the light of the *synthesis* Barth provides via his doctrine of election for relating the church to the broader sphere of human culture. The approach taken will be to compare briefly Barth with one of the fathers of Christendom, Augustine, and from the reverse angle, to compare Barth with the progeny of the great heroes of Europe's emancipation from Christendom, Nietzsche.

One of the most influential proposals in the history of Christian thought for viewing the relation between the sacred and secular domains is Augus-

52. See Jüngel, *Theological Legacy,* p. 121.

53. Jüngel, *Theological Legacy,* p. 121. The attempt will now be made to set forth briefly Barth's view of the relation of law and gospel and their relation to election as it bears upon the question of sanctification. In *Church Dogmatics,* II/2, Barth writes, "Election is the sum of the Gospel because of all words that can be said or heard it is the best" (p. 3). Later, in the same volume, he claims, ". . . ethics interprets the Law as the form of the Gospel, i.e., as the sanctification which comes to man through the electing God" (p. 509). For Barth, "Ruling grace is commanding grace. The Gospel itself has the form and fashion of the Law. The one Word of God is both Gospel *and* Law" (p. 511). In the context of his discussion of these texts, Jüngel writes that the gospel and law are conceived in supralapsarian terms in Barth's theology (Jüngel, *Theological Legacy,* p. 119). That is to say, the gospel and law logically precede creaturely existence in the same way that redemption precedes creation in the ordering of the divine decrees. In this light, one can see how it is that the sanctifying command of God bears relevance for all people, since it accompanies the inclusive word of election that encircles the life of the human creation, shaping that life as the gospel's form.

tine's *City of God.*[54] In his introduction to the work, John O'Meara writes that Augustine was in many ways an optimist regarding humanity.[55] However, he draws attention to the fact that Augustine's doctrine of predestination, "although not prominent," appears "grim and sombre in the *City of God.*"[56]

Consideration will be given to this point shortly. However, before doing so, it is worth reflecting further on Augustine's estimable optimism. Much of this optimism is due to Augustine's doctrine of providence. According to O'Meara, "The great lesson of the *City of God* is that out of all things comes good."[57] Was it not on this basis that Augustine was able to devise "a charter for a Christian future, not only for Rome but for all the world,"[58] even at a time of great social turmoil within the empire?[59] Was it not on account of his belief in divine providence that he was able to envision an "assimilation" of Christianity and Rome and give pre-eminence to "fulfilment" over against "destruction"?[60] Was it not for this reason that Augustine could ultimately refrain from attacking the Roman Empire?[61] Indeed, it was. For Rome was "a vehicle ordained by Providence for the benefit of Christianity in relation to which she would have a new and enduring future."[62] And was it not Augustine's belief in providence, coupled with the doctrine of the goodness of God's creation,[63] that enabled him to refrain from dismissing the *civitas terrena,* and inspired him to concern himself with this city's "future"?[64] Yes, here too the answer is in the affir-

54. John O'Meara writes, "The practical problem with which Augustine had to deal was the problem of a spiritual Church in a secular world: the city of God in the city of this world." John O'Meara, introduction to *Concerning the City of God, Against the Pagans,* by St. Augustine, trans. Henry Bettenson (London: Penguin Books, 1972; introduction copyright, 1984), p. ix. For a recent analysis of the church's role in relating to secular culture, see Carl E. Braaten and Robert W. Jenson, eds., *The Two Cities of God: The Church's Responsibility for the Earthly City* (Grand Rapids: Eerdmans, 1997).

55. O'Meara, introduction, p. vii.

56. O'Meara, introduction, p. vii.

57. O'Meara, introduction, p. ix.

58. O'Meara, introduction, p. ix.

59. See O'Meara, introduction, p. ix.

60. See O'Meara, introduction, p. ix.

61. O'Meara argues that the aim of the *City of God* was not to "attack . . . the Romans or the Roman Empire," but to work toward an appropriate, beneficial synthesis involving Christianity and the empire (O'Meara, introduction, p. xxvi).

62. O'Meara, introduction, p. xxvi.

63. On the creation, see O'Meara, introduction, p. ix.

64. O'Meara, introduction, p. xx.

mative. But what is to be made of that counter-movement in his thought, his particular understanding of the doctrine of predestination, however inconspicuous it might be in his great apology for Christendom?

Laying aside Augustine's *magna carta* for Christendom, and the fact that his age was that of the *"tempora Christiana,"*[65] what bearing might it have on the Christian's perception of the city of the world to view the eternal destiny of most of its inhabitants as determined in advance to a most pessimistic state? And what is to be made of Augustine's identification of the *civitas terrena* with the *civitas Cain?*[66] Lastly, the question may be posed as to how central Christ is to Augustine's understanding of the relation of the two cities. No doubt, Christ is the crown of creation, the author of redemption and Lord of God's coming kingdom. But is he truly the *basis* of creation, and the *ground* on which the city of this world, including the state, is founded?[67]

Chapter Five will consider Barth's view of the relation of church and state. Let it only be said at present that for Barth, the state as well as the church belongs to the sphere of redemption.[68] In this light, Barth rejects

65. O'Meara, introduction, p. xx. It should be noted, however, as O'Meara points out, that in Augustine's version of Christendom there is no false assumption that all of Christendom was Christian, that view upon which Barth looks so unfavorably (see the opening section of this chapter). In fact, even though "in a very general way" Augustine equates the church itself with the city of God, he argues that there are no doubt some in the church who belong to the city of this world and certain in that city who belong to the city of God (O'Meara, introduction, p. xxxi).

66. In Book XV, chapter one, which is entitled, "The two lines of descent of the human race, advancing from the start towards different ends," Augustine writes, "By two cities I mean two societies of human beings, one of which is predestined to reign with God for all eternity, the other doomed to undergo eternal punishment with the Devil." St. Augustine, *Concerning the City of God, Against the Pagans,* with an introduction by John O'Meara, trans. Henry Bettenson (London: Penguin Books, 1972), p. 595. Augustine states that Cain "belonged to the city of man" whereas Abel "belonged to the City of God." Cain founded a city while Abel did not, for the city to which he belongs is above (p. 596). See also Augustine's discussions of Cain and the city of this world in *The City of God,* Book XV, chapters seven, eight, and seventeen. On the subject of predestination, see also pages 591-92, 1023.

67. One of the invaluable features of Barth's theology is his application or extension of the Trinitarian and Christological doctrine of *perichoresis* to theology generally. Thus, he is able to conceive all doctrines in a Trinitarian manner. In this way, Barth views the creation, not simply as the work of the first person of the Trinity, but also as the work of Christ in mediating the creation to God.

68. See, for example, Karl Barth, "Community, State, and Church," in *Community, State,*

Augustine's negative view of the origin of the state, whereby he equates the "*civitas terrena* with the *civitas Cain.*"[69] Does one not find here in Augustine the view that the state belongs to the order of preservation wherein the ultimate purpose of the state is to hold in check the forces of human sinfulness?[70] Over against this way of conceiving the civil authority, should one not view the state as belonging to the order of creation, even redemption as Barth maintains, given the fact that the kingdom of Christ is itself a state, and that the state on earth "will one day contribute to the glory of the heavenly Jerusalem, and will inevitably bring its tribute thither"?[71] For all Augustine's optimism, what is to be made of such fundamental divisions between the two cities? Just as the *corpus christianum* may give rise to a destructive optimism, a division such as found here may, if left unchecked, lead to an equally pernicious pessimism. Whatever the case may be, it certainly leads to a tension in Augustine's thought, given his otherwise positive outlook on the city of this world.

In Augustine, one finds the danger of a *division* between the sacred and secular spheres due in part to the failure to conceive Christ as the basis for their relation.[72] In Nietzsche, on the other hand, the culmination of humanity come of age, Renaissance man, the "final European"[73] (as Barth refers to him), one finds the *repudiation* of the crucified God, the neighbor.[74] In Christ's place, one finds Dionysius and the *Übermensch,*[75] who is the true

and Church: Three Essays, with an introduction by Will Herberg (Gloucester, Mass.: Peter Smith, 1968), p. 114.

69. Barth, "Community, State, and Church," p. 125.

70. See Herberg's discussion in his introduction to *Community, State, and Church,* pp. 25-26.

71. Barth, "Community, State, and Church," p. 125.

72. In the introduction to this chapter, the problem with Christendom was noted, namely, its failure to *distinguish* between the church and the non-Christian world. Here, however, the problem concerns a failure to connect adequately the two spheres. In view of these imbalances, the ideal is to conceive the two in terms of dialectical distinction in inseparable relation.

73. Karl Barth, *Church Dogmatics,* III/2, *The Doctrine of Creation,* ed. G. W. Bromiley and T. F. Torrance (Edinburgh: T. & T. Clark, 1960), p. 236.

74. Nietzsche speaks of Christ as a neighbor in his work, *The Will to Power.* See Friedrich W. Nietzsche, *The Will to Power,* ed. Walter Kaufmann, trans. Walter Kaufmann and R. J. Hollingdale (New York: Random House, 1967), pp. 107-8. See also Barth, *Church Dogmatics,* III/2, pp. 239, 240.

75. For Nietzsche's opposition of Dionysius to the Crucified, see Friedrich W. Nietzsche, *Ecce Homo,* trans. Walter Kaufmann (New York: Vintage Books, 1969), pp. 332-35. See also Barth, *Church Dogmatics,* III/2, pp. 236-42.

goal of humanity. In contrast to Barth and Augustine, Nietzsche's doctrine of election is secular throughout, based wholly in natural selection, not, however, due to those impersonal forces of nature, but rather, due to the native will to power residing within the human individual.[76] One of the central problems with this view is that it ultimately leads to a *bifurcation* of humanity.[77] Here, however, the division is not one based on the sacred versus the secular since for Nietzsche the secular alone matters, the secular alone is truly real; rather, it is a division based on the strong versus the sickly. Although Nietzsche has great hopes for humanity, and is in many ways an optimist, he is no humanist. For the naturally elected or selected goal of humanity according to him is not humanity as such, but humanity *beyond* humanity, the superhuman or "overman."[78] It is for this reason that he feels nothing but disgust for Paul's doctrine of the crucified God, which

76. See Edward Craig's comments on the difference between Darwinism and the Nietzschean theory of human evolution in *The Mind of God and the Works of Man* (Oxford: Clarendon Press, 1987), p. 277.

77. Walter Kaufmann has argued that, contrary to what is often assumed, there is no bifurcation in Nietzsche's thought. See Paul Edwards, ed., *The Encyclopedia of Philosophy* (New York: Macmillan & The Free Press, 1967), s.v. "Friedrich Nietzsche," by Walter Kaufmann. The contention of this writer, however, is that for Nietzsche a bifurcation in humanity does exist, resulting from something being *gained (aufgegeben)* rather than something being *given (gegeben),* as in the case of Augustine. (See Kaufmann's discussion of the German terms.) Whereas for Augustine, who sees election as a gift given by God, super-added to the gift of creation, and Barth, who views election as a gift grounding the human creation, Nietzsche maintains that election, humanity's goal as superhuman, that form of existence beyond humanity, is something to be attained. For election, like creation, is nothing more than the result of one's own creative activity. Now since there is no God on Nietzsche's account, the individual alone is responsible for its destiny, acting alone and attributing values to its actions. However, given that Nietzsche calls on people to be creators rather than mere creatures and imitators, is not the individual led to look at others as objects, which the individual must seek to bring under its control? For is not the world about the individual simply the playing field for its own creative exploits? And does not the individual find its value solely in the sheer act of creating? If the individual's identity is somehow dependent on the imposition of its will on its surroundings, as Craig argues (Craig, *The Mind of God,* p. 277), is it not the case that to retain its identity and self-worth the individual must impose its creative will on others whose own identity and worth are nothing more than the products of the individual's own creative judgment? At least, there is nothing to safeguard against this move. In the end, does not this supposedly innocuous bifurcation, if employed by less than virtuous souls, become the most sinister division of all?

78. Nietzsche writes, "Not 'mankind' but *overman* is the goal!" (*The Will to Power,* no. 1001, p. 519).

he believes has kept humanity down, disabling it so that it cannot ascend to new heights.[79] But who is on the heights on Nietzsche's view? Is it not the solitary individual, setting itself apart from "mass-man,"[80] that herd,[81] over which it triumphs, incorporating the crowd into its own "sphere of potency,"[82] even if supposedly it does so on behalf of humanity?

During Barth's day, Nietzsche's idea of the *Übermensch* was being applied with urgency and forcefulness to the establishment of a new society in which the strong prevail and the weak are scorned and the Jewish race is trampled underfoot. In view of this, Barth championed the doctrine of the crucified God, who is incarnate as a Jewish male.[83] And it is only through this crucified God and Jewish man that humanity finds its basis for true humanity.[84] The crucified God, the neighbor, is able to serve as a guard

79. Nietzsche writes that with the doctrine of the crucified God "a nobler attitude of mind was destroyed. . . ." Christian morality, for Nietzsche, champions the ignoble, the forlorn, not the noble. For "everything that suffers, everything that hangs on the cross, is *divine.*" Friedrich W. Nietzsche, *The Antichrist* (New York: Alfred A. Knopf, 1918), pp. 146-47.

80. Barth, *Church Dogmatics,* III/2, p. 239.

81. See Nietzsche's discussion of "The Herd" in *The Will to Power,* pp. 156-62.

82. Craig, *The Mind of God,* p. 277.

83. One thinks here of Barth having written his doctrine of election, centered in the Jewish identity of Jesus Christ, during the height of Hitler's campaign against the Jews. Scott Bader-Saye points out that "it was no mere coincidence" that as war broke out in 1939, Barth was beginning work on the doctrine of election for the *Church Dogmatics.* He adds that "Barth's reformulation of the object of election can be read as a response to the modern rise of national supersessionism, especially in Germany." Scott Bader-Saye, *Church and Israel After Christendom: The Politics of Election,* Radical Traditions: Theology in a Postcritical Key (Boulder, Colo.: Westview Press, 1999), p. 74.

84. Barth faced opposition for what many, including Brunner, considered a preposterous idea, namely, that salvation did not simply arise from the Jews, but "'comes from the Jews,' put in the present tense." Eberhard Busch, *Karl Barth: His Life from Letters and Autobiographical Texts* (London: SCM Press, 1976), p. 313. As Bader-Saye writes, "By making Israel a continuing and necessary part of the one chosen community, Barth stands over against the tradition of supersessionism and affirms the unconditional and eternal election of the Jews. God will not forsake God's people." Nonetheless, he takes special exception to Barth speaking of Israel and the church as two forms of the one elect people of God whereby Israel stands for humanity's rejection of God; he also objects to Barth's claim in *Church Dogmatics* II/2, p. 311 that the election of the community serves as the vehicle for the ultimate goal of the election of the individual (p. 76). He argues that although Barth sees the Jews as God's covenantal people, even "without becoming Christians," Barth's thought nonetheless "remains latently supersessionist, and thus he also fails to avoid the danger of spiritualizing and individualizing the covenant" (p. 75). Although Barth is correct to stress the need for the dimension of

against a bifurcation in humanity. And as the elected ground of humanity, calling humanity as a whole, not simply the strong or the spiritual, to live out its essence as defined by his life, Jesus Christ, the focal point of Barth's doctrine of election, serves to preserve unity in the midst of various forms of distinction. Such unity does not come about despite Christ, but because of him. And because of him, the word of election addressed to secular culture, not simply the church, is convicting and challenging, yet also motivating and comforting.

Having spoken specifically of Barth's doctrine of election and its positive implications for the relation of the sacred and secular spheres, we will now turn our attention to the consideration of Barth's doctrine of creation. The reason for this move is that the Word through whom God elects humanity also serves to create humanity, for creation follows on from election.[85] For election is the basis of the covenant,[86] and the covenant is the internal basis of the creation. Therefore, ultimately speaking, election itself is the internal basis of the creation. As the electing Word, Jesus Christ is the efficient cause of creation, its formal cause, and lastly, its final cause. He is the origin, the ground, and goal of creation. However, there is a tension in the way Barth conceives the relation of the constitutive being of the Word to the creation, arising from his notion that the Word is the crucified, that is, the Word of the covenant of reconciliation, the Word of reconciled creation, and this alone. The creation exists for redemption. For Barth, there is only one covenant, the covenant of reconciliation. There is no covenant of creation as such. The creation is but the outer basis of the covenant of reconciliation, proving problematic for the distinct existence of creation, as shall be argued.

Covenant and Creation

In volume III/1 of the *Church Dogmatics,* Barth writes that the creation is the outer or external basis of the covenant, that is, the covenant of recon-

---

human response to one's election in Christ, whether Jew or Gentile, Bader-Saye points to the need to revisit consideration of the corporate aspect of election, which includes Israel.

85. The Word creates the world so that he might redeem the world elected in him. This point will be discussed in the section that follows.

86. Jüngel writes, "... the doctrine of the election of grace is" for Barth "the basis of the covenant" (*Theological Legacy,* p. 120).

ciliation.[87] There are several commendable features to be noted here. First, the doctrine of *creation* has no existence independent from the person of Jesus Christ. As the arena in which God's eternal election in the covenant in Jesus Christ is fulfilled, the doctrine of creation is inseparably related to Jesus Christ. By this means, Barth is able to dismiss those claims of natural theology put forth to defend and justify the rise of such movements as the Third Reich, which appeal to the supposed orders of creation.[88]

87. See Karl Barth, *Church Dogmatics,* III/1, *The Doctrine of Creation,* ed. G. W. Bromiley and T. F. Torrance (Edinburgh: T. & T. Clark, 1958), pp. 94-97.

88. Is it simply a coincidence that volume III/1 of the *Church Dogmatics* was written during the reign of Hitler, and published in 1945? In his discussion of two pastors associated with the "Thüringian 'German Christians,'" Julius Leutheuser and Siegfried Leffler, Arthur Cochrane speaks of their failure to ground pastoral theology in theology proper. As a result, he writes, "the aspirations and desires of the people became normative. When these became increasingly nationalistic in character, it was a short step to preaching the divine election of the German people and the saving work of Adolf Hitler and to finding God's revelation, not in the text of Scripture, but in the events of history." Arthur C. Cochrane, *The Church's Confession Under Hitler* (Philadelphia: Westminster Press, 1962), p. 76. There are two items to be noted here. First, one finds in Barth a countervailing movement, grounding pastoral theology in dogmatics, thereby insuring a constructive, yet also critical response to the needs of church and culture. Barth is for one very much concerned to speak to the situation of his day; the difference between him and the theologians mentioned above concerns a difference in starting points. Barth always moves from God in his Word addressed to the world rather than from the world that addresses itself to God. Second, the quotation from Cochrane illumines the context in which Barth's doctrines of election and creation are formulated. The inseparable relation of God's covenant in Christ to creation serves as a critical check on the pseudo-gospel of the election of the German race to salvation in the "Führer" as disclosed in the history of the creaturely sphere. One also thinks of Barth's repudiation of those supposed orders of creation, which were so readily employed to justify the positions taken by the "German Christians." It is interesting to note here Barth's discussion with Bultmann on the topic of the breakup of Neo-orthodoxy. Barth cites Gogarten's doctrine of the "states of life" as one factor in the movement's dissolution. Karl Barth, letter to Rudolf Bultmann, in Karl Barth and Rudolf Bultmann, *Letters, 1922-1966,* ed. Geoffrey W. Bromiley (Edinburgh: T. & T. Clark, 1982), p. 59. In his discussion of Neo-orthodoxy's decline, Cochrane refers to Barth's observation of Gogarten's decision to join the "German Christians" (which he eventually left in 1933) as the unambiguous indication of what Gogarten had always believed in and desired (Cochrane, *The Church's Confession,* p. 71). Perhaps Barth has in mind here Gogarten's doctrine of the "states of life" mentioned above. See Karl Barth, "No!," in Karl Barth and Emil Brunner, *Natural Theology,* with an introduction by John Baillie, trans. Peter Fraenkel (London: Geoffrey Bles/Centenary Press, 1946), pp. 85-86, for Barth's comments on the supposed orders of creation. Note also Busch's discussion of Barth's analysis of German Christianity's confusion of creation's "mystery" with an all-too-

Second, the way in which Barth relates creation to covenant implies that *humanity* itself has no existence independent of this covenant relationship, thereby guarding against ontological alienation. Although the *saeculum* may reject God, God never rejects humanity, only humanity's rejection, electing the creature to participate in fellowship with God.[89]

Third, Barth's understanding of creation and history as serving as the stage on which the history of the covenant of redemption is realized indicates that God's redemption is not to be viewed as a flight from history. God does not abandon history, but is infinitely concerned for his finite and fallen creatures, setting before them the true basis for hope, which stands in the face of their self-incurred alienation and destruction. Over against the possibility that the creature may reject God, seeking enlightened emancipation, that is, the ultimate secularization of life (which is nothing more than alienation from one's true self and God), God ever exists for his creature as demonstrated in the eternal election of all in the history of Jesus Christ.[90]

---

natural or naturalistic view of the German race and nation (Busch, *Karl Barth: His Life,* p. 243).

89. See, for example, Barth, *Church Dogmatics,* II/2, pp. 349, 449-50.

90. The point was made under footnote 21 above that Barth's incarnational theology comes into full bloom in *Church Dogmatics,* II. Yet it should be noted at this point that Braaten and Richard Roberts are critical of Barth on the subject of history. Braaten argues that Barth's lack of attention to historical questions suggests that his theology is not able to guard sufficiently against the threat posed by Neo-paganism. For only by placing due emphasis on kerygma, dogma, *and history* can one guard against the subjectivist orientation of Neo-paganism (Braaten, "The Gospel for a Neopagan Culture," pp. 9, 11, 13-15). Roberts critiques Barth from another angle, claiming that Barth's "ontological dogma of the Incarnation loses its roots in the shared and public reality of the world in which we live; it hovers above us like a cathedral resting upon a cloud." R. H. Roberts, "Barth's Doctrine of Time: Its Nature and Implications," in *Karl Barth: Studies of His Theological Method,* ed. S. W. Sykes (Oxford: Clarendon Press, 1979), p. 145. Roberts argues that Barth alienates "his theology" from the "natural" or secular sphere (p. 145), giving rise, among other things, to "the Marxist critique of religion as alienation of the self" (p. 145). In response, to the extent that Barth fails to identify the history of Christ with our history, he fails to guard against the threat of Neo-paganism and secularism noted above. Along these lines, one is reminded of Gilkey's claim set forth in Chapter Two that Neo-orthodoxy gave rise to secular theology. Now although one could not make a *necessary* link between Barth and secular theology given his understanding and emphasis on the incarnation, it cannot be denied that from a *historical* point of view, certain students of Barth did become key figures in the movement. See for example Langdon Gilkey's discussion of Paul van Buren in *Naming the Whirlwind: The Renewal of God-Language* (Indianapolis and

Having spoken of certain commendable features in Barth's approach to relating creation and covenant, we will now consider a point of tension that arises in his thought, resulting from the way in which he conceives creation in relation to the eternal covenant of redemption. The creation is the stage on which redemption is accomplished, existing for the sake of redemption, especially the redemption of the human creation. The creation

---

New York: Bobbs-Merrill, 1969), pp. 124-25. But it should be noted here that van Buren makes clear that Barthian theology in no way influenced his becoming an advocate of secular theology. Again, see Gilkey, pp. 124-25. The reason why no necessary link can be established is because Barth is quite emphatic on Christ assuming a human nature that is like our humanity's in every way, and because (in opposition to Bultmann) he champions the doctrine of the bodily resurrection of Jesus Christ, to which Roberts also draws the reader's attention. (See Barth, *Church Dogmatics,* III/2, p. 455; see Roberts, "Barth's Doctrine of Time," p. 138; Roberts writes that there is possibly an inconsistency between Barth's assertion at this point and his overall position on time, p. 138.) Over against the criticisms made of Barth by Braaten and Roberts, one needs to keep in mind the difference between an analysis of history and historical positivism, the latter being that view which approaches history from the standpoint of the canons of modern science. With good reason, Barth is suspicious of the preoccupation with historical analysis arising from this Procrustean bed. To the extent that Barth's wariness of historical considerations is a response to this orientation, Barth is justified in his "silence." Braaten himself asks why the church should not take up the historical pursuit of Jesus based on the pillars of "kerygma and dogma" rather than "the neopagan elements at the base of Enlightenment modernity" (Braaten, "The Gospel for a Neopagan Culture," p. 14). It is interesting to note in this context what McCormack says of the move in Barth's thought around the time of 1924. Barth redefines "Urgeschichte" as "pre-history," replacing its meaning as "unhistorical" (McCormack, *Karl Barth's Critically Realistic Dialectical Theology,* p. 363). If "pre-history" simply refers to the notion of the dialectic of revelation, namely, that God is hidden in revelation, or to the idea that Christ's history is the ground of all history, there is no problem with Barth's approach to history. For it guards against the objectification of revelation, that is, historicism. But if what is meant by this is that Christ's history is of a different order from ours, Barth's theology could indeed be taken to encourage others to foster a theological orientation that is wholly secular in kind. There is perhaps a tension in Barth's thought at this point. But the conclusion drawn here is that Barth believes that Christ does indeed inhabit human history (transforming it in the process), though not as defined by those modern canons of historical analysis. *Divine* revelation does indeed occur in *our* history, but in a manner free of "all *direct* intuitability," as McCormack writes (*Karl Barth's Critically Realistic Dialectical Theology,* p. 363; italics added). See Colwell's helpful discussion of "Urgeschichte" in Barth's thought (Colwell, *Actuality and Provisionality,* pp. 84-95). One item to be noted here is Colwell's definition of "Urgeschichte" as "primordial" or "primal history," over against "pre-history" (p. 84). See also Jüngel, *Trinity,* pp. 75-76.

is good as God's creation.[91] But from its inception, the ultimate redemption of creation overshadows its goodness.[92]

For reasons that will be given, it is more advantageous to speak of two covenants, the covenant of creation and the covenant of reconciliation.[93] And yet, there is a close relationship between these two covenants in that it is the *logos ensarkos* who is both Lord and partner in each covenant. In what follows, one will find the affirmation of Barth's Christological concentration, but also the rejection of his singular conception of the mediation of Jesus Christ in the history of the world.

Before we proceed further, it would be good to pause and return to the discussion of election proper. Barth's theology is supralapsarian, although of a very interesting sort. One might attempt to classify Barth's approach to election by considering it against the backdrop of the framework of the classical supralapsarian position, while placing in italics Barth's divergence from that tradition. With this framework in mind, one might reinterpret the logical ordering of the eternal decrees as follows. First, God *in Christ* decrees to bring glory to himself through the election of *all* in *Christ,* the crucified one, *who is himself* both the reprobate and elect of God. Second, God decrees the creation of the human race for the sake of his plan. Third, God decrees to permit the fall of humanity. And fourth, God decrees to provide reconciliation *for all* in Christ.

91. Barth claims, "What God has created is as such well done. . . . And if something is not good, it can be clearly recognised not to have been created by God, but to belong to the kingdom of the non-real" (*Church Dogmatics,* III/1, p. 331). Barth later writes of the creation, "because it may be by God, it may also be good." Again, ". . . it is good to the extent that it is, and it is therefore right for God and before Him, in the judgment of the One to whom it owes its existence." Barth adds, "This is valid without reservation or qualification" (p. 366).

92. Barth writes, "Even in Gen. 1:31 the assertion that God found all that He had made to be very good cannot be understood in isolation from its context as a description of the cosmos. Of course, the Creator justifies the cosmos as such. But He does so *only because* the latter is created according to His will and plan, *and therefore with the purpose of* instituting and fulfilling the covenant between the divine Creator and man" (*Church Dogmatics,* III/1, p. 369, italics added). The "covenant" here is the covenant of reconciliation. On page 370, Barth also speaks of the goodness of creation in a utilitarian manner, namely, in terms of its service to God's covenantal work of reconciliation or redemption in Christ. It is ultimately deemed good because it stands in "correspondence to the work of God's own Son as resolved from all eternity and fulfilled in time. . . . What is creaturely exists in order to be serviceable to the glory of God in the work of His Son. Because it lies under this determination, it is not evil but good, and not imperfectly but perfectly good" (*Church Dogmatics,* III/1, p. 370).

93. One may alternately speak of one covenant with two dispensations.

Is this ordering of the decrees true to Barth's view? Or is it the case that there is really only one decree in his thought, namely, the election of the reconciliation of fallen humanity in Christ? For Barth, the first decree is not simply about the eternal election of humanity. It is specifically the election of fallen humanity in Jesus Christ, the crucified one. Now if this Jesus, this Word, is present to God from the beginning, does this not imply that the fall, the creation, and reconciliation are encapsulated in the decree to elect? Because Christ is central to Barth's doctrine of eternal election, the one who from the very beginning is the electing God and elected human, and as such the crucified one, the second, third, and fourth decrees are encapsulated in the first. That is to say, creation, the fall, and reconciliation stand within election in the crucified. Not only are the distinct decrees eliminated, but also given the close relationship of logic and ontics in Barth's thought, namely, that logic and noetics follow ontology, being shaped by it, the collapsing of the decrees into one might suggest an ontological fusion of the contents of the decrees.

If it were not for Barth being adamant that the creation is good as created by God, one might be led to believe that for Barth the creation is in need of redemption from its inception. For if the Word of election (both as the electing God and elected human) *is* the crucified Word, and if creation stands within the framework of election in *this* Word, then the creation would appear to be in need of redemption from its inception.[94] The ten-

94. Gunton suggests that Barth comes close to advocating the Origenist-Augustinian doctrine of eternal creation according to which God is bound to create. For if God eternally loves the creature in Christ, is not God bound by necessity *to create* the creature? Colin E. Gunton, *The Triune Creator: A Historical and Systematic Study* (Edinburgh: Edinburgh University Press, 1998), p. 163. Gunton refers the reader to Robert Jenson's work, *Alpha and Omega*, for a striking comparison of Barth's doctrine of Christ with the Platonist doctrine of the eternal forms. See Robert W. Jenson, *Alpha and Omega: A Study in the Theology of Karl Barth* (New York: Thomas Nelson & Sons, 1963), especially page 140. Barth, of course, denies that his theology gives rise to the charge of necessitarianism. See Colwell's defense of Barth against a Platonist reading of his position on the subject of time and eternity (*Actuality and Provisionality*, pp. 278, 282). There is, however, a related concern that arises in the light of Barth's doctrine of election. If Jesus Christ, the *crucified* Word, is the electing God and elected human, not simply logically, but also ontically, not simply in history, but also from the standpoint of eternity, is not God eternally bound *to redeem* the creature? The most judicious reading of Barth would suggest that Barth approaches the relation of time and eternity at this point through the employment of the Trinitarian category of *perichoresis*. Hunsinger points out in his discussion of secular witness that Barth conceives eternity in

sion in Barth's thought is due to the absence of consideration being given to the Word's ministry of mediation in creation in distinction from reconciliation and redemption. *The creation is good as created. But its* ***perfection*** *rests with its ultimate redemption. Thus, although the creation is not fallen from its inception, it is created* ***in order to*** *be redeemed.*

At this point, it is beneficial to introduce Irenaeus's conception of the relation of Christ to creation. In what follows, Irenaeus's particular view of Christ's mediation will be set forth as a corrective to Barth's model in certain respects. Both Irenaeus and Barth refuse to approach the doctrine of the Word from any other vantage point than that of the *logos ensarkos.*[95] But Irenaeus views creation as distinct from reconciliation. Douglas Farrow writes that for Irenaeus, the Word's humanity "is not a consequence of the fall, a position that doubtless appeared to concede far too much to

---

perichoretic relation to itself and time: "Eternity is conceived, in Barth's theology, as perichoretic not only in itself, but also in its reception of history." George Hunsinger, *How to Read Karl Barth: The Shape of His Theology* (Oxford: Oxford University Press, 1991), p. 241. In this light, one could argue that Barth can safeguard against necessitarianism in that time is ever present to eternity just as pre-temporal, supra-temporal, and post-temporal eternity are ever present to one another in perichoretic relation. Time is present to eternity, being enclosed and penetrated by eternity in its various forms without in any way being confused with eternity. In this way, Barth's doctrine of election would be preserved from the charge that God is eternally bound to redeem humanity. Not only would the employment of *perichoresis* at this point guard against the charge of necessitarianism, but also it would shield Barth's theology from the accusation that the origin of the fall is located in the divine life, in eternity.

95. Jenson writes that for Irenaeus, ". . . his Logos, preexistent or whatever, is never a mere divine offshoot, but is always the historical man Jesus, the Christ." Robert Jenson, *The Triune Identity: God According to the Gospel* (Philadelphia: Fortress Press, 1982), p. 69. Jenson refers the reader to Irenaeus's work, *Against Heresies,* Book III/9.2-3; II/6.1; III/12-13. Jenson also quotes from Irenaeus, citing II/4.3 of the same work: "Neither is Christ one person and Jesus another; the Word of God, who is the Savior of all and the ruler of heaven and of earth, who is Jesus [!], who assumed flesh and was anointed by the Father with the Spirit, was made to be Jesus Christ." The citation is found on pages 69-70 of Jenson's work. Douglas Farrow says that for Irenaeus, "there is a twofold pre-existence of the Word corresponding to his twofold generation as divine and human." Douglas Farrow, "St. Irenaeus of Lyons: The Church and the World," *Pro Ecclesia* 4 (1995): 344, n. 39. For his own part, Barth writes, "In the *eternal decree* of God, Christ is God and man. Do not ever think of the second Person of the Trinity as only *Logos.* That is the mistake of Emil Brunner. There is no *Logos asarkos,* but only *ensarkos.*" John D. Godsey, ed., *Karl Barth's Table Talk,* Scottish Journal of Theology Occasional Papers (London: Oliver and Boyd, 1963), p. 49. Barth adds that on Brunner's model "the *Logos* becomes an abstract principle" (p. 49).

the gnostics."[96] Thus, it does not follow for Irenaeus that as the *logos ensarkos* the Word is thereby the crucified Word. For Barth, on the other hand, given his singular notions of both the Word and the covenant, Jesus is the crucified one throughout eternity in relation to time.

Both Irenaeus and Barth say that the creation exists so that the Son would not come in vain.[97] However, according to Farrow, this statement is an exception to the rule in the theology of Irenaeus, inconsistent with his general position.[98] For Barth, on the other hand, it is the rule, which governs his theology: "Because *servatio,* therefore *creatio* and therefore *conservatio.*"[99] As Farrow argues, "For Barth there can be no incarnation without the cross, and by implication no creation without the fall."[100] For both Irenaeus and Barth, Christ is central to God's dealings with humanity. However, for Irenaeus, Christ is central in the first place for his ministry of mediation in the creation, not reconciliation. Thus, his Christological construal of mediation resonates with the infralapsarian position on election, at least insofar as that model sets forth creation as the first of God's decrees, whereas Barth's doctrine of mediation depends upon his novel supralapsarian conception of election.

Although Barth's particular supralapsarian model allows him the freedom to move beyond certain difficulties in the traditional formulation by emphasizing the centrality of God's work of reconciliation *in Christ,* it raises difficulties for the doctrine of creation. Although creation is an indispensable companion to the covenant of God, it is the *outer* circle. Moreover, its honor is "improper," in contrast to the "proper" honor awarded to

96. Farrow, "St. Irenaeus of Lyons," p. 344. Irenaeus holds that the Word has always "co-existed with His creatures." If he had not, God would be guilty of "carelessness and neglect." James Donaldson and Alexander Roberts, eds., *Ante-Nicene Christian Library,* vol. 1, *The Writings of Irenaeus,* by St. Irenaeus, trans. Alexander Roberts and W. H. Rambaut (Edinburgh: T. & T. Clark, 1867), p. 389.

97. In one place, Irenaeus argues, "For inasmuch as He had a pre-existence as a saving Being, it was necessary that what might be saved should also be called into existence, in order that the Being who saves should not exist in vain" (*The Writings of Irenaeus,* p. 361).

98. Farrow, "St. Irenaeus of Lyons," p. 344, n. 42. See also the discussion of the same point in Douglas Farrow, *Ascension and Ecclesia: On the Significance of the Doctrine of the Ascension for Ecclesiology and Christian Cosmology* (Grand Rapids: Eerdmans, 1999), p. 296.

99. Barth, *Church Dogmatics,* III/3, p. 80. See H. Paul Santmire's discussion of this text in his work, *The Travail of Nature: The Ambiguous Ecological Promise of Christian Theology* (Philadelphia: Fortress Press, 1985), p. 152.

100. Farrow, *Ascension and Ecclesia,* p. 296.

reconciliation in Christ.[101] Although the creation plays an indispensable role, it is subordinate to redemption. It is a means to an end, the end of reconciliation, which suggests that Barth does not give enough space to creation in relation to the covenant. There is distinction, but distinction that sees the creation as a means and the covenant as an end. Over against Barth's view, here it is argued that the creation is itself an end, an end in itself as God's creation in Christ. For Barth, on the other hand, since creation is the outer basis of the covenant and not in any way an end in itself, since covenantal grace is always reconciling grace, the creation always anticipates reconciliation and redemption.

Reference was made above to Farrow's point that for Irenaeus, the Word's humanity "is not a consequence of the fall, a position that doubtless appeared to concede far too much to the gnostics." By conceiving the mediation of Christ in a twofold manner, that is, in creation and redemption, Irenaeus is able to guard against any suggestion that the creaturely sphere is less than good. The Word assumes human flesh to mediate the creation to God, taking the creation forward to perfection as created, not simply as redeemed. Here, too, Irenaeus's model is to be championed. Barth also conceives creation in a manner that includes eschatological perfection, distinguishing him from much of the tradition, which viewed creation as already perfected from its inception.[102] However, the way in which Barth conceives creation's perfection causes it to be overshadowed by redemption. Irenaeus, on the other hand, conceives eschatological perfection of the creation *as created,* without in any way subsuming creation under redemption. Barth is right to envision progression. But he does so at the expense of the distinct space awarded to creation, which is ultimately overshadowed by redemption.

Following Irenaeus, space is to be affirmed for the creation in relation to the covenant of reconciliation. One could approach the matter through viewing the creation itself as requiring the mediation of the incarnate Word for the sake of the perfection of creation. On this interpretation, the Word is destined originally to be incarnate, though not crucified, thereby emphasizing the significance of Christological mediation for the creation

101. Barth, *Church Dogmatics,* III/4, p. 652.

102. In his study of creation, Gunton draws the reader's attention to Barth's statement in *Church Dogmatics,* III/1, p. 366. "The only thing which can be better than what is by God (apart from God Himself) is what is to develop out of what is in its communion and encounter with God." (See also Gunton, *Triune Creator,* p. 164.)

whereby space is made for the creation in relation to the covenant of reconciliation. According to this perspective, the creation of all things through Christ is the first of God's decrees logically conceived. The merit of this position is found in the space it generates for the doctrine of creation in relation to the covenant of reconciliation while, at the same time, centering the creation in Christ.[103] Thus, the creation is not merely a

103. Having said this, one fully sympathizes with Barth's concern to guard against the danger posed by Marcion on the one hand and Schopenhauer on the other. (See Barth, *Church Dogmatics,* III/1, pp. 334ff.) The separation of creation from God's covenantal purposes in Christ so easily leads to a pessimistic view of creation. Marcion champions covenant over creation, losing sight of the creation in the covenant, thereby dismissing the creation as evil (pp. 334, 339). Schopenhauer loses sight of the covenant in creation (p. 339). Yet Schopenhauer, like Marcion, views the creation in a most pessimistic light. The basis for this twofold pessimism is set forth in Barth: "Where the covenant is no longer seen in creation, or creation in the covenant, the affirmation that creation is benefit cannot be sustained" (p. 334). The present study's call for greater distinction between the creation and covenant does not invoke separation since the creation and covenant of reconciliation are centered in Christ Jesus, mediator of what has been called the covenants of creation and reconciliation. How can there be any room for pessimism if, as is maintained, the eternal Word of God eternally elects the creation, and determines to become incarnate to mediate the creation to God, perfecting it, and this independent of the contingent event of the fall in history? To turn briefly to consider a related matter, the way in which the creation and the covenant of reconciliation are distinguished in this study also safeguards against Macken's charge that nature is subsumed under grace in particular examples of Barthian theology. See Macken's criticisms of a Barthian position on pages 151 and 168 of his work, *Autonomy Theme.* Although the term "creation" is preferable to "nature," Macken has a point. However, over against the position Macken and Balthasar with him (see Macken, *Autonomy Theme,* p. 151) appear to advocate, that is, grace perfecting nature, it is still better to speak of grace founding and perfecting creation, that is, the grace of Christ, who is the Word in creation. However, the grace in mind here is distinct from reconciling and redeeming grace (i.e., Barth), and is better conceived as creaturely grace (not to be confused with created grace), following on from the distinction made between the Word's mediation in creation and reconciliation. Thus, there is both creaturely grace and reconciling grace, guarding against what Macken sees as the collapsing of nature into grace (reconciling grace), and preserving what he calls "the contingency of sin and reconciliation" (Macken, *Autonomy Theme,* p. 168). On the view taken here, the Word enfleshed in creation creates, centers, and completes the creation. But given the fall, this Word's mediation in and perfection of the creation takes on new shape. On the subject of the shape or form of the incarnation in light of the fall, Farrow writes that for Irenaeus, "only the humble form or stance of that humanity is related to the fall" (Farrow, "St. Irenaeus of Lyons," p. 344). In any event, the *logos ensarkos* not only perfects or fulfills creation, but also founds and fills it.

means to an end, the end of the redemption of the fallen creation, but *an* end itself as created by God in and for Christ.[104]

104. In all fairness to Barth, it should be noted that not only does his doctrine of election enable him to steer clear of certain pessimistic and oppressive characteristics associated with the traditional model of election bound up with double predestination and the *decretum absolutum,* but also it enables him to conceive creation and redemption in inseparable relation to one another. As Gunton notes, Barth's conception of their relation enables him "to begin a move towards the integration of that which the tradition tended to hold apart, the spheres of creation and redemption, of divine action in the beginning and in the middle, and to do it by means of christology." Gunton also points out that on Barth's model "salvation is bound up systematically with creation, and is not a late intervention to make the best of a bad job" (Gunton, *Triune Creator,* p. 165). The infralapsarian model, on the other hand, has difficulty guarding against this problem. However, the conclusion drawn here is that it is more advantageous to speak of two phases to the one plan than to argue that the creation exists for the sake of redemption and that the incarnation is due to the fall. Now as it concerns the integration of creation and redemption, the attempt to conceive the *logos ensarkos* in distinction from the crucifixion, as the ground of creation, makes possible the uniting of creation and redemption in such a way that redemption does not overshadow the creation. It is the same Word, Jesus Christ. But his mediation in history is not bound up *necessarily* with redemption. It should be noted that as it concerns the problem of evil, Barth believes he is able to guard against the charge that his supralapsarian model makes God responsible for the fall. As R. Scott Rodin points out, key to Barth's defense against the charge that God is the author of sin is the distinction made between *"homo labilis"* and *"homo lapsus."* See R. Scott Rodin, *Evil and Theodicy in the Theology of Karl Barth* (New York: Peter Lang, 1997), pp. 118-19. Barth writes, "God wills *homo labilis,* not in order that he may fall, but in order that when he has fallen he may testify to the fulness of God's glory" (Barth, *Church Dogmatics,* II/2, pp. 141-42). Thus, God wills *homo labilis,* "man sinful and lost" (p. 143), but not *homo lapsus,* that is, the sin of humanity. Attention should be drawn to the fact that while Barth sees certain merits in the infralapsarian position, he rejects it. The reason for his rejection stems from the fact that infralapsarianism, the view that election has as its object *homo lapsus,* what Colwell defines as "man already . . . fallen" (Colwell, *Actuality and Provisionality,* p. 238), "cannot apprehend the idea of Jesus Christ the *Logos ensarkos,* as the eternally Elect sinful man" (Rodin, *Evil and Theodicy,* p. 119). For Barth, "Jesus Christ is the merciful and just God who elects from all eternity, and also *homo labilis* who is elected from all eternity" (Barth, *Church Dogmatics,* II/2, p. 143). Barth's dismissal of infralapsarianism is due in large part to its ordination of "another decree over and above that of predestination" (Barth, *Church Dogmatics,* II/2, p. 143), that is, above Christ's ministry in election, which would mean that, "there were two divine decrees at the beginning of all things" (Barth, *Church Dogmatics,* II/2, p. 144). Along similar lines, Rodin notes that Barth's repudiation of infralapsarianism "is consistent with his entire theological agenda which seeks to hold together creation and redemption, and to center both in Jesus Christ" (Rodin, *Evil and Theodicy,* p. 117). Lastly, it should be pointed out that Barth contends that the precedence given to the economy of natural providence over against "the whole economy of predestination" in infralapsarianism

Although Barth affirms the goodness of the creation as created, redemption overshadows such affirmation in that, *at its heart,* from the inception of creation, eschatological perfection involves the redemption of creation. In this light, there is a tension in Barth's thought when he writes of both the bird and Mozart that by simply making music, by simply being what they in fact are *as created* by God, they glorify God.[105] For the glory these creatures bring to God as created is overshadowed by the fact that they exist for redemption. If taken to an extreme whereby creation gives way ultimately to an otherworldly redemption, the sacred dimension would overwhelm the secular domain.

Fortunately, the tension inherent in Barth's model of the relation of creation to redemption does not give rise to this extreme. For although re-

led inevitably to natural theology (Barth, *Church Dogmatics,* II/2, p. 144). Here, it is worth mentioning G. C. Berkouwer's refutation of Barth's claim set forth in *Church Dogmatics,* II/2, p. 136, where Barth argues that the particular objections raised by adherents of the infralapsarian position helped bring about "the later cleavage between natural and revealed theology." Berkouwer comments that although he does not affirm what he terms "an objectionable arrangement of succession" in infralapsarianism, "the deepest motive is not to make creation independent of the counsel of God" but to guard against "monism." Its concern is not the "*oeconomia naturalis providentiae* as such, but . . . the significance of creation and the disturbance of sin." The "creation and fall" on this account are not "simply a means to realize God's prime decree." Although the doctrine "does not solve anything," according to Berkouwer, it guards against presenting God as the ultimate cause of evil, even while asserting God's sovereignty over evil. G. C. Berkouwer, *Divine Election* (Grand Rapids: Eerdmans, 1960), pp. 272-73. Now in response, although it is certainly the case that infralapsarianism "cannot apprehend" the Word as "the eternally Elect sinful man . . ." (see Rodin, *Evil and Theodicy,* p. 119), it can apprehend him as the *logos ensarkos.* Not only supralapsarianism, but infralapsarianism, too, can be construed along Christological lines, that is, if one views the decree of creation in the light of the *logos ensarkos* who exists to perfect the creation as created. Thus, if one defines election simply as *constitution* in the light of Christ, one need not equate predestination with election, but view creation and redemption as integrally related to one another through the dual ministry of mediation of the person of Jesus Christ. This view also removes any hint of conceiving the incarnation as simply the consequence of the fall, which may give rise to dangerous implications if taken up and developed by those with gnostic leanings. Lastly, the position adopted here has the further advantage of being able to guard against the charge that God is the author of sin. For although Barth's God does not will the fall, his election of sinful humanity, given Barth's supralapsarian model, makes the fall inevitable. This claim is made regardless of the fact that Barth's God does not order sin, but simply assumes it in the orchestration of election. For the exposition of Barth's position here, see Rodin, *Evil and Theodicy,* pp. 120 and 122, n. 41.

105. See Chapter Six of this study.

demption *overshadows* the creation, it certainly does not *overwhelm* or displace the creation. In fact, the beauty of Barth's model is that even as redeemed, the creation remains and is given space for the expression of authentic forms of secularity. For redemption is *not* accomplished *at the expense of creation* and certain forms of secular existence, *but on behalf of them.* Thus, in spite of the tension present in his thought at this point, Barth displays a healthy appreciation for creation and the secular domain in its own right. Barth is no sacramentalist, nor a secularist for that matter. He is able to steer a course between these two extreme poles because he envisions that in its very creatureliness and secularity, the creation is in a sense sacred, and that this sacredness manifests itself in the creation as it offers God its secular praise.

One is struck by the secular sentiment in Barth's theology, especially in the light of his Christocentric concentration. In Chapter Six, it will be shown that Barth's doctrine of the Word is at least partly responsible for generating such secular sentiment. In this chapter, however, it has been argued that Barth's doctrine of the same Word, Jesus Christ, enables him to offer a *synthesis* between the sacred and secular spheres without displacing the *diastasis* proper to that relation.

Beyond Modernity and the Heavenly City

In *The Heavenly City of the Eighteenth-Century Philosophers,* historian Carl Becker writes that, contrary to what is often assumed, "the *Philosophes* demolished the Heavenly City of St. Augustine only to rebuild it with more up-to-date materials."[106] One need not be too learned a historian to know how accurate an assessment of these moderns Becker offers. Of course, this paradox does not confine itself to them. One can also discern it in the movements and views of moderns who followed after Voltaire and Diderot.

One readily thinks of the French Revolution with its crusade against Christendom, which paradoxically involved the desecration of the cathedral of Notre Dame and veneration of the goddess of Reason, followed by Robespierre's worship of the supreme being, and still later the rise of

106. Carl L. Becker, *The Heavenly City of the Eighteenth-Century Philosophers* (New Haven & London: Yale University Press, 1960), p. 31.

"theophilanthropy."[107] The established church had been overthrown, but not religion itself.[108] Indeed, religion never really dies; it only takes new forms. Modern humanity substituted civil religion for the church. And what a religion it was, requiring more faith than was needed during the age of faith, given its belief in the inevitable perfection of humanity and utopian civilization created by human hands. Becker writes that both the thirteenth and eighteenth centuries coupled faith with reason. "In a very real sense it may be said of the eighteenth century that it was an age of faith as well as of reason, and of the thirteenth century that it was an age of reason as well as of faith."[109]

Faith, and with it mystery and dogma, did not cease with the full flowering of humanism in the eighteenth century, but spilled over and continued to take on new forms in the centuries that followed. Does one not find striking evidence of their ongoing existence in the founder of scientific positivism, Auguste Comte, who came to see increasingly his philosophy as setting forth the framework "for a new 'religion of humanity,'" indeed, as the only religious candidate beneficial to human life in the scientific age?[110] And what is one to make of the utopian vision hailing from Marx

107. See, for example, Alec R. Vidler, *The Church in an Age of Revolution: 1789 to the Present Day,* The Pelican History of the Church, ed. Owen Chadwick (Harmondsworth: Penguin Books, 1971), p. 17.

108. In a recent essay, Peter Berger has spoken of "the relation between religion and modernity" as "rather complicated." Peter Berger, "The Desecularization of the World: A Global Overview," in *The Desecularization of the World: Resurgent Religion and World Politics,* ed. Peter Berger (Washington, D.C.: Ethics and Public Policy Center, and Grand Rapids: Eerdmans, 1999), p. 3. While noting exceptions, such as Western Europe, which stands in marked contrast to America, and the educated elite of the international community, "composed of people with Western-type higher education" (pp. 9-10), Berger claims that, "The assumption that we live in a secularized world is false" (p. 2). While noting exceptions, he argues that, "The world today . . . is as furiously religious as it ever was, and in some places more so than ever" (p. 2). The resurgence of conservative religion, whether it be Christian, Muslim, or Hindu, bears witness to the fact that "at the very least . . . *counter*-secularization is at least as important a phenomenon in the contemporary world as secularization" (p. 6). Berger argues that modernization does not necessarily lead to secularization (p. 6), and that those religious institutions and organizations that have made concessions to secularization, following the strategy of "adaptation," are in many circles on the decline (pp. 4, 6).

109. Becker, *The Heavenly City,* p. 8.

110. Henry D. Aiken, ed., *The Age of Ideology: The 19th Century Philosophers,* The Mentor Philosophers (New York: New American Library, 1956), pp. 115, 122. At one point, Aiken remarks that, "Comte's mystical adoration of Humanity came perilously close to the sort of

and Engels, whose economic historiography and ideology of liberation calling for radical change have been enshrined as sacred writings? One thinks also of their followers, such as Lenin, Mao, and Kim Il Sung, who have been and, in some cases, still are, treated as gods and worshiped by the pilgrims of the revolution.[111] Various citizens of the secular city, far from overcoming Christendom and religion, have rebuilt the heavenly city in new guise.

Barth is too much a modern to long for the return of Christendom. As stated at the outset of this chapter, he looks favorably on the rise of modernity in that it laid the medieval synthesis to rest. That does not mean, however, that he is content for the church to sit quietly by, or is committed to pursuing peaceful coexistence and relational symmetry with modern civilization, whereby the church softens its claims and surrenders its center in fear of appearing offensive to its cultured despisers. For in place of elliptical Christendom, Barth sets forth the singular Christ.

Such a stance does not spell the dismissal of secularity, but its liberation from secularism. That is to say, secularity must be conceived anew. It must be viewed in inseparable relation to the Word event as Jesus Christ, who grants space in which authentic forms of secularity may flourish, as shall be shown.[112] Thus, Barth exhibits a profoundly secular sentiment while forging a new synthesis based in Jesus Christ.

The synthesis Barth offers is grounded in the universal reality of Jesus Christ, whose centrality is conceived neither as a transhistorical form (i.e., the ancients), nor as a mere historical particular (i.e., the moderns), but as that particular whose story is universal history. That is to say, it is the story within which humanity is to place itself. As Robert Jenson writes,

> The old method of exhibiting the historical event of Jesus as the object of faith has become impossible to continue. It is this crisis which has made the sentence "Christianity is an historical religion" into a cliché and a symptom. For theology is thus thrown back upon history, upon the flux of time, *in itself.* The preacher must, if he is to be understood, exhibit the events of 4 B.C. to A.D. 30 as containing the

animistic reification of a concept which he himself had exposed in the thinking of the theological and metaphysical stages" (p. 138).

111. Becker draws the reader's attention to this phenomenon in the former Soviet Union (Becker, *The Heavenly City*, p. 165).

112. Here reference is made to Chapters Five and Six.

> meaning of his hearers' lives without recourse to sources of meaning above time, without assuming that his hearers already suppose they *ought* to reflect justice and beauty in their lives. He must exhibit Jesus Christ, "crucified under Pontius Pilate," this personage of long ago, as himself, in his own unadulteratedly temporal reality, the sole meaning of human history, of each of our histories. He must show the meaning which life has, not in itself and not in atemporal abstractions, but in Jesus the Christ.[113]

Over against the orator of religion, Barth is this preacher who exhibits Christ's life as the meaning of life, the ground and goal of human existence.

Jesus Christ centers reality as the electing God and elected creature, whose eternity is wed to a temporal history on behalf of humanity generally. It is he who provides the grounds for a synthesis between the sacred and secular spheres, church and society, covenant and creation. For he is Lord of these spheres.

The problem with Barth's doctrine of creation is not that he refuses to tackle the questions of natural science, but that he so emphasizes redemption in Christ as the goal of creation that the distinctive reality of the creation is overshadowed by its ultimate redemption. As Gunton argues in a slightly different context,

> The weakness of Barth's theology of creation is not found in the fact that he did not have the time to go into the complications of the question of science, but in his repetition, albeit in improved form, of the Western tendency so to subordinate creation to redemption that the status of the material world as a whole is endangered. In this case, as the field on which election takes place, the created order is treated rather too externally to that which takes place on it.[114]

Having said this, we can conclude that Barth's attempt to form a synthesis of covenant and creation is a noble one. For apart from the justification of creation as benefit provided by the Word of hope as Jesus Christ, what is to prevent the advance of the pessimism of Marcion and Schopenhauer noted previously (see note 103 on p. 113 above), due to their disregard for God's

113. Jenson, *Alpha and Omega*, p. 16.

114. Gunton, *Triune Creator*, p. 165.

covenantal purposes in creation,[115] or for that matter, the near nihilism of Nietzsche, in the creaturely domain? For the isolation of religion in the modern period has done very little to advance the utopian vision of its progenitors in the secular sphere.

The rejection of the sacred sphere does not lead to the betterment of society. For the sacred only reappears, unnoticed perhaps, though in more sinister guise. Nor is the answer to be found in a return to Christendom, but in a synthesis beyond the heavenly cities of Augustine and Diderot, where space is made for both the sacred and secular, albeit in dialectical relation. Barth's doctrine of election can be conceived as such an attempt. And although it is not free of faults, it does point toward a possible resolution by which to bridge the impasse.

The problem with the medieval synthesis was that it did not make space for the *radical difference* between the sacred and secular spheres. The problem with the Enlightenment project, on the other hand, was that by *dismissing* or at least *privatizing* the institution of religion, the secular created a vacuum it was unable to fill. A new form of mediation was required, one that would celebrate the distinct existence of each, one that would welcome otherness. The medievals rejected *radical otherness.* The moderns simply rejected *the divine other.* In spite of its flaws, Barth's model falls prey to neither charge. Barth recognizes the radical otherness between the two spheres. But he also cherishes the distinctive role each plays on behalf of the kingdom of the Word in which they stand in distinct though inseparable relation.

The *distinction* between the sacred and secular will be discussed in Chapters Five and Six. However, consideration now turns to the theme of connections between Christ and culture from the standpoint of Christian and secular words of witness, especially the latter. Having spoken of the significance of Barth's doctrine of election as a novel and promising way by which to synthesize Christ and culture, discussion will center now on the analysis of *connections* from the standpoint of revelation and secular witness. Among other things, it will be shown that for all its *difference,* the secular word *need not* produce *dissonance,* but may prove to be to the sacred an invaluable counterpart.

115. Refer back to footnote 103.

4

The Commandeered Word and Secular Witness

Particularity and Accessibility: The Word and the Question of Witness

In *The Göttingen Dogmatics,* Barth argues that one must proceed cautiously when entertaining the question of the possibility of witness to revelation *extra muros ecclesiae.* On the one hand, he is unwilling to side quickly with Luther and Calvin in their vehement condemnation of Zwingli for being so eager "to people the Christian heaven with a whole series of noble pagans."[1] For "to shout 'Impossible' might be a sign of culpable obduracy."[2] Moreover, the Christian has "properly no reason to maintain the absoluteness of Christianity. It is revelation that is absolute."[3] Yet, on the other hand, he is quick to point out that if the pagans are to meet the test of bearing witness to the truth, it must be shown that they bear witness to

1. Karl Barth, *The Göttingen Dogmatics: Instruction in the Christian Religion,* vol. 1, trans. Geoffrey W. Bromiley (Grand Rapids: Eerdmans, 1990), pp. 149-150. See also Barth's discussion of Zwingli in Karl Barth, *Church Dogmatics,* IV/3.1, *The Doctrine of Reconciliation,* ed. G. W. Bromiley and T. F. Torrance (Edinburgh: T. & T. Clark, 1961), p. 135, where he writes that unlike Zwingli he has "deliberately refrained" from appealing to prototypical examples of pagan witnesses to the kingdom. Regardless of his differences from Zwingli, one finds here a constant thread in Barth's thought. It is not simply the later Barth of *Church Dogmatics,* IV/3 who is open to the possibility of unsuspecting witnesses to the kingdom, but also the early Barth not far removed from the completion of the second edition of *Romans.*

2. Barth, *Göttingen Dogmatics,* p. 150.

3. Barth, *Göttingen Dogmatics,* p. 150.

> the one revelation at all events, that is, indirect communication of the hidden God who is as such the revealed God, God's encounter with us, and hence the cross and the resurrection, offense and faith. This is the issue in the canon, in the OT and the NT. This is what the witness to revelation, to the incarnation, to Christ, is all about.[4]

One must be careful then not "to shut the gate of the castle," nor "to tear down the gates as though this were always self-evidently the issue throughout religious history."[5]

In light of the preceding discussion, it should be clear that while Barth *does not rule out* the possibility of witnesses to God arising from outside the walls of the church, all such witnesses *must be ruled by* the particularity of the "indirect communication"[6] of God, the incarnation, that is, revelation as Jesus Christ. The scandal of the particularity of revelation is the criterion by which to judge potential claims. But the indirectness of revelation as the incarnation proves equally scandalous from another angle in that it negates the possibility of accessibility to this revelation by means of a supposed native capacity for revelation. Accessibility to revelation is wholly dependent upon the divine Word's condescension in the event of revelation.

Protestant thought has traditionally been marked by its emphasis on the Word of God. Such is the case for Barth, whose theology can be described as a theology of the Word, namely, the living Word as witnessed to by the Word's written and spoken forms. In this vein, Stuart McLean writes, "Barth implies that the auditory and the temporal analogies more faithfully depict the essential character of the relationships between God and man, and man and man than do 'visual' and 'spatial' ones." McLean goes on to write, "it is not incidental that Barth's thought stresses the im-

4. Barth, *Göttingen Dogmatics,* p. 150. Now although Barth considers it possible that correspondence and witness may occur, arising from such figures as Lao-Tse and Buddha (p. 149), Barth claims that Christian and Islamic monotheism are irreconcilable in view of their disagreement on the Trinity, and that Christian and Amida Buddhist accounts of grace are incompatible on account of Christian grace being determined fundamentally by the personal reality of Jesus Christ. See Karl Barth, *Church Dogmatics,* II/1, *The Doctrine of God,* ed. G. W. Bromiley and T. F. Torrance (Edinburgh: T. & T. Clark, 1957), pp. 448-49; and Karl Barth, *Church Dogmatics,* I/2, *The Doctrine of the Word of God,* ed. G. W. Bromiley and T. F. Torrance (Edinburgh: T. & T. Clark, 1956), pp. 340-44.

5. Barth, *Göttingen Dogmatics,* p. 150.

6. Barth, *Göttingen Dogmatics,* p. 150.

portance of the Word and preaching and Roman Catholic thought, substance and the beatific vision."[7]

Barth's theology of the Word goes hand in hand with his rejection of the *analogia entis.* Barth rejects the analogy of being because he believes the concept expresses a form of relation whereby static, necessary, substantial threads of continuity exist between God and the creation, including an innate capacity of the mind for apprehension of things divine. For Barth, on the other hand, the analogy between God and the world is an *event* of language. As God creates all things out of nothing by his Word, so too, he *creates* analogies between himself and the world by that same Word in the history of revelation. In this light, Barth replaces the *analogia entis* with the *analogia fidei.*[8]

The *analogia fidei* expresses that event whereby God in his grace *creates* correspondence between himself and that reality which is totally different from God.[9] It should be noted that this event of correspondence endures

7. Stuart McLean, *Humanity in the Thought of Karl Barth* (Edinburgh: T. & T. Clark, 1981), p. 13.

8. Note Barth's discussion of God's hiddenness, human incapacity, and the miracle of divine grace in revelation in *Church Dogmatics,* II/1, p. 182.

9. Barth wishes to safeguard the biblical teaching of God's freedom from any links with the creation that are other than voluntary. In one place, Barth points to the tension inherent in the Thomist position, which classes God and the rest of reality together under a concept of being and how that conflicts with Aquinas's insistence that God does not belong to a class (*Church Dogmatics,* II/1, pp. 310-11). How can one reconcile the notion that all effects are like their causes with the idea that God does not belong to a class? Aquinas himself attempts to solve the problem by arguing that God and the creature share the attribute in question, but that God possesses the attribute in question in a way superior to human understanding. See Thomas Aquinas, *Summa Theologica* (London: Burns, Oates & Washbourne, 1920), Part 1, Question 4, Article 3, 49-51, 4.3. Brian Davies writes that Aquinas espouses "two apparently opposing conclusions. We may say, for example, that I am good and that God is good. But we must also insist that properties or attributes ascribable to God and creatures differ in the way they are exemplified." Brian Davies, *The Thought of Saint Thomas Aquinas* (Oxford: Clarendon Press, 1993), p. 65. Regarding Aquinas's point that God possesses the attribute in question in a way superior to human understanding, Frederick Ferre writes that the net result of such a position is to make all knowledge claims of God entirely vacuous. Moreover, he also raises suspicion concerning the underlying "metaphysical assumption" that upholds the doctrine of the analogy of intrinsic attribution, "namely, that some significant likeness must exist between all causes and their effects," wondering if there is sufficient "evidence to support such a principle," and whether it can "sustain modern criticism." Ferre, "Analogy in Theology," in *The Encyclopedia of Philosophy,* ed. Paul Edwards, vol. 1 (New York: Macmillan & The Free Press, 1967). In contrast to the Thomist position, and in keeping with his affir-

only so long as God sustains it. Moreover, as McCormack argues, the *analogia fidei* is "an *inherently dialectical concept,*" signifying the veiling and unveiling of God in both the event of revelation and witness to revelation.[10] The Word event of God in history in the person of Jesus Christ both wholly reveals God and wholly hides God at the same time.[11]

In light of the foregoing discussion, it should be evident that the possibility exists in principle that witness to the revelation of the kingdom of the Word may occur outside the confines of the church, and in the church for that matter. However, access to this revelation is wholly dependent on

---

mation of the analogies of faith and relation, Barth affirms the analogy of extrinsic attribution. Central to Barth's employment of this analogy is his belief that there is no capacity for the divine inherent in the human constitution. Along these lines, it is interesting to note that in the *Church Dogmatics* Barth takes aim at Quenstedt for his doctrine of analogy. Barth does so, not for the latter's rejection of the analogies of inequality and proportionality, nor for his acceptance of the analogy of attribution, but because of his acceptance of the analogy of intrinsic attribution (*Church Dogmatics,* II/1, pp. 238-43). Over against those advocates of the analogy of intrinsic attribution, Barth champions extrinsic attribution (pp. 238-43), for he believes it is the only possible doctrine of analogy that safeguards the concept of God from the ultimate deification of humanity. In the incarnation of Jesus Christ, the wholly other God establishes an analogy with humanity and the world, thereby safeguarding against the charge of agnosticism, while at the same time preserving the radical distinction between the divine and human spheres. God is wholly revealed and completely concealed in the incarnation of God as he who is God's creaturely other. See Bruce McCormack, *Karl Barth's Critically Realistic Dialectical Theology: Its Genesis and Development, 1909-1936* (Oxford: Clarendon Press, 1995), pp. 16-18. In addition to McCormack, see the following for discussions of Barth's doctrine of analogy: Alan J. Torrance, *Persons in Communion: Trinitarian Description and Human Participation* (Edinburgh: T. & T. Clark, 1996), chapter 3; Battista Mondin, *The Principle of Analogy in Protestant and Catholic Thought* (The Hague: Martinus Nijhoff, 1963); Henry Chavannes, *The Analogy Between God and the World in Saint Thomas Aquinas and Karl Barth,* trans. William Lumley (New York: Vantage Press, 1992).

10. McCormack, *Karl Barth's Critically Realistic Dialectical Theology,* pp. 16-18.

11. McCormack speaks of two extreme forms of conceiving Barth's dialectic. The first is to absolutize the positive side of the dialectic, namely, the unveiling of God. The second is to absolutize the negative side, that is, the veiling of God. Bruce McCormack, *English Language Barth Research Today,* paper given in the Research Institute in Systematic Theology, King's College London, 23 April 1996. For an example of the latter, see Graham Ward, *Barth, Derrida and the Language of Theology* (Cambridge: Cambridge University Press, 1995). There are merits to Ward's analysis of Barth and his comparison of him with Derrida. But his claim that "The revelation of the Word does not occur and cannot occur in Barth's theology, and so its meaning is maintained in mystery" is mistaken (Ward, p. 250). Barth himself speaks against absolutizing either knowledge or ignorance. (See Barth, *Church Dogmatics,* II/1, pp. 342-43; see also Barth, *Kirchliche Dogmatik,* II/1, p. 385.)

the divine initiative whereby God *commandeers* secular words to become parables of the kingdom. In what follows, consideration will be given to Barth's claim *that* secular and Christian witness to revelation occurs. Attention will also be given to *how* it is that witness outside the sphere of Christianity occurs, *what* it is that happens to words in the event of witness, and *how significant* creaturely forms such as words and human flesh are in the event of witness.

Actuality and Identity: The Reality of Witness

Barth maintains *that* the *logos ensarkos,* the Word in all his scandalous particularity, is the *lux mundi* to whom lesser lights, including those *extra muros ecclesiae,* bear witness. As such, the secular words of the world become parables of the kingdom. All parables of the kingdom model those parables of Christ in the gospels. Although the parables of Jesus themselves arise from the "everyday sphere," the characters employed by Jesus "are very strangely shaped, and their actions no less strangely directed, by an invisible hand which obviously estranges them from the everyday sphere in which they are set."[12] Jesus employs the ordinary, giving "them the mark of the extraordinary."[13] He commandeers human words, actions, and persons, giving to them a new sense, causing them to bear witness to the kingdom, which in and of themselves they could not do.[14]

Witnesses to revelation, whether sacred or secular, are not by nature able to bear witness to God or his Word. As Barth writes,

> Nothing could be further from our minds than to attribute to the human creature as such a capacity to know God and the one Word of God, or to produce true words corresponding to this knowledge. Even in the sphere of the Bible and the Church there can be no question of any such capacity. If there are true words of God, it is all miraculous. How much more so, then, in this wider field! What we have in both cases is the capacity of Jesus Christ to raise up of the stones children to Abraham, i.e., to take into His service, to empower

12. Barth, *Church Dogmatics,* IV/3.1, p. 112.
13. Barth, *Church Dogmatics,* IV/3.1, p. 113.
14. Barth, *Church Dogmatics,* IV/3.1, p. 113.

> for this service, to cause to speak in it, men who are quite without any capacity of their own.[15]

Witness ever depends on the divine prerogative, for God is always Lord in revelation. And yet, God in his mercy sees fit to elevate human words in the event of the Word of revelation to bear witness to the reconciliation of all things to God in Christ, not only in the Bible and the church, but also in the world at large. For as Barth makes clear, "Our thesis is simply that the capacity of Jesus Christ to create these human witnesses is not restricted to His working on and in prophets and apostles and what is thus made possible and actual in His community. His capacity transcends the limits of this sphere."[16]

The commandeered word of witness takes three forms. The word of witness as Scripture is entitled the "direct witness" whereas the word of witness in the church is labeled the "indirect witness," reflecting the relative proximity of each to the Word of Christ.[17] Words of the secular world, on the other hand, when commandeered by the Word of God, are what Hunsinger calls "unwitting" witnesses.[18] In contrast to the Bible and the church, which together make up the inside sphere, words of witness in the world belong to the "outside"[19] or "wider sphere."[20] It should be noted that this wider sphere, which Barth designates to refer to the "secular world," is further distinguished into "a closer and a more distant periphery . . . , between a secularism which approximates to a pure and absolute

15. Barth, *Church Dogmatics,* IV/3.1, p. 118. Just prior to this statement, Barth contends that in speaking of "true words from without" he is not appealing to natural theology, which involves nothing more than "abstract impartations." Rather, he appeals to those "attestations of the self-impartation" of God, which can be judged as true witnesses by their conformity to the witness of Scripture and the church (p. 117). Hunsinger notes that in his discussion of witness Barth is consistent with what he says elsewhere about the movement involving God and humanity, namely, "that there is no way from us to God, but only from God to us." George Hunsinger, *How to Read Karl Barth: The Shape of His Theology* (New York: Oxford University Press, 1991), p. 257. Such a movement is "irreversible" (p. 257). Thus, one moves from consideration of the Word to consideration of words in view of the Word, and not vice versa (p. 257).

16. Barth, *Church Dogmatics,* IV/3.1, p. 118.

17. Barth, *Church Dogmatics,* IV/3.1, p. 96.

18. Barth, *Church Dogmatics,* IV/3.1, pp. 96-99. Hunsinger, *How to Read Karl Barth,* p. 247.

19. Barth, *Church Dogmatics,* IV/3.1, p. 96.

20. Barth, *Church Dogmatics,* IV/3.1, p. 118. See also Hunsinger, *How to Read Karl Barth,* p. 247.

form and another which is mixed and relative."[21] Absolute or pure secularism refers to those who "stand unwittingly in full isolation from the Gospel in its biblical and churchly form" and whose "reaction to it" would likely "be hostile."[22] Relative secularism, on the other hand, denotes nominal Christianity.[23] Barth adds that it is possible, contrary to what might be assumed, that the nominally secular sphere may actually be more resistant to the gospel given its familiarity with and ability to acquiesce to the Word in certain ways while remaining virtually unaffected by the Word due to its subtle opposition to the gospel. Regardless though, the Word as Jesus Christ is able to raise up witnesses both from the "closer" and "more distant periphery"[24] of this outer sphere. Because of Christ, Barth holds out hope for the twofold secular dimension, since "for Him neither the militant godlessness of the outer periphery of the community, nor the intricate heathenism of the inner, is an insurmountable barrier."[25] The Word is able to commandeer these words just as he does those of Scripture and the church. What unites the various forms of witness that arise from within these various spheres is their inclusion in Christ by grace. What distinguishes them is their relative proximity to the Word coupled with the awareness or unawareness of each.

21. Barth, *Church Dogmatics,* IV/3.1, p. 118.

22. Barth, *Church Dogmatics,* IV/3.1, p. 118.

23. Barth, *Church Dogmatics,* IV/3.1, pp. 119-20.

24. Barth, *Church Dogmatics,* IV/3.1, p. 118.

25. Barth, *Church Dogmatics,* IV/3.1, p. 121. It appears safe to assume that implicit in Barth's statements that it is possible that witnesses to revelation may arise from within the "secular world" (for the use of the term, see p. 118) is the idea that witnesses may also emerge from within the context of the non-Christian religions. Here then "secular world" is taken to refer to the *whole* domain, which stands outside the parameters of the Bible and the church. This interpretation is in part dependent on the belief that Barth's statements about Lao-Tse and Buddha in *The Göttingen Dogmatics* (see note 4) represent his mature view of witness set forth in *Church Dogmatics,* IV/3. Having said this, while other religions must be "valued and taken seriously," Christian missions must ever proclaim the gospel in opposition to these religions "in all its radical uniqueness and novelty, with no attempt at compromise or at finding points of contact and the like." Karl Barth, *Church Dogmatics,* IV/3.2, *The Doctrine of Reconciliation,* ed. G. W. Bromiley and T. F. Torrance (Edinburgh: T. & T. Clark, 1962), p. 875. Thus, as with other forms of witness, if witness to the gospel is to occur in this sphere, it will be *ad-hoc* and ephemeral. For a recent discussion of Barth's engagement of other faith traditions, see Trevor Hart's article, "Truth, the Trinity, and Pluralism," in *Regarding Karl Barth: Toward a Reading of His Theology* (Downers Grove, Ill.: InterVarsity Press, 1999), 117-38.

How is it though that the light of the Word as Jesus Christ, who is enfleshed in scandalous particularity, can illumine the world, raising up witnesses from beyond the sphere of the Bible and the church? At least part of the answer to this question is to be found in Barth's understanding of the relation of reconciliation and revelation. Reconciliation, for Barth, is itself revelation.[26] Thus, revelation must attest to the reconciling life of Jesus Christ.[27] "We cannot first speak generally and abstractly of the fact that revelation, as the revelation of the reconciliation of the world to God, takes place (as it did and will take place), and then come back to Him as the One who is perhaps no more than the prominent Revealer."[28] Barth goes on to say that, "As the reconciliation takes place in Him, its revelation takes place through Him."[29] Christ the reconciler lives. And be-

26. Barth, *Church Dogmatics,* IV/3.1, p. 38.

27. As Hunsinger points out, in *Church Dogmatics,* IV/3.1, there is a "subtle priority" given to event over word, life over light, even though they are inseparably related in that they both refer to the one reality of Jesus Christ (Hunsinger, *How to Read Karl Barth,* p. 235). Hunsinger is to be credited with setting Barth's treatment of secular parables against the backdrop of Barth's discussion of reconciliation as revelation, "which in turn presupposes" Barth's conception of the relation of the person of Jesus Christ to eternity (p. 236). The priority of place given to the event or life of Christ should not, however, be taken to mean that for Barth, the word or light is any less important. It, too, is vital. For one, the reconciling event or life is itself revelation. Moreover, in *Church Dogmatics,* IV/1, Barth writes that he wishes to guard against what he considers to have been insufficient attention given to the prophetic office in relation to the *munus sacerdotale* and *munus regium* during the "orthodox period." Barth adds that it led to the obscuring of the former, indeed, in some treatments, its abandonment. The result was a reversal of fortunes at the time of the Enlightenment. With the rise of the *Aufklärung,* an inordinate amount of attention was given to this office at the expense of Christ's roles as priest and king. Only by giving due emphasis to the Word of witness in relation to Christ's offices of priest and king can one guard against the countermove to reduce the work of Christ to that of teacher and example. Karl Barth, *Church Dogmatics,* IV/1, *The Doctrine of Reconciliation,* ed. G. W. Bromiley and T. F. Torrance (Edinburgh: T. & T. Clark, 1956), pp. 138-39. For Barth, Christ's role as prophet or witness is vital in that it *guarantees* what is accomplished in the twofold movement of reconciliation. Christ is the "Guarantor" (p. 143) of what is accomplished in his work as priest and king.

28. Barth, *Church Dogmatics,* IV/3.1, p. 38.

29. Barth, *Church Dogmatics,* IV/3.1, pp. 38-39. Does not this close correspondence of reconciliation and revelation serve as the basis for Barth's rejection of that "dualism" that separates "word and act" (p. 47)? In Christ's life, "there is no place for the well-known dualism of word and act, for the nervous tension between theory and practice. There is no such thing as pure, undynamic or non-actual reason, logic or speech. Nor is there any such thing as irrational, a-logical, mute or mumbling dynamism or actuality" (p. 47). How could such a du-

cause he lives, ". . . He is His own authentic Witness." Moreover, he alone is responsible for creating knowledge of his life, "making it actual and therefore possible."[30] Not only does he actualize witness to revelation from within the sphere of the church, but also he actualizes witness from without given that he himself bears witness to his own life of paramount glory and power. At the close of his subsection on parables of the kingdom, Barth writes, "Reduced to the simplest formula, what we have said is that Jesus Christ was, is and will be the light of life, and because the light of life, of His own reconciling life, therefore and to that extent the one light incomparable in its majesty and authority."[31] Jesus Christ himself is the light of his own reconciling life, and therefore, the great prophetic light,[32] which shines throughout the world reconciled to God by him.

The merit of this position is twofold. First of all, as stated above, it guards against abstractions. One cannot discuss revelation and reconciliation apart from one another for both belong to the work of Christ, and the reconciling event of Christ is itself revelation, to which Christ as the Word bears witness. Second, by classifying reconciliation as revelation, Jesus Christ's reconciling life as light, Barth is able to offer a way in which the particular is *universally present throughout history* as the light of the world. How is this so?

Because Jesus Christ's life is itself light, his light is the light of life.

---

alism exist if the Word, the prophet, the "Guarantor" (*Church Dogmatics,* IV/3.1; see also *Church Dogmatics,* IV/1, p. 144), is the light of his own reconciling life, the prophet who bears witness to his work as priest (see also *Church Dogmatics,* IV/1) and king? See also Karl Barth, *Church Dogmatics,* IV/2, *The Doctrine of Reconciliation,* ed. G. W. Bromiley and T. F. Torrance (Edinburgh: T. & T. Clark, 1958); for a discussion of the threefold office of Christ as priest, king, and prophet, see *Church Dogmatics,* IV/1, pp. 142-44. Is it not in the light of the reality of Jesus Christ, the one who is "Reconciler, Saviour and Mediator" (*Church Dogmatics,* IV/3.1, p. 47), that Barth claims, ". . . as reconciliation takes place, it also declares itself" (p. 10)? Jesus Christ is λύτρον. And as such, he is also μαρτύριον (p. 11). "The one mediatorial man is or works or acts both as ransom and witness, both as Reconciler and Revealer, and as the latter as and because He is the former" (p. 11). In the light of Jesus' threefold office in which he is shown to be life *and* light, indeed, *the* light, the guarantor of this one reconciling life, Barth is able to reject that dualistic orientation that separates act and word.

30. Barth, *Church Dogmatics,* IV/3.1, p. 46.

31. Barth, *Church Dogmatics,* IV/3.1, p. 135.

32. See Barth's discussion of the relation of life and light as it bears on Jesus' role as prophet on page 48 of *Church Dogmatics,* IV/3.1.

Since Jesus' life itself is the light, this light is the light of the world, for it is no ordinary life he lives.[33] Jesus Christ *lives.*[34] He lives as man, but also as God. Thus, his life is not resigned to the historical past. It is both the eternal life of God, and temporal life of humanity. It is that life in which eternity is present to time, whereby the eternal Word takes time to himself in the incarnation, enfolding it in the pre-, supra-, and post-temporality of his eternity. As a result, Christ's life is present throughout history, illumining history with the light of his life. Without undermining the distinction between eternity and time, and the distinctions inherent in time itself, Jesus Christ's life history transcends those distinctions within history.

> His life is bordered neither by a No more nor a Not yet. His history did not take place to take place no more. It has not to take place as though it had not yet taken place. It takes place, yet not as one which is merely present at a single point, but in the power of a history which has already taken place and will do so again. This means, however, that the life of Jesus Christ is eternal life, which does not extinguish but integrates and to that extent overcomes the differences between what we call past, present and future. For even as human life, it shares the sovereignty of the life of the divine Subject over these distinctions. And the upshot is the same if we say also that it is the life of the grace which was and will be addressed to man as such, and which is addressed to him precisely as that which was and will be.[35]

As in eternity, so too in time in relation to eternity, the distinctions between past, present, and future are integrated in such a way that the life of God in Christ is an ever-present reality, present both to the whole of time and eternity as they meet in him. One is reminded here of Hunsinger's statement quoted in Chapter Three that "Eternity is conceived, in Barth's theology, as perichoretic not only in itself, but also in its reception of history."[36] The Word is present to all time. That is to say, there is no point in world history where the Word of reconciliation and

33. Compare this with Hunsinger's discussion on pages 235-42 of *How to Read Karl Barth.*

34. Barth, *Church Dogmatics,* IV/3.1, p. 39. On page 44, Barth writes, "'He lives' is very different from an abstract 'He has lived' or an equally abstract 'He will live.'"

35. Barth, *Church Dogmatics,* IV/3.1, pp. 44-45.

36. Hunsinger, *How to Read Karl Barth,* p. 241. See also note 94 on p. 110 above.

revelation is not present. He is present to all time, and all time is present to his time given the perichoretic union of time and eternity in the Word.[37] In this way, it can be argued that the Word is present to all words throughout human history.[38]

Not only does Barth extend the use of *perichoresis* to conceive the relation of time and eternity in distinct though inseparable terms, but also he employs this Christological and Trinitarian category in his discussion of the relation of God to the world and Christ to culture. They are bound up together. Brief consideration will here be given to this point. In Chapter Two, mention was made of Hunsinger's claim that categories of "coexis-

37. In addition to the perichoretic relation of time and eternity in and through the person of Jesus Christ set forth in *Church Dogmatics,* IV/3.1, pp. 44-45 quoted above, one finds another instance of the perichoretic engagement of time and eternity in Barth's discussion of the "eternal preservation" of the creature's temporal existence in *Church Dogmatics,* III/3. There he writes that the creature's time ever remains distinct from God's eternity. Thus, "eternal preservation does not mean a continuation of the existence of the creature." Karl Barth, *Church Dogmatics,* III/3, *The Doctrine of Creation,* ed. G. W. Bromiley and T. F. Torrance (Edinburgh: T. & T. Clark, 1960), p. 88. And yet, the creature ever exists before God. For God "will allow it to partake of His own eternal life" (p. 90). The creature will continue to be, not by continuing to exist, but because it partakes of God's eternity, even "in its limitation, even in its limited temporal duration" (p. 90). How can this be? Is it not because "God is the One who was, and is, and is to come," with whom "the past is future, and both past and future are present" (p. 89)? God in his pre-temporal, supra-temporal, and post-temporal eternity surrounds the life of the creature in its limited temporality, and in this way preserves it in its circumscribed temporality from the standpoint of his eternity. God's own eternal past, present, and future are distinct from one another, yet ever present to one another since they are the past, present, and future of the eternal God. In the same way, the creature's temporality is not confused with God's eternity. But God allows it to partake of his eternity by embracing and enfolding its circumscribed temporality in his eternity.

38. But how can Christ's history be "contemporaneous and luminous in relation to *all* other historical moments and *creatures*"? (The quotation is taken from Hunsinger, *How to Read Karl Barth,* p. 243; italics added.) How is it that Christ's history can be present to *all* persons throughout history without consideration of space? In Hunsinger's revised translation of the quotation taken from page 45 of *Church Dogmatics,* IV/3.1, it reads that Christ's life "will be addressed to *each and every* human being as such . . ." (Hunsinger, *How to Read Karl Barth,* p. 242; italics added). Is not the doctrine of the *Extra Calvinisticum,* applied to Barth's analysis of culture elsewhere, relevant here? For even though the human nature of Christ is not omnipresent, the divine person of the Word is present to all places and persons in time. When coupled with Barth's employment of *perichoresis* or coinherence for conceiving the relation of time and eternity in the person of Christ, the framework is in place whereby Barth can speak of the Word being present to all creatures (all occupants of space) throughout time.

tence" and "coinherence" or *perichoresis* play important roles in Barth's theology.[39] Barth employs and extends these Christological and Trinitarian

39. Hunsinger writes, "The doctrine of the perichoresis, as explicated in the doctrine of the Trinity, is the paradigm for the pattern of dialectical inclusion or coinherence" (*How to Read Karl Barth,* p. 241). In an article in which he compares Barth and Jürgen Moltmann on the subject of *perichoresis* with reference to the doctrine of the Trinity, Trevor Hart suggests that Barth employs the term in a weaker sense. In Barth's understanding of the Trinity, *perichoresis presupposes* the divine unity *in the same way* that the communication of attributes between the divine and human natures *presupposes* the union of the natures in the divine person of the Son. In the latter case, what is predicated of one nature can be predicated of the other *because of* their mutual inclusion in the hypostatic union. Trevor Hart, "Person and Prerogative in Perichoretic Perspective: An Ongoing Dispute in Trinitarian Ontology Observed," *Irish Theological Quarterly* 58, no. 1 (1992): 53-54. Moltmann, on the other hand, employs the stronger sense of the term *perichoresis* in his doctrine of the Trinity. For him, the divine unity of the three persons *presupposes perichoresis.* In Moltmann's model of the Trinity, *perichoresis* signifies "ontological interpenetration" (Hart, p. 54). Consideration will now be given to Barth's use of *perichoresis* or coinherence from the standpoint of Christological mediation. For Barth, the Word serves as the basis or backdrop for the perichoretic relation of various tandems such as time and eternity, God and the world, Christ and culture. The use of *perichoresis* still presupposes a view of the person centering relations between distinct entities. However, there is a sense here in which for Barth the entities in question actually *interpenetrate* one another *ontologically,* albeit dialectically in and through the mediation of the person of Christ. Does one not see evidence of this outlook in Barth's discussion in "Church and State" where he writes that (in view of Christ) the church must "assume a 'certain' political character" and "must recognize, and honour, a 'certain' ecclesiastical character in the State"? Karl Barth, "Church and State," in *Community, State, and Church: Three Essays,* with an introduction by Will Herberg (Gloucester, Mass.: Peter Smith, 1968), p. 134. Hunsinger also speaks of the "mutual, inner participation" of "all relations between God and the world" in and through the mediation of Christ. (See Hunsinger, *How to Read Karl Barth,* p. 238.) Moreover, there are instances to be noted in Barth's thought where Christ himself actually *indwells* the sacred and secular spheres, while ever remaining distinct from them. See *Church Dogmatics,* IV/3.1, p. 111, where Barth speaks of coinherence or "indwelling" in his discussion of witness to Christ. The truth of the Word of God dwells within the words of witness. "Es müsste ihnen somit eben die dem einen Worte Gottes eigene Wahrheit ihrerseits *innewohnen.*" Karl Barth, *Kirchliche Dogmatik,* IV/3.1, *Die Lehre von der Versöhnung* (Zürich: Evangelischer Verlag, 1959), p. 123, italics added. See also pages 253 and 261 of Hunsinger, *How to Read Karl Barth,* for his comments on this text. Lastly, does not the view of *ontological penetration* also hold true for Barth's mature view of the *communio naturarum* itself? The natures penetrate one another ontologically, albeit dialectically and asymmetrically from the divine to the human and then from the human to the divine in and through the person of Christ. There is a "mutual participation" of the divine and human essences, which "takes place in and by Him" (Barth, *Church Dogmatics,* IV/2, p. 70). And yet, such mutuality is not "interchangeable" (p. 71). The participation "takes place from above to below first, and only

concepts to speak of diverse patterns of relation, including those of time and eternity and God and the world, including Christ and culture. The union of the divine and human natures in the person of Jesus Christ serves as the basis of mediation for the "coexistence" and "coinherence" of these other pairs.[40] As Hunsinger writes, in Barth's thought God and the world both coexist and inhere in one another in and through the mediation of Christ.[41] Barth himself says of coexistence,

> As God exists only together with this One, and so too the world, His existence as such is the fact in which God and the world, however they may oppose or contradict one another, are not of course one and the same, but do exist together in an inviolable and indissoluble co-existence and conjunction.[42]

The divine stands in a distinct though inseparable, active relation to the creature, yet always from the standpoint of "absolutely sovereign spontaneity" to the "conditioned and limited spontaneity" of the creature.[43] Not only does Barth extend this and related categories of thought to the God-world relationship, but also he brings them to bear directly on the relation of Christ to culture itself, including the subject of witness *extra muros*

---

then from below to above" (p. 71). For Barth, "the determination" of Christ's "divine essence is *to* His human, and the determination of His human essence *from* His divine" (p. 70). In this way, Barth believes he moves beyond the historic debate between the Lutheran and Reformed. It should be noted that Barth nonetheless gives pride of place to the Reformed emphasis on the *unio hypostatica* over against the Lutheran emphasis on the *communio naturarum* (p. 66). However, he also sees validity in the Lutheran emphasis and wishes to give due regard to it, approaching it in the light of his starting point, namely, the *unio hypostatica* (p. 69).

40. Hunsinger, *How to Read Karl Barth*, p. 238. However, as has already been noted in Chapter Two, in *Church Dogmatics*, IV/2, Barth sharply differentiates the *unio personalis* from the *sustentatio generalis* (*Church Dogmatics*, IV/2, p. 53). He argues that the two cannot be compared or exchanged with one another. Now although it is true that the two are distinct, given that the Word is not hypostatically related to the world, is it not also true that for Barth the *unio personalis* is the basis for the *sustentatio generalis*? Is it not in and through the mediation of Christ Jesus that the entire world lives and moves and has its being in the God who sustains it?

41. Hunsinger, *How to Read Karl Barth*, pp. 237-38. See Barth, *Church Dogmatics*, IV/3.1, pp. 39-43. See also Karl Barth, *Church Dogmatics*, II/2, *The Doctrine of God*, ed. G. W. Bromiley and T. F. Torrance (Edinburgh: T. & T. Clark, 1957), pp. 177-81.

42. Barth, *Church Dogmatics*, IV/3.1, pp. 39-40.

43. Barth, *Church Dogmatics*, IV/3.1, p. 40.

ecclesiae. Thus, not only does God coexist with the creature, but also the truth of the divine Word can "dwell within" creaturely words, including those of secular culture,[44] not simply in the remote past either, but throughout the entire history of the world. Here one sees that the coexistence of God and the world and Christ and culture manifests itself as coinherence. Hunsinger goes so far as to say that "coinherence" is "the *mode* by which all things coexist in and with Jesus Christ."[45]

The Word who is present to all points in time, the mediator who mediates all things to God in his person, raises up witnesses to himself in his role as prophet, not only in Scripture and the church, but also in broader culture. There is one who reconciles all things to God. And although there is one great prophet, namely, he who also reconciles, the possibility exists that this Word will raise up other *words* from the world reconciled to God to bear witness to his life, and this by means of indwelling them.[46] Such words of witness need not be sacred words because the Word of life has reconciled *all* things to God, being present to the whole of history. His dominion knows no bounds.[47] The Word of God as Jesus Christ is the center of creaturely reality as the truth. But he is also present to the circumference of creaturely reality throughout history as the one who indwells words of witness whereby they manifest truth.[48] Christ is present to the whole of creation and human culture, serving as both the center and as the one who is able to indwell words on the periphery, causing them to bear witness to himself.[49]

There is hope for witness, hope, too, that there are God-fearers among the nations, those in the mold of Cornelius, Naaman, the Magi, and Sheba's queen,[50] and hope still that all others will someday bear witness with their

44. Barth, *Church Dogmatics,* IV/3.1, p. 111.

45. Hunsinger, *How to Read Karl Barth,* p. 238.

46. Hunsinger compares Calvin and Barth on the topic of secular witness and says that whereas Calvin places stress on the Spirit and the human mind, Barth stresses the prophetic activity of Jesus Christ and the human word (Hunsinger, *How to Read Karl Barth,* p. 234).

47. Barth, *Church Dogmatics,* IV/3.1, p. 116.

48. Barth, *Church Dogmatics,* IV/3.1, pp. 122-23.

49. Is it not the case that in addition to being the center and the one who indwells true words, words of witness on the periphery, the Word as Jesus Christ is also the whole of the periphery or circumference? Barth does indeed identify the center and the whole of the periphery as Jesus Christ (*Church Dogmatics,* IV/3.1, p. 123). In Chapters Five and Six, it shall be argued that for Barth Christ serves as the center, and also as the circumference of creaturely reality, that is, as the one in whom all things dwell.

50. See Barth's discussion of such figures in *Church Dogmatics,* IV/3.2, p. 488.

lives and words to the light of life. What is the basis of this hope? It is simply this. Christ "*is* the light of the world. And therefore to be man is always to stand already, even if with closed or blind eyes, in this light, the light of life."[51] He is the light of life, indeed the light of all life. That is to say, in the reconciliation accomplished in the history of Jesus Christ, God has altered the general human situation. To be sure, there is a difference between the Christian community and the world at large, between the particular situation in which Christians stand in relation to God, and this general one between God and the world.[52] However, the basis for both the particular and general situations is the same, namely, the reconciliation of the world accomplished in Christ Jesus.[53] Thus, it is fair to say that, "There are no clear boundaries between them."[54] For Jesus Christ is the light of life in whom all stand, knowingly or unknowingly, "called" or "to be called."[55] The basis for the hope of "biblical universalism," over against that counterfeit universalism,[56] or the "historical relativism"[57] of Nathan the Wise, is surely to be found in "the human situation as universally altered and redetermined by the act and Word of God, by the existence and work of Christ,"[58] whose

51. Barth, *Church Dogmatics,* IV/3.2, p. 487. In *Church Dogmatics,* IV/3.1, Barth speaks of the Word enfolding the sphere of the prophets and apostles (*Church Dogmatics,* IV/3.1, p. 116) and dwelling within true words, the words of witness (p. 111). Here in *Church Dogmatics,* IV/3.2, one finds that all humanity stands in the light of Christ. "He *is* the light of the world. And therefore to be man is always to stand already, even if with closed or blind eyes, in this light, the light of life" (*Church Dogmatics,* IV/3.2, p. 487). Is it not fair to say that for Barth not only is Christ *able* to dwell within creaturely words, causing them to bear witness, but also all humanity *actually* stands within him, albeit in a perichoretic manner? For Barth, words bear witness when Christ indwells them. But even outside the event of witness, Christ is present to humanity and human words in that humanity and its words dwell within him. Indications of the words of witness at the periphery dwelling in Christ himself can be found in *Church Dogmatics,* IV/3.1, pp. 122-23. On page 123, Barth identifies Jesus Christ not simply as the "centre," but also as "the whole of the periphery." See also Hunsinger's discussion of the relationship between center and periphery at this point on pages 260-61 of *How to Read Karl Barth.*

52. Barth, *Church Dogmatics,* IV/3.2, pp. 489-90.

53. Barth, *Church Dogmatics,* IV/3.2, pp. 489-90.

54. Barth, *Church Dogmatics,* IV/3.2, p. 487.

55. Barth, *Church Dogmatics,* IV/3.2, p. 490.

56. Here one has in mind the erroneous nullification of the distinction between the particular situation in which the church is placed and that "new determination of the general human situation," to which Barth refers on page 489 of *Church Dogmatics,* IV/3.2.

57. Barth, *Church Dogmatics,* IV/3.2, p. 488.

58. Barth, *Church Dogmatics,* IV/3.2, p. 490.

light shines even in the dark regions beyond the Christian sphere of witness to his light.

How is it though that the nominal and especially the secular serve as witnesses given the particularity of the Word? In the attempt to answer this question, one might offer the following explanation. Particularity does not imply prohibition. In fact, it is the particular reality of this Word that makes witness possible and actual, both in the church and outside it. Moreover, if it were not for *this* Word, the living and active Word, there would be no instances of witness whatsoever given the fact that there is no access to God apart from disclosure through his Word.

Now the particularity *and exclusivity* of the Word of Christ spell the rejection of competitors and companions. But the Word of Christ does not exclude all other words. It is not the only word that is true. But it is the basis of all true words, being itself the true Word. Thus, Barth wishes to affirm two things. First, the Word of Christ is the truth; and second, he is the basis for all true words about God and humanity.[59] How could it be otherwise when Christ creates, sustains, centers all things, and indwells words, causing them to bear witness to God in him?[60]

The question may still persist in the mind of the reader though as to the cogency of Barth's claim that there exist non-particular words of witness to the particular Word. One calls to mind here T. F. Torrance's comment on Barth's discussion of Jesus Christ as ascended in *Church Dogmatics,* IV/3, where Torrance writes, ". . . Christ seemed to be swallowed up in the transcendent Light and Spirit of God, so that the humanity of the risen Jesus appeared to be displaced by what he called 'the humanity of God' in his

59. Barth, *Church Dogmatics,* IV/3.1, p. 122. On page 8 of the same volume, Barth writes that the truth as Jesus Christ "is *the* truth, in which all truths, the truth of God particularly and the truth of man, are enclosed, not as truths in themselves, but as rays or facets of its truth." Not only are all truths *enclosed* in the truth of the Word, but also as Hunsinger points out, for Barth the "center and periphery . . . are regarded as two forms of single truth" (Hunsinger, *How to Read Karl Barth,* p. 261). In addition, center and periphery, whole and part, *entail* one another (Hunsinger, *How to Read Karl Barth,* p. 261; see also Barth, *Church Dogmatics,* IV/3.1, p. 122).

60. Hunsinger makes use of Tillich's categories of autonomy, heteronomy, and theonomy in his exposition of the light and lights. (See Hunsinger, *How to Read Karl Barth,* pp. 262-63.) Other lights do not exist *"alongside"* the light. Thus, "simple autonomy" is excluded (p. 262). Nor do they exist *"outside"* the light. Therefore, "simple heteronomy" is also excluded (pp. 262-63). Other lights only exist as lights by dwelling *within* the light (theonomy) (pp. 243, 262-63).

turning toward us."[61] In spite of Barth's concern to champion particularity over against abstraction as witnessed in his rejection of the *logos asarkos,* and in spite of his own denials, his discussion of secular witness may suggest to many that he himself is guilty of promoting "abstract impartations."[62]

In the last chapter, attention was drawn to Barth's criticism of Brunner for thinking "of the second Person of the Trinity as only *Logos.*"[63] Barth believes Brunner's regard for the "*Logos asarkos*" is the basis for the latter's natural theology. At the hands of Brunner, "the *Logos* becomes an abstract principle."[64] Now although the Logos for Barth is always concrete and particular, that is, *logos ensarkos,* and although witnesses to the Logos are always the result of particular events of divine commandeering, how is it that secular words of witness reflect the particularity of this *Logos?* How is it that they do not fall prey to the danger of abstraction? Barth responds by arguing that the "abstraction" of such words is "only apparent" since they point beyond themselves to the one Word of God, the "centre and totality."[65] "They do not express partial truths . . . ," for the one Word of God, Jesus Christ, "declares Himself in them."[66] Thus, through his indwelling presence, ". . . they express the one and total truth from a particular angle. . . ."[67] They may bear witness to the Word from the angle or standpoint of pointing to "the goodness of the original creation," or the "jeopardising" of the creation, "its liberation," or its future glory.[68] Even so,

61. T. F. Torrance, *Karl Barth, Biblical and Evangelical Theologian* (Edinburgh: T. & T. Clark, 1990), p. 134.

62. See Barth, *Church Dogmatics,* IV/3.1, p. 117.

63. John D. Godsey, ed., *Karl Barth's Table Talk,* Scottish Journal of Theology Occasional Papers (London: Oliver and Boyd, 1963), p. 49.

64. Barth, *Table Talk,* p. 49.

65. Barth, *Church Dogmatics,* IV/3.1, p. 123.

66. Barth, *Church Dogmatics,* IV/3.1, p. 123.

67. Barth, *Church Dogmatics,* IV/3.1, p. 123. One is reminded here of the divine perfections, each representing the one God in his entirety from a particular angle.

68. Barth, *Church Dogmatics,* IV/3.1, p. 123. Concerning witness to the Word from the standpoint of the "jeopardising" of the creation, one finds a potential parallel in the Hindu philosopher, Sarvepalli Radhakrishnan's statement that, "The everlasting vagrancy of thought, the contemporary muddle of conflicting philosophies, the rival ideologies which cut through national frontiers and geographical divisions, are a sign of spiritual homelessness. *The unrest is in a sense sacred,* for it is the confession of the failure of a self-sufficient humanism with no outlook beyond the world." Sarvepalli Radhakrishnan, "The Hindu View

even from such "particular" angles, they are witnesses of the truth because they bear witness to the one kingdom of God revealed in his Word.[69] Their witness is implicit, not explicit.[70] These words of true witness "indirectly point" to him, the Word, who "indirectly declares" himself in them.[71] Nonetheless, their witness faithfully reflects "the one light of the one truth" as a "particular refraction."[72] These words are words of witness, true words bearing witness to the Word who is the truth, their truthfulness being conditioned, "presupposed and implied" in view of their "connexion with the totality of Jesus Christ and his prophecy."[73]

The fundamental difference between Barth and Brunner here is twofold. It is because the Word *as* Jesus Christ indwells these words that they bear witness. Moreover, one only comes to know that such words bear witness to the Word by proceeding from the Word himself to these words (or from the Word as he manifests himself in the more direct forms of witness in Scripture and the church), rather than from these words to the Word. In view of the Word who causes them to bear witness, and through whom one knows *that* they bear witness, however indirectly, one knows they bear witness, not abstractly, but concretely from the standpoint of their "particular orientation."[74] *How* though does one actually discern which words in the secular community bear witness to the Word of Christ? How will one know which words in the secular sphere bear witness to the particular Word when such words do not explicitly reflect that particularity? For Barth, these words demonstrate their truthfulness by calling the church to the Word of Christ. Such witnesses are attested by Scripture and "will not lead us away from, but more deeply into, the *communio sanctorum* of all ages which is attested in these documents."[75]

Now even though Barth explains how secular words of truth demonstrate their truthfulness, he does not give examples of such acts of secular witness. His reasoning for this is that he does not wish to "make pro-

---

of Life," in *The Ways of Religion: An Introduction to the Major Traditions*, ed. Roger Eastman, 3rd ed. (New York: Oxford University Press, 1999), pp. 21-22 (italics added).

69. Barth, *Church Dogmatics*, IV/3.1, p. 123.

70. Barth, *Church Dogmatics*, IV/3.1, p. 123.

71. Barth, *Church Dogmatics*, IV/3.1, p. 123.

72. Barth, *Church Dogmatics*, IV/3.1, p. 123.

73. Barth, *Church Dogmatics*, IV/3.1, p. 123.

74. Barth, *Church Dogmatics*, IV/3.1, p. 123.

75. Barth, *Church Dogmatics*, IV/3.1, pp. 126-27.

nouncements on matters on which" Jesus Christ "has already spoken or will perhaps do so."[76] He simply wishes to point out that Christ is able to raise up words of witness "even *extra muros ecclesiae*."[77] Having said this, elsewhere Barth points to Mozart as one such parable of witness.[78] In its own particular way, the music of one such as Mozart may in the light of the Word bear witness to him in all his particularity and glory as through a parabolic veil, calling the church "more deeply into . . . the *communio sanctorum*" of the ages.[79]

Now *what* transpires when human words of stone are enabled to praise the divine Word? If words in and of themselves are not able to bear witness to the Word, if they do not bear capacities for the divine, as Barth claims, God must *commandeer* them, creating an *analogia gratiae* between the divine Word and human words. What happens then to the words themselves in the event of the divine commandeering of language?

On Barth's view, in the divine commandeering of language in the event of witness to the Word, does God *eradicate* secular words? Does grace *destroy* nature? Given Barth's repudiation of the *analogia entis,* one might assume that Barth advocates such a stance. However, it would be a misrepresentation of his position. For Barth does not believe grace destroys nature. The divine commandeering of words does not involve the destruction of their secularity. Now if the divine commandeering of language does not destroy secular words, does it lead to the transformation of words? Does grace perfect nature? *(gratia non tollit sed perficit naturam)*. No, on Barth's view, grace does not transform or perfect nature whereby words undergo metamorphosis or transubstantiation. Instead, grace *elevates* nature. God *elevates* words, giving to them new functions, capacities or uses, without

76. Barth, *Church Dogmatics,* IV/3.1, p. 135.

77. Barth, *Church Dogmatics,* IV/3.1, p. 135.

78. Karl Barth, "Mozart's Freedom," in *Wolfgang Amadeus Mozart* (Grand Rapids: Eerdmans, 1986), pp. 56-57. See also Robert J. Palma, *Karl Barth's Theology of Culture: The Freedom of Culture for the Praise of God,* Pittsburgh Theological Monographs, ed. Dikran Y. Hadidian (Allison Park: Pickwick Publications, 1983), p. 80.

79. In Chapter Six, consideration will be given to Mozart. In this chapter, attention has focused on words, both sacred and secular, bearing witness to the Word. There analysis will center on secular witnesses bearing witness to God's glory *because* they are secular. Whereas in this chapter (and Chapter Three), discussion has concentrated on the fact that in Barth's thought, space is *made* for oneness in otherness between the sacred and secular spheres in and through the Word as Jesus Christ, Chapter Six (as well as Five) will concentrate on space being *given* for secular otherness in view of the one Word of God as Jesus Christ.

thereby transforming the words themselves in the process. In this vein, Barth writes,

> Assuming that it does this, this implies for the human words which are claimed that, without losing their secular character or undergoing any inner transformation, without any question of transfiguration or transubstantiation, they acquire a function and capability as thus exercised which they did not have in themselves as elements of general human speech, but which they may now receive and have as they are claimed by the omnipotent Word of God.[80]

Barth goes on to draw a comparison between this view of witness and the Reformed understanding of what occurs in the celebration of the Lord's Supper.

> *Ceteris imparibus,* we are reminded of the eating and drinking of bread and wine, which do not have in themselves, but which, without ceasing to be what they are, acquire and have in the Lord's Supper, the function and capability of indicating and confirming the fellowship of the community with its Lord, its participation in His body and blood and its attachment to His person. Thus, even though these human words do not cease to be elements of general human speech which may be used and understood or misunderstood by all, nevertheless, not by the men who speak them but by the omnipotent God who calls these men to the service of His Word and uses their secular words, they are given the power to bear testimony to His Word. Pronounced by these men in the service of His Word, they do not merely say what they might say in their secular sense; beyond this they speak of God and His will and work revealed in His Word, calling Him to mind, pointing to Him, drawing attention to Him, mediating His promise and claim. For why should it be impossible for God as the Lord of His creation and especially of His people to do this, to dispose of human speech in this sense?[81]

According to the Reformed model of the Eucharist, Christ is present spiritually or virtually *(praesentia spiritualis sive virtualis)*. The Lord is truly present to the elements, but not physically present as in transubstantiation, con-

80. Barth, *Church Dogmatics*, IV/3.2, p. 737.
81. Barth, *Church Dogmatics*, IV/3.2, p. 737.

substantiation, and the Lutheran doctrine of real presence following as it does on the heels of the doctrine of the ubiquity of Christ. According to the Reformed position, Christ is spiritually present in the Lord's Supper to the persons of faith through an act of the Spirit. In the event of communion, the community is lifted up to the throne of God for communion with Christ: *sursum corda*. Thus, the bread and wine remain completely intact, both externally and internally. Now just as Christ's body and blood are communicated to the elements in the Lord's Supper through faith by the Spirit, so too an analogy between the divine and human is created through the divine commandeering of human flesh and language. The elements of the Lord's Supper are not transformed into the body and blood of Christ. Nor are words divinized through the creation of the *analogia gratiae*. Just as hearts are lifted up *(sursum corda)* to partake in the Supper without the properties of the elements undergoing change, so too human words are elevated to bear witness to the Word in the event of the divine commandeering of language by the Word without undergoing transformation.

Through the divine act of grace, God's Word stands in, with, and *over* the word of culture, not parallel to it, not becoming one with it nor descending to it, but following the Reformed model, elevating culture's word to participate in the life of the Word. The word of culture becomes the Word of God in a virtual sense, in effect, though not in a formal manner, reflecting the notion of the spiritual and virtual presence of God in the sacrament *(praesentia spiritualis sive virtualis)*. Christ is "in, with and over"[82] the activity of the creature, elevating the creature to bear witness without changing it in any way. When God's Word becomes present to culture's word, it is not a matter of God's Word becoming culture's word or of culture's word becoming God's Word, except in a virtual sense. The word of culture can never be viewed as becoming *the* Word of God. It does not ascend to the Word whereby it is perfected and transformed into *the* Word. In the event of the divine commandeering, God does not perfect or transform the internal properties of words and their meanings, but rather, gives them *new* meaning, *elevating* them to bear witness to the Word while preserving them in their creaturely integrity.[83]

82. See Barth, *Church Dogmatics*, III/3, pp. 132, 135-37, where Barth discusses the relation of God's activity to that of the creature in terms of "in, with and over."

83. Hunsinger also speaks of the *elevating* of the word of the creature in the event of witness on page 254 of *How to Read Karl Barth*.

In view of the Word, a semantic shift takes place when human words are commandeered for divine service. Words acquire a new "function and capability"[84] through the event of the divine commandeering of language. Human forms, including words, are not the innate bearers of the divine Word; and yet, they are not incapable of being the bearers of the divine Word. Such instruments are "neutral" in this respect. Words in and of themselves are neither religious nor secular. They do not *possess* meaning, secular or otherwise. Instead meaning comes to be *associated* with words *through use.*[85] Words are flexible instruments, which serve the ends of those who use them. Thus, words can be appropriated from a variety of contexts to bear witness to Christ. However, the key is not the human forms themselves, however flexible they may be, but the God who in his grace enables creaturely forms both to bear the divine and to bear witness to the divine. This holds true not only for the human form in which the Word of God was incarnate, but also for human words themselves. As McCormack argues, "The ability of God to take up a creaturely medium like human language and bear witness to Himself in and through it is demonstrated prin-

84. Barth, *Church Dogmatics,* IV/3.2, p. 737.

85. Thus, meaning is dependent on usage rather than on supposed inherent relations between words and things; for words do not have or possess meaning, standing for or naming particular objects. If then, one wishes to know the meaning of a word, one needs to observe how it is used in a particular "language game," as Wittgenstein argues. Ludwig Wittgenstein, *Philosophical Investigations* (New York: Macmillan, 1958), p. 24. See also his related critique of Augustine's view of language on pages 2-4. Fergus Kerr notes that Wittgenstein claims to have read one of Barth's works, which Kerr believes to be *Church Dogmatics,* I/1. Fergus Kerr, *Theology After Wittgenstein,* 2nd ed. (London: SPCK, 1997), p. 152. See also Alan Torrance's analysis of Barth and Wittgenstein in *Persons in Communion,* especially pages 29, 98, and 177. Consider, too, Torrance's observation on the relevance of *anhypostasia* and *enhypostasia* for the discussion of theological reference set forth in that context (p. 177). On a different note, the flexibility of words signifies that words can be made the instruments of new disclosures. Perhaps inherent in that model of language in which words *possess* meaning is the belief that words have a limited number of predetermined connotations. Thus, words according to such a model must always carry with them their prior associations of meaning for sense to be made. However, the model of language "as use" fosters the idea that words can be used for new disclosures. Thus, similar to their usage in science, words, when used for describing God, may be stretched and groomed, sometimes even shattered, to portray the reality envisaged in startling new ways. For a discussion of metaphor serving as an instrument of new disclosure, see Janet Martin Soskice, *Metaphor and Religious Language* (Oxford: Clarendon Press, 1985; reprint, New York: Clarendon Press, 1989).

cipally in the fact that He has taken up a human nature and lived a human life in and through it."[86]

Words do not *possess* meaning. Nor are they innate bearers of revelation. Rather, words are particularized through use as the divine Word commandeers them for his service in a way similar to the Word of God particularizing an anhypostatic human nature in the incarnation. The Word takes to himself *(enhypostasis)* a concrete, non-individuated human nature, filling it with divine content in order to consummate the reconciliation of the world, while at the same time preserving intact the integrity of the secular form. The human nature is particularized; but it is not divinized. For it stands in dialectical relation to the divine nature through the divine person of the Word, ever dependent upon the divine Word for its secular form to be of service. So too, the eternal Word whose human history is present to the whole of history commandeers human words, particularizing and indwelling them, elevating them to bear witness without divinizing them, preserving intact the integrity of the divine and human in the dialectical activity of the divine commandeering of language.

God elevates words in their secular form, preserving them intact. But *how important or significant* is the identity of the secular form in the witnessing event? The answer to this question can be found by analyzing Barth's understanding of the reality of Jesus Christ: for Barth the commandeering of words in the event of witness runs parallel to his notion of the commandeering of flesh in the incarnation of the Word. In each case, one is speaking of the manifestation of divine content through the veil of secular form.

On the subject of the *communicatio operationum* in the hypostatic union, Barth writes, "It is where the divine rules and reveals and gives that the human serves and attests and mediates."[87] Both the divine and the human are active participants in the event of revelation and reconciliation, albeit in *different* ways. The divine and human natures perform *different functions* in the *one event*. As the divine nature reveals, the human attests. These functions occur simultaneously. In the light of Barth's claim that the human "attests" the divine, Charles Waldrop remarks that Barth

86. McCormack, *Karl Barth's Critically Realistic Dialectical Theology*, p. 367.

87. Barth, *Church Dogmatics*, IV/2, p. 116. The German reads, "Genau da, wo das Göttliche herrscht, offenbart, schenkt, genau da dient, bezeugt, vermittelt das Menschliche." Karl Barth, *Kirchliche Dogmatik*, IV/2, *Die Lehre von der Versöhnung* (Zürich: Evangelischer Verlag, 1955), p. 129.

awards a certain "degree of independence to the human nature," contributing "to the hypothesis that he is an Antiochian thinker."[88] However, Waldrop concludes that ultimately Barth does not award enough indepen-

88. Charles T. Waldrop, *Karl Barth's Christology: Its Basic Alexandrian Character,* Religion and Reason: Method and Theory in the Study and Interpretation of Religion, ed. Jacques Waardenburg, no. 21 (Berlin: Mouton Publishers, 1984), p. 172. Waldrop points to Henri Bouillard's claim that Barth's Christology is Nestorian on account of the particular emphasis he gives to the separation of the divine and human natures (pp. 202-3, n. 6). See Henri Bouillard, *Karl Barth: Parole de Dieu et Existence Humaine,* vol. 2 (Aubier: Editions Montaigne, 1957), p. 122. Waldrop also refers the reader to Regin Prenter's study of Barth, which Waldrop claims is likely the most thorough argument defending the assertion that Barth is Nestorian (Waldrop, *Karl Barth's Christology,* p. 203, n. 6). See Regin Prenter, "Karl Barths Umbildung der traditionellen Zweinaturlehre in lutherischer Beleuchtung," *Studia Theologica* 11, no. 1 (1957): 1-88. Now a case can be made for conceiving Barth's entire theology as a sustained effort to uphold the Christological implications of the *atreptos kai asynchytos* of Chalcedon in Christology proper and by extension the distinction between God and the world in opposition to the modern drive toward deification. (See Barth's discussion of Hegel, Feuerbach, and the Lutheran doctrine of the *communio naturarum* in *Church Dogmatics,* IV/2, p. 83.) Along these lines, Waldrop notes Barth's adherence to the Reformed tradition's emphasis on the distinction in the union of the divine and human natures (Waldrop, *Karl Barth's Christology,* p. 172). At this point, one recalls McCormack's statement that Barth further radicalized the Reformed position on the union of the natures by "actualizing the hypostatic union." The divine Logos "continually wills to assume the human nature" (McCormack, *Karl Barth's Critically Realistic Dialectical Theology,* p. 365). In *Church Dogmatics,* IV/2, Barth says that in its debate with the Lutherans the Reformed "naturally came under the suspicion of a Nestorian tendency" (Barth, *Church Dogmatics,* IV/2, p. 68). Given Barth's radicalization of the Reformed position, some may be led to view him with even more suspicion regarding the problem of Nestorianism. However, as discussed briefly in footnote 39 of this chapter, it is important to note how Barth moves *beyond* the historic debate between the Reformed and their Lutheran counterparts on the subject of the *unio personalis.* For Barth conceives a "mutual participation" of the natures in the person of Christ (*Church Dogmatics,* IV/2, p. 70), which takes place in an asymmetrical manner in which "the determination" of Christ's "divine essence is *to* His human, and the determination of His human essence *from* His divine" (p. 70). Over against the attempt to characterize Barth's Christology as either Alexandrian or Antiochene, Hunsinger argues that one must take into consideration Barth's "dialectical strategy of juxtaposition," following the model set forth in the New Testament. George Hunsinger, "Karl Barth's Christology: Its Basic Chalcedonian Character," in *Disruptive Grace: Studies in the Theology of Karl Barth* (Grand Rapids: Eerdmans, 2000), pp. 136-37. Hunsinger claims that "Barth is probably the first theologian in the history of Christian doctrine who alternates back and forth, deliberately, between an 'Alexandrian' and an 'Antiochian' idiom" (p. 135). Analysis of Barth's Christology always falters when one focuses on one side of the dialectic to the exclusion of the other (p. 137).

dence to Christ's humanity.[89] He writes, "In the final analysis, the degree of independence which the human nature has is extremely slight. It serves and attests God because God determines it to be that which serves and attests him."[90]

On the whole, Waldrop classifies Barth as a representative of the Alexandrian tradition,[91] and claims that Barth is weakest where he is strongest,

89. Waldrop, *Karl Barth's Christology,* p. 174. In this vein, Waldrop criticizes Barth saying, ". . . it is difficult to see how this human nature can fail to obey and serve God" (p. 174). Waldrop's analysis is flawed at this point. To contextualize John Webster's response to Nigel Biggar's criticism of grace and moral freedom in Barth's theology to the present discussion, it appears that "lurking within" such a criticism is a view of human freedom involving "spiritual neutrality," according to which humans stand "in relative isolation from the formative activity of God." John Webster, *Barth's Ethics of Reconciliation* (Cambridge: Cambridge University Press, 1995), pp. 226-27. It seems that Waldrop fails to conceive moral freedom as "situated freedom," a phrase Webster employs in this context (Webster, p. 227). Webster refers the reader to Charles Taylor's works, *Hegel and Modern Society* (Cambridge: Cambridge University Press, 1979), pp. 135-69, and *Hegel* (Cambridge: Cambridge University Press, 1975), pp. 537-71, for the term and its use in the modern discussion on self and morality. (See Webster, *Barth's Ethics of Reconciliation,* p. 227, n. 36.) As Webster makes clear, Barth is neither an advocate of "abstract divine monergism" nor an apologist of modernity's rejection of the former by way of autonomous moral agency (p. 57; see also pp. 6, 17-18). In place of creaturely passivity and autonomous, isolated human activity, Barth conceives moral agency as corresponding to the divine summons. Free, authentic, human action does not occur in a moral vacuum, but rather, within the framework of covenantal participation, which involves a positive response to God's gracious calling. (See pp. 54-58.) Properly conceived, dogmatics centers on God's gracious being in action directed toward humanity. And for its part, ethics arises from dogmatics as the study of humanity's active "conformity" to that divine activity. (See pp. 4, 57.) God in his Word initiates an active encounter between God and the human counterpart, situating that encounter in the context of the covenant, and graciously eliciting from humanity a response of authentic moral agency in the form of free and active "correspondence." (See pp. 8, 54-58.)

90. Waldrop, *Karl Barth's Christology,* p. 174.

91. Waldrop, *Karl Barth's Christology,* p. 172. Waldrop draws attention to Wolfhart Pannenberg's claim that Barth is the leading proponent of Alexandrian Christology in modern Protestant theology (Waldrop, p. 202). Pannenberg writes, "The Christological procedure 'from above to below' is followed in modern Protestant dogmatics by Karl Barth especially." Wolfhart Pannenberg, *Jesus — God and Man,* 2nd ed., trans. Lewis L. Wilkins and Duane A. Priebe (Philadelphia: Westminster Press, 1977), p. 33. Waldrop also refers to John Thompson's study of Barth's Christology, which claims that although Barth's theology starts *from above,* there is a return movement from the humanity of Christ to God, which has God as its cause and which is one with the divine descent. See Waldrop, *Karl Barth's Christology,* p. 202, and also John Thompson, *Christ in Perspective: Christological Perspectives in the Theology of Karl Barth* (Grand Rapids: Eerdmans, 1978), p. 17.

voicing the suspicion that Barth's "emphasis" on "the divinity of Christ" fails to do "sufficient justice to his humanity."[92] He points to Barth's conception of the human nature's role in revelation, saying, "Although he states that Jesus Christ has limited knowledge and can be anxious, these features of Jesus play no significant role in Christ's revealing activity."[93] According to Waldrop, Barth fails to give sufficient consideration to

> Jesus' growing awareness of God in his life or to the fact that his beliefs and ideas about God may have changed over time. Jesus' faith is treated as a constant. . . . The actual form of the service of Jesus' human nature is not related specifically to the ideas, teachings, feelings or actions of Jesus as a man.[94]

Although Barth "insists upon the affirmation that the eternal Son became man, it is not clear to what extent Barth can say that Jesus Christ is an ordinary man as other men are."[95]

In view of Waldrop's contention, it is important to consider what Barth

92. Waldrop, *Karl Barth's Christology*, p. 172. Megas Pharantos argues that Barth's idea of *enhypostasis* is correct, though not his use of it. Pharantos writes that Barth understands the union in a Protestant manner, underestimating the active participation of the human nature in its unity with the divine Logos. He adds that the sixth ecumenical council did not underestimate the human will, nature, and operation, unlike the Monophysites. Megas Pharantos, *Christologia 1. To Enhypostaton* (Athens: n.p., 1972), pp. 10-18. Now mention has been made of various opinions regarding Barth's relation to Alexandrian and Antiochene theology. In this context, it is interesting to note that the extreme forms of these traditions, Eutycheanism and Nestorianism, for all their differences, may not be so far apart. To illustrate, in his debate with Maximus, Pyrrhus raises the question, "How? Was not the flesh moved by the decision of the Word Who is united with it?" See Maximus the Confessor, *The Disputation with Pyrrhus*, trans. Joseph P. Farrell (South Canaan: St. Tikhon's Seminary Press, 1990), p. 16. The English editor of the translation writes, "The idea of 'flesh' being moved by the Word is Apollinarian both in language and content" (p. 16). In fact, the sixth ecumenical council condemned Pyrrhus (after death) for Apollinarianism. In contrast to the preceding, Maximus's reply to Pyrrhus indicates that Maximus believes Pyrrhus entertains Nestorian ideas. Maximus responds, "Thou dividest Christ by talking like this!" (p. 16). Maximus's reply to the "Apollinarian" Pyrrhus intimates that for all their apparent differences, Nestorianism and Apollinarianism (in the discussion here, Eutycheanism) are closely related. For the points made about the texts considered in this footnote, the author is indebted to discussions with Dr. Demetrios Bathrellos.

93. Waldrop, *Karl Barth's Christology*, p. 174.

94. Waldrop, *Karl Barth's Christology*, p. 175.

95. Waldrop, *Karl Barth's Christology*, p. 172.

has to say about revelation as it bears upon the subject of the human nature of Christ. In the *Göttingen Dogmatics,* Barth argues, "The content of revelation as well as the subject is God alone."[96] God alone is the revealer and the content, the revelation itself.[97] Bound up with this twofold declaration is Barth's adherence to the doctrines of *anhypostasis* and *enhypostasis.*[98] Only by coming to terms with the fact that "the person of the God-man is exclusively the Word, the Logos of God"[99] can one guard against the zealous preoccupation with

> the man Jesus of Nazareth, . . . the hero, the religious personality, his inner life so far as we may know it, his view of God and the world and life, the "fairest Lord Jesus," . . . revelation being now found in the teaching, loving, and suffering Jesus — the accents might vary — but at any rate in the living Jesus, not in the crucified and risen Jesus, as in Paul and the Reformers.[100]

Confronted with the obsession with the historical Jesus that arose in the modern period, the "proponents" of which include Schleiermacher and Zinzendorf,[101] Barth emphasizes instead the divine subject, seeking to guard against the "confusion of above and below, a deifying of the creature."[102] Faced with the "ardent worship" of the Jesus of history, of the man Jesus, Barth argues that one must "be less christocentric and therefore . . . more objective . . . giving God the significance that is his due." God, not "the historical fact of Jesus of Nazareth, . . . *alone* is the content of revelation."[103] As McCormack argues, Barth is here "rejecting any confusion of revelation with the medium in which it veils itself."[104]

96. Barth, *Göttingen Dogmatics,* p. 90.

97. Barth, *Göttingen Dogmatics,* p. 89.

98. See McCormack's discussion on p. 352 of *Karl Barth's Critically Realistic Dialectical Theology* for his exposition of pages 89-90 of Barth's work, *The Göttingen Dogmatics.*

99. Barth, *Göttingen Dogmatics,* p. 90.

100. Barth, *Göttingen Dogmatics,* p. 90.

101. Barth, *Göttingen Dogmatics,* p. 90. However, later Barth gives high praise to Zinzendorf and his Christocentrism (albeit with qualifications), considering him an ally. See Eberhard Busch, *Karl Barth: His Life from Letters and Autobiographical Texts* (London: SCM Press, 1976), pp. 446-47.

102. Barth, *Göttingen Dogmatics,* p. 91.

103. Barth, *Göttingen Dogmatics,* p. 91.

104. McCormack, *Karl Barth's Critically Realistic Dialectical Theology,* p. 352.

Now Barth's rejection of the idea that the human nature or form belongs to the content of divine revelation is consistent with his position generally on the relation of the divine and human: the finite is incapable of the infinite.[105] In one place, Barth goes so far as to say that the human form "contradicts" the revelation of God ("Ihre Gestalt ist ihr gerade nicht entsprechend, sondern widersprechend").[106] Yet there is a sense in which the human reveals God, namely, as the form in which the revelation is concealed. The form is itself revelation ("obwohl und indem sie ihre Gestalt ist!").[107] In speaking of this paradoxical state, Waldrop says that, "While the one Jesus Christ reveals through both natures, he reveals in spite of his human nature."[108] This assessment of Barth's position appears extreme. A more adequate accounting would suggest that Barth wishes to stress two things. First, the form is "not the content" of revelation. But second, the content is inseparable from the form. For "except in this form there is no revelation."[109]

One sympathizes with Barth's concern to preserve the inseparability of the divine person of the Word and his humanity, that is, his rejection of the quest for the historical Jesus apart from the resurrected Christ,[110] thereby guarding against abstraction. For if it is indeed the case that the humanity has no existence independent of the divine person *(anhypostasis),* that humanity abstracted from the divine person is illusory, non-existent.[111] There

105. Barth, *Göttingen Dogmatics,* p. 90.

106. Barth, *Church Dogmatics,* IV/1, p. 178; Karl Barth, *Kirchliche Dogmatik,* IV/1, *Die Lehre von der Versöhnung* (Zürich: Evangelischer Verlag, 1953), p. 195.

107. Barth, *Church Dogmatics,* IV/1, p. 178; Karl Barth, *Kirchliche Dogmatik,* IV/1, p. 195.

108. Waldrop, *Karl Barth's Christology,* p. 174.

109. Barth, *Göttingen Dogmatics,* p. 89.

110. See Busch, *Karl Barth: His Life,* p. 448. In *Church Dogmatics,* IV/2, Barth speaks of those biographers of Jesus who fail to account for the humanity of Jesus Christ because they abstract his humanity from its subject, namely, the divine Son (*Church Dogmatics,* IV/2, p. 102). Barth writes, "It is no accident that the New Testament material for" constructing a biography of Christ's "life and character . . . is so sparse and unsatisfactory" (p. 102). For Barth, "As God cannot be considered without His humanity, His humanity cannot be considered or known or magnified or worshipped without God" (p. 102). The biographer of Jesus always misses "the decisive thing — the vertical movement in which Jesus Christ is actual, the history in which" God becomes human (p. 102).

111. That is not to say that the human nature of Christ lacks personality. For to reiterate a point made in Chapter Two, the Latin term *impersonalitas,* sometimes used for *anhypostasis,* means that Christ's humanity has no existence independent of his divine person, not that his human nature lacks a personality. Karl Barth, *Church Dogmatics,* I/2, *The Doctrine of the Word*

is also much to be said for the dialectical emphasis found in Barth's doctrine of revelation according to which God is wholly revealed in hiddenness and wholly hidden in revelation, guarding against any hint of humanity's deification. And yet, although Barth safeguards against the confusion of the divine and human, does not his emphasis on the former lead to some extent to the neglect of the latter? Although the human is not overwhelmed, is it not *overshadowed?* And what does the significance or lack of it given to human flesh in the event of the divine commandeering imply for the divine commandeering of human language? How important is the form employed in the witnessing event?

If the form contradicts revelation, in what sense then is the form revelation? Does not the humanity of Jesus Christ itself serve as content of revelation? Does not the form *reveal* that God is ever the God of humanity? And given the intimate relation of the immanent and economic Trinities (as Barth himself propounds), namely, that the second person of the Trinity is ever conceived as the *logos ensarkos,* must not the humanity of Christ on this account reveal something of God? God is ever the God *of man,* this man, and therefore, all humanity in him. Thus, even in its otherness from the divine nature, the humanity of Jesus Christ reveals something about God. Revelation does not simply have God as its content. Humanity is included. The incarnation does not simply reveal divine content; it *reveals human* content as well. The divine content of revelation does not simply stand in a distinct though inseparable relation to the human *form;* it also stands in a distinct though inseparable relation to the human *content* of revelation as disclosed through that form.

The humanity of Christ reveals God, albeit indirectly though, and not in itself as such, but because of God, indicating that God is the God *of humanity,* telling the recipients of revelation something about God that they would not otherwise know. God is never God apart from humanity, ever choosing to be the God of humanity. Revelation also tells its recipients that

of God, ed. G. W. Bromiley and T. F. Torrance (Edinburgh: T. & T. Clark, 1956), p. 164. In this way, Barth and other defenders of *anhypostasis* and *enhypostasis* are able to ward off the charge that Christ's humanity is unlike the rest of humanity. Barth's doctrine of Christ is indeed incarnational. Does Barth not suggest that if during the modern period greater consideration had been given to the content of the doctrine of the *anhypostasis,* coming to terms with its meaning, instead of theologians having gotten "worked up about it," Christology would have been spared consideration of the humanity of Christ in abstraction from the eternal Word? (See Barth, *The Göttingen Dogmatics,* p. 90.)

humanity is ever the humanity *of God,* indeed *this* God, God in Jesus Christ, thereby telling them something about humanity that they would not otherwise know. Humanity is not humanity apart from God in Christ. Thus, God and man reveal God and man. For the humanity of God reveals God as the God of humanity and humanity as the humanity of God. The humanity of God does not reveal God's deity as such, but only God in relation to humanity, a human nature steeped in creaturely features, including a human personality. Is it not in light of God becoming human, in light of the humanity of God, that it is revealed to people that God's being is in becoming other than who God is, with all that it implies for the constancy of divine being? And does not the humanity of Christ, the humanity of the eternal Word, reveal to people what it means to be truly human, to develop and grow in faith in God and to think, act, and feel in a holistic manner, pleasing to God?

The preceding remarks should not be taken to mean the complete rejection of Barth's dialectical understanding of revelation according to which the human conceals the divine and is wholly distinct from it. What is rejected here is Barth's claim that the human form is simply the vessel or medium of revelation and not revelatory content, too.[112] God does not simply reveal God. God and God's humanity reveal God and that humanity, yet always in such a way that the relation between God and God's humanity is asymmetrical (from above) as well as dialectical (indirect).

One needs to make clear at this point that, in suggesting that the humanity of Christ itself is to be deemed content *of revelation,* one is not claiming that the human nature or secular form possesses a capacity for

112. For Barth, God reveals God by God alone. See, for example, Karl Barth, *Church Dogmatics,* I/1, *The Doctrine of the Word of God,* ed. G. W. Bromiley and T. F. Torrance (Edinburgh: T. & T. Clark, 1975), pp. 295-304. That is to say, God alone is the subject, content, and means by which revelation occurs. God alone is "Revealer, Revelation, and Revealedness" (p. 295). Although objection has been made to Barth's claim that the content of revelation is God alone (and not also God's humanity), Waldrop's assertion that Barth's claim that the bearer of the human nature of Christ is divine, not human, giving to Barth's Christology "an Apollinarian appearance" (Waldrop, *Karl Barth's Christology,* p. 173), is also to be rejected. For if the doctrine of *enhypostasis,* as Barth understands it, is correct, how could the bearer of the human nature be human? If the bearer were human, would it not result in the division of Christ into two persons, one divine, and the other human? Although Christ has a fully human personality (Barth, *Church Dogmatics,* I/2, p. 164), the bearer of that human personality is the divine person of the Word. The human nature does have a personal center, not in itself as such, but in the divine person in whom it exists.

revelation. Rather, the revelatory content of the form is totally the work of the grace of God. There is nothing special about the secular form as such. It has no sacred property, which somehow makes it a native bearer of revelation. Thus, one cannot deduce the divine-human content of revelation from the human form. One can only conceive such divine-human content *a posteriori,* that is, in light of God becoming human. To be sure, there is nothing special, that is, revelatory, about the human nature of Jesus Christ, or of humanity generally, for that matter, apart from the divine commandeering. But that does not necessitate the conclusion that the content of revelation is exclusively divine, whereby the secular human form is simply the medium of divine revelation, which, in the end, spells the overshadowing of the human in view of the divine. In Barth's theology, the humanity of the Word, and by extension creaturely words of witness, are overshadowed to some extent given the lack of emphasis on the identity of the secular form in the event of revelation.

Now one must say "overshadowed" and not "overwhelmed" given Barth's doctrine of the inseparability of form and content. Barth refuses to give consideration to the doctrine of the *Logos* apart from *ensarkos,* for again, the form is inseparable from the content. The same can be said of witness. For God bears witness to God solely through creaturely mediums such as words. Regarding the incarnation, Barth highlights the fact that the Word became flesh, entering a particular time and a particular space as Jesus of Nazareth. The Word in Barth's theology is not amorphous, but incarnate. Indeed, ". . . in virtue of the eternal Word . . . Jesus Christ exists as a man of flesh and blood in our sphere, as a man like us, as an historical phenomenon."[113]

Now, as incarnate, the Word is not generic humanity, but Jewish flesh. Thus, the Word is not simply incarnate. The Word is also enculturated. Here again one sees that the divine content does not overwhelm the humanity of the Word, for Barth places great emphasis on Jesus' Jewish identity. For Barth, one cannot retain Jesus Christ if one severs his Jewish identity from him. For "Jesus Christ would not be what He is, were He not the Christ, the Commissioner who comes out of *Israel,* who is the *Jew* Jesus."[114] Christ's Jewish identity is the "starting-point" for understanding

113. Barth, *Church Dogmatics,* I/2, p. 165.

114. Karl Barth, *Dogmatics in Outline,* trans. G. T. Thomson (London: SCM Press, 1949; reprint, SCM Press, 1958), p. 72.

who he is.[115] However, one cannot stop there. For this Jewish Jesus "would not be the person He is, were He not God's Commissioner, were He not Christ who causes Israel's life and meaning to gleam as a light in the Gentile world and in the whole of humanity."[116] Thus, to understand him, one cannot simply view him in terms of his "starting-point." One must also view him in relation to his "goal" as the light of the entire world.[117]

It is fair to say that because of the emphasis placed on this "starting-point," that is, the Jewish particularity of the Word in his theology, Barth creates space for the enculturation of the Word in the whole host of particular cultures, he who is the light of life, the true witness of God who bears witness to the "goal" of his own life, the redemption of the world. For by becoming particularized in this one culture, the Word affirms the particularization of his light in other cultures in the event of witness to his life. In light of the foregoing, it is important to note that although there are occurrences in Barth's thought where the divine content *overshadows* the secular form of the divine Word and secular words of witness to the Word, it does not *overwhelm* them. For attestation to the divine does not take place in a celestial vacuum, but in the form of creaturely life in the manifold expressions of human culture.

Continuity and Discontinuity: The Enculturated and Transcultural Word

Perhaps the central component of any culture's identity is the language of its people. As Lesslie Newbigin argues, "The language of a people provides the means by which they express their way of perceiving things and of coping with them."[118] And yet, regardless of its importance, no matter if it be possessed by a high degree of sophistication, inspiring though it may be from the standpoint of fostering poetic genius, there is nothing inherent in a language, or a culture for that matter, that enables it to serve as a witness to the Word. Surely, the incarnation suggests that the divine Word does not require lofty forms of cultural identity to reveal his glory, having revealed his majesty

115. Barth, *Dogmatics in Outline,* p. 72.

116. Barth, *Dogmatics in Outline,* p. 72.

117. Barth, *Dogmatics in Outline,* p. 72.

118. Lesslie Newbigin, *Foolishness to the Greeks: The Gospel and Western Culture* (Grand Rapids: Eerdmans, 1986), p. 3.

supremely through the most lowly veil of all. The Word is indeed free and able to appropriate human words from whatever context, commandeering them for his service in a way similar to his commandeering of human flesh.

The foregoing should not be taken to suggest that the Word is detached from the words and patterns of cultural life. In fact, as Newbigin claims, "The idea that one can or could at any time separate out by some process of distillation a pure gospel unadulterated by any cultural accretions is an illusion."[119] Barth's theology itself is a culturally conditioned work, that is, a critical though constructive response to the cultural situation of his day. Moreover, for Barth, the Word of Christ has and does take up residence within cultural forms, taking them to himself, and yet without being dependent on or domesticated by them. In this light, the role of the church in any given culture in bearing witness to the Word is to aim toward the contextualization of the Word without such appropriation resulting in the Word's domestication. In this vein, Newbigin writes that, "The word of God is to be spoken in every tongue, but it can never be domesticated in any."[120] How though does one advocate the incarnation of the Word in culture without promoting the domestication of the Word in this or that particular cultural form?

One thing that is required is a model of the Word that is truly incarnational: contextual, affirming the Word's embodiment in culture, and yet, at the same time, dialectical, safeguarding against the syncretistic union of gospel and culture. On the whole, Barth's doctrine of the Word provides such a model of Christ and culture, one that affirms the incarnation of the Word while guarding against the domestication of the gospel, and also against the cultural imperialism that so easily results from such syncretism when the church of one culture offers its supposedly unadulterated gospel to another people. Barth's theology of the Word, including his anhypostatic-enhypostatic Christology and conception of the *unio personalis,* enables him to affirm the incarnation of the divine Word in human history, and to protect the distinction between the divine and human natures in that incarnate life. The Word becomes incarnate as a human, as a Jewish male, in history. However, the Word is not exhausted by that enculturation. For the divine nature ever remains distinct from the human in their union in the person of the Word.

119. Newbigin, *Foolishness to the Greeks,* p. 4.
120. Newbigin, *Foolishness to the Greeks,* p. 147.

Here one calls to mind Barth's notion of the fundamental distinction that exists between the divine and human natures and what it *implies* for the Word's relation to the world of culture. Because the Word is not exhausted by or reduced to his incarnate existence, the Word as Jesus Christ can enable other words to bear witness to himself and take form in other cultures, again without being overwhelmed by those cultural forms. For although the attributes of the divine and human natures are predicated of the divine person directly and undialectically, the natures themselves relate to one another indirectly and dialectically.[121] In this way, one can maintain the balance between celebrating and critiquing particular cultural forms. God became wholly other than he is, becoming human, even as Jesus of Nazareth. And yet, God also remained wholly other in that union. Only by maintaining the distinction between the divine and human natures in their union in the Word is the Word preserved from being overwhelmed by a particular culture and able to enable the words of other cultures to bear witness to his incarnate life.

The incarnation is a dialectical reality. By entering the human sphere, the Word is not thereby fused with a particular culture, not even the culture in which the Word entered time and space as a human being, but is sovereign in relation to culture. Thus, not only is the Word enculturated, but also it is *transcultural.* The enculturation of the Word does not lead to the overwhelming of that same Word by a particular culture. For the Word transcends culture even in its enculturation.

Both the enculturation and transcultural reality of the Word *imply* that the Word makes space for Christ's church in every culture to bear witness to the Word through its own cultural forms. For one, no culture has a handle or corner on the Word. In this way, provision is made to safeguard against imperialistic forces at work in one culture's church as it presents its gospel to other cultures. Newbigin calls on Western Christianity to become aware of its own syncretistic tendencies, urging the Western church to listen to the gospel message as it presents itself through the categories of the non-Western world. By listening to these other portrayals of Christ, by gazing at their portraits, Western peoples come to understand better their own enculturated gospels and perceive more clearly how to speak the

121. See page 365 of McCormack's work, *Karl Barth's Critically Realistic Dialectical Theology,* for his discussion of Barth's work, "Unterricht in der christlichen Religion," pp. 47-48, where such terms are employed.

gospel to their culture, realizing, too, that the gospel is not limited to their Western conceptions, but rather, transcends them.[122]

It is only by coming to terms with the enculturation of the Word within one's own culture and those of others that one is able to guard against cultural imperialism. The only truly international gospel is one that accounts for the incarnation of the Word in the plethora of cultures. By denying such enculturation of the Word, one fails to guard against the absolutizing of one's own culture's particular appropriation of the Word. Was this not true of the German Christians and National Socialists? In refusing to acknowledge the fundamentally Jewish quality of Christ's humanity, they absolutized the German context in the appropriation of the gospel.

Now a universal, amorphous Christianity, one that stresses the *logos asarkos,* may ultimately be the most adulterated in cultural form, the most syncretistic in shape, and, in turn, the most imperialistic in its missionary enterprise. Only by accounting for the particularity of the gospel, both in its original and consequent manifestation, is one able to make space for its universality.[123]

122. Newbigin, *Foolishness to the Greeks,* pp. 146-47.

123. The same point holds for American Christianity. Mention was made in Chapter Three of the Puritan John Winthrop's dream for America becoming a spiritual nation founded on Christian Scripture. Winthrop invoked biblical covenantal imagery pertaining to Israel, applying it to the Massachusetts Bay Colony, which he governed. Such a move, which involved the supersession of Israel as the covenant elect of God, created a vacuum, opening the door for a more heinous form of supersessionism in Manifest Destiny in the nineteenth century. As Bader-Saye argues, "Later generations, not so steeped in Scripture and more enamored of national power, would come to take it as their right, too, to draw up their own articles." Manifest Destiny went so far as to reverse election, "making it a reward for America's goodness rather than a witness to God's grace," thereby turning "the claim to chosenness into a justification of American power rather than a vocation to be a holy people." Scott Bader-Saye, *Church and Israel After Christendom: The Politics of Election,* Radical Traditions: Theology in a Postcritical Key (Boulder, Colo.: Westview Press, 1999), p. 67. In contrast to Winthrop's view that the church has superseded Israel, see Bader-Saye, p. 67. Dispensational theology, which has also had widespread influence in American Christianity, including its foreign missions enterprise, safeguards against the notion that the church is the replacement of Israel. And yet, it has traditionally viewed the church and Israel as completely separate from one another: the church, which is made up of Jews and Gentiles, stands at the center of God's present administrative plan as a *new,* spiritual people, whereas Israel as a national, political, and ethnic people will be reinstated as the focal point of God's plan after the close of the church age. Recently, some dispensationalist writers have argued

As indicated above, a supposedly non-enculturated, amorphous, international Christianity is in danger of being an imperialistic Christianity. Only by fostering and being aware of a national gospel can one be open to a truly international gospel, one that welcomes the particular manifestations of the gospel in diverse cultural fields, while, at the same time, critiquing them in light of the Word. An amorphous Christianity, on the other hand, gives rise to the subsuming of Christ, and other Christian subcultural construals of Christ, under a particular form. This point is well put by Kanzo Uchimura, a leading Japanese Christian scholar of the Meiji era.

> A Japanese by becoming a Christian does not cease to be a Japanese. On the contrary, he becomes more Japanese by becoming a Christian. A Japanese who becomes an American or an Englishman, or an amorphous universal man, is neither a true Japanese nor a true Christian.[124]

He goes on to speak of Paul, Luther, and Knox as those who "were not characterless universal men, but distinctly national, therefore distinctly human, and distinctly Christian."[125] He adds that Japanese who are converted as "'universal Christians' may turn out to be no more than denationalized Japanese, whose universality is no more than Americanism or Anglicanism adopted to cover up their lost nationality."[126]

The Word is ever enculturated. By coming to terms with this reality, one is better able to guard against the imposition of one's own enculturated gospel on those of other cultures and the overwhelming of their

---

that by viewing the church as a new "race of humanity different from Jews and Gentiles, some earlier dispensationalists have not been as sensitive as they should have been to actually existing ethnic and cultural differences within the body of Christ today. Lack of sensitivity here leads to the cultural domination of one group over another within the church (such as the Gentilization of Jewish Christians, or the Anglicization or Americanization of third-world Christians)." Craig A. Blaising and Darrell L. Bock, *Progressive Dispensationalism* (Wheaton, Ill.: A BridgePoint Book, 1993), pp. 50-51.

124. Kanzo Uchimura, "Japanese Christianity," in *Sources of Japanese Tradition,* vol. 2, ed. Ryusaku Tsunoda, Wm. Theodore de Bary, and Donald Keene (New York: Columbia University Press, 1958); reprint, H. Byron Earhart, ed., *Religion in the Japanese Experience: Sources and Interpretations,* The Religious Life of Man Series, ed. Frederick J. Streng (Belmont, Mass.: Wadsworth, 1974), p. 113.

125. Uchimura, "Japanese Christianity," p. 113.

126. Uchimura, "Japanese Christianity," p. 114.

distinctive cultural engagement with the gospel. The Word is also transcultural, guarding against its domestication in any culture whereby it is overwhelmed by that culture. Space is *made* for the gospel to take root in culture, even for words to become witnesses to the Word in their otherness without words and the world of culture overwhelming the Word, or the Word overwhelming them.

In this chapter, attention has been directed largely to the topic of the commandeering, the elevating of secular forms, *in order that* they may bear witness to divine truth. In Chapter Six, analysis will center on secular forms bearing witness to God's glory *because* they are secular. Whereas in this chapter, and the one preceding it, discussion has focused on the fact that in Barth's thought, space is *made for oneness in otherness* between the divine and human and the sacred and secular spheres in and through the Word as Jesus Christ (connections), Chapters Five and Six will concentrate on space being *given for secular otherness* in view of the *one* Word of God as Jesus Christ (distinctions). Thus, not only is space *made* for unity in otherness in light of Barth's doctrine of the Word, but also as shall be shown, space is *given* for the celebration of secular otherness in view of this same Word.

PART III

DISTINCTIONS

5

The Prophetic Word and the Secular State

"Theological Politics" and the Question of Repristination[1]

The two loves of Barth outside the realm of theology proper are politics and Mozart. The concern of this chapter is to discuss Barth's distinctive view of the relation of church and state, and how it safeguards the secular vocation of the state. In the next chapter, discussion will center on those tenets of Barth's theology that enable him to affirm certain secular enterprises and endeavors, including Mozart's creation of music, through consideration of his doctrine of the Word in creation. In these two chapters, it will be argued that although politics, the arts, the sciences, and human existence generally are not often viewed in *direct* relation to the subject matter of theology, Barth brings theological, more specifically, Christological categories to bear *directly* on these subjects, yet in such a manner as to award space to these subjects for the expression of authentic forms of secularity. Discussion will shortly turn to Barth's concept of the state in its relation to the church from this angle. However, before we turn to consider how Barth's Christological model promotes space for the pursuit of the secular vocation of the state, we will give some attention to the

1. Here appropriation is made of Alan Torrance's phrase, "theological politics," taken from the following source: Alan J. Torrance, introduction to *Christ, Justice and Peace: Toward a Theology of the State in Dialogue with the Barmen Declaration*, by Eberhard Jüngel, trans. D. Bruce Hamill and Alan J. Torrance (Edinburgh: T. & T. Clark, 1992), p. xx.

question of what relevance if any Barth's dogmatic approach to culture bears for the political situation of his day.

The reader will recall Paul Tillich's criticism of Barth's "kerygmatic" theology noted in Chapter One. According to Tillich, Barth is partly responsible for strengthening the "trends toward a theology of repristination in Europe." The basis for Tillich's criticism of Barth is that the latter brings "ultimate truth" to bear "directly" on every situation (a "method" that Tillich calls "neo-orthodox"), for example, "deriving the duty of making war against Hitler from the resurrection of the Christ."[2] Contrary to Tillich's assessment of Barth, it will be argued that, if anything, Barth's dialectical, incarnational theology of the Word provided a much needed, carefully nuanced response to *the* cultural "situation,"[3] namely, the political crisis in Europe during Hitler's reign of terror.[4]

In Barth's Christological model, one finds the basis both for *diastasis* and *synthesis,* the critique of the political situation of his day, but also a constructive response to it. Far from relegating theology to a state of repristination, Barth's paradigm provided the foundation stone for a theological rejoinder that was thoroughly equipped to address key aspects of the political crisis in Germany in the thirties and forties. It was not the introduction of these Christological categories that endangered theology's place in the public, political debate at that time, but the lack of consideration given them by others, as shall be argued.

Will Herberg writes that Barth's Christological perspective on the state stands in marked contrast to the model of natural law and the Augustin-

2. Paul Tillich, *Systematic Theology,* vol. 1 (Chicago: University of Chicago Press, 1951), p. 5. Here Tillich refers the reader to Karl Barth's essay, "A Letter to Great Britain from Switzerland," in *This Christian Cause* (New York: Macmillan, 1941).

3. Barth would later reflect that it was not he who changed, but the situation with which he was confronted in Germany in the early thirties, necessitating from him a response in the form "of a summons, a challenge, a battle cry, a confession." Karl Barth, *How I Changed My Mind,* with an introduction and epilogue by John D. Godsey (Richmond, Va.: John Knox Press, 1966), p. 46.

4. Far from being considered irrelevant or a feeble challenge to the Hitler regime, the essay to which Tillich refers was banned by the Swiss authorities. The rationale behind the ban was that Barth, in keeping with "his earlier writings," used "his theological framework to support a position hostile to a foreign state, holding up a mirror to the Confederation in a way which is likely to disturb correct relations between Switzerland and this other state." Karl Barth, letter to Dr. Bally-Gerber, 6 August 1941; quoted in Eberhard Busch, *Karl Barth: His Life from Letters and Autobiographical Texts* (London: SCM Press, 1976), p. 310.

ian-Reformation archetype. For Barth, advocates of natural law wrongly conceive there to be substantial continuity between the divine and human realms and mistakenly champion the inherent goodness of humanity. On the other hand, Barth blamed the Reformers for dividing creation and redemption.[5]

In contrast to the Reformers, and many Protestant divines in his own day, Barth contends that human justice *(Recht)* and the justification of the human *(Rechtfertigung)* belong to the second article of the creed.[6] Barth argues that although the Reformers did not set human justice and divine justification in opposition to one another, they nonetheless failed to connect them sufficiently.[7] The result of this failure was twofold: "pietistic sterility on the one hand, and the sterility of the Enlightenment on the other."[8] The former results from Christian indifference to the sphere of "human justice" in favor of concern for the soul. The latter results from indifference to "the Reformers' juxtaposition of human justice and divine justification," favoring instead a "secular gospel of human law and a secular church," in which God and human justice are conceived along very different lines.[9] In place of the Reformers' "juxtaposition" of the two, which gives rise to "the temptation to those separations" noted above,[10] Barth argues that Scripture not only speaks "of the *conflict* between" the church and state, but also highlights "the *positive* connection between the two realms,"[11] thereby safeguarding against such separations.

Barth finds in the gospel accounts of Pilate's "encounter" with Christ not simply a basis for the doctrine of the "separation" of "Church and State," but also support for their vital connection.[12] Barth maintains that "the Roman governor" is the "virtual founder of the Church,"[13] arguing that Pilate "belongs not only to the Creed but to its second article in partic-

5. Will Herberg, introduction to *Community, State, and Church: Three Essays,* by Karl Barth (Gloucester, Mass.: Peter Smith, 1968), p. 29.

6. See Karl Barth, "Church and State," in *Community, State, and Church: Three Essays,* with an introduction by Will Herberg (Gloucester, Mass.: Peter Smith, 1968), pp. 101-14.

7. Barth, "Church and State," pp. 102-5.

8. Barth, "Church and State," p. 105.

9. Barth, "Church and State," p. 105.

10. Barth, "Church and State," p. 106.

11. Barth, "Church and State," p. 107.

12. Barth, "Church and State," pp. 108-9.

13. Barth, "Church and State," p. 111.

ular!"[14] If it had not been for the unjust Pilate, the representative of the "'demonic' State," who, after declaring Christ a righteous man and attempting to free him, gave him over to be crucified, there would have been no provision made for the justification of sinners. Failing to be just, Pilate "became the involuntary agent and herald of divine justification." Now if, on the other hand, Pilate had been true to "human justice," "the State would have had to grant legal protection to the Church!"[15] And Pilate would have had to recognize the church's "right to proclaim divine justification."[16] Regardless though, even in acting unjustly, the supposed guardian of human justice could not but serve divine justification.

What does Barth's Christological model and understanding of Pilate imply for Barth's response to the political situation in Germany under Hitler? For one, in view of the close relation of human justice to divine justification in Barth's thought, he is able to guard against a pessimistic view of the state. The state is not to be demonized. For "the heavenly Jerusalem is also a State" to which even the most corrupt state will in the end "bring its tribute."[17] For Barth, the state does not ultimately belong to the order of the fallen creation, but the order of redemption, just as Pilate himself belongs to the second article of the creed.[18] Thus, the church must take the state most seriously. There is no place for Augustine's identification of "the *civitas terrena* with the *civitas Cain*."[19]

Not only does Barth's model rule out a pessimistic view of the state, but also it protects against an unduly optimistic conception of the civil authority. Thus, in addition to guarding against the demonizing of the state, one must beware of divinizing the human state, "not because there is no divinity of the State, but because" such divinity belongs not "to the *earthly* State," but to "the *heavenly* Jerusalem."[20] And how could one divinize the state anyway when its chief symbol, Pilate, contributed to divine justification, not by exercising human justice, but by failing to be just?

In keeping with his repulsion of a pessimistic view of the state, Barth rejects *indifference* on the part of the church to the state. For how can the

14. Barth, "Church and State," p. 114.
15. Barth, "Church and State," pp. 112-13.
16. Barth, "Church and State," pp. 113-14.
17. Barth, "Church and State," p. 125.
18. Barth. "Church and State," p. 114.
19. Barth, "Church and State," p. 125.
20. Barth, "Church and State," p. 125.

church remain indifferent since the church and state indwell one another in and through Christ, who is the basis for the union of human justice and divine justification? Is it not in the light of him that the church "has had to assume a 'certain' political character" and "must recognize, and honour, a 'certain' ecclesiastical character in the State"?[21] The ministers of the state "'to a certain extent' actually stand within the sacred order, not — as was later said, with far too great a servility — as *membra præcipua,* but as *ministri extraordinarii ecclesiæ.*"[22] Not only though must the church guard against indifference to the state, but also the state must beware of indifference to the church. For Christ is the Lord of both spheres. Thus, there can be no privatizing of religion.

Alan Torrance points out that the rise of nationalism in Germany led to spiritual subjectivism and to the relativizing of the "imperatives of the Gospel."[23] The move was made at this time to relativize or spiritualize the law of the gospel for the sake of advancing the *Volksnomoi.*[24] For only by privatizing the law of Christ could the path be cleared for what Barth writes of "Stapel's theological dictum," namely, the equation of "the law of God . . . with the law of the German people."[25] Indeed, the seeds of pri-

21. Barth, "Church and State," p. 134.

22. Barth, "Church and State," p. 135.

23. Alan Torrance, introduction to *Christ, Justice and Peace,* p. xi.

24. With the rise of nationalism in Germany, which Barth refers to as "these recent troubled times," one finds the invention of the "Volksnomoi." Karl Barth, "Gospel and Law," in *Community, State, and Church: Three Essays,* with an introduction by Will Herberg (Gloucester, Mass.: Peter Smith, 1968), p. 91. Herberg writes of this movement that "like 'proletarian justice' in Russia," the People's Law "had become the slogan under which all the protections of custom and law were being contemptuously trampled under foot" (Herberg, introduction to *Community, State, and Church,* p. 43). In contrast to the law of Christ that liberates people, the "People's Law" suppressed them. Now Barth's own approach to the law, namely, the reversal of the order of law and gospel in "Gospel and Law," served to preserve *the* law and at the same time relate it inseparably to Christ. In this way, Barth safeguarded against the imposition of a new and foreign law that was in reality *anti*-nomian, that is, the *anti*-Christian repudiation of law as the preservation of human well-being. Barth writes in one place that unless Christ is the "goal" of the interpretation of the law, "its interpretation . . . will vacillate unsteadily between . . . *nomianism* . . . and *antinomianism*" (Barth, "Gospel and Law," p. 91). See Busch's discussion of the importance of Barth's essay, "Gospel and Law" (Busch, *Karl Barth: His Life,* p. 266). Does not the nomianism or antinomianism mentioned above arise from the rejection of God's gracious love in Christ and the grateful service to God and others in favor of self-love and service to self?

25. Karl Barth, "Abschied," *Zwischen den Zeiten* (1933): 539; quoted in Eberhard Busch,

vatization had already been sown given the influence of Neo-Kantian thought in certain sectors of German culture, according to which religion was relegated to the realm of the "*Individuum.*"[26]

In contrast to the Neo-Kantian privatization of religion, the second article of Barmen, for which Barth was in large part responsible, states that in all areas of life Jesus Christ is Lord of the Christian community. "We reject the false doctrine that there could be areas of our life in which we would belong not to Jesus Christ but to other lords, areas in which we would not need justification and *sanctification* through him."[27] In his opposition to the "German Christians," Barth maintains that Christ is "der Hohepriester, aber auch der König, wie auch er allein der Prophet ist."[28] He is not only the high priest of God's people. He is also king, just as he alone is the prophet of God, not only in the church, but also in the context of the state. Over against the attempt to *isolate* Christ and the church, relegating them to the private domain of otherworldly religion, the church is called upon to submit to *Christ's* lordship in the public sphere of the state. Thus, there could be no compromise with Hitler's forces. For the oath to

---

Karl Barth: His Life from Letters and Autobiographical Texts (London: SCM Press, 1976), p. 229. See the full context of this statement in Busch, pp. 229-30. Cochrane also draws attention to Barth's remarks on Stapel's identification of "God's law" with the law of the "German people," quoting Barth as saying the equation made by Stapel is "treason against the gospel." Barth adds that it "amounts to setting up the Man-God of the eighteenth and nineteenth centuries in a form that is much worse than in the Harnack-Troeltsch era because it is much more axiomatic and much more concrete." Arthur C. Cochrane, *The Church's Confession Under Hitler* (Philadelphia: Westminster Press, 1962), p. 71, quoting Karl Barth, *Zwischen den Zeiten* (1939): 539.

26. See Alan Torrance, introduction to *Christ, Justice and Peace,* p. xi.

27. Douglas S. Bax, trans., "The Barmen Theological Declaration: A New Translation," *Journal of Theology for Southern Africa* 47 (June 1984): 79 (italics added). Barth and two Lutheran theologians, Hans Asmussen and Thomas Breit, were given the task of formulating the declaration of Barmen. (See Busch, *Karl Barth: His Life,* p. 245.) However, Barth writes that while his co-authors slumbered, the Reformed church stayed alert, revising the declaration in full. Barth writes, "I don't want to boast, but it was really my text." Karl Barth, conversation with Tübingen students, 2 March 1964; quoted in Eberhard Busch, *Karl Barth: His Life,* p. 245. For a discussion of the historical context that gave rise to the formulation of "The Barmen Declaration," see Douglas S. Bax, "The Barmen Declaration: Its Historical Background," *Journal of Theology for Southern Africa* 47 (June 1984): 12-20.

28. The quotation is taken from Karl Barth, "Barmen," in *Protestantismus Heute,* ed. Fritz Heinrich Ryssel (Frankfurt: Ullstein Bücher, 1959), p. 83.

Hitler involved a total submission of the "whole" person, that is, "his actions, his thoughts and his conscience" to the "will" of Hitler, "which is subject to no control or superior law."[29]

Not only does Barth attack *indifference* to the gospel in the sphere of political considerations, but also he rejects the *identification* of political programs and propaganda with the gospel. For the gospel is Jesus Christ, and him alone. He "is the one Word of God." In the light of him, the church rejects "other events, powers, historic figures . . . , and truths . . . as God's revelation."[30] In the light of the one Word of God, Jesus Christ, Barth dismisses natural theology, that *"formulation of a system* which claims to be theological, . . . whose *subject,* however, differs fundamentally from the revelation in Jesus Christ and whose *method* therefore differs equally from the exposition of Holy Scripture."[31] "Ist Jesus Christus das eine Wort Gottes."[32] There is no other word of God existing independently of him. Thus, there can be no ascent to God through race or culture according to

29. Karl Barth, *The German Church Conflict,* Ecumenical Studies in History, no. 1 (Richmond, Va.: John Knox Press, 1965), p. 68.

30. Bax, "Barmen Theological Declaration," p. 79. Bax points out that the "'German Christians' spoke of Hitler as the German Moses" (p. 79, n. 9). He also draws attention to Ernst Wolf's exegesis of this passage. According to Wolf, "events" refer to Hitler's seizure of office in 1933, "powers" as *"Blut und Boden,"* "figures" as Hitler, and "truths" as the doctrines of the *"Volk"* (Bax, "Barmen Theological Declaration," p. 79, n. 10). See Ernst Wolf, *Barmen. Kirche zwischen Versuchung und Gnade* (München: Chr. Kaiser, 1957), p. 104. Barth describes the "German Christians" as those who preached "Christ *and* Hitler; the Bible *and* the glorious present! Cross *and* Swastika!" (Barth, *German Church Conflict,* p. 42). Originally published in German in 1956, the work is a collection of pieces written by Barth between the years 1933 and 1939. Due to the syncretism so prevalent in the ideology of the "German Christians," Barth boldly states that, "We have different beliefs, different spirits and a different God." Karl Barth, *Gottes Wille und unsere Wünsche,* p. 4; quoted in Eberhard Busch, *Karl Barth: His Life,* p. 242. For an in-depth discussion of the "German Christian" movement, see Cochrane, *The Church's Confession Under Hitler,* pp. 74-89.

31. Karl Barth, "No!," in Karl Barth and Emil Brunner, *Natural Theology,* with an introduction by John Baillie, trans. Peter Fraenkel (London: Geoffrey Bles/Centenary Press, 1946), pp. 74-75. Barth would later write that his harsh response to Brunner in "No!" was in large part due to the poor timing of the publication of Brunner's essay. It emerged during the heat of the battle in the German church conflict as the "German Christians" were practicing natural theology, employing it to their own ends. Against this background, Brunner's "Nature and Grace" attacked Barth "from the rear at the worst possible moment." Karl Barth, letter to Pastor Max Schoch, in *Letters, 1961-1968,* ed. Geoffrey Bromiley (Grand Rapids: Eerdmans, 1981), p. 270.

32. Barth, "Barmen," in *Protestantismus Heute,* p. 82.

nature, no spiritual significance to "Nordic blood."[33] For contact between God and his human creature always depends upon divine initiative in that the justification of the human pertains not simply to justification by faith, but also to the justification of human knowledge in the light of the Word whose Spirit generates the knowledge of faith.[34] In the face of Hitler and the "German Christians" who employed natural theology for the propagation of the Aryan gospel, inspired as it was by the orders of creation and the evolutionary movement of history, Barth championed the theology of the Word. This Word comes to humanity from above, calling into question all mere human words. Such a dialectical orientation enabled Barth to critique that pseudo-gospel that identified the kingdom of God with the Third Reich, which was supposedly based on a "second source of revelation" in addition to the Christ revealed in Scripture.[35] It was this claim of a second revelation that served as the ultimate reason for Barth's "protest"[36] and critique.[37]

33. Barth refers to this potent symbol in his discussion of the relation of modernism to the rise of nationalism in *Church Dogmatics,* I/1, *The Doctrine of the Word of God,* ed. G. W. Bromiley and T. F. Torrance (Edinburgh: T. & T. Clark, 1975), p. xiv.

34. See Barth's "No!" to Brunner in *Natural Theology,* especially pp. 101-2. For Barth, the proper extension of the Reformers' credo that salvation comes by grace alone is that knowledge of God comes by grace alone.

35. Barth, *German Church Conflict,* p. 16.

36. Barth, *German Church Conflict,* p. 16.

37. It was not only Barth's doctrine of the *divinity* of the Word that served as a form of critique of Hitlerism. One should also take into account his doctrine of the humanity of the same Word. In opposition to the theology of German Aryanism, which gave rise to the oppression of people groups deemed inferior, Barth proclaimed the theology of the crucified God. This God, the divine Word, demonstrates his deity in his humiliation, in service as the neighbor of all, in the incarnation. Is it any wonder Barth has been hailed a forerunner of the theology of liberation? Refer to Barth's essay, "The Humanity of God," in *The Humanity of God* (Atlanta: John Knox Press, 1960), pp. 37-65, his discussion of Friedrich Nietzsche's doctrine of the *Übermensch* in *Church Dogmatics,* III/2, *The Doctrine of Creation,* ed. G. W. Bromiley and T. F. Torrance (Edinburgh: T. & T. Clark, 1960), pp. 231-42, and his treatment of the advent of Christ in *Church Dogmatics,* IV/1, *The Doctrine of Reconciliation,* ed. G. W. Bromiley and T. F. Torrance (Edinburgh: T. & T. Clark, 1956), p. 130, for his exposition of this theme. In the last of these works mentioned, Barth argues that the gods show themselves to be false by their exclusion of "self-humiliation. False gods are all reflections of a false and all too human self-exaltation" (Barth, *Church Dogmatics,* IV/1, p. 130). Barmen itself has been hailed as a paradigmatic text in the struggle against oppression. For discussions of the relevance of Barmen for the war against oppression, see the following two works: John W. De Gruchy, "Barmen: Symbol of Contemporary Liberation?," *Journal of Theology for Southern*

Consideration of Barth's critical, Christological response to the crisis of culture under Hitler is not yet finished. "The Barmen Declaration" and Barth's essay, "Church and State," served as the theological and exegetical backdrop for his critique of the political problem of his day, the totalitarian threat of National Socialism. Central to this threat was Hitler's attack on the Jewish people, which is analyzed in Barth's work, *The Church and the Political Problem of Our Day.*[38] There Barth writes, "Anti-Semitism is sin against the Holy Ghost. For anti-Semitism means rejection of the *grace* of God. But National Socialism lives, moves, and has its being in anti-Semitism."[39] The one "who rejects and persecutes the Jews rejects and persecutes Him who died for the sins of the Jews — and then, and only *thereby* for our sins as well."[40] Barth's attention to the Jewish particularity of Christ and his understanding of the narrative of the whole of Scripture bearing witness to Christ enabled him to contest the Aryan Marcionites, the "German Christians" and their political messiah.[41]

In the light of the foregoing, it is concluded that contrary to Tillich's assessment, one does not find in Barth's Christological response to Hitler the repristination of theology or the "splitting" of "hairs,"[42] but the *advance*

Africa 47 (June 1984): 59-71; Desmond Tutu, "Barmen and Apartheid," *Journal of Theology for Southern Africa* 47 (June 1984): 73-77. For an opposing view to the claim noted above in this footnote that Barth's doctrine of God is a model of authentic liberation, see Falk Wagner, "Theologische Gleichschaltung: zur Christologie bei Karl Barth," in *Die Realisierung der Freiheit,* ed. Trutz Rendtorff (Gütersloh: Gütersloher Verlagshaus Gerd Mohn, 1975), pp. 10-43.

38. See Mueller's discussion of the relation of "Church and State" and *The Church and the Political Problem of Our Day* in his introduction to *Church and State,* pp. xxvi-xxvii.

39. Karl Barth, *The Church and the Political Problem of Our Day* (London: Hodder and Stoughton, 1939), p. 51.

40. Barth, *The Church and the Political Problem of Our Day,* p. 51.

41. It is worth noting Bader-Saye's critique of Barth's doctrine of election at this point: although Barth guards against the view that the German people possess "elect status," he does not go far enough to guard against the privatizing of Christianity given what is deemed to be a spiritualized and noetic construal of election. Instead of promoting "a politics of election embodied in church and Israel, Barth spiritualizes election," placing the emphasis on the knowing individual. According to Bader-Saye, and Nicholas Healy, whom he quotes, such spiritualization promotes, albeit unwittingly, the very privatization of Christianity found in the Culture Protestant, German Christian movement, which Barth so vehemently opposed. Scott Bader-Saye, *Church and Israel After Christendom: The Politics of Election,* Radical Traditions: Theology in a Postcritical Key (Boulder, Colo.: Westview Press, 1999), p. 77.

42. In "A Letter to Great Britain from Switzerland," in *This Christian Cause,* the object of

ment of the Christian cause. Barth is not a *political theologian,* imposing on theology and religion a political agenda. But he does engage in the *theologizing of politics* in the light of his Christological focus,[43] providing the basis for *diastasis* and *synthesis,* that is, constructive critique and critical construction.[44] For Barth, Christ distinguishes the church and true religion

---

Tillich's criticism, in which Barth bases his protest against Hitler on the resurrection, Barth writes that those arguments against Hitler based on natural law prove inadequate from a *Christian* perspective. In defending himself against the charge that he is simply engaging in "splitting hairs" (p. 17), Barth writes that the fundamental issue in effectively repelling the Hitler menace revolves around an either-or. "The question" is "Jesus Christ or Natural Law?" (p. 18). A response based on natural law does not distinguish the Christian claim from that of the "Hindu, Buddhist or Atheist" (p. 16). The *Christian* Church must base its "resistance to Hitler" on the "sure foundation," resisting him "unequivocally in the name of Jesus Christ" (p. 17). Those responses based on natural law, on the other hand, "are Janus-headed. They do not lead to the light of clear decisions, but to the misty twilight in which all cats become grey. They lead to — Munich" (p. 17). The church must resist this form of engagement, turning straightaway to its alternative, Jesus Christ. Because of Christ, the church cannot shrink back from its "obligations" (p. 19). Christians "are not aliens in the political sphere" (p. 19). For ". . . Jesus Christ does not dwell in some mystic, ritualistic, pietistic, individual-ethical or theological hinterland beyond the political sphere, so that life in real fellowship with Christ begins only outside its bounds" (p. 19). Only by basing their response as Christians on Christ can they stand firm as Christians in their political resistance to Hitler. For if they do otherwise, if they base their offensive on "Natural Law," the very real danger exists that it will "inevitably lead to a division between the political and Christian spheres" (p. 20). Of all people, Christians "have no right whatsoever to fear and respect" the reign of Hitler and other terrors "or to resign" themselves "to the fact that" these forces "are spreading throughout the world as though they know neither bounds nor lord" (pp. 10-11). For the church to give in to such fears and doubts would be to trivialize Christ's resurrection and to deny his kingly "reign" (p. 11). The "enterprise" of Hitler is that "of an evil spirit," which God has "apparently allowed . . . for a time in order to test" the church's "faith in the resurrection of Jesus Christ, and above all to test" its "obedience to that faith" (p. 11). In the light of the resurrected Christ who already reigns from "the right hand of the Father" the church must not be shaken in its hope that Christ will make all things new (pp. 10-11). In view of this hope in him, the resurrected and reigning Christ, the church must "come to grips spiritedly and resolutely with these evil spirits" (p. 11). In the light of the foregoing, the posing of the question of "Jesus Christ or Natural Law" is anything but needless speculation or the splitting of hairs. (There is no page numbering in this volume; the page numbers given are based on numbering from the first page of the essay in question.)

43. The author is indebted at this point to Alan Torrance's discussion of "political theologies" and "theological politics" in his introduction to *Christ, Justice and Peace* (p. xx).

44. Timothy Gorringe argues that Barth addresses the political concerns of his time — as a specifically Christian theologian, even in the *Church Dogmatics.* See Timothy Gorringe,

from the state, and is himself distinct from both church and state. But Christ also serves as the basis for conceiving the relation of church and state in integral terms. In this way, Barth was able to offer a critical and constructive response to the political crisis of the thirties and forties. As stated at the outset of this section, the problem in Barth's day was not the application of "ultimate truth," of Christological categories to the public, political debate during the time of Hitler, but the lack of such extensions on the part of many of Barth's theological peers.

Having discussed the significance of Barth's Christocentrism for the political crisis under Hitler, we will now consider whether Barth's Christocentric framework promotes a theocratic model of the state or makes space for the pursuit of a state that is secular in orientation, albeit within limits. The remainder of this chapter and the one that follows will be devoted to analyzing whether or not Barth's Christological model of the Word provides the theological parameters for the state, and broader culture generally, to pursue their vocation in such a way that authentic forms of secularity may flourish.

The Secular State of the Kingdom

The question was raised above as to whether or not Barth's theology advances that concept and form of government that is theocratic in shape. The answer is in the negative since for Barth, political considerations are distinct from the theological constructs that give rise to them. Just as one would be at fault for divorcing consideration of politics from theology, so too, one would be at fault for collapsing politics into theology.[45] What though is the basis for Barth's way of conceiving the inseparable yet distinct relation of theology and politics, church and state? Is not the answer

---

Karl Barth Against Hegemony, Christian Theology in Context (New York: Oxford University Press, 1999), pp. 19-20. Gorringe asserts that Barth's multifaceted approach to engaging the subject matter of Jesus Christ gives rise to Barth's theology making a most significant contribution to the theme of "human liberation" (p. 288).

45. Equally important, one should not collapse theology into politics in that theology is the basis of politics. As Jüngel writes, "Simply put, for Barth, the political is surely a predicate of theology, but theology is never a predicate of the political." Eberhard Jüngel, *Karl Barth: A Theological Legacy,* trans. Garrett E. Paul (Philadelphia: Westminster Press, 1986), p. 104.

to this question to be found in Barth's conception of Christ and his kingdom? Indeed it is, for as Barth argues in *Against the Stream,* the church is the inner circle and the state the outer circle of the one kingdom of God.[46] In this way, the two stand in a distinct relation to one another in the one kingdom of Christ.

Further to the discussion in the previous section, Barth's particular conception of the church-state relation leads him to conceive matters very differently from much of the tradition since, for Barth, the state is conceived in the light of Christ, standing not outside the kingdom, but *within* it, yet without being identified with it. At this point, it will prove beneficial to pause briefly to analyze Barth's conception of the relation of the church and state to the kingdom of Christ before proceeding to consider the relation of the church to the state itself.

One way of looking at Barth's idea of the kingdom of God, comprising both church and state, encompassing and penetrating both church and state without being exhausted by them, and ever remaining distinct from them, is to relate it to the so-called *Extra-Calvinisticum.* As stated in Chapter Two of this study, Barth himself employs the concept in his discussion of the general relation of Christ to culture.[47] In his analysis of the relation of the church and state to Jesus Christ in *Against the Stream,* Barth writes that Jesus Christ

> is the Alpha and Omega, the beginning and the end, the standpoint from which it must always be judged whether or not the Church is on the right road. He is the "whole," within which the change of political systems takes place, within which the Church has its mission and commission. It must therefore pray that it may always be ready and willing to serve its Lord with an integrity in accordance with His wholeness.[48]

46. See, for example, Karl Barth, "The Christian Community and the Civil Community," in *Against the Stream: Shorter Post-War Writings, 1946-1952,* ed. R. G. Smith, trans. E. M. Delecour and S. Godman (London: SCM Press, 1954), pp. 32-33.

47. See Karl Barth, "Church and Culture," in *Theology and Church: Shorter Writings, 1920-1928,* with an introduction by T. F. Torrance, trans. Louise Pettibone Smith (New York: Harper & Row, 1962), pp. 342-43.

48. Karl Barth, "The Christian Community in the Midst of Political Change," in *Against the Stream: Shorter Post-War Writings, 1946-1952,* ed. R. G. Smith, trans. E. M. Delecour and S. Godman (London: SCM Press, 1954), p. 93.

Does one not find here in Barth's discussion of the church and "political systems" parallels to his discussion of the relation of the church to culture generally, a relation *based* in the eternal Word who became flesh? For how could it be that the Word who exists as the man Jesus Christ is the "whole"[49] in whom the church and state stand if it were not for Barth's conception of the *unio personalis?* For as discussed in Chapter Two, in light of the *Extra-Calvinisticum,* Barth argues that the Word in all his particularity, who is "wholly man in Jesus of Nazareth,"[50] not only is the "Church's own invisible truth," but also is "truth . . . beyond the visible reality of the Church."[51] The eternal Word, though identified with no creature save the human nature of Jesus Christ, nonetheless enfolds and indwells all creaturely reality, including human culture, which includes the state.

Barth's model of the relation of the kingdom to church and state follows the same path as his exposition of the overall relation of Christ to church and culture. In each case, Jesus Christ is the center, sustenance, and circumference of creaturely reality, standing in a distinct though inseparable relation to it. As it concerns Christ and his kingdom, the kingdom of God enfolds all creaturely reality, encompassing both church and state. And yet, the kingdom is not to be identified with any aspect of creaturely reality, save Jesus of Nazareth, in whom the kingdom has been inaugurated, and in whom it will be fully realized. Neither the church nor the state is to be identified with the kingdom of God.[52] The church and state last only so long as Christ tarries, ceasing to exist upon his return.[53]

Barth's doctrine of the revelation of the *coming* kingdom serves as a critical limit to any such identification of the kingdom with particular ecclesial and political models, or the manifestations of them in history. For just as God's revelation in Christ commandeers people, concepts, words, institutions, and rites without being contained by them, so too for Barth, the revelation of God's *coming* kingdom in Christ limits both particular models of the state and the manifestations of these models without being limited by them.[54]

49. Barth, "The Christian Community in the Midst of Political Change," p. 93.

50. Barth, "Church and Culture," p. 342.

51. Barth, "Church and Culture," p. 342.

52. Barth, "The Christian Community and the Civil Community," p. 32.

53. Barth, "The Christian Community and the Civil Community," p. 32.

54. One finds here in Barth's doctrine of the revelation of the kingdom a parallel to his

In addition to distinguishing the Word and the kingdom of the Word from the church and state, Barth distinguishes them from one another in the one kingdom of Christ. As already stated, the church is the inner circle whereas the state is the outer circle. What is it that gives rise to this particular distinction?

The basis for the distinction between church and state in Barth's theology is his doctrine of revelation. The church is the *inner* circle because it is called to bear witness to the enfleshed Word who has revealed himself to it. The state, on the other hand, is the *outer* circle of the one kingdom because of its *exclusion* from participation in the manifestation of *revelation.* God has revealed himself to the church but not as yet to the state. In a way, this is a reversal of the biblical statement, "Many are called, but few are chosen." For Barth, many are elect, but few are called, called to serve as witnesses to the election of the entirety of the human creaturely domain, which is to exist to honor Christ and his kingdom.

The church has a knowledge of the Word incarnate and thus of the eternal Word as well. However, the state has no such insight, that is, unless God chooses to raise up witnesses from within the outer circle. The church is the recipient of the Word of God. The state, on the other hand, bases its claims on natural law.[55] *Both church and state are elect* by and in the Word to serve the kingdom of the Word, Christ Jesus; *but only the church is called* to bear witness to that Word who is the center of all things, the same Word who also contains all things, even the state. Thus, the church serves as the inner circle of the kingdom, bearing witness to the revelation of the personal, divine-human center and circumference of all reality, namely, Jesus Christ. The state, on the other hand, serves as the outer circle of the king-

doctrine of *enhypostasis* and also his doctrine of the *unio personalis* (particularly as the latter bears upon his understanding of the *communicatio idiomatum*). For one, witnesses to the revelation of the kingdom are *not* as witnesses *self-subsistent,* but exist as witnesses only so long as they *subsist in* God's work by divine enablement. Moreover, the event of the divine commandeering involves the *assumption* of creaturely forms, but *not* the *communication* of itself to these forms. Neither the church nor the state is to be *identified* with the kingdom of the Word. And yet, neither the church nor the state exists *independently* of the kingdom, which is to come. In discussing the church, Barth writes that ". . . even at its best the Church is not an image of the Kingdom of God" ("The Christian Community and the Civil Community," p. 32). And yet, the church is called to bear witness to the kingdom. Although the church is not to be identified with the kingdom, it is nonetheless inseparably related to the kingdom.

55. Barth, "The Christian Community and the Civil Community," pp. 27-28.

dom since it only has indirect access to the Word of revelation through the witnessing agency of the church.[56]

Attention has been given to what distinguishes church and state. But what actually connects them other than the fact that they are in the one kingdom? Are their *vocations* in the one kingdom so distinct that Barth *in effect* advocates the Lutheran doctrine of the two kingdoms?

Election and the Interpenetration of the Ecclesial and Political Vocations

Barth rejects the Lutheran model of the two kingdoms according to which the church subordinates itself to the state in the sphere of the state.[57] As he sees it, the church must concern itself with the affairs of the civil community, i.e., the state, because both belong to the kingdom.[58] But how is it that the church is to be active in the sphere of the state? The church for its part is called to bear witness to the state concerning their respective roles in the kingdom through life and word. Exemplification and proclamation are the *church's* tasks in the political realm whereas the state is called to govern society in a just manner befitting the one kingdom, which includes granting the church freedom to proclaim the Word of election and its im-

56. Barth, "The Christian Community and the Civil Community," pp. 27-28. On page 23, Barth speaks of the church as belonging "to the inner circle." As such, its members "are also automatically members of the wider circle." He adds, "They cannot halt at the boundary where the inner and outer circles meet." The church must manifest "faith, love and hope," albeit in a different way, in the "civil community" with which it "shares common interests" (p. 23). The church and state have a "common centre," which the church is called to represent. It is called upon "to represent the inner within the outer circle" (p. 48).

57. Barth disagrees with Luther's translation of Romans 13. According to Barth, "Luther's translation speaks of 'being *subject*' . . . , which is something dangerously different from what is meant here. The last thing this instruction implies is that the Christian community and the Christian should offer the blindest possible obedience to the civil community and its officials" ("The Christian Community and the Civil Community," p. 24). For Barth, the church is called by Christ, not to subject itself to the state in blind obedience, but to Christ Jesus in the sphere of the state since Christ's kingdom includes both the church and the secular domain. Neither the church nor the state is an end in itself (Barth says this of the church in "The Christian Community and the Civil Community," p. 29). Both are instruments of the kingdom. Thus, they only submit to one another in their respective service to that kingdom.

58. Barth, "The Christian Community and the Civil Community," pp. 23-25.

plications for the whole of creaturely life.[59] Here one finds the coinherence of the church and state in the intersection of their respective vocations in one another's sphere.[60]

The distinction between the church and state concerns their respective proximity to the Word. The connection between the two, on the other hand, involves not only their joint election, but also the effectual exemplification and proclamation of the Word by the church to the state and the state's safeguarding freedom of speech for the church.

Barth says that since the church "is directly and consciously" assembled "around the common centre," it must shape "its own life" in such a way that it proves itself to be "the model and prototype of the real State," serving as "a source of renewal for the State and the power by which the State is preserved."[61] The church should indeed set an example for the state to follow because it is the inner circle of the *one* kingdom, that is, because it has more direct access to the revelation of that kingdom. The church has a responsibility in its sphere to exemplify for the state what community life should be in the secular sphere, that is, in the outer circle of the *one* kingdom.

The church is to set an example for the state to follow, not by functioning as the state, but by simply being the church. Thus, the church should neither create political parties nor seek to influence the state in such a way as to make its own ecclesial cause the cause of the state whereby the state becomes an extension of the church.[62] For its own part, the state should resist any attempt by the church to fashion the state into "the likeness of the Kingdom of God."[63]

Not only is the church called to set an example for the state to follow,

59. Further to what was stated about Barth's doctrine of election in Chapter Three, Christ and his kingdom have a constructive bearing, not only on the church, but also on the totality of the human sphere, including the political domain.

60. One is reminded here of the point made in the discussion of Barth's essay, "Church and State," in the first section of this chapter. The church and state intersect in a perichoretic manner. In and through Jesus Christ, who is Lord in the church and Lord over all, the church's vocation extends to the sphere of the state, and vice versa. Yet such cooperation and penetration concerning vocations does not thereby undermine the fundamental distinction between the two realms.

61. Barth, "The Christian Community and the Civil Community," p. 48.

62. Barth writes that the state must never become a church state in "The Christian Community and the Civil Community," p. 30.

63. Barth, "The Christian Community and the Civil Community," p. 31.

but also it is called to proclaim the kingdom to the state and exhort the state to be the state, legislating and ruling justly for the benefit of society. The church is called to preach the gospel of Christ, a gospel with political implications. Given that for Barth politics is a predicate of the gospel and theology, one rightly interprets Christian proclamation when one interprets it in a political manner, allowing the prophetic implications of the proclamation of the gospel to address the current political situation.[64]

When the church speaks, it should speak to the political situation of its day. It should be speaking to its times, not behind them.[65] It should speak to the concerns of the whole person, not simply a part.[66] Neither the Christian nor the church should be indifferent to politics;[67] for an "indifferent," that is, "a non-political Christianity" is ruled out as a possibility.[68] And so, it follows that, "The Christian Church that is aware of its political responsibility will demand political preaching; and it will interpret it politically even if it contains no direct reference to politics."[69]

The church will demand political preaching; but it will not demand of the state special privileges as its right.[70] Nor should it demand recognition in the political sphere.[71] Thus, as stated above, the church should resist any temptation to attempt to impose its will on the state. Now why is this? The reason is that when the church demands privileges and an audience in the secular sphere it forgets its own vocation and that of the state as well, thereby abandoning its freedom in the process. "Whenever the Church has entered the political arena to fight for its claim to be given public recognition, it has always been a Church which has failed to understand the special purpose of the State, an impenitent, spiritually unfree Church."[72]

Now if the church were to demand that the state accept its word, would not the church in effect displace the state? If so, how could the church continue to serve God and the state in a non-partisan way? Its word would then be bound, not free. Only as the church remains a spiritual insti-

64. Barth, "The Christian Community and the Civil Community," pp. 46-47.
65. Barth, "The Christian Community and the Civil Community," pp. 47-48.
66. Barth, "The Christian Community and the Civil Community," p. 46.
67. Barth, "The Christian Community and the Civil Community," p. 26.
68. Barth, "The Christian Community and the Civil Community," p. 22.
69. Barth, "The Christian Community and the Civil Community," p. 47.
70. Barth, "The Christian Community and the Civil Community," p. 30.
71. Barth, "The Christian Community and the Civil Community," p. 31.
72. Barth, "The Christian Community and the Civil Community," p. 31.

tution will it have secular, political responsibilities, namely, those of exemplifying the ideals of the kingdom to the state and of proclaiming God's word of the kingdom to the state. However, the reverse is not the case. If the church functions as a secular institution, it will forfeit its responsibilities in the sacred sphere.

The church must call on the state to listen to its Word, the Word of the kingdom, since the message of the kingdom concerns the state.[73] But it must not demand that the state listen. The church must not use force, the instrument of the state, imposing its message on its hearers, but must seek to persuade its addressees of the need to receive its message through reasoned argument alone in the event of Christian proclamation, appealing to the state to take to heart its word rather than compelling the state to do so.[74] The church must not demand but discuss, not presume upon but reason, appealing to the state to take its claims to heart, claims not about the centrality of the church, but about the centrality of the kingdom of which both church and state are parts. Now if in God's providential workings the state bestows on the church certain benefits and rights, even taking the church's message to heart, the church must not come to expect such benefits, rights, and respect as irrevocable, permanent privileges, which must be preserved at all costs, but rather as gifts from God's hand, gifts that may last but for a season.[75]

It was stated above that the church is to proclaim a political word. Does this mean that the church should promote this or that form of government or party to the exclusion of others? No, for as Barth reasons, the church

73. Since the state "belongs to the Kingdom of God, it has no autonomy, no independence over against the Church and the Kingdom of God" (Barth, "The Christian Community and the Civil Community," p. 32). Thus, the message of the kingdom concerns the state ultimately. And yet, without the church, that institution which bears witness to the kingdom, the state would have no knowledge of the kingdom and its place in it (p. 33). In view of these factors, the church must speak. And the state must listen.

74. Here one has in mind Barth's discussion of the purpose of speech acts, namely, an appeal to an audience to take a particular course of action. Along these lines, the vocation of the church is to bear witness to the kingdom with its words, calling forth a response of obedience to the Word. Karl Barth, "The Christian Understanding of Revelation," in *Against the Stream: Shorter Post-War Writings, 1946-1952*, ed. R. G. Smith, trans. E. M. Delecour and S. Godman (London: SCM Press, 1954), p. 214. Note also Barth's repudiation of the church taking up "political weapons" in "The Christian Community and the Civil Community," p. 29.

75. Barth, "The Christian Community and the Civil Community," p. 30.

must refrain from promoting the practice of Christians aligning themselves *as a collective* with a particular party. He contends that if the church were to support the cause of a particular party, the church would be supporting the cause of a select group of humans to the neglect of the interests of the whole. Such a move would be at variance with its commission to defend God's cause in Christ, that is, the common cause of election, the cause of all humanity.[76] Rather, Christians "must show that although they go their own special way, they are not in fact against anybody but unconditionally for all men, for the common cause of the whole State."[77] Thus, the church should not defend its own cause in the sphere of the state, but that of the state itself, which is the outer circle of the one kingdom.[78]

Now although it is the case that the church should resist any inclination to promote a particular party, it is appropriate for individual Christians to join political parties in keeping with their responsibilities as citizens of the state.[79] However, they should do so in an anonymous manner.[80] If Christians fail to speak as anonymous Christian *citizens* in the sphere of the state's *vocation,* failing to speak as citizens who simply happen to be Christians, but instead promote a particular agenda because it is "Christian," they will be fighting for the cause of the church rather than society as a whole. The result will be that "they will inevitably bring discredit and disgrace on the Christian name."[81] Christians must reason from their Christian convictions in the sphere of the state, yet without arguing for their positions because they are *Christian.* They should not leave their faith behind in the church. And yet, they should not bring *the church* to the assembly hall of the state. They must argue as anonymous Christians, as citizens, believing all citizens could make the same judgment, hoping all citizens will make the same judgment, regardless of their religious convictions.[82] Christians are to serve anonymously in their roles as citizens, calling for their views to be applied in the realm of the state, not because they themselves and their views are Christian, but simply because their positions are more sound.[83]

76. Barth, "The Christian Community and the Civil Community," p. 45.
77. Barth, "The Christian Community and the Civil Community," p. 45.
78. Barth, "The Christian Community and the Civil Community," pp. 29-30.
79. Barth, "The Christian Community in the Midst of Political Change," pp. 99-100.
80. See Barth, "The Christian Community and the Civil Community," pp. 44-46.
81. Barth, "The Christian Community and the Civil Community," p. 46.
82. Barth, "The Christian Community and the Civil Community," p. 46.
83. Barth, "The Christian Community and the Civil Community," pp. 45, 49.

As stated above, the church must resist the temptation to become the state, imposing its will on the state. The reverse is also true. The state must refrain from becoming the church. The church must ever resist moves by the secular authority to become a religious authority, using religion to serve its own secular ends.

The church may be called upon at times to speak out against an existing state for the sake of the true cause of the state. The state is to remain secular and not become a religious institution. The church is called on to resist those governments or political parties that speak from religious platforms, as in the case of National Socialism.[84] Just as the church should resist promoting a particular model of government to the exclusion of others,[85] the state should not exist to promote a religious ideology or a religious institution. When a state acts in an anti-Christian manner, putting itself forth as the kingdom, the church must speak out against it. Barth's view of the church-state relation provides space for the state to fulfill its *secular* calling, but also safeguards and preserves it from pursuing a *religious* one.

Barth's model provides distinct space for the secular vocation of the state. Can the same be said for the integral relation of church and state? Does Barth balance his emphasis on distinction with appropriate regard for connections? To answer this question, consideration will be given to Barth's varying responses to political situations, namely, his response to National Socialism on the one hand, and Soviet Socialism on the other.

According to Barth's own reasoning, which will soon be analyzed, he *spoke out prophetically* against National Socialism because it used religion to promote its own agenda. However, Barth did not raise his voice in protest against communist aggression in Eastern Europe, causing quite a stir. What was the rationale behind his decision? Was Barth's reasoning valid, or was he guilty of inconsistency? Could it be that he did not sufficiently balance consideration of the distinct existence of both church and state with appropriate concern for the ways in which they are connected, that is, in his analysis of Soviet Socialism? This latter possibility is in fact the case, as shall be argued in what follows.

84. This point will be discussed further in the treatment of Barth's rationale for his response to National Socialism in the next section.

85. Refer again to Barth, "The Christian Community and the Civil Community," p. 45.

The Modern Myths of Atheism and the Separation of Religion and State

In an open letter to Barth, Emil Brunner chastens him for failing to speak out against what has transpired in Eastern Europe under communism and charges Barth with inconsistency in his responses to political injustices. Why was it that Barth ardently spoke out against offenses committed under National Socialism in Germany and yet remains silent in the wake of the Soviet oppression of Hungary?[86]

Barth rejects Brunner's charge, arguing that his silence in the face of Soviet acts of injustice is consistent with his outcry against National Socialism. He contends that the church may take a different path today from the one it trod yesterday because it does not judge according to principles based on natural law, but according to "individual cases" in the light of "its living Lord."[87] Thus, the church may today remain silent even though yesterday it spoke relentlessly, its response depending on the divine directive in each situation.

The God who is always Lord in the event of revelation is always Lord in the event of the revelation of the divine command. One cannot predict or trace the way in which God might respond to a given situation. Thus, one cannot set forth necessary, universal principles to be applied in ethical matters. Just as one must wait for God to grant knowledge of himself, so too, one must wait for God to give knowledge of his ways and will, including his particular responses to particular offenses. Just as natural theology is ruled out, so too is natural law and casuistry in the sphere of the church.[88]

86. Barth, "The Christian Community in the Midst of Political Change," pp. 106-13.

87. Barth, "The Christian Community in the Midst of Political Change," p. 114.

88. Barth says that the state has no access to revelation, only natural law ("The Christian Community and the Civil Community," p. 31). Barth does not appear to rule out the employment of natural law in the sphere of the state by the state, only in the sphere of the church concerning the state. R. E. Hood points out that in *Church Dogmatics,* III/4, Barth "attacks natural theology and the use of it for the establishment of the state's authority, insisting that the foundation of the state for the Christian lay not in the *Schöpfungsordnung,* as natural theology would have to maintain, but rather in the *Bundesordnung* — that is, the realm of the covenant." R. E. Hood, "Karl Barth's Christological Basis for the State and Political Praxis," *Scottish Journal of Theology* 33 (June 1980): 229. In this context, Hood refers to Eckhard Lessing's work, *Das Problem der Gesellschaft in der Theologie Karl Barths und Friedrich Gogartens* (Gütersloh: Gütersloher Verlagshaus, 1972). According to Hood, Lessing argues that Barth will have nothing to do with natural law and natural theology. For if consider-

Thus, the theologian should be like the prophet, who speaks only when God calls on the prophet to speak, and who remains silent when God commands silence. And just as the prophetess may be called upon to give a different word today from the one given yesterday, so too the theologian's response today may vary from that response given yesterday.

Having said all this, Barth nonetheless gives Brunner reasons why his present course of action is compatible with his earlier stance. One reason for Barth's silence in the face of injustices committed under Soviet Communism is his conviction that speech would prove *ineffectual* in the present situation. He tells Brunner that Europe and America are already quite confident of the rightness of their crusade against the Soviets, and thus are in no need of moral support. Moreover, the Russians and Communists would only be dumbfounded by the Western church's response given that the same church had tolerated so much totalitarianism in the past, and still does at present. And lastly, the church that is behind the Iron Curtain, the church that is actually struggling "with the 'monster,'" would not profit from the Western church's declarations, words for which it has not asked, cheap words, words that cost the Western church nothing.[89] Things were quite different under National Socialism. The prior situation required prophetic speech. Such speech in the present situation, however, as far as he can tell, would profit no one.[90]

Barth also tells Brunner that it is *not necessary* to speak out against Soiet Socialism since so many other voices have been raised in protest. Such a state of affairs contrasts strongly with the situation under National Socialism where few protested against the abuses. So many had failed to speak out against the evils committed, whereas in the current situation, many voices outside the church can be heard. For Barth, it is not "the duty of Christians or of the Church to give theological backing" in such situations.

---

ation were to be given them, proper regard would not be given to the fact that the state belongs to the sphere of God's covenant with humanity. In turn, this would mean that proper criticisms of extreme instances of political rule could not be made from the perspective of the revelation of God in Christ Jesus. (See Hood, "Karl Barth's Christological Basis for the State and Political Praxis," p. 229, and Lessing, *Das Problem der Gesellschaft*, pp. 259-67.) In view of the foregoing considerations, it is concluded that for Barth, the state only has recourse to natural law and natural theology when left to its own devices, that is, apart from the witnessing activity of the church.

89. Barth, "The Christian Community in the Midst of Political Change," p. 117.

90. Barth, "The Christian Community in the Midst of Political Change," p. 117.

"No, when the Church witnesses it moves in fear and trembling, not with the stream but against it."[91]

Another reason why Barth remains silent in the face of Soviet Communism after having spoken out so fervently against National Socialism is due to the remoteness of the former and the proximity of the latter to Christian faith. Barth says of Hitler that he had many admirers both inside and outside Germany. They "had succumbed to Hitler's spell. He had become a spiritual and, almost everywhere, a political source of temptation," which attacked "body and soul."[92] Elsewhere in *Against the Stream,* Barth makes a similar point about National Socialism, contrasting it with Soviet Communism.

> The cause of the Russian-Communist East is doubtless a decidedly godless business: the cause of a false belief in accordance with which Christianity is seen and treated as an inconvenience from a pedagogical-tactical standpoint: tolerated for the moment, but in the expectation that in the process of development, that is, with the dawn of the great kingdom of socialist justice, it will vanish of its own accord, which does not, of course, exclude the possibility of a little coaxing if necessary. But please note that, in its relationship to Christianity, Communism, as distinguished from Nazism, has not done, and by its very nature cannot do, one thing: it has never made the slightest attempt to reinterpret or to falsify Christianity, or to shroud itself in a Christian garment. It has never committed the basic crime of the Nazis, the removal and replacement of the real Christ by a national Jesus, and it has never committed the crime of anti-Semitism. There is nothing of the false prophet about it. It is not anti-Christian. It is coldly non-Christian. It does not seem to have encountered the gospel as yet. It is brutally, but at least honestly, godless.[93]

This is the key charge and basis for Barth's change of action.

National Socialism clothed itself in Christian dress. Communism, on the other hand, does not clothe itself in Christian raiment, but in non-

91. Barth, "The Christian Community in the Midst of Political Change," p. 116.

92. Barth, "The Christian Community in the Midst of Political Change," pp. 114-15.

93. Karl Barth, "The Church Between East and West," in *Against the Stream: Shorter Post-War Writings, 1946-1952,* ed. R. G. Smith, trans. E. M. Delecour and S. Godman (London: SCM Press, 1954), p. 140.

Christian attire. This is one reason why, on the one hand, so many, though not all, were deceived by National Socialism and, on the other hand, why so many are alert to the dangers of Soviet Communism. And this is the reason why Barth spoke out against the former, and yet remains silent in the face of the latter. A wolf in sheep's clothing is always more dangerous than one wearing no disguise.

Barth does of course look disapprovingly on Soviet acts of aggression. And yet, it needs to be made clear at this point that while Barth looks unfavorably on those wrongs committed by the Soviet regime against other peoples, he does not look with disdain on socialism generally. Barth does not condemn the socialist political model (or any model for that matter), but only abuses of it as exemplified by certain policies pursued by the Soiet regime.[94] Thus, Barth writes that,

> The Church can never defend and proclaim — or even attack — abstract norms, ideals, historical laws and socio-political ideologies as such. Its concern must never be with political principles, creeds and catechisms but only with definite and concrete political constellations. It cannot make itself responsible either for any -ism or for rejecting it.[95]

Barth is unwilling to champion or reject democracy or communism as such. For him, the kingdom is not to be identified with any particular form of political rule; and yet, the kingdom is able to make use of any such form.[96] However, in one place, Barth does argue that the model of govern-

94. Marquardt argues that Barth's theology can be viewed from the standpoint of socialism, claiming that Barth was himself a committed socialist (Marquardt, *Theologie und Sozialismus*). See also George Hunsinger, ed., *Karl Barth and Radical Politics*, trans. George Hunsinger (Philadelphia: Westminster Press, 1976) for discussions of Barth's political views. Note also Barth's correspondence with Professor Joseph L. Hromadka in *Letters, 1961-1968*, pp. 104-5. There he speaks of communism in positive terms.

95. Barth, "The Christian Community in the Midst of Political Change," p. 91.

96. R. E. Hood refers to Barth's claim that culture is *"the promise originally given to man of what he is to become"* (Barth, "Church and Culture," p. 341; see Hood, "Karl Barth's Christological Basis for the State and Political Praxis," p. 235). Culture is itself reconciled to God (Hood, "Karl Barth's Christological Basis for the State and Political Praxis," p. 235). The "eschatological significance" of redeemed culture means that the Christian will not "underestimate or undervalue cultural and political phenomena" but will be liberated "to see these phenomena in light of the *telos* for which all cultural and political activity is striving" (p. 235). Bound up with *culture as promise* is the notion that the possibility exists for the cultural enti-

ment known as democracy, "'the rule of the people,'" moves closer to the notion of the Christian community than other forms of government, but adds that its concrete manifestations in modern states such as Switzerland, America, and France fail to image the Christian ideal. He also writes in the same place, however, that the Christian view "may equally well assume the form of a monarchy or an aristocracy, and occasionally even that of a dictatorship."[97] Lastly, from what he says of democracy, it can be inferred that for Barth, no state is immune to the dangers of corruption, lawlessness, and repression, even a democratic one.[98]

Barth's attempt to remain objective about the relation of the kingdom of Christ to the state, critiquing views of the state in the light of that kingdom which is to come, is commendable. Indeed, there is no existing state or form of government that images the kingdom. For the gospel of the kingdom stands in a position of transcendence in relation to this world's governments. In one place, Barth writes that the gospel "does not exclude individualism or collectivism," but "defends social freedom against the attacks of the West, and personal freedom against the attacks of the East."[99] He is not against "-isms" as such as long as their proponents do not seek to reconstruct the Christian message, interpreting the gospel in the light of party ideals and ends, thereby enslaving the gospel. However, Barth goes on the offensive when a particular ideology assimilates the gospel, altering it to achieve some particular end as in the case of National Socialism. Such alertness follows from his vigilance to safeguard the conceptual distinction between the kingdom, church, and state against attempts by either the

ties themselves to "illuminate the promise and the fact of reconciliation" (p. 235). Reconciliation occurs *in* culture rather than remaining external to it. The church itself plays a part in the reconciliation of culture in Christ as it shapes culture in its ministry to the state. (See also Hood, p. 236.)

97. Barth, "The Christian Community and the Civil Community," p. 44.

98. See Barth, "The Christian Community and the Civil Community," p. 44. Hood points out that for Barth there is no such thing as a "totally redeemed" or "totally unredeemed" state. Like the Christian, the state is both righteous and unrighteous. As unrighteous, the state is still "threatened" by sin and its powers. However, Hood also notes that as righteous, the state like the Christian is "'troubled'" in its sinful condition, redirected in the light of Christ's bearing on the cosmos (Hood, "Karl Barth's Christological Basis for the State and Political Praxis," p. 231).

99. Karl Barth, "The Christian Message and the New Humanism," in *Against the Stream: Shorter Post-War Writings, 1946-1952*, ed. R. G. Smith, trans. E. M. Delecour and S. Godman (London: SCM Press, 1954), p. 188.

church or state to identify itself with the kingdom or to displace the other.[100]

Once again, one finds that Barth's theology promotes space, not only for the kingdom and the church, but also for the state to fulfill its secular vocation. However, the investigation is not yet finished. For the question as to how Barth conceives the space itself has not yet been answered. Does he set the freedom awarded to the state to fulfill its secular vocation within the limits of inseparable relation to the church? This question will be approached by considering once again what Barth says of the atheistic state.

As noted above, Barth calls the atheistic state of the communist system false and godless. However, unlike the pseudo-religious state, it is innocent of the crime of willful deception.[101] It is not a state that uses religion for its own ends, camouflaging its real aims. Therefore, as he sees it, one need not necessarily speak out against it. The best course to follow is to wait and see.

Is this a valid move? Is the atheistic state truly innocent of the crime of deception? Is it really godless? Is not the atheistic state in reality a *pseudo-secular* state? For one, atheism is itself a form of belief, namely, the belief in no God.[102] Moreover, when the atheistic state disowns the church or insti-

100. In addition to *Against the Stream,* "The Barmen Theological Declaration" also speaks out against the church or state going beyond the "special commission" assigned to each in the errant attempt to fulfill the responsibilities of the other. See point five of the declaration in Bax, "The Barmen Theological Declaration," p. 80.

101. The term "pseudo-religious" is used here to denote that state which employs the symbols of the prevailing religious system in a particular society to advance its own political ends. In the case of National Socialism in Germany, one could refer to it as a "pseudo-Christian" state. However, the expression "pseudo-religious" has been chosen in light of the fact that the same abuse of religion occurs in countries where Christianity is not the prevailing religion.

102. Barth himself makes a similar point in his reply to Max Bense, a noted atheist, who championed "existential determinism." Barth argues that Bense's views, such as his belief in "infinite progress," are without basis, but are dependent on rigorous faith. Karl Barth, "The Rationality of Discipleship, (Karl Barth's Reply)," in *Fragments Grave and Gay,* ed. Martin Rumscheidt, trans. Eric Mosbacher (Glasgow: William Collins & Sons, 1971), pp. 40-41. On a different note, Michael Buckley points out that both Socrates and the first Christians were called atheists by their critics, arguing that the term "atheism" has often been used to denounce those who reject prevailing philosophical and religious views in favor of others. Michael Buckley, S.J., *At the Origins of Modern Atheism* (New Haven and London: Yale University Press, 1987), pp. 3-4. Buckley also reasons that the meaning and existence of atheism is dependent on the theism it denies, to which it is inseparably joined (pp. 14, 16).

tutional religion, it is only a matter of time before it replaces the church, becoming itself a religious institution.[103] When the state removes the church, or simply disowns and disregards it, the state succeeds the church, consciously or unconsciously stepping in to fill the void, championing its belief in no God and its belief in itself in the face of all contenders. In this light, is not the atheistic state in the end also anti-Christian, albeit in a different form from the quasi-religious state? Indeed it is. For this reason, Barth should have spoken out against the Soviet form of socialism instead of remaining silent.

It is wrong to think that one can have the state without religion. One simply has good or bad religion. Marx, for instance, may have been accurate in his criticism of the religion of his day serving as the opium of the masses. However, he oversimplified the nature of religion, failing to perceive the manifold forms it takes.[104] For one can disown the church or organized religion as the Soviet form of socialism in effect did. However, one cannot eradicate religion. Nor should one attempt to do so. For as Machiavelli argues, the state requires the observance of religion if the state itself is to function well.

> And as the observance of divine institutions is the cause of the greatness of republics so the disregard of them produces their ruin; for where the fear of God is wanting, there the country will come to ruin, unless it be sustained by the fear of the prince, which may temporarily supply the want of religion. But as the lives of princes are

103. The opposite was in some sense true of National Socialism. According to Barth, it first used religious groups such as the "German Christians" in the attempt to "destroy" the true church "in favour of a more or less sentimental reverence for the State, and in favour of the ethos of the 'political soldier,' in which the German man is to recognize his ultimate destiny." In the end, however, this movement would have had "nothing more at all to do with the Church." Most likely, the "'German-Christians,'" the "'German Faith Movement,' . . . all Rosenbergians" and "the enterprises" of the two "Ludendorffs" were "destined to provide only a prelude" to the "establishment" of the final "destiny" of the German people under National Socialism (Barth, *German Church Conflict*, p. 56). Even so, it would have been impossible for National Socialism to rid itself of religion. Religion would simply have taken on new forms.

104. One should take into account the paradoxical nature of Marx's doctrine. On the one hand, Marx repudiates religion (as he understands it); and on the other hand, he sets forth a utopian vision of heaven on earth. The author is indebted to Daniel Eshun for these points on Marx.

> short, the kingdom will of necessity perish as the prince fails in virtue.[105]

Although Machiavelli's wholly pragmatic espousal of religion is to be rejected, he is nonetheless correct in arguing that religion is a force that the state ignores to its own peril.[106]

Not only is it important for society that the state make space for religion, but also it is vital for the well-being of the state that it make space for the church. The state requires the coexistence of the ecclesial institution if it is to remain secular. Indeed, the state cannot adequately perform its secular vocation without the church as its counterpart,[107] for as Dostoyevsky writes, "the universal and everlasting craving of humanity" is "to find someone to worship."[108] Now if there is no church but only the state, the populace will be led to worship the state in due course. In the end, the state will become a sacred institution, laying aside its secular vocation. In the atheistic state, neither the church nor the state is able to fulfill its calling in that the church is displaced by the state. Ultimately, there is not enough space for either to function in its respective role. Why is this? Such distinction is absent because, ironically, the two stand in too distinct a relation to one another. That is to say, the distinction is too dramatic, leading ultimately to its opposite, namely, the amalgamation of vocations in favor of the state. In view of this danger, the church should demand to be heard,

105. Machiavelli, *Discourses,* in *The Age of Adventure: The Renaissance Philosophers,* ed. Giorgio de Santillana, The Meridian Philosophers (New York: New American Library, 1956), p. 118. Barth's critique of religion in the face of Christ should be noted here. Religion itself, according to Barth, belongs to "civilization," which is a *"lower"* layer, and *"not* the kingdom of love, *not* the final goal." Thus, regardless of the occasional and perhaps accurate statements made by leading citizens of society commending religion "as the indispensable ferment of civilization," one must remain sober as to the limitations of religion, and civilization for that matter, in the light of Christ and his kingdom of love. Karl Barth, "The Problem of Ethics Today," in *The Word of God and the Word of Man,* trans. Douglas Horton (London: Hodder & Stoughton, 1928), p. 165.

106. Voltaire says that the well-being of society requires belief in God. Thus, if God did not exist, it would be required of humanity to create God. "If God did not exist, it would be necessary to invent him." *The Oxford Dictionary of Quotations,* 2nd ed. (London: Oxford University Press, 1953), p. 557.

107. The reverse is of course also true.

108. Fyodor Dostoyevsky, *The Brothers Karamazov,* vol. 1, trans. Constance Garnett, with an introduction by Edward Garnett (London: J. M. Dent & Sons, 1927; reprint, London: J. M. Dent & Sons, 1967), p. 259 (page reference is to reprint edition).

not for its own sake or reputation, but for the well-being of the state. There must be distinction between the church and state, but not separation. If there is separation, a vacuum may result, in the light of which substitution may occur whereby the one takes on the role of the other, potentially leading to an abuse of power to the detriment of society's well-being.

The problem here is not isolated to the atheistic state, for example, Soviet Communism. What is to be made of the American ideal of the *separation* of church and state? Does it really exist? If so, why is it then that one finds the American flag behind the altar in so many churches there? Perhaps it is nothing more than an isolated example. But even if on the whole one finds in the American system the practice of the separation of church and state, one certainly does not find there the separation of religion and state.[109] It is not a question of bringing religion into or excluding religion from the sphere of the state, but of how one relates the two. Either it is coexistence and coinherence or amalgamation. The attempt to separate church and state jeopardizes the distinct existence of each since it is ultimately impossible to separate the sacred and secular domains. One can only distinguish or confuse them. Thus, one should not speak of separation, but of *distinction.*

In the case of the atheistic state, the state disowns the church, perhaps even displaces it. In the democratic state, on the other hand, especially of the American variety, the state ignores the church, privatizes it, perhaps even displaces it, if it is indeed the case that civil religion is the religion of the state.[110]

109. Herberg speaks of "the American Way of Life" as "the operative faith of the American people." Will Herberg, *Protestant, Catholic, Jew,* rev. ed. (New York: Anchor Books, Doubleday, 1960), p. 75. See also Hood, "Karl Barth's Christological Basis for the State and Political Praxis," p. 230.

110. Peter Berger has argued that the state/society cannot fulfill the deepest needs and desires of the people. If it seeks to do so, the individual is left ultimately in a state of despair. The moment religion is relegated to the private sphere, the worldview it generates is imprisoned given the dominance of the state, resulting in disillusionment for its adherents. See Peter Berger, *The Social Reality of Religion* (Harmondsworth: Penguin Books, 1967), p. 31. The state should not attempt to fulfill the spiritual needs of the populace since it is not transcendent and thus can never adequately address the individual's yearnings for the transcendent. Moreover, civil religion, the religion of the state, is even less able to provide spiritual and moral foundations for Western society today given that, not only organized religion, but it too, is in danger of extinction in light of the disappearance of the monolithic worldview that gave rise to it. As a result, religion can no longer be privatized. As Christoph Schwöbel has

Now given the dangers found in both the socialist and democratic models considered, Barth's attempt to remain objective in the face of the plethora of political systems is praiseworthy. Neither the atheistic state of the East nor the seemingly agnostic or indifferent state of the West is to be championed. Nonetheless, having said this, the church and state stand in too distinct a relation to one another in Barth's discussion of atheistic socialism. The church must not only speak out when the state is quasi-religious, but also when it is quasi-secular, as in its Soviet (or, for that matter, American) form. The state can only be truly secular if it has the church or perhaps another institutional religious form as its counterpart, serving as a check to its ambitions, reminding the state of the kingdom that transcends it.[111]

It is in the best interest of the state for the church to exist, playing an active role in the sphere of the state. In this light, the church should urge the state to give ear to its word, not for its own sake, but for the sake of the state, not because its view is Christian, but simply because its view makes sense. If the church were to be ignored, equilibrium would be lacking, leading perhaps to the displacement of the church in one form or another. Not only would this jeopardize the calling of the church, but also it would undermine the secular calling of the state, namely, its duty to govern society, preserving the individual and collective rights of its populace.

One is reminded here of Barth's statement that the communist state is brutally godless. This raises the question of human rights. Is it any coincidence that in the twentieth century crimes against humanity have escalated to astronomical proportions, often committed by states that are atheistic in outlook? Is it due simply to improved technology and efficiency? Or

---

pointed out, religion can only be privatized when a monolithic and all-pervasive form of civil religion exists in its place. Thus, in today's society, religion is becoming a very public matter. The point was made by Schwöbel during his series of lectures entitled *Identities, Differences and Dialogues: Christian Faith in the Context of Pluralism*, F. D. Maurice Lectures, 18 March to 20 March 1997, King's College London. In this light, public dialogue between the various voices in society is crucial. A unified voice is required, one that includes all voices, even those of the numerous forms of organized religious communities. The state must involve them. It can no longer ignore them.

111. The possibility that a form of institutional or organized religion other than the church may serve to delimit the vocation and ambitions of the state should not be ruled out in advance. Now the reason for speaking of institutional or organized religion here is due to this writer's conviction that it makes clear the distinction between religion and state. A clear line of distinction is necessary given the tendency for the state either to become a religious institution or to create one.

could it be that whenever the state destroys the church, or more generally, the institution of religion, it tends to displace it, perhaps even claiming to be the kingdom, brushing aside all checks to its authority? What is the result? Simply this: when the transcendent other is displaced, so too is the other.[112] Did not the one who said that religion is the opium of the masses also say that violence could be used to awaken the masses and guide them into the kingdom of socialism?[113] Of course, it is not only atheistic states, but also quasi-religious, even deeply religious states, which have been guilty of heinous crimes committed against humanity. However, the atheistic state moves in this direction much more readily than others given its conscious desire to depose God. For as Dostoyevsky argues, "If there's no everlasting God, there's no such thing as virtue, and there's no need of it."[114]

In light of the preceding, Barth's decision to remain silent on the ideology and activities of the atheistic Soviet state is problematic. As Colin Gunton has been quoted as saying, "Barth never remains silent on other occasions. So why here?"[115] In view of this silence, could it be that Barth's desire to preserve the concept of the secular state, especially in view of the menace posed by National Socialism and the "German Christians," causes him to lean in the direction of promoting the *separation* of church and state rather than the distinct existence of each in inseparable relation to the other in his consideration of Soviet Socialism, as a result of which he fails to see that there is ultimately no real distinction between the church (or re-

112. Although Barth seemed to be aware by and large of the crimes committed against humanity by the atheistic regimes of the Soviet empire, he was ignorant of the rampant anti-Semitism found in such states.

113. The truth of the theory of dialectical materialism by which history eventually moves toward the realization of the socialist state is confirmed or better proven by the overthrow of bourgeois capitalism by the workers. Marx's understanding of truth is reflected in his thesis that the essence of life is not to interpret the world, but "to *change* it." Karl Marx, "Theses on Feuerbach," in *The Age of Ideology: The Nineteenth Century Philosophers*, ed. Henry D. Aiken (New York: New American Library, 1956), p. 195. Although Marx's desire was to make the world a better place in which to live, his belief that truth is determined by action rather than by correspondence to the transcendent other opens the door to the possibility of anarchy and the displacement of the human other.

114. Fyodor Dostoyevsky, *The Brothers Karamazov*, vol. 2, trans. Constance Garnett, with an introduction by Edward Garnett (London: J. M. Dent & Sons, 1927; reprint, London: J. M. Dent & Sons, 1961), p. 288 (page reference is to reprint edition).

115. Colin Gunton, Interview by author, winter 1996, London.

ligion) and state in the Soviet system? And is it not fair to say that, *in effect,* Barth inadvertently advocates the Lutheran doctrine of the two kingdoms, and the danger inherent in it, by refusing to speak out against the menace posed by atheistic socialism?

Here there is found a reversal of fortunes from what was indicated in Chapters Three and Four of this study. There it was argued that there are instances in Barth's theology where the sacred or divine overshadows the secular or human. Here the opposite is the case. In Barth's discussion of Soviet or atheistic socialism, the sacred is in danger of being overshadowed by, indeed even overwhelmed by, the secular. The term "overwhelmed" is used in this context because, as has already been argued, Barth does not account for the paradoxical reality that atheistic socialism leads ultimately in the direction of religion, whereby the church is not simply ignored or marginalized, but is threatened ultimately with being *displaced by* the state.

In the end, Barth does not employ his own insight that both the church and state have duties to fulfill in the sphere of the other in his discussion of Soviet Socialism. How is it that the church can fulfill its vocation in the sphere of the state if it remains silent? Barth's claim that the church should for the time remain silent in the face of Soviet ideology and aggression militates against his understanding of the church-state relation whereby the church is ever called to bear witness to the kingdom in the sphere of the state, exhorting the state to take to heart the Word of the kingdom for the fulfillment of the state's political tasks, not despise or ignore it.[116] There is of course a time to remain silent. But the situation concerning which Barth speaks here is not such a time.[117] Not only must the church speak

116. Implicit in Barth's claim that the state has no existence independent of the kingdom and the church given that "the State is based on a particular divine ordinance" (Barth, "The Christian Community and the Civil Community," p. 32) is the view that the state should listen to the word of the church regarding the kingdom. And if the state is "to be saved from degeneration and decay it needs to be reminded of the righteousness which is a reflection of Christian truth" (p. 33). But how can it be reminded, how can it proceed toward "the execution of political responsibility" (p. 33) if it refuses to listen to the church, and if the church for its part does not speak out on behalf of the true state, which unlike its secular counterpart "has knowledge" (p. 33) of the kingdom? The state "*needs* the wholesomely disturbing presence, the activity that revolves directly around the common centre, the participation of the Christian community" (p. 33, italics added) for the fulfillment of its political tasks in view of the divine ordinance on which it is based (pp. 32-33).

117. Moreover, Barth's claim that the church does not go with the stream but against it could be seen as a piece of natural theology of the negative type. Who is to say? There may

out against the quasi-religious state as in the case of the German church under National Socialism, but also it must speak out against the quasi-secular state of atheistic socialism.

Barth may be aware of many of the dangers inherent in the atheistic state. But his claim that the church need not speak out against Soviet Communism because it is "honestly . . . godless"[118] betrays a misunderstanding of the atheistic state, including the full implications for human life and social well-being arising from it. Whatever the atheistic state is, it is not godless. It may not be pseudo-Christian, but it is not secular either. Moreover, the god it promotes is often, if not always, more oppressive than those gods it deposes.

Christological Mediation and the Preservation of the Secular

In this chapter, it has been argued that Barth is to a large extent successful in providing space for the secular vocation of the state, as exemplified in his discussion of National Socialism. However, in considering Barth's response to the problem posed by Soviet Socialism, we found that Barth's approach there was flawed, inclined toward conceiving the space for the state in its relation to the church as that of separation, given his silence on the subject. Having spoken of Barth's problematic response to Soviet Socialism, we must recall that, as narrated in the course of this chapter, *in theory,* Barth succeeds in distinguishing the church and state from one another *without* separating them given his Christological model. For he conceives the church and state as standing in distinct though inseparable relation to one another in and through the mediation of Jesus Christ.[119] Thus, the problem noted in the case of atheistic socialism *does not extend* to his theological analysis of the state as a whole. For given his dogmatic enterprise, in which he conceives the relation of church and state as involving patterns of coexistence and coinherence, he is in a position to correct the particular

be times when the church is called to speak *with* society against a certain form of evil and not always against the prevailing voice of society.

118. Barth, "The Church Between East and West," p. 140.

119. See especially in this regard his essay, "Church and State," and his work, *Against the Stream*. Refer also to Bax, "Barmen Theological Declaration," and the discussion of these texts in this chapter.

instance of imbalance noted here. For the problem does not concern his underlying dogmatic conception or model of the relation of church and state, but simply the application of that model in this particular instance. And as was shown in the discussion of Barth's response to the crisis that emerged with the rise of National Socialism and the "German Christians," Barth's model is indeed efficacious if applied appropriately to the "situation" with which the church finds itself confronted.

To conclude, Barth's Christological *model* of the relation of church and state is sound, balancing between an unhealthy fusion and an equally unsound polarization of the two, thereby preserving the *status* of the state as a *secular* institution. Will evidence of such preservation and celebration of the secular be found in the next chapter where consideration will focus on such things as Mozart and his music, on science, and on creaturely existence generally? There consideration will center on the question as to whether or not Barth is able to provide theological parameters for creaturely existence and cultural activity that balance between the sacramentalist and secularist orientations in favor of fostering authentic forms of secular expression. To this subject, discussion now turns.

6

The Creative Word and Creaturely Existence and Activity

Prelude

Attempts have often been made in theology to find a middle ground position between a variety of religious and non-religious perspectives in seeking to delineate what is admirable in the context of a pluralistic culture by going behind Christology to the doctrine of God or nature, or past Christology to Pneumatology.[1] One reason for such ventures is the desire to achieve some form of universal harmony or cohesion in terms of what is to be considered good in human culture, beyond the margins of the respective religious and ideological traditions. Now given the particularity and objectivity of God's Word in Christ in Barth's theology, does Barth in any way affirm human creativity beyond the frontiers of the church? It shall be shown that although Barth does not go the routes mentioned above to provide theological affirmation for non-Christian forms of cultural creativity, he does offer an alternative model.

1. On the religious front, James Sanders has gone so far as to call for doing away with "a distorted christocentric singularism"; what is required is the development of "canonically faithful monotheising pluralists." As he sees it, such a move is necessary in view of the oppressive intolerance of Christendom toward those of other religions throughout church history. James A. Sanders, "A Christian Response to Elliot Dorff: 'This is my God': One Jew's Faith," in *Three Faiths — One God: A Jewish, Christian, Muslim Encounter,* ed. John Hick and Edmund S. Meltzer, with a foreword by John David Maguire (New York: State University of New York Press, 1989), p. 34.

The Freedom of the Word and the Secular Praise of Creation

Barth views the creation as bearing witness to God. He even uses the term "mirror" in this context.[2] However, such imaging is different from how creation's witness is at times conceived, that is, in terms of some form of *ontological proximity.* Barth's position is radically dissimilar, for he conceives of creation's witnessing agency in the light of its *ontological otherness or distance.* That is to say, the creation glorifies God by being what it is in the freedom of its limits.[3] Thus, the truly secular is indeed sacred, or rather, compatible with the sacred. This point is admirably put by John Updike in his foreword to Barth's work on Mozart:

> Karl Barth's insistence upon the otherness of God seemed to free him to be exceptionally (for a theologian) appreciative and indulgent of this world, the world at hand. His humor and love of combat, his

2. Karl Barth, *Church Dogmatics,* III/3, *The Doctrine of Creation,* ed. G. W. Bromiley and T. F. Torrance (Edinburgh: T. & T. Clark, 1960), pp. 52-53.

3. Barth makes this point at several places in the *Dogmatics* when speaking of humanity. God has created and reconciled humanity with the intent for it simply to be itself, to revel in being human. In this light, the notion of divinization is to be replaced by that of humanization: in his death and resurrection, Jesus makes it possible for humanity to be simply human, indeed, to be truly human, not divine, and not less than human. See especially Karl Barth, *Church Dogmatics,* III/2, *The Doctrine of Creation,* ed. G. W. Bromiley and T. F. Torrance (Edinburgh: T. & T. Clark, 1960) and Karl Barth, *Church Dogmatics,* IV/2, *The Doctrine of Reconciliation,* ed. G. W. Bromiley and T. F. Torrance (Edinburgh: T. & T. Clark, 1958) in this regard. See also Karl Barth, "Mozart's Freedom," in *Wolfgang Amadeus Mozart,* with a foreword by John Updike (Grand Rapids: Eerdmans, 1986), pp. 43-60. In *Church Dogmatics,* III/3, Barth defines the life of the creature "within its limits" as not simply "a limitation to its own particular place. It means also a limitation of its possibilities and capacities, of its development and operation. Above all, it means a limitation of its existence in itself and as such" (*Church Dogmatics,* III/3, p. 87). See also pages 234-36 for a discussion on the limitations of human life. In "Church and Culture," Barth writes, "*Limit* is not a merely negative concept, it is also very positive. Our limit informs us of our situation. *God* is our limit. Is there anything better we could know about our situation? God who created men and reconciled them with himself in order to draw them to him for ever, God who is faithful, is over our faithlessness." Karl Barth, "Church and Culture," in *Theology and Church: Shorter Writings, 1920-1928,* with an introduction by T. F. Torrance, trans. Louise Pettibone Smith (New York: Harper & Row, 1962), p. 349. See also Barth's discussion of freedom within the limits of time, vocation, and honor in Karl Barth, *Church Dogmatics,* III/4, *The Doctrine of Creation,* ed. G. W. Bromiley and T. F. Torrance (Edinburgh: T. & T. Clark, 1961), pp. 565-685.

> capacity for friendship even with his ideological opponents, his fondness for his tobacco and other physical comforts, his tastes in art and entertainment were heartily worldly, worldly not in the fashion of those who accept this life as a way-station and testing-ground but of those who embrace it as a piece of Creation.[4]

The ontological otherness of God safeguards the distinct identity and existence of the creation. It also allows for the creation, including humanity in the exercise of its creativity within human culture, to give glory to God by simply being what it in fact is and by doing what it in fact does as created by God. One need not make music or tables with the goal in mind to glorify the creator. By *simply* working or playing, one glorifies God. There need be no theological ax to grind or message to send.[5] Workmanship is itself a form of doxology, affirmed by the God of creation. God is glorified in the very imaginative and enterprising acts of human creation and recreation.[6]

4. John Updike, foreword to *Wolfgang Amdaeus Mozart,* by Karl Barth (Grand Rapids: Eerdmans, 1986), p. 7.

5. Is Barth here guilty of a certain kind of artistic naïveté? Certain commentators on art say that all artists, including those who are Christian, whether conscious of it or not, impose meaning on the world through art, meaning that is not in the object of imagination itself. For such critics, artists always have a theological ax to grind or message to send. People are the creators of meaning. Aristotle's classic description of what transpires in the making of the Greek tragedies offers a different model for viewing the intention of the artist in the production of a work of art. Although order and meaning are not imposed on reality in the construction of the tragedy given Aristotle's belief in the moral order of the universe, nonetheless the artist orders the tragedy in such a way as to make sense of the pity and terror people experience, providing for them a means of catharsis. See Aristotle, *Poetics,* in *The Basic Works of Aristotle,* ed. Richard McKeon (New York: Random House, 1941), p. 1460. Where Aristotle and commentators sympathetic to him differ from that approach to art deemed to be Christian is found in the supposedly Christian attempt to portray through art the redemption of the cosmos. Aristotle for one knows nothing of redemption, simply the order of a moral universe. On a different note, Barth's talk of a thing simply being itself sounds like the Romantic view of nature according to which one loves nature for what it is, as it is. This leads to the following question: Is Barth's view of creation noted here shaped exclusively by revelation? Could it be that his view is influenced to some extent by Romanticism? The issues raised in this footnote were brought to the writer's attention by Brian Horne, in an interview by author, autumn 1996, London.

6. Although Barth argues that work itself may bring glory to God, he opposes the notion of work as an end in itself, that is, "work for work's sake." "Culture as an end in itself will always be an extra duty which man may accept or evade. But as a *parergon* of the *ergon*

Before God, there is room for free play. When the artist or carpenter or nursing mother revels in his or her work, content with it, and not wishing to go beyond it, it is then that even non-Christian cultural existence finds affirmation. One glorifies God and enjoys him by glorying in and enjoying the works of one's hands. Thus, the creation is not a means to an end of glorifying God. Its end is to be itself. And by being itself, it glorifies God.

The truly empirical perspective is to take the creation for what it is without importing into one's investigation a certain theology or philosophy. Nature is what it itself says it is. It speaks the glory of God by speaking about itself, the workmanship of God. But by speaking about itself, it glorifies God. The creation declares God's glory by speaking about itself and simply itself. It does not speak about itself by speaking about God. Rather, it says something about God by simply speaking about itself. God is not the negation of creation, but creation's ultimate affirmation in its otherness from God. One should not seek to read God out of nature, or into nature, but simply read nature. The marvels disclosed bespeak the glory of God, which are there to see, but are only seen by the eye of faith, the eye which is looking, which is trained to know how to look.

This view of creation contrasts strongly with certain forms of sacramentalism in which the creation is not allowed to be what it in fact is. According to such views, this world is regarded *simply* as a window for viewing another world, a door through which to pass. Along similar lines, Plato's theory of universals in which the immaterial forms exist outside time and space involves the tenet that this world possesses reality *to the extent* it models the immaterial world, that of the universal forms. There is only one real world, the world of the forms, which this shadowy sphere reflects and participates in to the degree it models that reality. Barth, on the other hand, is not arguing that this world is the only world, but that it, too, is *fully* real.

Certainly the creation bears witness to God; but it does so by *simply*

---

which is truly and essentially required, it is an obligatory duty which no one who is prepared to obey the call of God can overlook or neglect." Barth adds, "The idea of an independent value and existence of human culture, and the consequent requirement of work for work's sake, can only be dismissed. This means that, strictly speaking, it is only as a Christian, only as he is claimed for co-operation in the service of the Christian community and thus knows the meaning of work, that man finds himself summoned to it. Without faith and its obedience, man's work will always stand under the shadow of the most profound uncertainty" (Barth, *Church Dogmatics,* III/4, p. 523).

being what it in fact is. One of the implications arising from the doctrine of the Word, a doctrine championed by Barth,[7] is the idea that God *grants* to the creation, *not a separate, but a distinct* existence from that of his own by creating all things *ex nihilo* by his Word.[8] God is able to provide the creation with ontological space or otherness due to the nature of the agent of creation, namely, the divine Word, whose creative agency demonstrates the ontological difference between God and the creation. Creaturely reality is that which is commanded into existence out of nothing rather than an emanation that proceeds from an already existing life form, ultimately God. God also *affirms* the goodness of his creation and *orders* it to its proper end through the agency of this same Word. Moreover, the creation's existence is spoken to it. Its existence is something *from which* it proceeds rather than an existence *to which* it proceeds, as in the case of the beatific vision. The existence and goodness of creation are declared rather than envisioned. Or to put it another way, all forms of its anticipated, eschatological perfection *stand within* this original declaration. Thus, the creation has the God-given freedom to serve God by simply being itself. It need not be anything more. It simply proceeds from this position. As such, the truly secular is indeed sacred, or better, compatible with the sacred.[9]

The problem with many forms of secularity is that they are nothing more than disguised theologies. Just like some of their confessing religious counterparts, they impose a worldview onto this world. They *exploit* this world rather than *explore* it. Whether one looks on this world for what it says about God or some God surrogate, one forces this world to speak of something to which it does not directly speak. For it speaks about itself, and by speaking about itself, it speaks of God. It glorifies God by simply proclaiming the glories of its own reality, which is God's workmanship.

The creation speaks about God by speaking about itself. It is the doctrine of the creation of all things from nothing by God's Word that allows the creation to speak in this way, that is, by being itself, and not the embodiment of God by which one must say that the question of the constitu-

7. Recall Stuart McLean's claim discussed in the opening section of Chapter Four.

8. Through the course of this study, attention has been drawn to the distinct space awarded to culture in view of Barth's doctrine of the Word with whom it is inseparably related.

9. See Karl Barth, "Wolfgang Amadeus Mozart," in *Wolfgang Amadeus Mozart,* with a foreword by John Updike (Grand Rapids: Eerdmans, 1986), pp. 39-40.

tion of God and the creation are ultimately one.[10] God lets the creation be itself. And by being allowed to be itself, the creation glorifies God by simply existing. By being allowed to speak about itself, and not having to be viewed as some way station for viewing God, creation bespeaks the glory of God. This is what the creation says about God. God in his love gives the creation the freedom to praise God by simply being itself. The doctrine of the creation of all things out of nothing by God's Word reflects God's unconditional love and perfect freedom. And one of this doctrine's implications is that the creation is allowed to be itself, an end in itself.

The Christian doctrine of creation and the doctrine of the Trinity enable one to view the creation more appropriately. The creation does not help one to know how to view the being of God. Thus, one should not seek to find vestiges of the Trinity in creation. Rather, Christian doctrine offers the parameters on how to view creation. God creates all things *freely* by his Word. Moreover, he creates in view of the Word *enfleshed* who is the ultimate affirmation of the goodness of God's creative work.[11] It is the Son, the enfleshed Word, together with the Spirit, who *mediates* the creation to God. Such mediation, along with the free creative activity of the creator, who has taken on human flesh for time and eternity, is what provides space for the creation as an end in itself.

One way in which Christian thought has set the parameters for approaching the subject of creation can be seen from a historical study of Christianity's influence on science. There is space from oppressive theological constraints for the development of the natural sciences, not because of the absence of theological tenets, but because of their presence. Harold Nebelsick has argued that the Christian doctrine of creation, especially in

10. Harold Nebelsick writes that the Reformation emphasis on the Word (which, it should be noted, Barth shares) led to the further emphasis on the distinction between God and the world. "God is God and the world as the world is secular." Harold P. Nebelsick, *The Renaissance, the Reformation and the Rise of Science* (Edinburgh: T. & T. Clark, 1992), pp. 154-55. Nebelsick then quotes T. F. Torrance, "It is the sheer differentiation between God and nature which definitively overcomes both the sacramentalism of Augustinianism and the *aeternitas mundi* (the eternality of the universe) of Aristotelian philosophy. Thus, the concept of *deus sive natura* is finally dispensed with." Nebelsick, *The Renaissance, the Reformation and the Rise of Science,* p. 155, quoting Thomas F. Torrance, *Theological Science* (London: Oxford University Press, 1969), pp. 65-66.

11. Note the reflections on the positive implications for a theology of culture arising from the doctrine of the incarnation of the Word as Jesus Christ in Thomas F. Torrance, *Karl Barth: An Introduction to His Early Theology, 1910-1931* (London: SCM Press, 1962), pp. 208-17.

its Reformation form, was influential in the development of modern science. Because God created the universe out of nothing by his Word, science, *as long as it remains science,* has the freedom to explore nature on its own terms. Because there are two distinct orders, the uncreated (God) and the created (all things other than God), there are grounds for free, scientific investigation. Christian theology provides the intellectual basis of freedom for natural science given its doctrine of the free creation of all things out of nothing by God's Word.[12]

Inherent in certain problematic perspectives on sacramentalism is a failure to come to terms with this important implication stemming from the Christian doctrine of creation, namely, that as the creation of the God who is other, the universe is truly distinct from God and as secular as it is sacred. Where this implication is not recognized, the result is the imprisonment of free scientific exploration and artistic creativity. Along similar lines, William T. Jones comments on the sacramental outlook of the medieval mind:

> What makes Augustine and Thomas and all the other medieval thinkers so fundamentally alike, despite all differences, is the sacramental outlook they shared. What makes us differ so markedly from them is that we have largely lost this outlook and that we share the basically secular point of view of the Greeks. When we say that medieval men looked on this world as a sacrament, we mean, first, that they conceived this world to be but the visible sign of an invisible reality, thoroughly impregnated, as it were, with the energy, the purpose, and the love of its Creator, who dwells in it as He dwells in the bread and wine on the altar. And we mean, second, that medieval men conceived this world to be a sacrifice which they freely and gratefully dedicated to the all-good, all-true Giver. Thus, while to us and to the Greeks the world by and large means what it is, to the Middle Ages it meant something beyond itself and immeasurably better. While for us and for the Greeks our life here is its own end, for the Middle Ages life's true end was beyond this world.
>
> That this sacramental point of view was a block to progress — progress in knowledge of how to control the environment and utilize it for this-worldly purposes — can hardly be denied. . . .[13]

12. Nebelsick, *The Renaissance, the Reformation and the Rise of Science,* pp. 154-56.

13. William T. Jones, *A History of Western Philosophy,* vol. 1 (New York: Harcourt, Brace and Company, 1952), p. 524.

Perhaps Jones is too sweeping in his generalization in attributing this perspective to all medieval thinkers.[14] However, the outlook did captivate the minds of many.[15] One may also question Jones's assessment of the Greeks. Both Plato and Aristotle viewed reality very differently from their Greek predecessors given their logical and psychological systems, and doctrines of universals. For Plato, this world is a shadow of the ideal realm beyond time and space. Aristotle's logic and metaphysics, on the other hand, impregnated both his approach to and understanding of physical reality.[16] Such impregnation led Francis Bacon to assess the significance of the Greek Aristotle in a very different light. In contrast to Jones's positive estimation of the Greeks, Bacon attributes much of the blame for the slowness of science's progress up to his own day to the system of "the Philosopher." In the following quotation, Bacon takes aim at Aristotelian logic and scientific analysis.

14. In his interview with the author noted already (see footnote 5 above), Horne argues that Jones is wrong to say that for Thomas everything is sacramental. Horne claims that only the incarnation and those things belonging to the church are sacramental. For Thomas, the world is full of signs, but not sacraments. Thomas distinguishes between sacrament and sign. A sacrament is a form of a sign, which concerns the incarnate Lord. Thus, there is no such thing as a sacrament outside the church. Not only is Jones wrong in saying that all is sacramental for Thomas, but also he is wrong in saying that for Thomas, the world is but a sign. Rather, the world is both significatory and fully real. Horne adds that although Jones's criticism does not apply to Aquinas, it does indeed apply to later medievals who see the world as full of sacraments (Horne, interview).

15. Regarding the sacramental mindset of the later medievals, see J. Huizinga, *The Waning of the Middle Ages: A Study of the Forms of Life, Thought and Art in France and the Netherlands in the XIVth and XVth Centuries* (London: Edward Arnold & Co., 1937).

16. Nebelsick writes, "Like Plato who viewed nature as unreal, a shadow of the ideal, Aristotle considered matter to be of secondary importance. It was an 'accident' of the *substance* of reality. Added to that, Aristotle's 'metaphysics' so circumscribed his 'physics' with the contradictory characteristics of rigidity and capriciousness that investigation of nature was discouraged. The rigidity resulted from its claim that first and final causes both determined reality and interpenetrated it in such a way that all solutions could be gained from present principles by the simple application of deductive logic. At the same time and equally important, Aristotle's understanding of reality in organismic terms subjected nature to the unpredictable and capricious intervention of living and divine principles" (Nebelsick, *The Renaissance, the Reformation and the Rise of Science,* pp. x-xi). Nebelsick refers to Stanley Jaki's claim that the development of physics was influenced by Greek theology (p. xii). Jaki himself writes, "To a large extent, it was religious motivation that helped decide the course of physics for almost two thousand years when Aristotle, following Socrates' and Plato's lead, made physics serve the 'living and divine principles' that were believed to rule the cosmos." Stanley L. Jaki, *The Relevance of Physics* (Chicago: University of Chicago Press, 1966), p. 412.

> The understanding must not however be allowed to jump and fly from particulars to remote axioms and of almost the highest generality (such as the first principles, as they are called, of arts and things), and taking stand upon them as truths that cannot be shaken, proceed to prove and frame the middle axioms by reference to them; which has been the practice hitherto; the understanding being not only carried that way by a natural impulse, but also by the use of syllogistic demonstration trained and inured to it. But then, and then only, may we hope well of the sciences, when in a just scale of ascent, and by successive steps not interrupted or broken, we rise from particulars to lesser axioms; and then to middle axioms, one above the other; and last of all to the most general. For the lowest axioms differ but slightly from bare experience, while the highest and most general (which we now have) are notional and abstract and without solidity. But the middle are the true and solid and living axioms, on which depend the affairs and fortunes of men; and above them again, last of all, those which are indeed the most general; such I mean as are not abstract, but of which those intermediate axioms are really limitations.
>
> The understanding must not therefore be supplied with wings, but rather hung with weights, to keep it from leaping and flying. Now this has never been done; when it is done, we may entertain better hopes of the sciences.[17]

To this, let it be added, "of the theology of creation, too." One should view the creation, not as the theater of redemption, but as redemption's object, that is, as part of the drama itself.[18] By viewing the creation, not as a launching pad or way station, but as humanity's homeland, humankind is better able to see its way.

How does this view of the creation relate to the theology of culture generally? It has already been stated that, for Barth, when one simply works or plays one glorifies God. This now needs to be spelled out in greater detail.

17. Francis Bacon, "First Book of Aphorisms," in *The Age of Reason: The 17th Century Philosophers,* ed. Stuart Hampshire, The Mentor Philosophers (New York: New American Library, 1956), pp. 27-28. For Bacon, empirical observation and efficient recording were the essential traits of scientific study. However, he failed to appreciate the roles of hypothesis and theory formulation for scientific analysis.

18. Is this not the view of Irenaeus?

A Vestige of Creation: The Music of Mozart

Barth illustrates his position through consideration of the music of Mozart. It is not this writer's concern given the limits of time and space to discuss the merits and defects of Barth's historical-theological exegesis of Mozart.[19] What is of concern is the delineation of Barth's theological model for affirming space for non-Christian cultural creativity and existence illustrated through consideration of his interpretation of Mozart and his music.[20]

There is a parallel between Nebelsick's affirmation of the enterprise of natural scientific investigation mentioned above and Barth's affirmation of the music of Mozart. Barth sees in Mozart's music something symbolic of the creation, something that the Christian theologian can affirm. According to Barth, Mozart plays simply to make music. There is no worldview that Mozart imposes on his music. What Mozart's music symbolizes for Barth is nothing other than the celebration of creation.

> Mozart's music is not, in contrast to that of Bach, a message, and not, in contrast to that of Beethoven, a personal confession. He does not reveal in his music any doctrine and certainly not himself. . . . Mozart does not wish to *say* anything: he just sings and sounds. . . . Nor does he *will* to proclaim the praise of God. He just does it — precisely in that humility in which he himself is, so to speak, only the instrument

19. See Thomas Erne's article, "Barth und Mozart," *Zeitschrift für Dialektische Theologie* 3 (June 1988): 234-48. There he presents divergent views from that of Barth on the topic of Mozart's music.

20. It would perhaps prove an illuminating study to analyze Barth's correspondence with the poet Carl Zuckmayer, whose work he says affects him "'as if it were a part of me,'" alluding to the title of one of Zuckmayer's writings. See Karl Barth, letter to Dr. Carl Zuckmayer, in *Letters, 1961-1968*, ed. Geoffrey W. Bromiley (Grand Rapids: Eerdmans, 1981), p. 312. However, such correspondence is indeed sparse. In discussing Barth's appreciation of the works of culture, it makes best sense to consider his discussions of Mozart and politics (the latter being the subject of Chapter Five) given that he has written extensively about these subjects and most sparingly on others related to the present theme. To illustrate, at one point Barth says that he is not antagonistic toward modern art, simply ignorant of it and unable to appreciate it. "I have not passed a negative judgement on it and do not recall having ever said a bad word about modern art. It is just a sad fact that I have no understanding, no eyes, no ears for it." Karl Barth, letter to Pastor Kurt Lüthi, in *Letters, 1961-1968*, ed. Geoffrey W. Bromiley, p. 101. However, it may prove rewarding at some future date to develop the connection Barth makes between the music of Mozart and the paintings of Sandro Botticelli. (See Barth, "Mozart's Freedom," p. 59.)

> with which he allows us to hear what he hears: what surges at him from God's creation, what rises in him, and must proceed from him.[21]

Because music is the creation of God, the celebration of music is the celebration of creation, and in its own way, the celebration of God. The making of music and its enjoyment is an end, a created end. The making and enjoyment of music is only misdirected when one treats music as the ultimate end or when one imposes ideological constraints on it.

According to Barth, Mozart's music is an affirmation of the creation itself in its freedom to be what it is and nothing more or less. The simple celebration of creation in the music of Mozart is praiseworthy. Such music is free from Christian theology's critique, even though it does not expressly speak of Christ, because it does not promote non-Christian theologies, but instead encourages the free enjoyment of life as it is given, something which Christian theology itself establishes and promotes. Such music is free from theology's critique because it is in keeping with theology's claim.[22]

The Christian doctrine of creation out of nothing affirms both the free investigation of science and the equally free development and enjoyment of human life, including the arts, within limits. The creation mirrors God in and by way of its otherness; and because of its ontological otherness, there is space for cultural creativity that is pleasing, not only to its human creator, but also to the divine creator.[23]

The true danger to human culture is the pantheistic doctrine of God in which culture is a manifestation of the being of God, and thus only seemingly human in its origin as distinct from God. The Christian doctrine of creation affirms the otherness of creation in relation to God, and is thus

21. Barth, "Wolfgang Amadeus Mozart," pp. 37-38.

22. Robert Palma rightly observes that it is not in the setting aside of "his theological imagination" that Barth is able to affirm secular culture, but in the application of it. Robert J. Palma, *Karl Barth's Theology of Culture: The Freedom of Culture for the Praise of God,* Pittsburgh Theological Monographs, ed. Dikran Y. Hadidian (Allison Park: Pickwick Publications, 1983), p. 11. See his discussion of Hans Frei's analysis of Barth on the relation of Christ to culture found there.

23. A theology, a worldview, is always bound up with science. The question is thus not whether or not theology accompanies science, but rather *which* theology allows for science to be science and not religion. As argued earlier in this chapter, it is the conviction of this author that the Christian doctrine of the creation of all things out of nothing by God's Word offers science the best possible theological companion.

the basis for free culture.[24] Moreover, Barth's own emphasis on the otherness of God, as reflected in the Christian doctrine of creation by God's Word, when complemented by Barth's equally strong emphasis on the humanity of God in his Word, actually serves to promote the freedom of humanity in relation to God. God affirms the creation in its otherness, even to the extent of becoming one with creation in the person of his Son, elected from all eternity as the *logos ensarkos.*[25] The orthodox doctrine of Christ, in its opposition to all forms of docetism, affirms the goodness of creation and, together with the Christian doctrine of creation, is the ultimate basis for the affirmation of the goodness and freedom of the creation, including human culture, that is, when human culture affirms the limits of its own creaturely existence.

When humanity explores and creates from what is already given it, exploring and creating for the sheer joy of doing so, humanity affirms God's good creation. The word most fitting to express this idea is that of "play." True play is bound up with an understanding of creaturely freedom within limits, which involves a total disregard for self-conscious absorption. Even human work is to be as play. Humanity should not take itself too seriously, not be preoccupied with thoughts of self-importance or self-loathing, but should consider its work as play, serious play perhaps, but play nonetheless. When humans simply act within their range of potentialities and respec-

24. In *Church Dogmatics,* III/1, Barth writes that the intent of the Christian doctrine of creation is to make clear that God has indeed created the world and therefore is not the sole reality. The world is not an emanation from God. Thus, the world is awarded a distinct existence. It is granted freedom within the limits created and preserved by God. Moreover, the Christian doctrine of creation demonstrates that "we should have no less factual knowledge of this factual being of the world." Karl Barth, *Church Dogmatics,* III/1, *The Doctrine of Creation,* ed. G. W. Bromiley and T. F. Torrance (Edinburgh: T. & T. Clark, 1958), p. 5. In this same context, he rejects reflecting on God in relation to the world in favor of reflecting on the world in relation to God. He writes that theologians have often preoccupied themselves with only one side of the question, and as a result, "there has been a dangerous failure to realise that the question of creation is not less but even more concerned with the reality of the creature than that of the creator. Presupposing the certain knowledge of God in His Word, it is actually the case that the existence and being of the world are rendered far more problematical by the existence and being of God than *vice versa*" (p. 6).

25. See Karl Barth, "The Humanity of God," in *The Humanity of God* (Atlanta: John Knox Press, 1960), pp. 37-65. By placing emphasis not only on the deity of God (i.e., the otherness of God), but also on his humanity (i.e., the nearness of God), by which God supremely demonstrates his providential care and affirmation of the creation, Barth seeks to show that God sustains humanity through the granting of appropriate, authentic space.

tive interests, resting even in their work, simply reveling in, performing the existence which is theirs, which is given, they affirm God in their cultural endeavors, the God whose work is truly work.[26]

For Barth, play in this context does not mean frivolity as in superficiality. He writes of Mozart that, "behind his play there is an iron zeal."[27] Moreover, the "ever-present lightness" of Mozart's music "is not effortlessly accessible," but "possesses something very demanding, disturbing, almost provocative, even in the most radiant, most childlike, most joyful movements."[28] In speaking of the reason for his devout admiration for Mozart's music, Barth refers to this theme of play.

> How am I to explain this? In a few words perhaps this way: our daily bread must also include playing. I hear Mozart — both younger and older — at play. But play is something so lofty and demanding that it requires mastery. And in Mozart I hear an art of playing as I hear it in no one else. Beautiful playing presupposes an intuitive, childlike awareness of the essence or center — as also the beginning and the end — of all things. It is from this center, from this beginning and end, that I hear Mozart create his music. I can hear those boundaries which he imposed upon himself because it was precisely this discipline that gave him joy. And when I hear him, it gladdens, encourages, and comforts me as well. Not that I want to utter even one critical word against anyone else. But in this sense I can offer my testimonial to Mozart alone.[29]

Mozart glorified God in his mastery of play. And more than in any other, Barth finds in Mozart one who has perfected that playful song of praise.

Barth's emphasis on play may sound very postmodern at first sight. However, there is one important respect in which it is not. Mozart freely created and played music within the limits given him. Barth writes,

26. Barth takes cultural activity seriously as play, as "a serious game," adding that "the game might actually be played better and more successfully, the more it was recognized as a game. *Our* earnestness could not be impaired by making clear to ourselves that the game can never be ultimately serious, and never is; that the right and the possibility of being wholly in earnest is God's alone" (Barth, "Church and Culture," p. 349).

27. Barth, "Mozart's Freedom," p. 47.

28. Barth, "Mozart's Freedom," p. 48.

29. Karl Barth, "A Testimonial to Mozart," in *Wolfgang Amadeus Mozart* (Grand Rapids: Eerdmans, 1986), pp. 16-17.

> What was originally foreign to him, until he made it his own, became in his ears, in his head and spirit, and under his hands something which it had not been before: it became — Mozart. Even while he adapted, and precisely then, the man was creative. He certainly never merely imitated. From the beginning, he moved freely within the limits of the musical laws of his time, and then later ever more freely. But he did not revolt against these laws; he did not break them. He sought to be himself and yet achieved his greatness precisely in being himself while observing the conventions which he imposed upon himself.[30]

Barth says that Mozart did not simply imitate, but did indeed create music. He did so while remaining within the limits given rather than create by transcending those limits.[31] Is it not the case that for Barth, Mozart transforms music, not by way of transcending the limits of his day, but by way of working within those limits?

In contrast to Barth's view, a truly postmodern, secularist perspective on creative play allows for no pre-established, "creaturely" limits to human freedom. There are no limits, but infinite space and time for unlimited possibilities of discovery and creation. What limits do exist are but the creation of human minds and wills.[32] Thus, in the light of truly postmodern

30. Barth, "Mozart's Freedom," p. 46.

31. Barth, "Mozart's Freedom," p. 46.

32. Nicholas Rescher speaks of science's limitless freedom. He opposes "conversion" or "approximation" models of scientific inquiry. For him, science proceeds by way of "replacement" rather than "cumulation." Thus, science is immortal, not due to physical complexity or infinite discovery, but rather to the infinite possibilities for viewing physical reality generated by way of cognitive inquiry. Nicholas Rescher, *A System of Pragmatic Idealism,* vol. 1, *Human Knowledge in Idealistic Perspective* (Princeton: Princeton University Press, 1992), pp. 47-76. Be that as it may, Rescher's idealist and pragmatist program is not skeptical in outlook, for he argues that, "There is more to reality than can be compassed by instrumentalities of mind" (p. 76). However, science must nonetheless be conceived in idealist terms since, as he sees it, science is dealing with a *concept of* discovered reality rather than the real itself as discovered (p. 76). For Nietzsche, on the other hand, idealism and pragmatism give way to skepticism. The pragmatic drive for Nietzsche is nothing more than one's own determination for survival and supremacy. Kant had argued in his *Critique of Judgment* that the artist engages in an activity not governed by the laws of science or morality. See Immanuel Kant, *Critique of the Faculty of Judgment,* in *Kant Selections,* ed. Lewis White Beck, The Great Philosophers, ed. Paul Edwards (New York: Macmillan, 1988). There is so to speak free play. Nietzsche extends Kant's idealist conception of art (as ruleless) to that of truth and morality as well. For Nietzsche, truth is an illusion gen-

perspectives, Barth's talk of free play within limits may seem very enslaving, hierarchical, bourgeois and conservative, even religious. To this, however, Barth would likely respond that one only experiences freedom by living within the limits of God's creative purposes. Enslavement occurs when we break free from such parameters.[33]

Mozart did not seek to master music, but to serve it. Music must remain free. For example, the music must ever remain music no matter what passions one wishes to express.[34] In opera, poetry must serve music, and not the music poetry.[35] Even Mozart's life served his art.[36] He simply

---

erated by means of the will to power. See Friedrich Nietzsche, "On Truth and Lie in an Extra-Moral Sense," in *The Portable Nietzsche,* ed. Walter Kaufmann (New York: Viking, 1968), pp. 46-47. See also Friedrich Nietzsche, *The Will to Power,* ed. Walter Kaufmann, trans. Walter Kaufmann and R. J. Hollingdale (New York: Random House, 1967). According to Nietzsche, humanity has forgotten that "truths" are merely the creations of human minds. The key to reality is perpetual, creative generation. In this regard, see Edward Craig's discussion of Nietzsche in *The Mind of God and the Works of Man* (Oxford: Clarendon Press, 1987), pp. 272-81. In his work, Craig argues that modern philosophy is an evolution of thought, moving from that of imitation or understanding to creation or praxis. This contrast is typified in Marx's statement that the heart of the matter is not to understand history, but to change it. For Marx, praxis is fundamental. Kevin Vanhoozer charts a similar journey for an understanding of language, ending with Derrida in which *poiesis* replaces *mimesis.* See his article, "A Lamp in the Labyrinth: The Hermeneutics of 'Aesthetic' Theology," *Trinity Journal* 8 (Spring 1987): 38.

33. At the heart of Barth's consideration of humanity in the *Church Dogmatics,* one finds the claim that through the sin of pride, through the human struggle to exalt itself to the place of God, humanity becomes enslaved and *falls short* of its humanity. Related to this assertion, Colin Gunton argues in *The One, the Three and the Many* that although the moderns were justified in their efforts to release themselves from the shackles of an oppressive monotheism, they would have better served themselves and their successors through the employment of Trinitarian parameters in which to live. The end result of their "liberation" from religion and metaphysics has been a very pronounced increase in enslavement through the execution of atrocities committed against humanity under the various guises of humanism. The heart of the problem concerns an inability to conceive of otherness in a non-threatening manner. Gunton endeavors to show that it is only the Christian doctrine of the Trinity that provides the proper framework in which human culture can flourish. Colin E. Gunton, *The One, the Three and the Many: God, Creation and the Culture of Modernity, the 1992 Bampton Lectures* (Cambridge: Cambridge University Press, 1993), pp. 22-37. On a related note Barth writes, "It is only the heathen gods who envy man. The true God, who is unconditionally the Lord, allows him to be the thing for which He created him" (Barth, *Church Dogmatics,* III/3, p. 87).

34. Barth, "Mozart's Freedom," pp. 53-54. For Mozart, the emotions must serve music, and not *vice-versa.* See Barth, *Church Dogmatics,* III/3, p. 298.

35. Barth, "Mozart's Freedom," p. 52.

36. Barth, "Mozart's Freedom," p. 49.

sought to devote himself to music, not to *parade* his musical prowess, but simply *to pursue and play* music itself.[37] Updike speaks of Barth's admiration for Mozart's playing and his freedom in doing so.[38] The two go together. There is freedom for play within limits, indeed because of the limits given. It is within such limits that true play takes place. And it is only as the music is free that the musician is also free.

Barth's theology, for all its seriousness, is itself playful. And Barth's work on Mozart is perhaps the closest thing we have to an autobiographical account from the pen of Barth.[39] That is to say, the ideals Barth finds in Mozart's music bear traces of characteristic marks found in Barth's theology, including his concerns for objectivity,[40] self-restraint, earthiness, a combination of "gaiety" and tragedy, "lightness" and "gravity" in moderation,[41] in which one finds the "consoling turn" of grace overcoming demonic nothingness.[42] All this takes place in the free activity of play as one reflects upon one's subject matter in an objective manner.[43]

37. Barth, "Mozart's Freedom," p. 51.

38. Updike, foreword to *Wolfgang Amadeus Mozart,* p. 9.

39. Thomas Erne says something to the effect that Barth does not impose on Mozart's music a confession of himself. And yet according to Erne, Barth does view Mozart and his music as reflecting his own view of the gospel, and sees his own theology of freedom as advocating the human freedom of Mozart's music (Erne, "Barth und Mozart," pp. 236, 245).

40. Barth, "Mozart's Freedom," pp. 48-51.

41. Barth, "Mozart's Freedom," pp. 47-48, 53.

42. Barth, "Mozart's Freedom," pp. 54-56.

43. On the subject of objectivity, Barth writes that he has "a warm relationship" with "the blackbird" and "all God's creatures that refrain from regarding the self-understanding of their faith as the theme of theology." Karl Barth, letter to Prof. Ronald Gregor Smith, in *Letters, 1961-1968,* ed. Geoffrey W. Bromiley (Grand Rapids: Eerdmans, 1981), p. 112. On the same topic, Bromiley writes that Barth "said he had given up the idea of an autobiography since it would unavoidably have too much reference to himself." See Geoffrey Bromiley, editorial comment in *Letters, 1961-1968,* by Karl Barth, p. 242. Barth praises Mozart for his objectivity in making music. Because Mozart simply made music, because he listened to "creation unresentfully and impartially, he did not produce merely his own music but that of creation, its twofold and yet harmonious praise of God." Mozart was able to hear, and teaches those who listen what he heard, and which will not be heard or seen again "until the end of time — the whole context of providence" in which there is within creation light and shadow (though not darkness), and in which the light "breaks forth from the shadow." Barth believes no theologian has taught of the "total goodness" of creation as the seemingly nominally religious Mozart has, and thus argues, "Mozart has a place in theology, especially in the doctrine of creation and also in eschatology . . ." (Barth, *Church Dogmatics,* III/3, p. 298). For Barth, Mozart is the theologian of providence *par excellence* because he perceives the

According to Barth, Mozart's music does not promote a worldview. There is "no 'moral to the story.'"[44] Nor is there a "Mozartean metaphysics."[45] Is it not fair to say that for Barth, the language of Mozart's music is the language of creation? Mozart's music does not abuse the creation, but imitates it, explores it, creates from within the limits given. The creative genius of Mozart's music does not emerge as it were from the negation of the creation from which it springs. Rather, it moves in keeping with the limits given Mozart by creation and the music of his time.[46]

A theology of culture delineated along such lines affirms the scientist in the investigation of this world, which is the good creation of God. In this way, it is a theology *for* culture. But such a theology cannot affirm the scientist in the development of a doctrine of nature in which nature is viewed as a self-governing system, divine to be precise. When faced with such forms of naturalism, it is a theology *against* culture.

The creative Word is affirming of culture according to Barth when culture is *creaturely* in its existence, living within its limits and loving life for what it is, not for what it might be, nor for what one might make from it as if one could improve on God's work, but for what it is, loving it, playing

light breaking forth through the shadow. What then would Barth say in response to the claim that it is perfectly warranted for a composer or an artist to focus attention simply on the shadow, or even on the terrors of nothingness, bracketing off consideration of the light of grace? One might be led to think that Barth would look less favorably on such an approach to the subject matter. One might assume that Barth would argue that if one brackets off consideration of the light in creation, one distorts the shadow and night, falsely representing them. On this view, it would be assumed that Barth maintains instead that one must view the parts within the context of the whole drama of life, giving due attention to the light of divine grace. For an opposing view to this understanding of the relation of theology to music, see Francis Watson, "Theology and Music," *Scottish Journal of Theology* 51, no. 4 (1998): 435-63. Surprisingly though, Barth claims that not only words of the "liberation" and glorification of the creation may bear witness to the Word, but also those of the "jeopardising" of the creation. See Karl Barth, *Church Dogmatics*, IV/3.1, *The Doctrine of Reconciliation*, ed. G. W. Bromiley and T. F. Torrance (Edinburgh: T. & T. Clark, 1961), p. 123. For their "abstraction" is only "apparent." For "the one thing envisaged under all these aspects is the kingdom and deity of the one living God" (p. 123). Here, at this point, two questions arise. How can one glorify God in one's work without reflecting God's *glory* in that work? Following on from this, if one's work does not glorify God, directly or indirectly, can one's work truly be considered good in view of God's glory?

44. Barth, "Mozart's Freedom," p. 51.

45. Barth, "Mozart's Freedom," p. 53.

46. Barth, "Mozart's Freedom," pp. 46, 53.

within the parameters of the possibilities given. When cultural creativity takes place within these bounds, there is for Barth the divine affirmation of culture by the creative Word.

Humans live freely when they live within their limits, being what they are in the acts of their existence. They live in love when they simply enjoy life, loving it for what it is. This is the moral to be learned from Mozart and his music. Mozart made music within the limits given him. He simply played. In this way, even the atheist can glorify God. When the creature lives within the limits given it, rejoicing in the life it lives, and the life around it, the creature honors God.[47]

How is Barth's treatment of space within limits given to the creation by the creative Word different from Aquinas's separation of nature and grace? Is Barth not in effect contradicting his own principle of the covenant in Jesus Christ being the ground of creation? To support Barth, perhaps one could argue that the problem with Aristotle and Aquinas was that they were not empirical enough, that they did not give enough space, not enough *proper* space, to the created realm. Aquinas certainly did make a division between nature and grace in which nature has freedom within limits. But what kind of limits were they but those of Aristotelian physics, and indeed, metaphysics and logic? The issue may not be space so much as it is the *kind* of space. For Barth at least, space is awarded for the free play of the creature within the limits granted in creation.

Barth's doctrine of creation gives room to science to engage in scientific enquiry apart from theological constraints. His doctrine of creation sets the parameters within which the natural sciences have space for free enquiry. Because he safeguards against seeking vestiges of God within nature, because he is wary of making connections between revelation and scientific theories, and because he refuses to build his theology upon a natural foundation (whereas in the case of Aristotle, physics was closely joined to metaphysics), Barth is better able to make proper delimitations.

The view mentioned above concerns Barth's doctrine of creation gen-

47. The question here, however, is will the atheist live within these limits without knowing what they are? Could it be that the God of all grace will raise up witnesses from outside the confines of the confessing church to glorify him, enabling them to perceive the limits within which free creaturely existence may take place and, in the light of such perception, act? Or is the answer to be found elsewhere? Barth seems to suggest that by *simply existing,* one experiences and perceives the limits of one's createdness.

erally. The same cannot be said, however, for his doctrine of humanity.[48] For Barth, humanity and human freedom can only be viewed in terms of a positive orientation toward God and others, founded in Jesus Christ. Nonetheless, his emphasis on the Word and play allows for the affirmation of Christian and non-Christian alike, who engage in the simple affirmation of existence as given.

The Christian doctrine of creation, according to which God creates all things out of nothing by his Word and for his Word, the eternal Word who is also the Word enfleshed, sets the parameters for free play within limits. That is to say, the divine Word does not enslave human creativity, but grants it freedom within limits, Christological limits, to be precise. These Christological limits are not confined to the realm of the church, but extend beyond the church to include human culture generally.

Here one calls to mind once again Barth's employment of the *Extra-Calvinisticum* for his analysis of culture, to which attention has already been drawn at several places in this study. "The kingdom of the Word" is not "limited" to the incarnation,[49] though inseparable from it. Thus, the "invisible truth" of the church "is truth also beyond the visible reality of the Church."[50]

The divine Word, who creates *all* things in freedom, the ever-present Word, who is the circumference of creaturely reality, including the church and broader culture, which has its center in the *logos ensarkos,* grants free-

48. See the section entitled "Phenomena of the Human" in Barth, *Church Dogmatics,* III/2.

49. Barth, "Church and Culture," p. 341.

50. Barth, "Church and Culture," p. 342. Does not Barth's view of the joint relation of the eternal Word and *logos ensarkos* to that of broader culture find a parallel in the following statement of Athanasius? "For He was not circumscribed in the body; nor was so in the body as not to be elsewhere too. Nor, while He moved that, had He emptied the universe of His effectual working and providence; but, what is most marvelous, being the Word, He was not contained by anything, but rather contained all things Himself. And as, when present in the whole creation He is essentially distinct from it all, but in it all by His power, ordering all things, and unfolding His providence over all things in all, and quickening each and everything at once, containing the universe, and not being contained, but existing wholly in His Father alone in every respect; — so also, existing in human body and Himself quickening it, He was naturally quickening also the universe, and was present in every part, yet outside the whole. And being known from the body through His works, He was manifest too from His working of the universe." Athanasius, *De Incarnatione Verbi Dei,* trans. T. Herbert Bindley (London: The Religious Tract Society, 1903), p. 72.

dom to the creation. He does so by serving as its wholly other origin, the whole in whom it has space to be, and its creaturely center, having become incarnate to guide it to its creaturely (and not divine) eschatological end. The Word, who is Jesus Christ, ministers as creation's radically distinct origin and distinctive whole, center, and *telos,* granting it freedom within limits in mediating it to God.[51]

Such freedom in view of the Word is evidenced in the music of Mozart. For Mozart's music honors the divine Word, yet without being subservient to it. This is true even of his church music. Barth writes that Mozart's "music is a free counterpart to that word given him."[52] The music always has a life of its own, but one that always corresponds to the word received. It is "a music bound by the word but in this 'binding' still a sovereign shape with its own nature."[53]

Barth critiques the critics of Mozart's church music for not sensing the appropriateness of Mozart's music's relation to the word.[54] Their misunderstanding is based on two things: first, they confuse appropriate correspondence of music to the word with servitude; and second, they work from a false division of the sacred and secular.[55] For Barth, on the other hand, Mozart's church music is most appropriate for the word of Scripture given him, and "often in a very surprising way" (as is the music for his operas).[56] Barth reasons,

> This is perhaps because Mozart's sacred music, too, is heard to originate in a region from which vantage point God and the world are certainly not to be judged identical but which does allow church and world (these also not to be interchanged) to be recognizable and recognized in their merely relative difference, in their ultimate togetherness: both emanating from God, both going back to God.[57]

51. One could approach the topic of God, creation, and appropriate space from another angle, namely, the doctrine of the Trinity. Because God allows for distinctions within his own being, he can allow for distinctions in creaturely being, both in its own sphere and in relation to himself. The writer owes this point to Peter Robinson.

52. Barth, "Wolfgang Amadeus Mozart," p. 38.

53. Barth, "Wolfgang Amadeus Mozart," p. 39.

54. Barth, "Wolfgang Amadeus Mozart," p. 39.

55. Barth, "Wolfgang Amadeus Mozart," p. 39.

56. Barth, "Wolfgang Amadeus Mozart," p. 39.

57. Barth, "Wolfgang Amadeus Mozart," pp. 39-40. The word "emanating" here should not be understood in the pantheistic sense.

As Barth sees it, because God and the world are distinct,[58] and because both the sacred and the secular come forth from God, music is given the freedom to correspond as a companion rather than as a servant to the Word. For Barth, Mozart's music honors God by providing an appropriate counterpart to the Word given in its sacred and secular forms.[59]

In the light of what has been said throughout the course of this chapter, should it come as a surprise that Barth finds in Mozart and his music a parable of the kingdom? In the closing paragraphs of his address on "Mozart's Freedom," Barth writes,

> There is a question which I shall leave unanswered, but which surely has not escaped you. How can I as an evangelical Christian and theologian proclaim Mozart? After all he was so Catholic, even a Freemason, and for the rest no more than a musician, albeit a complete one. He who has ears has certainly heard. May I ask all those others who may be shaking their heads in astonishment and anxiety to be content for the moment with the general reminder that the New Testament speaks not only of the kingdom of heaven but also of *parables* of the kingdom of heaven?[60]

Why is Mozart and his music a parable of the kingdom?[61] Perhaps the key is to be found in Barth's statement that Mozart was "no more than a musician, albeit a complete one."

Mozart took advantage of the freedom within the limits given him to immerse himself in music, reveling in the playing and making of music.[62] This freedom conveyed itself through objectivity, resisting the utilization of music for purposes of self-expression.[63] Mozart did not employ music for the sake of morals or metaphysics.[64] He did not employ music at all.

58. It should be added that this distinction is due to God creating the world by his Word rather than from his being.

59. Does not the following contrast with Schleiermacher illumine Barth's position on the value of the secular sphere? Barth writes, "Mozart . . . has unceasingly accompanied and still accompanies me, as Schleiermacher said of his religion." Karl Barth, circular letter, in *Letters, 1961-1968*, ed. Geoffrey W. Bromiley (Grand Rapids: Eerdmans, 1981), p. 298.

60. Barth, "Mozart's Freedom," pp. 56-57.

61. Barth says of cultural achievements that they may serve as signs of the coming kingdom, but never its reality ("Church and Culture," p. 344).

62. Barth, "Mozart's Freedom," p. 46.

63. Barth, "Mozart's Freedom," pp. 48-49.

64. Barth, "Mozart's Freedom," pp. 51-53.

Rather, it employed him for its purposes of affirming life, and for consoling God's creatures that the divine "yes" manifest in creation will ultimately triumph over the nothingness that opposes it.[65] Mozart was music's instrument because he *simply* made and played music. And because he simply produced music, he fashioned the music of creation.[66] "He simply offered himself as the agent by which little bits of horn, metal and catgut could serve as the voices of creation, sometimes leading, sometimes accompanying and sometimes in harmony."[67] Because he was "no more than a musician, albeit a complete one," he and his music serve the kingdom as a parable, secular in form, divine in content.

Lingering Doubt and Enduring Hope

This writer finds much in Barth's theology of the Word appealing, convinced that it serves as the backdrop for his affirmation of certain secular forms of creaturely existence. For as stated in the course of this chapter, the ontological otherness of God as manifest in that Reformation-based theology of the Word, which Barth himself champions, safeguards the distinctive activity and existence of the creature. Space is thereby made for the creation, including humanity, to give glory to God simply by being what it in fact is and by doing what it in fact does as created by God. One need not produce or perform a sonata or conduct an experiment with the goal in mind to bring glory to the creator. For *simply* by working or playing, one glorifies God. There need be no theological ax to grind or message to send. Workmanship is itself a form of doxology, affirmed by the God of creation. For God in his Word is glorified in the very imaginative and enterprising acts of human creation and recreation.

But at this point, a doubt surfaces and lingers. Can one give glory to God simply by being what one in fact is and by doing what one in fact does as created by God? Can this claim hold up to investigation? What is one to make of Richard Dawkins's famous illustration of the digger wasp, which victimizes the caterpillar and lays its egg inside it? As the larva develops

65. Barth, "Mozart's Freedom," pp. 51, 55-56; Barth, *Church Dogmatics*, III/3, p. 298.

66. Barth, *Church Dogmatics*, III/3, p. 298.

67. Barth, *Church Dogmatics*, III/3, p. 298.

and grows, it slowly eats away the very life of its host.[68] Does such "creaturely" action actually glorify God? Many such seemingly chaotic and evil events occur in nature. Would one wish to ascribe them to the hand of a benevolent creator?

The answer to the preceding question is "No," for such acts are an abuse of the creation, the outworking of nothingness, that *absence* of good that *attacks* the good,[69] overturned only by the benevolent hand of the creator. Barth would of course resist any suggestion that such events in creation bring glory to God. This having been said, the dilemma still stands since for Barth, the event of witness in the creation noted in this chapter concerns creation as it is, not as it was. And given the radical presence of evil in the whole of the world, how can creaturely activity, not as originally created, but as it is, as "jeopardised,"[70] give glory to God?

Perhaps it is the case that the creation bears witness in its creatureliness, as it is as created and fallen, as though through a glass dimly. And yet, given the radicalness of evil, which casts a shadow over the creation,[71] could the creation be viewed with anything other than that pessimism characteristic of a Marcion or a Schopenhauer, that is, if it were not for the good pleasure of God who in his grace justifies the creation as good by creating it,[72] declaring it good,[73] imputing unfading honor to it in view of his Word?[74] It is

68. See Richard Dawkins, *River Out of Eden: A Darwinian View of Life* (London: Weidenfeld & Nicolson, 1995), pp. 95-96.

69. In mind here is Barth's exposition and affirmation of Augustine's conception of privation in *Church Dogmatics,* III/3, p. 318.

70. The term is taken from Barth's discussion of witness in *Church Dogmatics,* IV/3.1, p. 123.

71. It can hardly be maintained that Barth is unaware of the presence and magnitude of evil. For as he writes in *Church Dogmatics,* III/3, the "power and powers of falsehood" take a "thousand different forms." The question is not "Where?" but "Where not?" (*Church Dogmatics,* III/3, p. 527). One finds it at work in the human soul, in one's relationships, in humanity's "progress, equilibrium and retrogression, in the great common ventures of what is called culture, science, art, technics and politics, in the conflict and concord of classes, peoples and nations, in the savage dissensions but also the beautiful agreements and tolerances in the life of the Church, and not least in the *rabies* and even more so the *inertia theologorum*" (p. 528).

72. Barth, *Church Dogmatics,* III/1, p. 366.

73. Barth, *Church Dogmatics,* III/1, p. 366.

74. In *Church Dogmatics,* III/4, p. 652, Barth writes that honor is bestowed on humanity by God's Word in creation, that is, by the declaration of God in creation. This honor ("improper" honor in comparison with the "proper honour" spoken to humanity by God's Word

here that an answer is found to the question of doubt and suspicion to which reference was made above. It is only in light of the divine justification of the creation that the creation is deemed good and doubt is erased. For even though surrounded and threatened by the presence of evil, the Word is also present to the creation, ever ascribing honor to it.[75]

Turning once again to Barth's account of Mozart and his music, those who have ears with which to hear may find that the merit of Mozart's music depends upon that divine justification noted above. For Barth, it will be recalled, the beauty of Mozart's music lies in its playfulness and objectivity. For even in the negative or serious or somber note played, one finds an unassuming, joyful, childlike quality. Could it perhaps be that Barth finds in Mozart's music signs that Mozart did not face the darkness in creation in his own strength, forcing his way through it, but instead created and played his work of music as if it were sustained by grace (and this regardless of Mozart's view of the relation of divine grace to human works)? And is it not the case that in Mozart's music one finds evidence of the fact that creaturely work is play, work that is serious and masterful play,[76] but play nonetheless, when compared with that divine work that justifies and sustains?[77] And so, might it not be that he, whose work is truly serious, sustained this musician in order that he might play in all earnestness?

For Barth, Mozart's music *sounds* as if he did not take his music too seriously, as though he was not consumed with himself, that is, with self-conscious admiration. Is it not because of what Barth conceives as Mozart's concern for objectivity over against the expression of self, for work free of the pretense of self-importance and self-justification, immersed

---

of mercy, see p. 652) is spoken to humanity by God ("von Gott zugesprochen wird"). Karl Barth, *Kirchliche Dogmatik*, III/4, *Die Lehre von der Schöpfung* (Zürich: Evangelischer Verlag, 1951), p. 750. Humanity can "sin against" the honor conferred on it by God. Nevertheless, its honor before God remains "constant" because it "is from God." The honor bestowed on humanity by God is humanity's "own at least to the extent that it is ascribed to" humanity "by God," the God who is never "'man-less,'" even when humanity is "godless" (Barth, *Church Dogmatics*, III/4, p. 652).

75. Barth, *Church Dogmatics*, III/4, p. 652.

76. Refer to the earlier discussion in this chapter of Barth's "A Testimonial to Mozart," pp. 16-17, on the theme of play.

77. One calls to mind once again Barth's claim that all cultural activity is to be understood as "a serious game," for human "earnestness . . . can never be ultimately serious, and never is; that the right and the possibility of being wholly in earnest is God's alone" (Barth, "Church and Culture," p. 349).

rather in the simple joy of playing, that one who has ears to hear may find therein a witness to that "consoling turn" whereby God's grace overturns and overcomes demonic nothingness?[78] And again, could it not be that Mozart's music rested in the justifying Word of God in creation who creates and sustains the creation, and who leads it forth to its created end, rather than resting in the presumption of human pride and the justification of self and one's work, which in the end would but lead to condemnation? In this way and in this way alone could Mozart's creaturely songs sing clear praise to the creator, piercing the shadow of nothingness that so immerses the creation.

Having spoken of the problem of evil and how nothingness casts its *shadow* over the creation and how it seems that for Barth Mozart's music breaks free of the shadow by resting in the justifying work of God's Word in creation, one calls to mind the point made in Chapter Three, namely, that the Word of redemption *overshadows* creation. For creation's proper end is redemption. The argument set forth in Chapter Three will not be repeated here, given that a resolution to this particular point of tension in Barth's thought was offered there. Instead, the direction of argument will now be reversed. For there is a sense in which there must always exist a point of tension between creation and redemption, between what is and what will someday be, given the presence of evil in the creation. Indeed, redemption *overshadows* the creation in Barth's thought. But given the *shadow* cast on creation by the jeopardizing of the creation by nothingness, the creation surely stands in need of redemption. Thus, while not wishing to speak of the honor of creation as "improper,"[79] it is only proper that one looks forward to its redemption given the present state of the creation. There is in fact space for the creation as created in Barth's thought, however overshadowed it might be by its liberation and ultimate redemption. But if it were not for the present liberation and ultimate redemption of the world in view of the Word of reconciliation, there would be no basis ultimately for that "consoling turn" in Mozart's music, for there would be no end to creation's groan.

As argued in this chapter, Barth's doctrine of the Word makes space for

78. See Barth, "Mozart's Freedom," pp. 54-56.

79. Refer back to note 74 as well as to the discussion of the relation of covenant to creation in Chapter Three where the improper honor awarded to creation in Barth's theology is discussed.

the celebration of authentic forms of secularity. The creation bears witness to God in its secularity because in this secular form it adheres *simply* to being what it in fact is as created, not out of God, but out of nothing by the Word of God. Thus, the creation does not serve as a *sacramentalist* stepping stone or means to an otherworldly end. It is not a window through which to pass. The glory it gives to its creator, the witness it bears to him, is found in bearing witness to its own creaturely designs, that is, in its work that is truly play.

Now just as one would be wrong to conceive the creation as a window through which to pass, one would be equally mistaken to view the cosmos as self-contained, for it is not cut off from the craftsman who formed it. The true work of creation, although earthen and *secular,* leaves no room for the orientation of the *secularist,* who absolutizes creaturely work, as if it were divine. For the space that is made by the Word for creation is not absolute but relative to the absolute space of God, in relation to whose work creaturely work, though real and taken seriously by God, is but serious play.[80] God grants authentic space to the creation, not absolute space, but space relative to his own.[81] Thus, being situated in freedom, the cre-

80. Palma's criticism that Barth's view of cultural activity as a game is inadequate should not go unchallenged. (See Palma, *Karl Barth's Theology of Culture,* p. 80.) For only by devaluing play can one devalue creaturely activity; far from serving as a sign of disregard for humanity and human culture, Barth's talk of play credits creaturely activity with much value. For true play, as represented in the music of Mozart, requires unparalleled skill (Barth, "A Testimonial to Mozart," pp. 16-17) and "iron zeal" (Barth, "Mozart's Freedom," p. 47). Moreover, it must be kept in mind that, for Barth, human activity is regarded as play *when compared with* the earnestness of God's activity (Barth, "Church and Culture," p. 349). As Palma understands, Barth views culture's activity as "ultimately ineffective" (Barth, "Church and Culture," p. 349) so as to safeguard against confusing it with God's redemptive work in history. (See Palma, *Karl Barth's Theology of Culture,* p. 80.) Nonetheless, Barth maintains that cultural activity is to be taken with the utmost seriousness, "with the highest possible evaluation" (Barth, "Church and Culture," p. 349). This is *not* because of its work as such in the present, but because of the eschatological goal toward which it strives when the "Redeemer" will "make all things new," including human culture (p. 349). In view of the redeemer's promise, Barth does not view human culture in a pessimistic or degrading light, but "confronts society" with "boundless hope" (p. 349).

81. God can make space for the creation because God in God's self also has space. Here one has in mind Barth's discussion in Karl Barth, *Church Dogmatics,* II/1, *The Doctrine of God,* ed. G. W. Bromiley and T. F. Torrance (Edinburgh: T. & T. Clark, 1957), pp. 468-69. If it were not for the fact that God is triune, there would be no space for the creation. As in the Godhead, so too in relation to creation, the "presence" of God does not spell "identity, but to-

ation is not left to its own devices, separated from, abandoned by God, not even in its self-imposed alienation. For it comes forth through God's act in creation through his Word, and returns to God through that same Word who redeems it from the threat of nothingness, bringing hope out of despair, light out of the shadows.

In this light, there is enduring hope, hope for the creation, for the church and for broader culture, not because grace as such triumphs, but because Jesus Christ is "'Victor.'"[82] In view of him, "there is no justification for doubt."[83] For nothingness, that force without a "basis for its being,"[84] which casts its shadow on creation, giving rise to the latter's present plight, is without a future. For the Word who justifies the creation and imputes honor to it even at this time will bring glory to the creation at the end of time. The "'triumph of grace'" is no "easy" victory.[85] But in view of him who has waged and won the "battle," the hope of certain and enduring victory is already assured.[86]

---

getherness at a distance" (pp. 468-69). In the light of revelation, one sees that God does not begrudge humanity its existence, does not envy it, but makes space for creaturely otherness. How is this so? Barth argues that because God has space within his own being for otherness as the triune God (albeit space that is wholly different from that of the creation), God is able to make space for the creation as other (pp. 468-69). It is not the Christian doctrine of God, the doctrine of the Trinity, but pantheism that threatens the space required for free, creaturely action. And moreover, as already indicated in this chapter, over against that modern mythical disposition that calls the existence of the creator into question, it is really the creation that is in danger of being called into question by the existence of God (Barth, *Church Dogmatics,* III/1, p. 6). If it were not for the fact that God is triune (i.e., having space within his own being for otherness), the distinctive existence of the creaturely world would in fact be called into question by the existence of God.

82. Barth, *Church Dogmatics,* IV/3.1, p. 173. Here Barth is responding to G. C. Berkouwer's critique of his theology. See G. C. Berkouwer, *The Triumph of Grace in the Theology of Karl Barth* (Grand Rapids: Eerdmans, 1956).

83. Barth, *Church Dogmatics,* IV/3.1, p. 176.

84. Barth, *Church Dogmatics,* IV/3.1, p. 178.

85. Barth, *Church Dogmatics,* IV/3.1, p. 179. Again, Barth is responding to Berkouwer here.

86. Barth, *Church Dogmatics,* IV/3.1, p. 180.

Conclusion

Barth's survey of theology in relation to Kierkegaard set forth in *Fragments Grave and Gay* sums up well Barth's own theological pilgrimage and its bearing on his approach to culture. There, in "A Thank-You and a Bow — Kierkegaard's Reveille," Barth writes that there are many theologians who *pass by* Kierkegaard as if he had "lived, suffered, and struggled in vain."[1] Regardless of their diverse theological orientations and ministerial concerns, such theologians have much in common, for each of them is marked by an eternal optimism and "cheerfulness," knowing nothing of that sense of alarm inspired by Kierkegaard's Christianity.[2] For in passing by Kierkegaard's message, they avoid confronting the wholly otherness and "no" of God. They embrace only the divine "yes."[3] These divines are secure in their status and roles as "representatives" of Christianity in society.[4] Their occupation causes them no sense of embarrassment in that they are oblivious to its strangeness and the alien nature of the faith.[5] Is it not fair to say that for Barth, they know nothing of "the infinite message of the Bible"[6] and the

1. Karl Barth, "A Thank-You and a Bow — Kierkegaard's Reveille," in *Fragments Grave and Gay*, ed. Martin Rumscheidt (Glasgow: William Collins & Sons, 1971), p. 102.

2. Barth, "Kierkegaard's Reveille," pp. 102-3.

3. Barth, "Kierkegaard's Reveille," pp. 102-4.

4. Barth, "Kierkegaard's Reveille," p. 102.

5. Barth, "Kierkegaard's Reveille," p. 102.

6. Karl Barth, "The Need of Christian Preaching," in *The Word of God and the Word of Man*, trans. Douglas Horton (London: Hodder and Stoughton, 1928), p. 100.

"riddle"[7] it poses, nor "the infinite contradiction" and "riddle" of human existence, preoccupied as they are from the outset with achieving a synthesis between Christ and culture?[8]

But there are others, those endowed with a different spirit, who *pass their days, abiding in* Kierkegaard's dialectic.[9] These theologians know only the "no" of God, nothing of the divine "yes."[10] In place of affirmation and security, they exist in an eternal "state of suspension" and "negations."[11] They are possessed by a "seriousness" that does not permit them to be truly "serious."[12] For they have consigned themselves with a sense of finality to enduring the extreme otherness of God, possessed, consumed, and broken by it. "To them Kierkegaard has become a system."[13] In them, one finds that *diastasis* has become absolutized, the opposition of Christ to culture.

Lastly, there are those theologians who *pass through* Kierkegaard. They, too, know that sense of alarm, inspired by Kierkegaard's "no," overtaken by fear and trembling. They too have been shaken and struck by him, awakened so as never to return to that state of "merely aesthetical piety."[14] Nor will they return to those "flesh-pots of a bourgeois Christianism and a churchiness of either ancient or modern coloration."[15] They are alert to the divine rejection. But they are not fixated by or entrenched in it. They have gone "beyond Kierkegaard"[16] and those theologians suspended in negation. For these divines embrace God's "'no' enfolded" as it is "in God's 'yes.'"[17] They have come to realize that God's "no" is but "the fire of His love."[18] And so, "their desperation" has "changed to confident desperation," the "*desperatio fiducialis*" of Luther.[19] With the comfort and hope that emerges from such despair, these voices have "become really serious

7. Karl Barth, "The Need of Christian Preaching," p. 100.
8. Karl Barth, "The Need of Christian Preaching," p. 100.
9. Barth, "Kierkegaard's Reveille," pp. 102-3.
10. Barth, "Kierkegaard's Reveille," pp. 102-3.
11. Barth, "Kierkegaard's Reveille," p. 103.
12. Barth, "Kierkegaard's Reveille," p. 103.
13. Barth, "Kierkegaard's Reveille," p. 103.
14. Barth, "Kierkegaard's Reveille," p. 103.
15. Barth, "Kierkegaard's Reveille," p. 103.
16. Barth, "Kierkegaard's Reveille," p. 103.
17. Barth, "Kierkegaard's Reveille," p. 103.
18. Barth, "Kierkegaard's Reveille," pp. 103-4.
19. Barth, "Kierkegaard's Reveille," p. 104.

and also" have "burst into peals of laughter."[20] Such confident despair, despair of themselves in the face of God's grace to humanity, with its ensuing seriousness and accompanying laughter, has in turn "enabled" them "to become a little more human."[21]

Barth had studied in Kierkegaard's school, and so was equipped to pass judgment on the ominous syntheses of Christ and culture in his day. It was with the weapons furnished him by a Kierkegaard, an Overbeck, a Jeremiah, and a Paul that he was able to speak forth the word of the *diastasis* between Christ and culture. And yet, in time, Barth would come to see that on its own *diastasis* could not meet the challenges posed to the theologian by the concerns of the day. He came to understand that although God's "no" must be spoken, it must be spoken from within the framework of the divine "yes." Thus, gone was that false optimism; so too, however, the temptation of an equally flawed pessimism. Thus, gone was the Kierkegaard with whom Barth had acquainted himself. And in the place of the wholly otherness of God, which when absolutized threatens to annihilate humanity, one finds in Barth concentration on God's oneness with humanity, which includes due consideration of divine otherness. For Barth had come to see that *diastasis* is only truly divine *diastasis* when viewed from the standpoint of the *synthesis* God provides for mediating the world to God in the incarnation of Jesus Christ.

One finds in *this* Barth neither the progeny of Pelagius (neither in pure nor diluted form) nor the descendant of Münzer,[22] nor of Marcion.[23] For he steers a course between the uncritical *identification* of Christ with culture and the *polarization* of them. And in place of either the *deification* of culture or the *secularization* of it, the latter arising from Christ and culture's polarization, one witnesses in Barth's theology the *humanization* of the creaturely domain whereby humanity is free to go about its tasks, free "to

20. Barth, "Kierkegaard's Reveille," p. 104.

21. Barth, "Kierkegaard's Reveille," p. 104.

22. As stated in the preface, Harnack had "compared" Barth "with Thomas Munzer." Eberhard Busch, *Karl Barth: His Life from Letters and Autobiographical Texts* (London: SCM Press, 1976), p. 113.

23. In his correspondence with Barth, Harnack suggests there may be a link between Barth and Marcion, who had severed "every link between faith and what is human." Adolf von Harnack, "An Open Letter to Professor Karl Barth," in *The Beginnings of Dialectical Theology*, vol. 1, ed. James M. Robinson, trans. Keith R. Crim and Louis De Grazia (Richmond, Va.: John Knox Press, 1968), p. 172.

become a little more human."[24] One is now free to laugh in all seriousness, for hope is now firmly based in the incarnate reality of the divine Word.

That is not to say that the doctrine of the divine Word is incarnate in a pristine state in Barth's thought, that is, free from enculturation. For as Tillich correctly perceives, even kerygmatic theologians, who for him include Barth, make use of modern conceptualities.[25] The real issue for Barth though is neither *synthesis* nor *diastasis,* the immersion of one's thought forms in modern categories or the repudiation of them, but *how* it is one employs such categories. As Trevor Hart has argued in his analysis of Clement of Alexandria and Athanasius, both used the tools of their day to speak of the Word, but only Athanasius reshaped them in light of the Word. In contrast to Athanasius, Clement accommodated his thought forms to the worldview of his day, thereby giving rise to a somewhat syncretistic picture of the Word's relation to the world.[26] Like Athanasius before him, Barth enfleshes his doctrine of the Word in a particular cultural context, a social milieu, yet ever remaining critical of that context, reshaping its conceptualities in view of the Word made flesh.

In light of the foregoing discussion, it is evident that Barth's theology of the Word is indeed modern and not a return to the distant past,[27] yet without proving a sellout to modernity. As stated above, just as there is no *logos asarkos,* there is no culture-free gospel either: the gospel is always enfleshed, always enculturated. But this is not the last word, for the gospel in turn critiques the culture in which it is clothed. Newbigin says it well in his own articulation of the relation of Christ to culture.

> The idea that one can or could at any time separate out by some process of distillation a pure gospel unadulterated by any cultural accretions is an illusion. It is, in fact, an abandonment of the gospel, for the gospel is about the word made flesh. Every statement of the gospel in words is conditioned by the culture of which those words are a part, and every style of life that claims to embody the truth of the gospel is

24. Barth, "Kierkegaard's Reveille," p. 104.

25. Paul Tillich, *Systematic Theology,* vol. 1 (Chicago: University of Chicago Press, 1951), p. 7.

26. Trevor Hart, "The Two Soteriological Traditions of Alexandria," *Evangelical Quarterly* (1989): 239-59.

27. Here one has in mind Tillich's statement about Barth to which reference was made in Chapter One. See Tillich, *Systematic Theology,* p. 5.

> a culturally conditioned style of life. There can never be a culture-free gospel. Yet the gospel, which is from the beginning to the end embodied in culturally conditioned forms, calls into question all cultures, including the one in which it was originally embodied.[28]

One can go further though and claim that for Barth, the critical encounter between the Word and world is itself set forth within the larger framework of condescension whereby God takes the world to himself in the Word. *Diastasis* always accompanies *synthesis* as the latter's middle word, bordered and enfolded by it. Thus, the dialectical *point of tension* is itself a positive one, enclosed as it is in Barth's doctrine of the incarnate Word.

Barth's extension of his particular Christological model of the Word enables him by and large to mediate between the divinization and utter secularization of culture. To draw a parallel to Christology proper, in his *Reformed Dogmatics,* Heppe refers to Riissen's claim that in Christology one must steer a course between Nestorianism on the one hand and Eutycheanism on the other.[29] Given Barth's extension of Christological categories to the analysis of culture noted in this study, one could argue analogically that in Barth, one finds a balanced approach to Christ and culture, mediating between the "Nestorian" *polarization* of the divine and human, sacred and secular, and the "Eutychean" *overwhelming* of the human and secular by the divine and sacred, and vice versa.

Barth is able to mediate between this Scylla and Charybdis through recourse to his Christological doctrine of the Word. However, instances in Barth's thought have been noted where the divine and sacred *overshadow* the human and secular, namely, in his discussions of the relation of creation to redemption and the relation of the divine to the human in revelation and witness. Attention was also drawn to the reversal of fortunes for the relation of the sacred and secular in view of Barth's silence in the face of the threat posed by atheistic socialism for the existence of the church and the secular vocation of the state whereby the former is in danger of being overshadowed, indeed, *overwhelmed,* by the latter.

28. Lesslie Newbigin, *Foolishness to the Greeks: The Gospel and Western Culture* (Grand Rapids: Eerdmans, 1986), p. 4.

29. Heinrich Heppe, *Reformed Dogmatics: Set Out and Illustrated from the Sources,* with a foreword by Karl Barth, ed. Ernst Bizer, trans. G. T. Thomson (London: George Allen & Unwin, 1950; reprint, Grand Rapids: Baker, 1978), p. 433.

Having highlighted certain points of tension or problematic features in Barth's consideration of themes bearing upon the theological engagement of culture, nonetheless, this writer has viewed Barth's Christological model as a *template* on the basis of which to proceed. The key feature that is found to be so attractive here is the way in which Barth combines constructive engagement with critical awareness, the incorporation of *diastasis* into his proposed synthesis in view of his doctrine of the Word. And it is this very enfolding of *diastasis* in synthesis, otherness in oneness, in his Christological model of the Word, that makes Barth's engagement of Christ and culture so difficult to categorize according to standard classifications.

One cannot classify Barth's model as "Christ *against* culture," since for Barth, Christ and the church ever exist for the world, granting culture space to be truly secular rather than serve as a front for the sacred. The secular vocation of culture is viewed as an end in itself in distinct relation to the sacred rather than simply as a means to the end of the sacred. The secular exists as secular, neither in opposition to the sacred nor in spite of the sacred, but because of its union with the sacred. Nor can Barth's view be classified as "Christ *of* culture" given how the Word judges the world of culture. Space is awarded to human culture *within* the critical limits set by the divine Word.

Not only is it difficult to classify Barth's theological engagement of culture according to the two models discussed here, but also it is difficult to categorize Barth's position according to other common ways of conceiving the Christ-culture relation.[30] The reason for this is the *positive* albeit *dialectical* relation of the two whereby Barth views the world, including culture, as neither confused with nor separated from the Word and church. The Word who mediates the church to broader culture is wholly other

30. One has in mind here those types represented in H. Richard Niebuhr's study, *Christ and Culture* (New York: Harper & Brothers, 1951). Palma also argues that Barth's position does not fit easily any of Niebuhr's categories for viewing the Christ-culture relation but speculates as to the possibility of locating Barth somewhere between "Christ and Culture in Paradox" and "Christ the Transformer of Culture." Palma concludes, however, by choosing to allow what he calls the *"sui generis"* quality of Barth's theology to disclose the unique character of his view of Christ's relation to culture rather than attempt to label his position. Robert J. Palma, *Karl Barth's Theology of Culture: The Freedom of Culture for the Praise of God*, Pittsburgh Theological Monographs, ed. Dikran Y. Hadidian (Allison Park: Pickwick Publications, 1983), pp. 6-7.

than the world of culture, and yet embraces it in and through his incarnation. In this light, it is argued that Barth conceives the relation of Christ to culture in a revolutionary manner, going beyond typical categorizations.

The Word of Christ is both "against culture" and "for culture." The Word of Christ stands against culture, critiquing it. And yet, the divine critique gives way to the divine confirmation, which is ever spoken in connection with the Word of judgment. Thus, the Word of Christ is "for culture" in that culture is ultimately "of Christ." The Word of Christ is the transcendental ground and goal of culture, making its existence possible, even to the extent of providing limits within which culture glorifies God in its sheer otherness from God. For Barth, the Word of Christ radically critiques culture, but only for the ultimate confirmation of culture as eschatological promise.

The Word critiques culture, but not it only. The Word critiques the church as well, for the church is neither the kingdom nor an image of the kingdom. But the church has a role to play, namely, that of witness, in view of the coming kingdom, which is the goal of both church and broader culture. The Word critiques in order to safeguard both the secular vocation of culture and the sacred calling of the church. Moreover, the Christian, too, is called to fulfill a secular vocation, one that does not hinder the cause of Christ, but which is part and parcel of that cause. Thus, Barth's theology weds the scandal of particularity to robust secularity in and through the one Word of God, who safeguards the distinctive vocations of the sacred and secular stewards of the kingdom.

Key to Barth's understanding of the Christ-culture relation in view of his doctrine of the Word is his novel employment of the doctrines of *anhypostasis, enhypostasis,* and the *unio personalis.* Barth's particular model of the Word shapes his views on election, revelation, and creation, and through them, his approach to culture, bearing implications for a variety of societal concerns, including the relation of the sacred and secular spheres. For Barth, the divine person of the eternal Word fills and enfolds both the humanity of Christ and, albeit in a different way, the creation and the world of culture in distinct though inseparable relation. As elect in Christ, both the church and society are integrally related to him, although not in the same manner. The former stands in closer proximity to the revelation of Christ, having come to participate in the event of revelation, and thus serves as a witness to the rest of humanity of the reality of Christ in which the latter, too, is constituted *de jure.* However, it is not the church but Christ himself who mediates the presence of God to the world, and in such a manner that he himself is the basis of authentic culture, not simply existing alongside culture, but also filling and enfolding it, enabling culture to bear witness to him, even in its otherness. To reiterate the point made in the introduction to this work, for Barth, "Christ and culture" does not mean Christianity and culture, but Jesus Christ and culture. As he sees it, Jesus Christ does not simply stand in relation to culture through the witness of the church. Culture also stands in a direct relation to Jesus Christ, who is the basis for culture and the basis for the relation between the church and broader culture.[31]

Barth's doctrine of the Word enables him to give a critical yet constructive response to culture whereby space is also made for the secular other in relation to the sacred. That is to say, the *dedivinization* and *desecularization* of culture lead to its *humanization,* that is, the affirmation of the secular. As Palma so insightfully points out, it is not in the setting aside of "his theological imagination" that Barth is able to affirm secular culture, but in the application of it.[32] As this study has attempted to demonstrate, especially Chapters Five and Six, it is not in spite of Barth's doctrine of the Word that he can affirm certain secular enterprises, activities, and forms of existence,

31. In contrast to that paradigm of engaging culture directly from the vantage point of the church, Barth's Christological focus provides an invaluable resource for speaking to an age in which "reverence for Jesus has grown" even as "respect for the organized church has declined," to quote Pelikan. Jaroslav Pelikan, *Jesus Through the Centuries: His Place in the History of Culture,* with a new preface by the author (New Haven: Yale University Press, 1985; new preface copyright, 1999), p. 232. Barth's critique of Christendom and his call to return constantly to the center of Christian faith in the person of Jesus Christ and begin anew suggests that Barth would affirm Pelikan's assessment that "there is more in" Jesus "than is dreamt of in the philosophy and Christology of the theologians. Within the church, but also far beyond its walls, his person and message are, in the phrase of Augustine, a 'beauty ever ancient, ever new,' and now he belongs to the world" (pp. 232-33; Pelikan's quotation from Augustine is taken from the *Confessions,* 9.27.38).

32. Palma, *Karl Barth's Theology of Culture,* p. 11. Although Palma speaks of instances of the bracketing off of or suspension of the "theological dimension" in Barth's consideration of culture, he quickly adds that such bracketing on the part of Barth "should not lead one to suspect that he ever really places himself outside of the theological circle of activity, or that he ever really places himself beyond the perimeter of the theological context wherein he is situated. He was too much a committed theologian to be able to do that" (pp. 10-11). In this vein, Palma draws attention to the theme of Christ's dominion in the present age and how it "made" Barth "free for letting a cultural scene be seen on its own terms and for what it is in itself" (p. 11).

but because of it. Hans Frei, whose claim Palma also notes,[33] goes so far as to argue, "I believe there was in Barth a self-conscious secularity of sensibility far, far beyond that shown by any of those modern Christian apologists who would make theological hay out of this very state of affairs."[34] Yet, as Palma argues, and as this writer has attempted to make clear, such a conclusion should not be taken to mean that Barth rejects the idea that true words can be found *extra muros ecclesiae* or that Barth is "content" to offer no more than "a bare phenomenological account of cultural phenomena."[35] For although one finds in Barth a capacity to let culture be, it is not in spite of, but in view of, his theology that culture is free to be the secular reality it is.

The assessment given here of Barth resonates with that of Wood, who argues, "Barth's unique accomplishment . . . is to have genuinely honored human achievement without conflating its truth with the Gospel's own suprahuman gladness."[36] How wrong it is then that the one who challenged Schleiermacher's programmatic attempt to win over the faith's "cultured despisers" could be deemed a despiser of culture. For although the original intent of Barth's critique of his great theological predecessor and the program he inaugurated was to preserve the deity of God, it nonetheless resulted in the preservation of culture as human, and not divine or semi-divine. Thus, as Wood writes,

> It is extremely unfortunate . . . that Barth should have become renowned as a despiser of culture and a hater of humanism. The truth

33. Palma, *Karl Barth's Theology of Culture*, p. 11.

34. Hans Frei, "Karl Barth — Theologian," in *Karl Barth and the Future of Theology: A Memorial Colloquium Held at the Yale Divinity School, January 28, 1969*, ed. David L. Dickerman (New Haven: Yale Divinity School Association, 1969), p. 9. Frei's assessment of "those modern Christian apologists" and their secular concerns (p. 9) calls to mind Barth's own observation of Gogarten. "I always had the impression that Gogarten was almost more interested in secularity as a background to the gospel than in the gospel itself." Karl Barth, conversation with Tübingen students; quoted in Eberhard Busch, *Karl Barth: His Life from Letters and Autobiographical Texts* (London: SCM Press, 1976), p. 194. In contrast to this orientation, attention is drawn to Wood's claim that Barth's decision to begin "with the Gospel rather than the world" enables him "to make a fairer estimate of both biblical faith and secular culture than . . . the Christian humanist who, having sought natural evidence for God within the world, then makes it serve as the foundation for revealed faith." Ralph C. Wood, *The Comedy of Redemption: Christian Faith and Comic Vision in Four American Novelists* (Notre Dame: University of Notre Dame Press, 1988), p. 57.

35. Palma, *Karl Barth's Theology of Culture*, p. 11.

36. Wood, *The Comedy of Redemption*, p. 57.

> of the matter is exactly the reverse. Barth can look favorably upon the glory and beauty of human creation and discovery because, and only because, he does not seek to squeeze salvation from the turnip of culture.[37]

In Barth's theology, humanity is free to be human, and not divine, yet never apart from but only in view of the divine preservation of it and its culture. This point is admirably put by Barth in his discussion of "The Divine Preserving" of the creature and creaturely activity. There he writes that because the creature is "freely created by God" rather than proceeding from the being of God, the creature cannot and should not "in any way forfeit or surrender its autonomy in face of" God.[38] In contrast to the pantheistic conception of reality, "which does violence and injustice"[39] to the actuality and activity of both God and God's creature, the biblical doctrine of "the divine preservation" spells that God's creature "may be actual within its limits."[40] The creature is granted freedom "within the limits marked off for it" for the exercising of its existence.[41] In view of the divine preserving of the creature, "God does not begrudge . . . or deprive" the creature its situated freedom within which to act. Indeed, "there is a delighting or sport in which first the Creator and then the creature has a part."[42] In light of this preservation of the actuality and activity of the creature,

> "Man goeth forth unto his work and to his labour until the evening" (Ps. 104:23); to which it belongs that he can use his senses and understanding to perceive that two and two make four, and to write poetry, and to think, and to make music, and to eat and drink and to be filled with joy and often with sorrow, and to love and sometimes to hate, and to be young and to grow old, and all within his own experience and activity, affirming it not as half a man but as a whole man, with head uplifted, and the heart free and the conscience at rest: "O Lord, how manifold are thy works" (Ps. 104:24). It is only the heathen gods

37. Wood, *The Comedy of Redemption,* p. 60.

38. Karl Barth, *Church Dogmatics,* III/3, *The Doctrine of Creation,* ed. G. W. Bromiley and T. F. Torrance (Edinburgh: T. & T. Clark, 1960), p. 86.

39. Barth, *Church Dogmatics,* III/3, p. 86.

40. Barth, *Church Dogmatics,* III/3, p. 86.

41. Barth, *Church Dogmatics,* III/3, p. 87.

42. Barth, *Church Dogmatics,* III/3, p. 87.

> who envy man. The true God, who is unconditionally the Lord, allows him to be the thing for which He created him.[43]

Barth's theology, a theology driven by the love and freedom of the triune God who creates and preserves, elects and addresses humanity in and through the person of the Word, Jesus Christ, safeguards the *distinction* between God and the world, Christianity and broader culture, while also *connecting* the two spheres, the divine and human, sacred and secular, in an integral manner. In this way, it serves well those in the church who would speak out against the ever-present threats of the divinization and secularization of culture in favor of a culture that is truly human. Like all theologies, Barth's theology, too, is dated. And yet, it continues to speak, even in the postmodern present, offering wisdom on how to proceed in mediating between Christ and culture.[44] It does so, not with naïve optimism or scath-

43. Barth, *Church Dogmatics,* III/3, p. 87.

44. Bernard Ramm has argued in *After Fundamentalism* that the Evangelical church will find in Barth a guide for being completely modern while upholding the central convictions of Christian faith. Bernard Ramm, *After Fundamentalism: The Future of Evangelical Theology* (San Francisco: Harper & Row, 1983). However, given that the church exists today — after modernity — Evangelicals must find a way to speak within a postmodern context while remaining steadfast to the Christian calling. Fortunately, Barth provides guidance here as well. For as Gary Dorrien argues, due to Barth's dialectical emphasis on presence and absence, Barth's "perspective . . . has more to contribute to the possibility of a compelling postmodern theology of Word and Spirit than much of the neorthodox movement that his work engendered." Gary Dorrien, *The Barthian Revolt in Modern Theology: Theology without Weapons* (Louisville: Westminster/John Knox Press, 2000), p. 3. Other recent works demonstrating that Barth's theological engagement of culture served as a prophetic voice in his own day, and still speaks, addressing the theological and cultural concerns of our own include the following: Timothy Gorringe, *Karl Barth Against Hegemony,* Christian Theology in Context (New York: Oxford University Press, 1999); Trevor Hart, *Regarding Karl Barth: Toward a Reading of His Theology* (Downers Grove, Ill.: InterVarsity Press, 1999); William Stacy Johnson, *The Mystery of God: Karl Barth and the Postmodern Foundations of Theology,* Columbia Series in Reformed Theology (Louisville: Westminster/John Knox Press, 1997). Barth's twofold program of providing a critical though constructive engagement of culture suits well the postmodern cultural scene. Regarding the critical dimension, Barth ever calls into question the prevailing thought forms of bourgeois culture, including Christianity, not as an end in itself, but as a means to the end of exhorting culture and the church to aspire to and attain their lofty ideals set before them. Johnson, who sees this same characteristic in postmodernity, argues that Barth's view of theology "as an ongoing response to divine mystery" rather than "a repristination of past orthodoxy" gives rise to this particular orientation (Johnson, *The Mystery of God,* p. 5). Regarding the constructive dimension, Barth ever seeks

ing pessimism, but with boundless hope, based not on culture's achievements, but in view of culture's goal, when the redeeming Word of eschatological promise renews the world.

to bridge the modern divide between the sacred and secular. In his study, *A Time to Be Born — A Time to Die,* Robert Short argues that Dietrich Bonhoeffer's attempt to build bridges between the sacred sphere and secular culture by means of "religionless Christianity" was inspired by Ecclesiastes and Barth. Robert L. Short, *A Time to Be Born — A Time to Die* (New York: Harper & Row, 1973), p. 79. Short points to Barth as a theologian who understands well the spiritual significance of secular Ecclesiastes, namely, the relation of the cosmos, including man, to the creator. (See pages 78-79, 84 of Short.) Barth writes that Ecclesiastes is "Epicurean in appearance only." Upon quoting Ecclesiastes 9:7-10, Barth claims that, "One surely fails to know the Gospels if he thinks Jesus could not also have said this. It is quite in his character." He adds, "To perceive the *absolute vanity* of life under the sun in the light of the heavenly life of God is also to perceive its *relative potentiality:* it is to perceive that it possesses no insignificant nor inglorious *authorization.*" Karl Barth, "The Christian's Place in Society," in *The Word of God and the Word of Man,* trans. Douglas Horton (London: Hodder and Stoughton, 1928), p. 301. Barth's view of the secular as an invaluable counterpart to the sacred, supplying the form for spiritual content, can provide a much needed platform for engaging secular culture, including the irreligious spirituality of many postmoderns today. For a discussion of the interface of spirituality with this particular cultural field, see Tom Beaudoin's work, *Virtual Faith: The Irreverent Spiritual Quest of Generation X,* with a foreword by Harvey Cox (San Francisco: Jossey-Bass Publishers, 1998).

Bibliography

Works by Karl Barth

Against the Stream: Shorter Post-War Writings, 1946-1952. Edited by R. G. Smith. Translated by E. M. Delecour and S. Godman. London: SCM Press, 1954.

Anselm: Fides Quaerens Intellectum, Anselm's Proof of the Existence of God in the Context of His Theological Scheme. The Library of Philosophy and Theology. Edited by John McIntyre and Ian T. Ramsey. London: SCM Press, 1960.

"Barmen." In *Protestantismus Heute.* Edited by Fritz Heinrich Ryssel, pp. 77-86. Frankfurt: Ullstein Bücher, 1959.

The Church and the Political Problem of Our Day. London: Hodder and Stoughton, 1939.

Church Dogmatics. I/1, *The Doctrine of the Word of God.* Edited by G. W. Bromiley and T. F. Torrance. Edinburgh: T. & T. Clark, 1975.

Church Dogmatics. I/2, *The Doctrine of the Word of God.* Edited by G. W. Bromiley and T. F. Torrance. Edinburgh: T. & T. Clark, 1956.

Church Dogmatics. II/1, *The Doctrine of God.* Edited by G. W. Bromiley and T. F. Torrance. Edinburgh: T. & T. Clark, 1957.

Church Dogmatics. II/2, *The Doctrine of God.* Edited by G. W. Bromiley and T. F. Torrance. Edinburgh: T. & T. Clark, 1957.

Church Dogmatics. III/1, *The Doctrine of Creation.* Edited by G. W. Bromiley and T. F. Torrance. Edinburgh: T. & T. Clark, 1958.

Church Dogmatics. III/2, *The Doctrine of Creation.* Edited by G. W. Bromiley and T. F. Torrance. Edinburgh: T. & T. Clark, 1960.

Church Dogmatics. III/3, *The Doctrine of Creation.* Edited by G. W. Bromiley and T. F. Torrance. Edinburgh: T. & T. Clark, 1960.

Church Dogmatics. III/4, *The Doctrine of Creation*. Edited by G. W. Bromiley and T. F. Torrance. Edinburgh: T. & T. Clark, 1961.

Church Dogmatics. IV/1, *The Doctrine of Reconciliation*. Edited by G. W. Bromiley and T. F. Torrance. Edinburgh: T. & T. Clark, 1956.

Church Dogmatics. IV/2, *The Doctrine of Reconciliation*. Edited by G. W. Bromiley and T. F. Torrance. Edinburgh: T. & T. Clark, 1958.

Church Dogmatics. IV/3.1, *The Doctrine of Reconciliation*. Edited by G. W. Bromiley and T. F. Torrance. Edinburgh: T. & T. Clark, 1961.

Church Dogmatics. IV/3.2, *The Doctrine of Reconciliation*. Edited by G. W. Bromiley and T. F. Torrance. Edinburgh: T. & T. Clark, 1962.

Church Dogmatics. IV/4, *The Doctrine of Reconciliation, Fragment, Baptism as the Foundation of the Christian Life*. Edited by G. W. Bromiley and T. F. Torrance. Edinburgh: T. & T. Clark, 1969.

Church Dogmatics. IV/4, *The Doctrine of Reconciliation, Lecture Fragments, The Christian Life*. Translated by G. W. Bromiley. Grand Rapids: Eerdmans, 1981.

Community, State, and Church: Three Essays. With an introduction by Will Herberg. Gloucester, Mass.: Peter Smith, 1968.

Dogmatics in Outline. Translated by G. T. Thomson. London: SCM Press, 1949; reprint, SCM Press, 1958.

The Epistle to the Romans. 6th ed. Translated by Edwyn C. Hoskyns. London: Oxford University Press, 1933.

"Fifteen Answers to Professor von Harnack." In *The Beginnings of Dialectical Theology*, vol. 1, edited by James M. Robinson, translated by Keith R. Crim and Louis De Grazia, pp. 167-70. Richmond, Va.: John Knox Press, 1968.

Fragments Grave and Gay. Edited by Martin Rumscheidt. Translated by Eric Mosbacher. Glasgow: William Collins & Sons, 1971.

The German Church Conflict. Ecumenical Studies in History, no. 1. Richmond, Va.: John Knox Press, 1965.

The Göttingen Dogmatics: Instruction in the Christian Religion, vol. 1. Translated by Geoffrey W. Bromiley. Grand Rapids: Eerdmans, 1990.

How I Changed My Mind. With an introduction and epilogue by John D. Godsey. Richmond, Va.: John Knox Press, 1966.

The Humanity of God. Atlanta: John Knox Press, 1960.

Karl Barth — and Rudolf Bultmann. *Letters 1922-1966*. Edited by Geoffrey W. Bromiley. Edinburgh: T. & T. Clark, 1982.

"Die Kirche und die Kultur." In *Die Theologie und die Kirche*. Gesammelte Vorträge, vol. 2. München: Chr. Kaiser Verlag, 1928.

Kirchliche Dogmatik. II/1, *Die Lehre von Gott*. Zürich: Evangelischer Verlag, 1942.

Kirchliche Dogmatik. II/2, *Die Lehre von Gott*. Zürich: Evangelischer Verlag, 1942.

Kirchliche Dogmatik. IV/1, *Die Lehre von der Versöhnung*. Zürich: Evangelischer Verlag, 1953.

Kirchliche Dogmatik. IV/2, *Die Lehre von der Versöhnung.* Zürich: Evangelischer Verlag, 1955.

Kirchliche Dogmatik. IV/3.1, *Die Lehre von der Versöhnung.* Zürich: Evangelischer Verlag, 1959.

Kirchliche Dogmatik. I/1, *Die Lehre vom Wort Gottes: Prologomena zur Kirchlichen Dogmatik.* Zürich: Evangelischer Verlag, 1942.

Letters, 1961-1968. Edited by Geoffrey W. Bromiley. Grand Rapids: Eerdmans, 1981.

"No!" In Karl Barth and Emil Brunner. *Natural Theology.* With an introduction by John Baillie. Translated by Peter Fraenkel. London: Geoffrey Bles/Centenary Press, 1946.

"The Paradoxical Nature of the 'Positive Paradox': Answers and Questions to Paul Tillich." In *The Beginnings of Dialectical Theology,* vol. 1, edited by James M. Robinson, translated by Keith R. Crim and Louis De Grazia, pp. 142-54. Richmond, Va.: John Knox Press, 1968.

Protestant Theology in the Nineteenth Century: Its Background and History. London: SCM Press, 1972.

"Rudolf Bultmann — An Attempt to Understand Him." In *Kerygma and Myth: A Theological Debate,* vol. 2, edited by Hans-Werner Bartsch, translated by Reginald H. Fuller, pp. 83-132. London: SPCK, 1962.

Theology and Church: Shorter Writings, 1920-1928. With an introduction by T. F. Torrance. Translated by Louise Pettibone Smith. New York: Harper & Row, 1962.

The Theology of Schleiermacher: Lectures at Göttingen, Winter Semester of 1923/24. Edited by Dietrich Ritschl. Translated by Geoffrey W. Bromiley. Edinburgh: T. & T. Clark, 1982.

This Christian Cause. New York: Macmillan, 1941.

Wolfgang Amadeus Mozart. With a foreword by John Updike. Grand Rapids: Eerdmans, 1986.

The Word of God and the Word of Man. Translated by Douglas Horton. London: Hodder and Stoughton, 1928.

Works on Barth

Andresen, Dieter. "Karl Barth und die Kultur," *Pastoraltheologie* 77 (1988): 220-40.

Balthasar, Hans Urs von. *The Theology of Karl Barth.* Translated by Edward T. Oakes, S.J. San Francisco: Communio Books, Ignatius Press, 1992.

Barth, Markus. "Response," *Union Seminary Quarterly Review* 28 (Autumn 1972): 53-54.

Bax, Douglas S. "The Barmen Declaration: Its Historical Background," *Journal of Theology for Southern Africa* 47 (June 1984): 12-20.

———, translator. "The Barmen Theological Declaration: A New Translation," *Journal of Theology for Southern Africa* 47 (June 1984): 78-81.

Berkouwer, G. C. *The Triumph of Grace in the Theology of Karl Barth*. Grand Rapids: Eerdmans, 1956.

Bouillard, Henri. *Karl Barth: Parole de Dieu et Existence Humaine*, vol. 2. Aubier: Editions Montaigne, 1957.

Bromiley, Geoffrey W. *Introduction to the Theology of Karl Barth*. Edinburgh: T. & T. Clark; Grand Rapids: Eerdmans, 1979.

Busch, Eberhard. *Karl Barth: His Life from Letters and Autobiographical Texts*. London: SCM Press, 1976.

Chavannes, Henry. *The Analogy Between God and the World in Saint Thomas Aquinas and Karl Barth*. Translated by William Lumley. New York: Vantage Press, 1992.

Colwell, John. *Actuality and Provisionality: Eternity and Election in the Theology of Karl Barth*. Edinburgh: Rutherford House Books, 1989.

Dorrien, Gary. *The Barthian Revolt in Modern Theology: Theology without Weapons*. Louisville: Westminster/John Knox Press, 2000.

Erne, Thomas. "Barth und Mozart," *Zeitschrift für Dialektische Theologie* 3 (June 1988): 234-48.

Ford, David. *Barth and God's Story: Biblical Narrative and the Theological Method of Karl Barth in the "Church Dogmatics."* Frankfurt am Main: Lang, 1981.

Frei, Hans. "Karl Barth — Theologian." In *Karl Barth and the Future of Theology: A Memorial Colloquium Held at the Yale Divinity School, January 28, 1969*, edited by David L. Dickerman, pp. 5-12. New Haven: Yale Divinity School Association, 1969.

Godsey, John D., ed. *Karl Barth's Table Talk*. Scottish Journal of Theology Occasional Papers. London: Oliver and Boyd, 1963.

Gorringe, Timothy. *Karl Barth Against Hegemony*. Christian Theology in Context. New York: Oxford University Press, 1999.

Hart, Trevor. "Person and Prerogative in Perichoretic Perspective: An Ongoing Dispute in Trinitarian Ontology Observed," *Irish Theological Quarterly* 58, no. 1 (1992): 46-57.

———. *Regarding Karl Barth: Toward a Reading of His Theology*. Downers Grove, Ill.: InterVarsity Press, 1999.

Hauerwas, Stanley. *With the Grain of the Universe: The Church's Witness and Natural Theology*. Grand Rapids: Brazos Press, 2001.

Herberg, Will. Introduction to *Community, State, and Church: Three Essays*. Gloucester, Mass.: Peter Smith, 1968.

Hood, R. E. "Karl Barth's Christological Basis for the State and Political Praxis," *Scottish Journal of Theology* 33 (June 1980): 223-38.

Hunsinger, George. *Disruptive Grace: Studies in the Theology of Karl Barth*. Grand Rapids: Eerdmans, 2000.

———. *How to Read Karl Barth: The Shape of His Theology.* Oxford: Oxford University Press, 1991.

———, ed. *Karl Barth and Radical Politics.* Translated by George Hunsinger. Philadelphia: Westminster Press, 1976.

Jenson, Robert W. *Alpha and Omega: A Study in the Theology of Karl Barth.* New York: Thomas Nelson & Sons, 1963.

Johnson, William Stacy. *The Mystery of God: Karl Barth and the Postmodern Foundations of Theology.* Columbia Series in Reformed Theology. Louisville: Westminster/John Knox Press, 1997.

Jüngel, Eberhard. *The Doctrine of the Trinity: God's Being Is in Becoming.* Grand Rapids: Eerdmans, 1976.

———. *Karl Barth: A Theological Legacy.* Translated by Garrett E. Paul. Philadelphia: Westminster Press, 1986.

———. *Unterwegs zur Sache. Theologische Bemerkungen, Beiträge zur evangelischen Theologie.* Theologische Abhandlungen 61. München: Kaiser, 1972.

Kim, Heup Young. *Wang Yang-Ming and Karl Barth: A Confucian-Christian Dialogue.* Lanham, Md.: University Press of America, 1996.

Lang, U. M. "Anhypostatos-Enhypostatos," *Journal of Theological Studies* 49, no. 2 (October 1998): 630-57.

Lessing, Eckhard. *Das Problem der Gesellschaft in der Theologie Karl Barths und Friedrich Gogartens.* Gütersloh: Gütersloher Verlagshaus, 1972.

Macken, John, S.J. *The Autonomy Theme in the "Church Dogmatics": Karl Barth and His Critics.* Cambridge: Cambridge University Press, 1990.

Marquardt, Friedrich-Wilhelm. *Theologie und Sozialismus: Das Beispiel Karl Barths.* München: Chr. Kaiser Verlag, 1972.

McCormack, Bruce. *English Language Barth Research Today.* Paper given in the Research Institute in Systematic Theology, King's College London, 23 April 1996.

———. *Karl Barth's Critically Realistic Dialectical Theology: Its Genesis and Development, 1909-1936.* Oxford: Clarendon Press, 1995.

McLean, Stuart. *Humanity in the Thought of Karl Barth.* Edinburgh: T. & T. Clark, 1981.

Mondin, Battista. *The Principle of Analogy in Protestant and Catholic Thought.* The Hague: Martinus Nijhoff, 1963.

Mueller, David L. Introduction to *Church and State,* by Karl Barth. Translated by G. Ronald Howe. Church Classics. Greenville: Smyth & Helwys, 1991.

Palma, Robert J. *Karl Barth's Theology of Culture: The Freedom of Culture for the Praise of God.* Pittsburgh Theological Monographs. Edited by Dikran Y. Hadidian. Allison Park: Pickwick Publications, 1983.

Phillips, Donald E. *Karl Barth's Philosophy of Communication.* Philosophische Texte und Studien, vol. 2. Hildesheim: Georg Olms Verlag, 1981.

Prenter, Regin. "Karl Barths Umbildung der traditionellen Zweinaturlehre in lutherischer Beleuchtung," *Studia Theologica* 11, no. 1 (1957): 1-88.

Ramm, Bernard. *After Fundamentalism: The Future of Evangelical Theology.* San Francisco: Harper & Row, 1983.

Rendtorff, Trutz. "Radikale Autonomie Gottes: Zum Verständnis der Theologie Karl Barths und ihrer Folgen." In *Theorie des Christentums.* Gütersloh: Gütersloher Verlagshaus Gerd Mohn, 1972.

Rhee, Jung Suck. *Secularization and Sanctification: A Study of Karl Barth's Doctrine of Sanctification and Its Contextual Application to the Korean Church.* Amsterdam: VU University Press, 1994.

Roberts, Richard H. "Barth's Doctrine of Time: Its Nature and Implications." In *Karl Barth: Studies of His Theological Method,* edited by S. W. Sykes, pp. 88-146. Oxford: Clarendon Press, 1979.

Rodin, R. Scott. *Evil and Theodicy in the Theology of Karl Barth.* New York: Peter Lang, 1997.

Shults, F. LeRon. "A Dubious Christological Formula: From Leontius of Byzantium to Karl Barth," *Theological Studies* 57 (September 1996): 431-46.

Smith, Steven G. *The Argument to the Other: Reason Beyond Reason in the Thought of Karl Barth and Emmanuel Levinas.* American Academy of Religion Academy Series. Edited by Carl Raschke, no. 42. Chico, Calif.: Scholars Press, 1983.

Stickelberger, Hans. *Ipsa assumptione creatur. Karl Barths Rückgriff auf die klassische Christologie und die Frage nach der Selbständigkeit des Menschen.* Basler u. Berner Studien zur historischen und systematischen Theologie, no. 38. Bern: Lang, 1979.

Stroble, Paul E., Jr. *The Social Ontology of Karl Barth.* San Francisco: Christian University Press, 1994.

Thompson, John. *Christ in Perspective: Christological Perspectives in the Theology of Karl Barth.* Grand Rapids: Eerdmans, 1978.

Torrance, Alan J. *Persons in Communion: Trinitarian Description and Human Participation, with special reference to Volume One of Karl Barth's "Church Dogmatics."* Edinburgh: T. & T. Clark, 1996.

Torrance, Thomas F. *Karl Barth: An Introduction to His Early Theology, 1910-1931.* London: SCM Press, 1962.

———. *Karl Barth, Biblical and Evangelical Theologian.* Edinburgh: T. & T. Clark, 1990.

———. Introduction to *Theology and Church: Shorter Writings, 1920-1928,* by Karl Barth. Translated by Louise Pettibone Smith. New York: Harper & Row, 1962.

Updike, John. Foreword to *Wolfgang Amadeus Mozart,* by Karl Barth. Grand Rapids: Eerdmans, 1986.

Wagner, Falk. "Theologische Gleichschaltung: Zur Christologie bei Karl Barth." In *Die Realisierung der Freiheit,* edited by Trutz Rendtorff, pp. 10-43. Gütersloh: Gütersloher Verlagshaus Gerd Mohn, 1975.

Waldrop, Charles T. *Karl Barth's Christology: Its Basic Alexandrian Character.* Religion and Reason: Method and Theory in the Study and Interpretation of Religion. Edited by Jacques Waardenburg, no. 21. Berlin: Mouton Publishers, 1984.

Ward, Graham. *Barth, Derrida and the Language of Theology.* Cambridge: Cambridge University Press, 1995.

Webster, John. *Barth's Ethics of Reconciliation.* Cambridge: Cambridge University Press, 1995.

White, Roger. "Notes on Analogical Predication and Speaking about God." In *The Philosophical Frontiers of Christian Theology: Essays Presented to D. M. MacKinnon,* edited by Brian Hebblethwaite and Stewart Sutherland, pp. 197-226. Cambridge: Cambridge University Press, 1982.

Wood, Ralph C. *The Comedy of Redemption: Christian Faith and Comic Vision in Four American Novelists.* Notre Dame: University of Notre Dame Press, 1988.

Other Works

Aiken, Henry D., ed. *The Age of Ideology: The Nineteenth Century Philosophers.* The Mentor Philosophers. New York: New American Library, 1956.

Allen, Diogenes. *Philosophy for Understanding Theology.* Atlanta: John Knox Press, 1985.

Aquinas, Saint Thomas. *Summa Theologica,* Part 1, Question 4. London: Burns, Oates & Washbourne, 1920.

Aristotle. *Poetics.* In *The Basic Works of Aristotle,* edited by Richard McKeon. New York: Random House, 1941.

Athanasius, Saint. *De Incarnatione Verbi Dei.* Translated by T. Herbert Bindley. London: The Religious Tract Society, 1903.

Augustine, Saint. *Concerning the City of God, Against the Pagans.* With an introduction by John O'Meara. Translated by Henry Bettenson. London: Penguin Books, 1972.

Bacon, Francis. "First Book of Aphorisms." In *The Age of Reason: The 17th Century Philosophers,* edited by Stuart Hampshire, pp. 24-29. The Mentor Philosophers. New York: New American Library, 1956.

Bader-Saye, Scott. *Church and Israel After Christendom: The Politics of Election.* Radical Traditions: Theology in a Postcritical Key. Boulder, Colo.: Westview Press, 1999.

Beaudoin, Tom. *Virtual Faith: The Irreverent Spiritual Quest of Generation X.* With a foreword by Harvey Cox. San Francisco: Jossey-Bass Publishers, 1998.

Beck, Lewis White, ed. *Kant Selections.* The Great Philosophers, edited by Paul Edwards. New York: Macmillan, 1988.

———. *Studies in the Philosophy of Kant.* Indianapolis: Bobbs-Merrill, 1965.

Becker, Carl L. *The Heavenly City of the Eighteenth-Century Philosophers.* New Haven & London: Yale University Press, 1960.

Benedict, Ruth. *The Chrysanthemum and the Sword: Patterns of Japanese Culture.* Tokyo: Charles E. Tuttle Company, 1974.

Berger, Peter. "The Desecularization of the World: A Global Overview." In *The Desecularization of the World: Resurgent Religion and World Politics,* edited by Peter Berger, pp. 1-18. Published jointly: Washington, D.C.: Ethics and Public Policy Center and Grand Rapids: Eerdmans, 1999.

———. *The Social Reality of Religion.* Harmondsworth: Penguin Books, 1967.

Berkouwer, G. C. *Divine Election.* Grand Rapids: Eerdmans, 1960.

Blaising, Craig A., and Darrell L. Bock. *Progressive Dispensationalism.* Wheaton, Ill.: A BridgePoint Book, 1993.

Bock, Paul, ed. *Signs of the Kingdom: A Ragaz Reader.* With a foreword by M. Douglas Meeks. Grand Rapids: Eerdmans, 1984.

Bonhoeffer, Dietrich. *Christology.* London: William Collins & Sons, 1966.

———. *Letters and Papers from Prison.* Edited by Eberhard Bethge. New York: Collier Books, Macmillan, 1972.

Borg, Marcus J. *Meeting Jesus Again for the First Time: The Historical Jesus and the Heart of Contemporary Faith.* San Francisco: HarperSanFrancisco, 1994.

———. "A Vision of the Christian Life." In Marcus J. Borg and N. T. Wright, *The Meaning of Jesus: Two Visions,* pp. 229-50. San Francisco: HarperSanFrancisco, 1999.

Braaten, Carl E. "The Gospel for a Neopagan Culture." In *Either/Or: The Gospel or Neopaganism,* edited by Carl E. Braaten and Robert W. Jenson, pp. 7-21. Grand Rapids: Eerdmans, 1995.

Braaten, Carl E., and Robert W. Jenson, eds. *The Two Cities of God: The Church's Responsibility for the Earthly City.* Grand Rapids: Eerdmans, 1997.

Brunner, Emil. "Nature and Grace." In *Natural Theology.* With an introduction by John Baillie. Translated by Peter Fraenkel, pp. 15-64. London: Geoffrey Bles/The Centenary Press, 1946.

Buckley, Michael, S. J. *At the Origins of Modern Atheism.* New Haven and London: Yale University Press, 1987.

Bultmann, Rudolf. Introduction to *What Is Christianity?,* by Adolf Harnack. New York: Harper & Row, 1957.

———. *Jesus Christ and Mythology.* New York: Charles Scribner's Sons, 1958.

Chan, Sze Chi. TMs. Presented to author of dissertation by Colin E. Gunton, London, Spring 1997.

Chapman, Mark D. "Troeltsch, Kant and the Quest for a Critical Public Theology," *Zeitschrift für neuere Theologiegeschichte* 5, no. 1 (1998): 29-59.

Cochrane, Arthur C. *The Church's Confession Under Hitler.* Philadelphia: Westminster Press, 1962.

Copleston, Frederick, S.J. *A History of Philosophy.* Book 3, vol. 7, *Fichte to Nietzsche.* New York: Image Books, 1985.

Craig, Edward. *The Mind of God and the Works of Man.* Oxford: Clarendon Press, 1987.

Daley, Brian. "The Origenism of Leontius of Byzantium," *Journal of Theological Studies* 27 (October 1976): 333-69.

Davies, Brian. *The Thought of Saint Thomas Aquinas.* Oxford: Clarendon Press, 1993.

Dawkins, Richard. *River Out of Eden: A Darwinian View of Life.* London: Weidenfeld & Nicolson, 1995.

De Gruchy, John W. "Barmen: Symbol of Contemporary Liberation?" *Journal of Theology for Southern Africa* 47 (June 1984): 59-71.

Donaldson, James, and Alexander Roberts, eds. *Ante-Nicene Christian Library,* vol. 1, *The Writings of Irenaeus,* by Saint Irenaeus. Translated by Alexander Roberts and W. H. Rambaut. Edinburgh: T. & T. Clark, 1867.

Dostoyevsky, Fyodor. *The Brothers Karamazov,* vol. 1. With an introduction by Edward Garnett. Translated by Constance Garnett. London: J. M. Dent & Sons, 1927. Reprint, London: J. M. Dent & Sons, 1967.

———. *The Brothers Karamazov,* vol. 2. With an introduction by Edward Garnett. Translated by Constance Garnett. London: J. M. Dent & Sons, 1927. Reprint, London: J. M. Dent & Sons, 1961.

Edwards, Paul, ed. *The Encyclopedia of Philosophy.* New York: Macmillan & The Free Press, 1967. S.v. "Analogy in Theology," by Frederick Ferre.

———. *The Encyclopedia of Philosophy.* New York: Macmillan & The Free Press, 1967. S.v. "Friedrich Nietzsche," by Walter Kaufmann.

———. *The Encyclopedia of Philosophy.* New York: Macmillan & The Free Press, 1967. S.v. "Neo-Kantianism," by Lewis White Beck.

Eliade, Mircea. *The Sacred and the Profane: The Nature of Religion.* Translated by Willard R. Trask. New York: Harper & Row, 1961.

Evans, David B. *Leontius of Byzantium: An Origenist Christology.* Washington, D.C.: Dumbarton Oaks Center for Byzantine Studies, Trustees for Harvard University, 1970.

Farrow, Douglas. *Ascension and Ecclesia: On the Significance of the Doctrine of the Ascension for Ecclesiology and Christian Cosmology.* Grand Rapids: Eerdmans, 1999.

———. "St. Irenaeus of Lyons: The Church and the World," *Pro Ecclesia* 4 (1995): 333-55.

Ferguson, Sinclair B., David F. Wright, J. I. Packer, eds. *New Dictionary of Theology.* Downers Grove, Ill.: InterVarsity, 1988. S.v. "Monophysitism," by H. D. McDonald.

———. *New Dictionary of Theology.* Downers Grove, Ill.: InterVarsity, 1988. S.v. "Hypostasis," by David F. Wright.

Feuerbach, Ludwig. *Lectures on the Essence of Religion.* Translated by Ralph Manheim. New York: Harper & Row, 1967.

Findlay, J. N. *Hegel: A Re-examination.* London: George Allen and Unwin, Ltd., 1958.

Fisher, George Park. *History of Christian Doctrine.* New York: Charles Scribner's Sons, 1911.

Friedrich, Otto. "New Age Harmonies." *Time,* 7 December 1987, pp. 62-66, 69, 72.

Gilkey, Langdon. *Naming the Whirlwind: The Renewal of God-Language.* Indianapolis and New York: Bobbs-Merrill, 1969.

Gunton, Colin E. Interview by author. Winter 1996. London.

———. *The One, the Three and the Many: God, Creation and the Culture of Modernity, the 1992 Bampton Lectures.* Cambridge: Cambridge University Press, 1993.

———. "The Trinity, Natural Theology, and a Theology of Nature." In *The Trinity in a Pluralistic Age,* edited by Kevin J. Vanhoozer, pp. 88-103. Grand Rapids: Eerdmans, 1997.

———. *The Triune Creator: A Historical and Systematic Study.* Edinburgh: Edinburgh University Press, 1998.

———. *Yesterday and Today: A Study of Continuities in Christology.* Grand Rapids: Eerdmans, 1983.

Hamilton, William. "The Death of God Theologies Today." In *Radical Theology and the Death of God,* edited by Thomas J. J. Altizer and William Hamilton, pp. 23-50. Indianapolis, New York, Kansas City: Bobbs-Merrill, 1966.

Harnack, Adolf von. "Fifteen Questions to Those Among the Theologians Who Are Contemptuous of the Scientific Theology." In *The Beginnings of Dialectical Theology,* vol. 1, edited by James M. Robinson, translated by Keith R. Crim and Louis De Grazia, pp. 165-66. Richmond, Va.: John Knox Press, 1968.

———. *History of Dogma,* vol. 2. Translated by Neil Buchanan. London: Williams & Norgate, 1896.

———. "An Open Letter to Professor Karl Barth." In *The Beginnings of Dialectical Theology,* vol. 1, edited by James M. Robinson, translated by Keith R. Crim and Louis De Grazia, pp. 171-74. Richmond, Va.: John Knox Press, 1968.

———. *What Is Christianity?* With an introduction by Rudolf Bultmann. New York: Harper & Row, 1957.

Hart, Trevor. "The Two Soteriological Traditions of Alexandria," *The Evangelical Quarterly* (1989): 239-59.

Hegel, Georg Wilhelm Friedrich. *Introduction to the Philosophy of History.* In *The European Philosophers from Descartes to Nietzsche,* edited by Monroe C. Beardsley, pp. 537-608. New York: The Modern Library, 1960.

———. *Phenomenology of Spirit.* With a foreword by J. N. Findlay. Translated by A. V. Miller. Oxford: Clarendon Press, 1977.

Heppe, Heinrich. *Reformed Dogmatics: Set Out and Illustrated from the Sources.* With a foreword by Karl Barth. Edited by Ernst Bizer. Translated by G. T.

Thomson. London: George Allen & Unwin, 1950. Reprint, Grand Rapids: Baker, 1978.

Herberg, Will. *Protestant, Catholic, Jew.* Rev. ed. New York: Anchor Books, Doubleday, 1960.

Horne, Brian. Interview by author. Autumn 1996. London.

Huizinga, J. *The Waning of the Middle Ages: A Study of the Forms of Life, Thought and Art in France and the Netherlands in the XIVth and XVth Centuries.* London: Edward Arnold & Co., 1937.

Irenaeus, Saint. *Five Books of Irenaeus, Bishop of Lyons, Against Heresies.* Translated by John Keeble. Library of the Fathers. Oxford: James Parker and Co., 1872.

Jaki, Stanley L. *The Relevance of Physics.* Chicago: University of Chicago Press, 1966.

Janik, Allan, and Stephen Toulmin. *Wittgenstein's Vienna.* New York: A Touchstone Book, published by Simon and Schuster, 1973.

Jenson, Robert W. *The Triune Identity: God According to the Gospel.* Philadelphia: Fortress Press, 1982.

Johnson, Roger A. *The Origins of Demythologizing: Philosophy and Historiography in the Theology of Rudolph Bultmann.* Leiden: E. J. Brill, 1974.

Jones, William T. *A History of Western Philosophy,* vol. 1. New York: Harcourt, Brace and Company, 1952.

Kant, Immanuel. *Critique of the Faculty of Judgment.* In *Kant Selections,* edited by Lewis White Beck, pp. 341-409. The Great Philosophers, edited by Paul Edwards. New York: Macmillan, 1988.

———. *Religion within the Limits of Reason Alone.* Translated, with an introduction and notes by Theodore M. Greene and Hoyt H. Hudson. New York: Harper & Row, 1960.

———. "What Is Enlightenment?" In *Foundations of the Metaphysics of Morals and What Is Enlightenment?* Translated and with an introduction by Lewis White Beck. Indianapolis: Bobbs-Merrill, 1959.

Kelly, J. N. D. *Early Christian Doctrines.* Rev. ed. San Francisco: Harper & Row, 1978.

Kelsey, David H. *The Fabric of Paul Tillich's Theology.* New Haven: Yale University Press, 1967.

———. *The Uses of Scripture in Recent Theology.* Philadelphia: Fortress Press, 1975.

Kerr, Fergus. *Theology After Wittgenstein.* 2nd ed. London: SPCK, 1997.

Kierkegaard, Søren. *Philosophical Fragments.* Edited and translated by Howard V. Hong and Edna H. Hong. Princeton: Princeton University Press, 1985.

———. *Training in Christianity and the Edifying Discourse which "Accompanied" It.* With an introduction by Walter Lowrie. Princeton: Princeton University Press, 1947.

Lynch, John J. "Leontius of Byzantium: A Cyrillian Christology," *Theological Studies* 36 (1975): 455-71.

Machiavelli. *Discourses.* In *The Age of Adventure: The Renaissance Philosophers,* edited by Giorgio de Santillana, pp. 112-28. The Meridian Philosophers. New York: New American Library, 1956.

Marx, Karl. "Theses on Feuerbach." In *The Age of Ideology: The Nineteenth Century Philosophers,* edited by Henry D. Aiken, pp. 193-95. The Mentor Philosophers. New York: New American Library, 1956.

Maximus the Confessor, Saint. *The Disputation with Pyrrhus.* Translated by Joseph P. Farrell. South Canaan: St. Tikhon's Seminary Press, 1990.

McDowell, Jeanne, and Richard N. Ostling. "Buddhism in America." *Time,* 13 October 1997, pp. 72-77, 80-81.

Meyendorff, John. *Christ in Eastern Thought.* Crestwood, N.Y.: St. Vladimir's Seminary Press, 1975.

Miller, Perry. *Errand into the Wilderness.* Cambridge: Belknap Press of Harvard University Press, 1956.

Muller, Richard A. *Dictionary of Latin and Greek Theological Terms: Drawn Principally from Protestant Scholastic Theology.* Grand Rapids: Baker, 1985.

Nebelsick, Harold P. *The Renaissance, the Reformation and the Rise of Science.* Edinburgh: T. & T. Clark, 1992.

Newbigin, Lesslie. *Foolishness to the Greeks: The Gospel and Western Culture.* Grand Rapids: Eerdmans, 1986.

Niebuhr, H. Richard. *Christ and Culture.* New York: Harper & Brothers, 1951.

Nietzsche, Friedrich W. *The Antichrist.* New York: Alfred A. Knopf, 1918.

———. *Ecce Homo.* Translated by Walter Kaufmann. New York: Vintage Books, 1969.

———. "On Truth and Lie in an Extra-Moral Sense." In *The Portable Nietzsche,* edited by Walter Kaufmann, pp. 42-47. New York: Viking, 1968.

———. *Thus Spake Zarathustra.* With an introduction by Henry David Aiken. Translated by Thomas Common. New York: Heritage Press, 1967.

———. *The Will to Power.* Edited by Walter Kaufmann. Translated by Walter Kaufmann and R. J. Hollingdale. New York: Random House, 1967.

O'Meara, John. Introduction to *Concerning the City of God, Against the Pagans,* by Saint Augustine. Translated by Henry Bettenson. London: Penguin Books, 1984.

Pannenberg, Wolfhart. *Jesus — God and Man.* 2nd ed. Translated by Lewis L. Wilkins and Duane A. Priebe. Philadelphia: Westminster Press, 1977.

Pelikan, Jaroslav. *Jesus Through the Centuries: His Place in the History of Culture.* New Haven: Yale University Press, 1985; new preface, 1999.

Pharantos, Megas. *Christologia 1. To Enhypostaton.* Athens: n.p., 1972.

Prestige, G. L. *God in Patristic Thought.* 2nd ed. London: SPCK, 1952. Reprint, London: SPCK, 1977.

Radhakrishnan, Sarvepalli. "The Hindu View of Life." In *The Ways of Religion:*

An Introduction to the Major Traditions, edited by Roger Eastman, 3rd ed., pp. 16-22. New York: Oxford University Press, 1999.

Relton, Herbert. *A Study in Christology: The Problem of the Relation of the Two Natures in the Person of Christ.* With a preface by Arthur C. Headlam. London: Society for Promoting Christian Knowledge, 1917.

Rescher, Nicholas. *A System of Pragmatic Idealism.* Vol. 1, *Human Knowledge in Idealistic Perspective.* Princeton: Princeton University Press, 1992.

Rupp, George. *Culture-Protestantism: German Liberal Theology at the Turn of the Twentieth Century.* American Academy of Religion Studies in Religion Series, edited by Stephen Crites, no. 15. Missoula, Mont.: Scholars Press, 1977.

Sanders, James A. "A Christian Response to Elliot Dorff: 'This is my God': One Jew's Faith." In *Three Faiths — One God: A Jewish, Christian, Muslim Encounter,* edited by John Hick and Edmund S. Meltzer, pp. 30-34. New York: State University of New York Press, 1989.

Santmire, H. Paul. *The Travail of Nature: The Ambiguous Ecological Promise of Christian Theology.* Philadelphia: Fortress Press, 1985.

Sato, Toshio. "The Second Generation." In *A History of Japanese Theology,* edited by Yasuo Furuya, pp. 43-82. Grand Rapids: Eerdmans, 1997.

Schleiermacher, Friedrich. *On Religion: Speeches to Its Cultured Despisers.* With an introduction by E. Graham Waring. New York: Frederick Ungar Publishing Company, 1955.

Schmid, Heinrich. *The Doctrinal Theology of the Evangelical Lutheran Church.* 3rd ed. Translated by Charles A. Hay and Henry E. Jacobs. Minneapolis: Augsburg Publishing House, 1899.

Schwöbel, Christoph. *Identities, Differences and Dialogues: Christian Faith in the Context of Pluralism.* F. D. Maurice Lectures, 18 to 20 March 1997, King's College London.

Short, Robert L. *A Time to Be Born — A Time to Die.* New York: Harper & Row, 1973.

Smit, D. J. "A *Status Confessionis* in South Africa?" *Journal of Theology for Southern Africa* 47 (June 1984): 21-46.

Soskice, Janet Martin. *Metaphor and Religious Language.* Oxford: Clarendon Press, 1985. Reprint, New York: Clarendon Press, 1989.

Strauss, David. *The Life of Jesus, Critically Examined.* Translated by Marian Evans. New York: Published by Calvin Blanchard, 1855.

Taylor, Charles. *Hegel.* Cambridge: Cambridge University Press, 1975.

———. *Hegel and Modern Society.* Cambridge: Cambridge University Press, 1979.

———. *Sources of the Self: The Making of the Modern Identity.* Cambridge: Cambridge University Press, 1989.

Tillich, Paul. "Invocation: The Lost Dimension in Religion." In *The Essential Tillich: An Anthology of the Writings of Paul Tillich,* edited by F. Forrester Church. New York: Macmillan, 1987.

———. *The New Being.* New York: Charles Scribner's Sons, 1955.

———. *Systematic Theology,* vol. 1. Chicago: University of Chicago Press, 1951.

———. *Theology of Culture.* Edited by Robert C. Kimball. New York: Oxford University Press, 1959.

Torrance, Alan J. Introduction to *Christ and Context: The Confrontation between Gospel and Culture.* Edited by Hilary D. Regan and Alan J. Torrance with Antony Wood. Edinburgh: T. & T. Clark, 1993.

———. Introduction to *Christ, Justice and Peace: Toward a Theology of the State in Dialogue with the Barmen Declaration,* by Eberhard Jüngel. Translated by D. Bruce Hamill and Alan J. Torrance. Edinburgh: T. & T. Clark, 1992.

Tutu, Desmond. "Barmen and Apartheid," *Journal of Theology for Southern Africa* 47 (June 1984): 73-77.

Uchimura, Kanzo. "Japanese Christianity." In *Sources of Japanese Tradition,* vol. 2, edited by Ryusaku Tsunoda, Wm. Theodore de Bary, and Donald Keene. New York: Columbia University Press, 1958. Reprint, *Religion in the Japanese Experience: Sources and Interpretations,* edited by H. Byron Earhart, pp. 113-14. The Religious Life of Man Series, edited by Frederick J. Streng. Belmont, Mass.: Wadsworth, 1974.

Vanhoozer, Kevin J. "A Lamp in the Labyrinth: The Hermeneutics of 'Aesthetic' Theology," *Trinity Journal* 8 (Spring 1987): 25-56.

Vidler, Alec R. *The Church in an Age of Revolution: 1789 to the Present Day.* Harmondsworth: Penguin Books, 1971.

Voltaire. *"Épîtres xcvi. A l' Auteur du Livre des Trois Imposteurs."* Quoted and translated in *The Oxford Dictionary of Quotations,* 2nd ed., p. 557. London: Oxford University Press, 1953. Reprint, London: Oxford University Press, 1964.

Waring, E. Graham. Introduction to *On Religion: Speeches to Its Cultured Despisers,* by Friedrich Schleiermacher. New York: Frederick Ungar Publishing Company, 1955.

Watson, Francis. "Theology and Music," *Scottish Journal of Theology* 51, no. 4 (1998): 435-63.

Wiles, Maurice, "Christianity Without Incarnation?" In *The Myth of God Incarnate,* edited by John Hick, pp. 1-10. Philadelphia: Westminster Press, 1977.

Wittgenstein, Ludwig. *Philosophical Investigations.* New York: Macmillan, 1958.

Wolf, Ernst. *Barmen: Kirche zwischen Versuchung und Gnade.* München: Chr. Kaiser, 1957.

Index